setsu

Vol. 7

Story & Art by
Chika Shiomi

Characters

Rasetsu Hyuga

A powerful 19-year-old exorcist, Rasetsu has a flowerlike mark on her chest—a memento left by a demon. Rasetsu eats lots of sweets to recharge her psychic powers. She's currently looking for a boyfriend.

Yako Hoshino

An ace psychic who controls water, Yako was headhunted by Rasetsu. After much ado, he finally realizes that he has feelings for her.

Hiichiro Amakawa

The chief of the agency where Rasetsu and Yako work. A very powerful psychic.

Kuryu Iwatsuki

A psychic who uses *kotodama* (spiritual power manifested through words). His power works on humans and animals alike.

Aoi Kugi

Does administrative work for the agency. Ever since Yako came to the office, however, he's been left with nothing to do.

Story

The Hiichiro Amakawa Agency deals with exorcisms, and Rasetsu, Kuryu and Yako are psychics who work there. Rasetsu is actually cursed by an evil spirit, and the only way for her to break the curse is to find true love before she turns 20! Rasetsu tells Yako that she's in love with him, but Yako doesn't know what to feel. Meanwhile, he doesn't like how Kuryu is openly affectionate with Rasetsu. With a little help from his friend Mei Tendo, Yako realizes that he actually has feelings for Rasetsu too…

Rasetsu

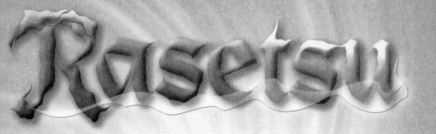

Volume 7

Contents

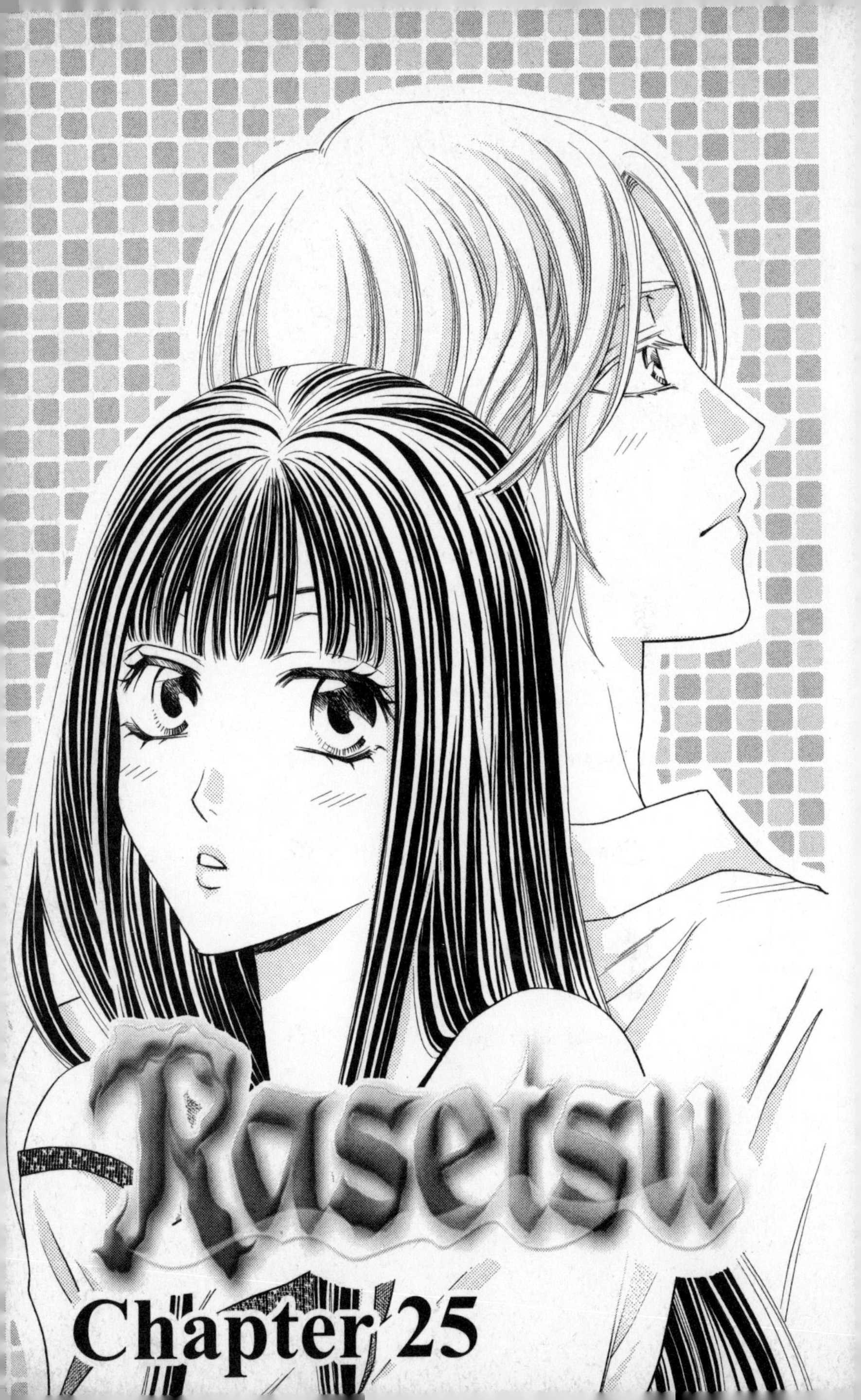
Rasetsu
Chapter 25

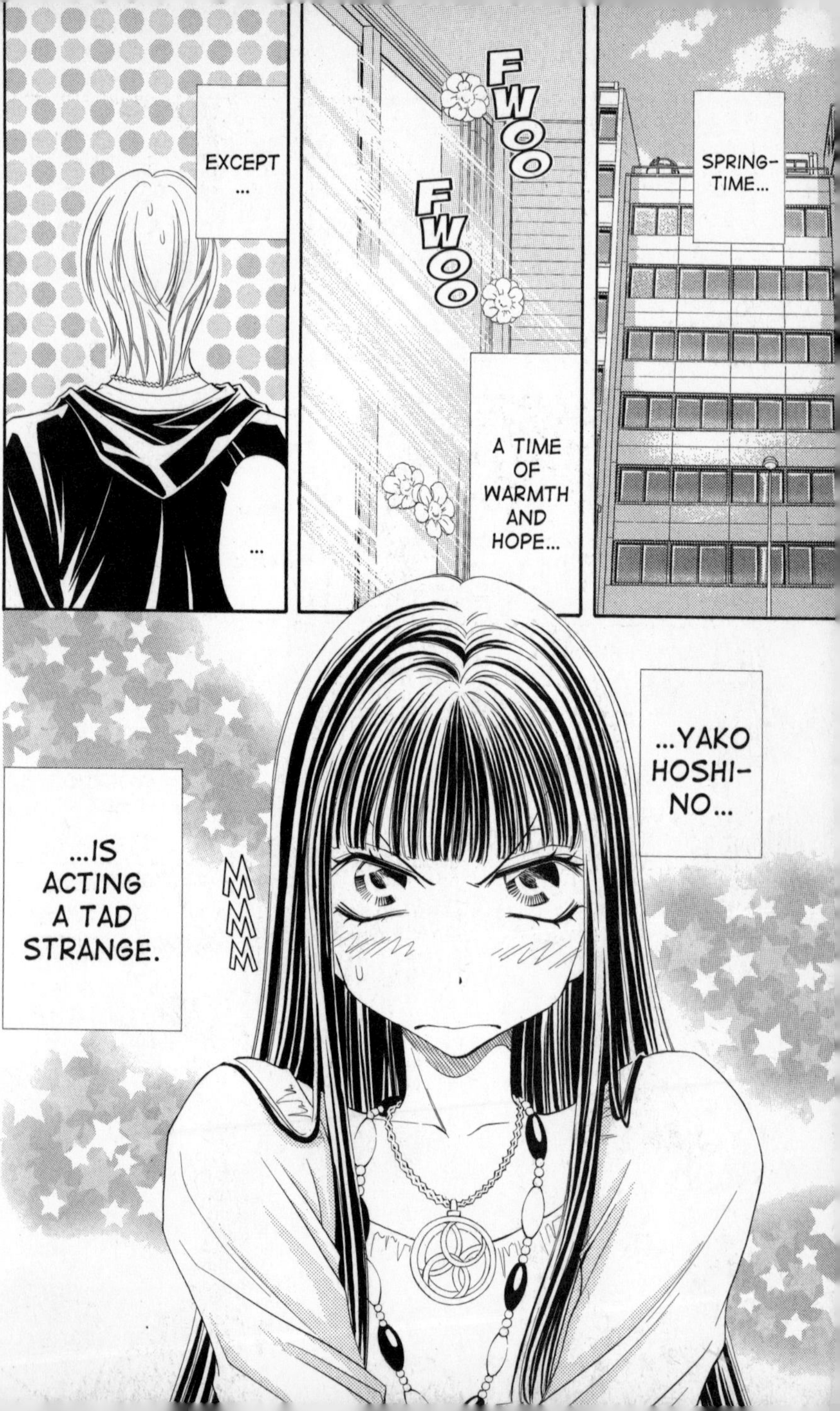
SPRING-TIME...
FWOO
FWOO
A TIME OF WARMTH AND HOPE...
EXCEPT...
...
...YAKO HOSHI-NO...
MMMM
...IS ACTING A TAD STRANGE.

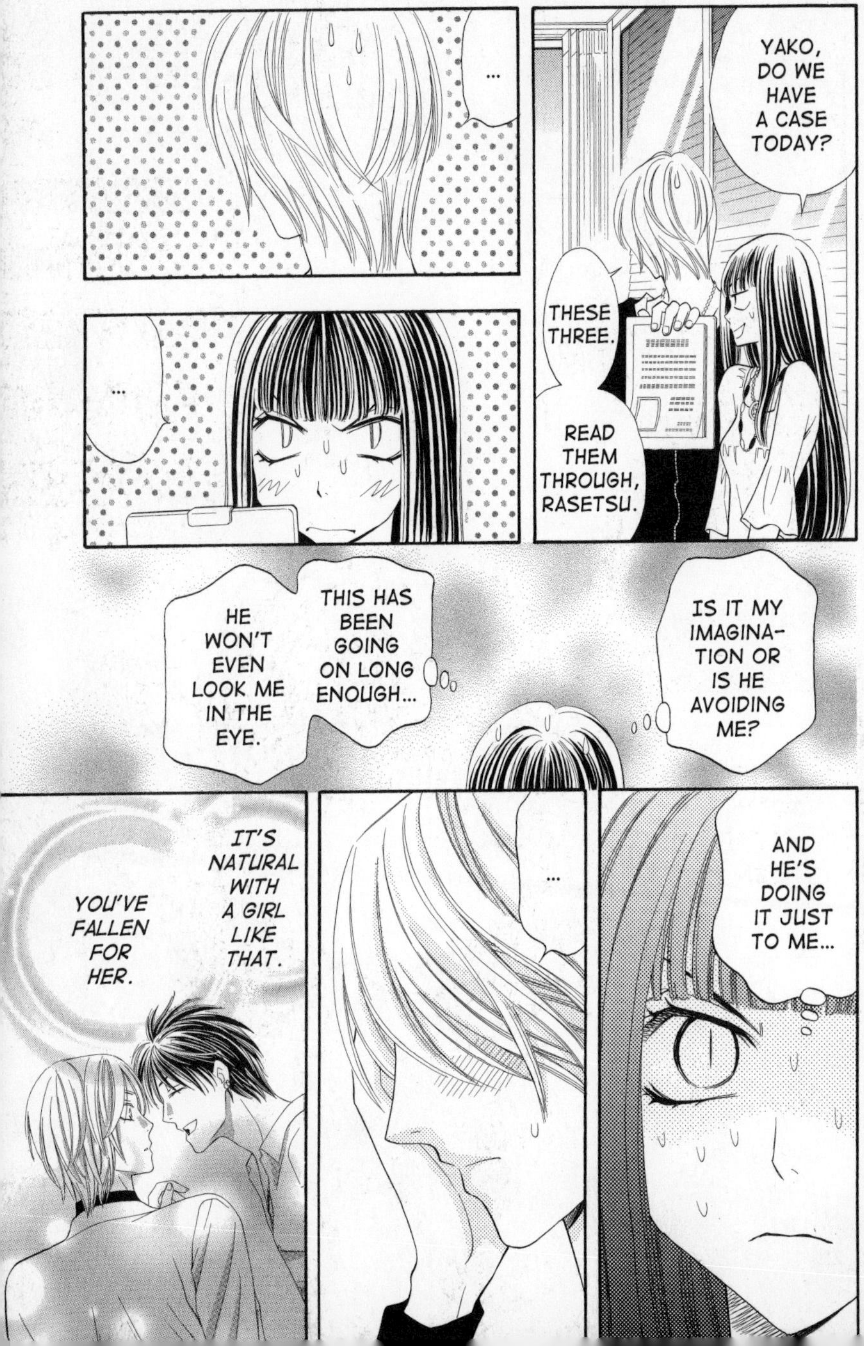
YAKO, DO WE HAVE A CASE TODAY?
THESE THREE.
READ THEM THROUGH, RASETSU.
...
...
IS IT MY IMAGINATION OR IS HE AVOIDING ME?
THIS HAS BEEN GOING ON LONG ENOUGH...
HE WON'T EVEN LOOK ME IN THE EYE.
AND HE'S DOING IT JUST TO ME...
...
IT'S NATURAL WITH A GIRL LIKE THAT.
YOU'VE FALLEN FOR HER.

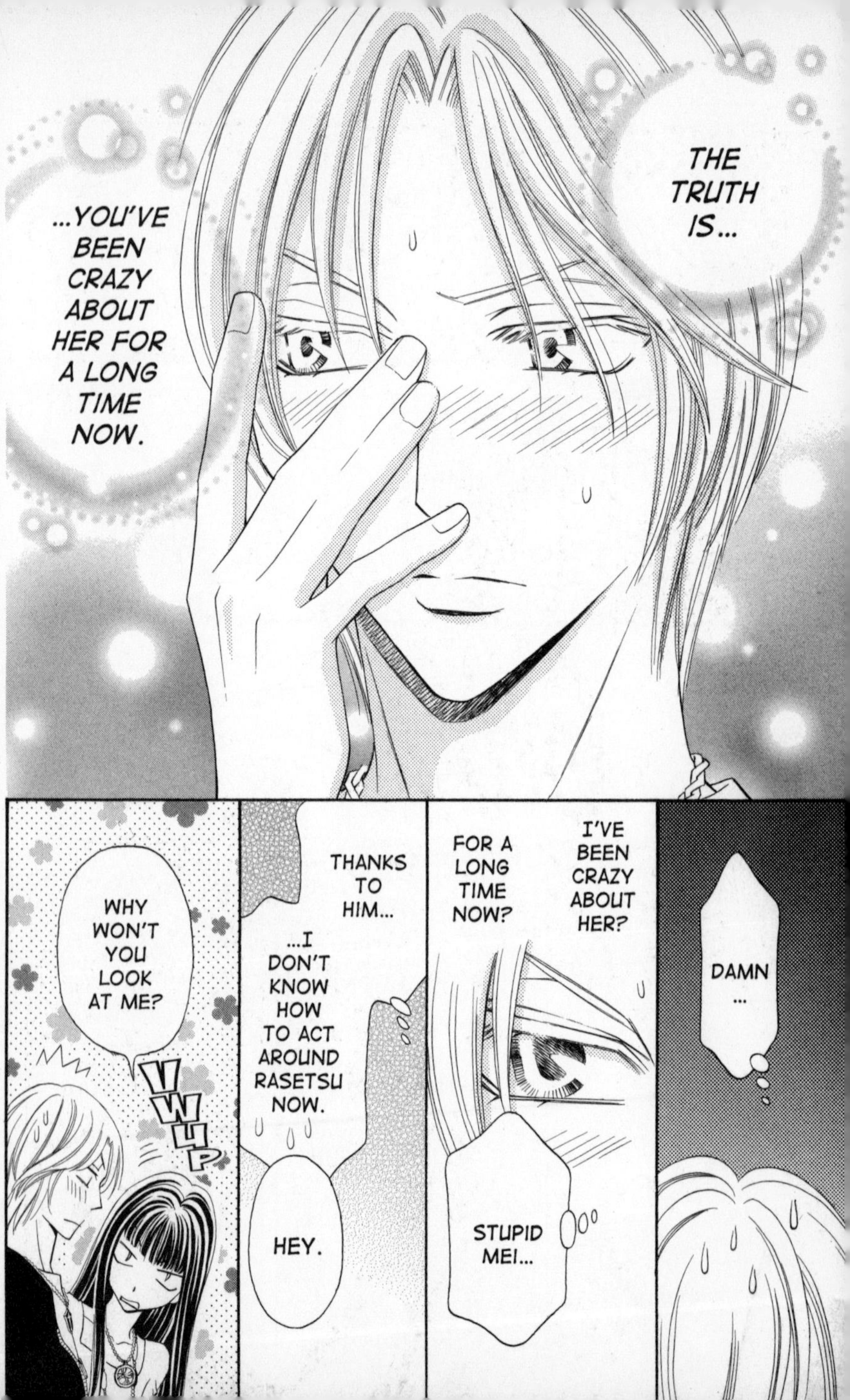
THE TRUTH IS...
...YOU'VE BEEN CRAZY ABOUT HER FOR A LONG TIME NOW.
DAMN...
I'VE BEEN CRAZY ABOUT HER?
FOR A LONG TIME NOW?
STUPID MEI...
THANKS TO HIM...
...I DON'T KNOW HOW TO ACT AROUND RASETSU NOW.
HEY.
WHY WON'T YOU LOOK AT ME?
WHUP

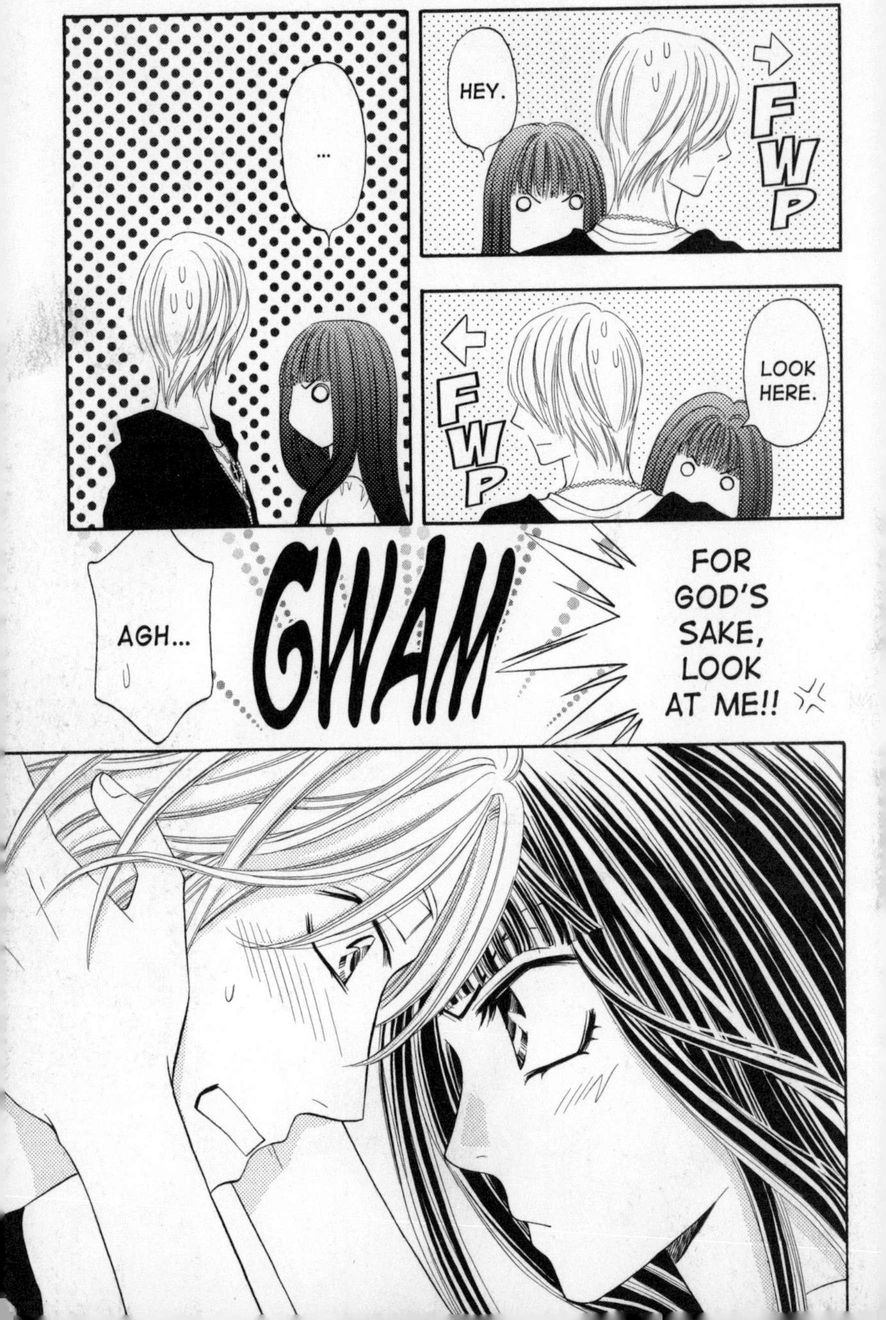
HEY.
FWP
LOOK HERE.
FWP
...
FOR GOD'S SAKE, LOOK AT ME!!
GWAM
AGH...

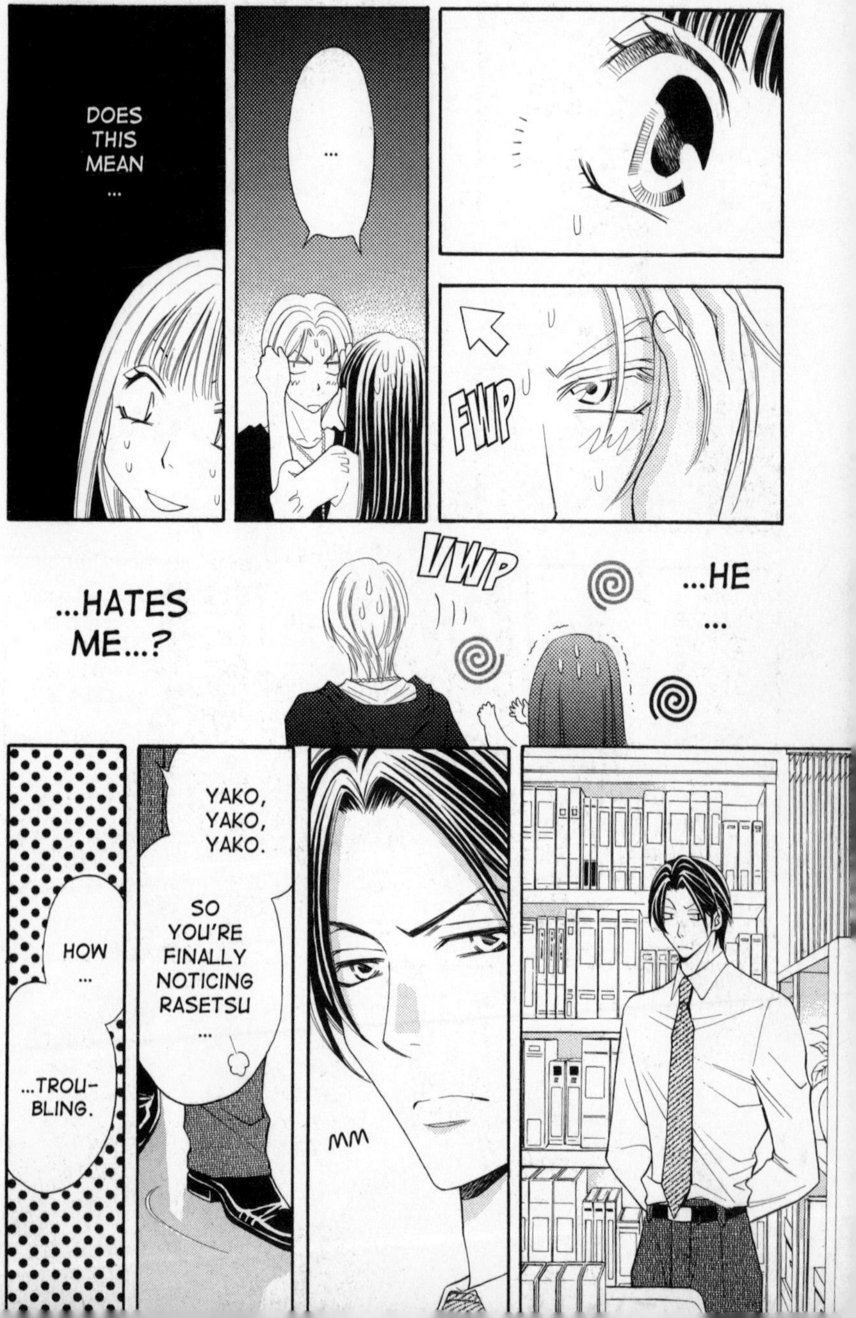
FWP
...
DOES THIS MEAN ...
...HE ...
VWP
...HATES ME...?
MM
YAKO, YAKO, YAKO.
SO YOU'RE FINALLY NOTICING RASETSU ...
HOW ...
...TROU-BLING.

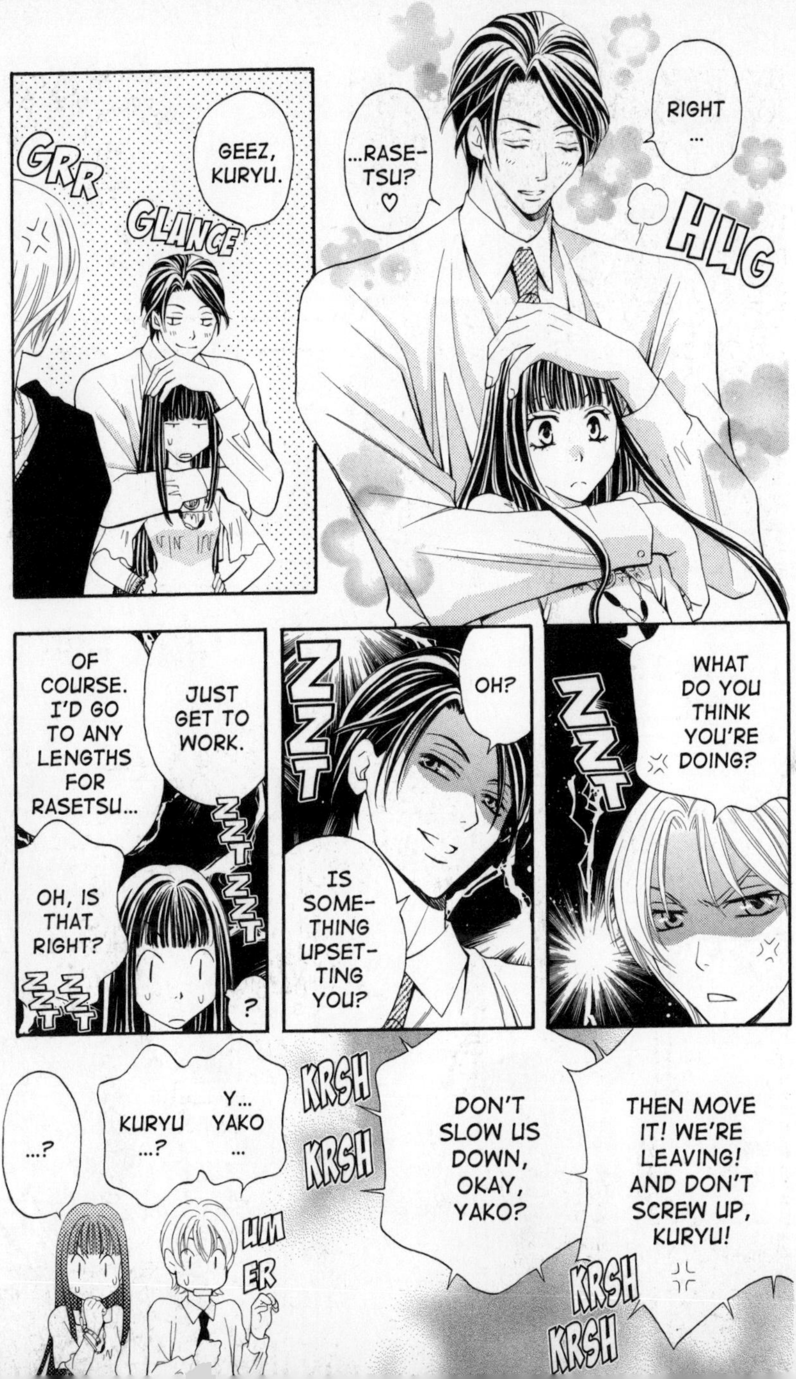
RIGHT ...
...RASE-TSU? ♡
HUG
GEEZ, KURYU.
GLANCE
GRR
WHAT DO YOU THINK YOU'RE DOING?
ZZZT
OH?
ZZZT
IS SOME-THING UPSET-TING YOU?
JUST GET TO WORK.
OF COURSE. I'D GO TO ANY LENGTHS FOR RASETSU...
ZZZT ZZZT
OH, IS THAT RIGHT?
?
ZZZT ZZZT
THEN MOVE IT! WE'RE LEAVING! AND DON'T SCREW UP, KURYU!
DON'T SLOW US DOWN, OKAY, YAKO?
KRSH
KRSH
Y... YAKO ...
KURYU ...?
...?
UMMER
KRSH
KRSH

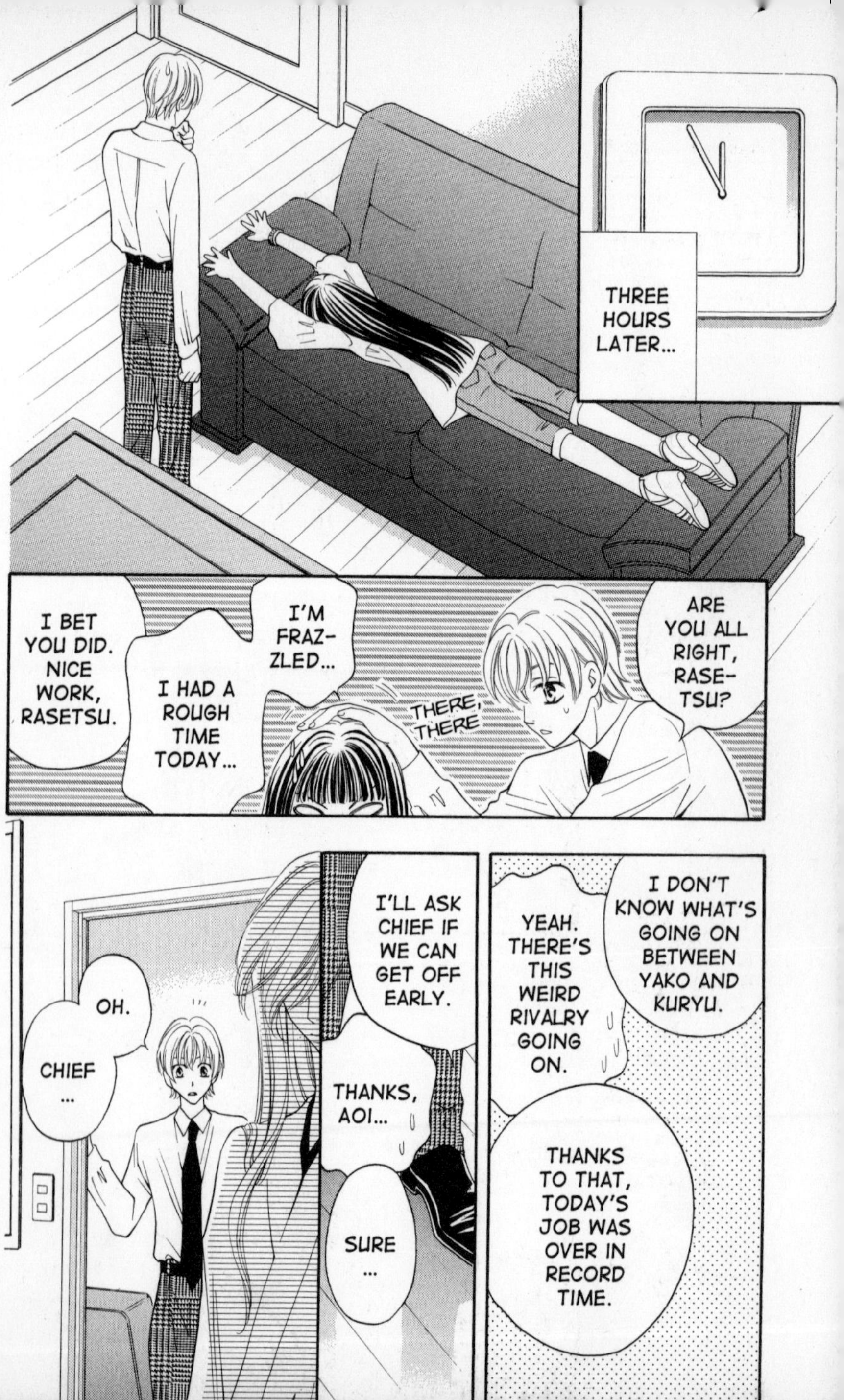
THREE HOURS LATER...
ARE YOU ALL RIGHT, RASETSU?
THERE, THERE
I'M FRAZZLED...
I HAD A ROUGH TIME TODAY...
I BET YOU DID. NICE WORK, RASETSU.
I DON'T KNOW WHAT'S GOING ON BETWEEN YAKO AND KURYU.
YEAH. THERE'S THIS WEIRD RIVALRY GOING ON.
THANKS TO THAT, TODAY'S JOB WAS OVER IN RECORD TIME.
I'LL ASK CHIEF IF WE CAN GET OFF EARLY.
THANKS, AOI...
SURE...
OH.
CHIEF...

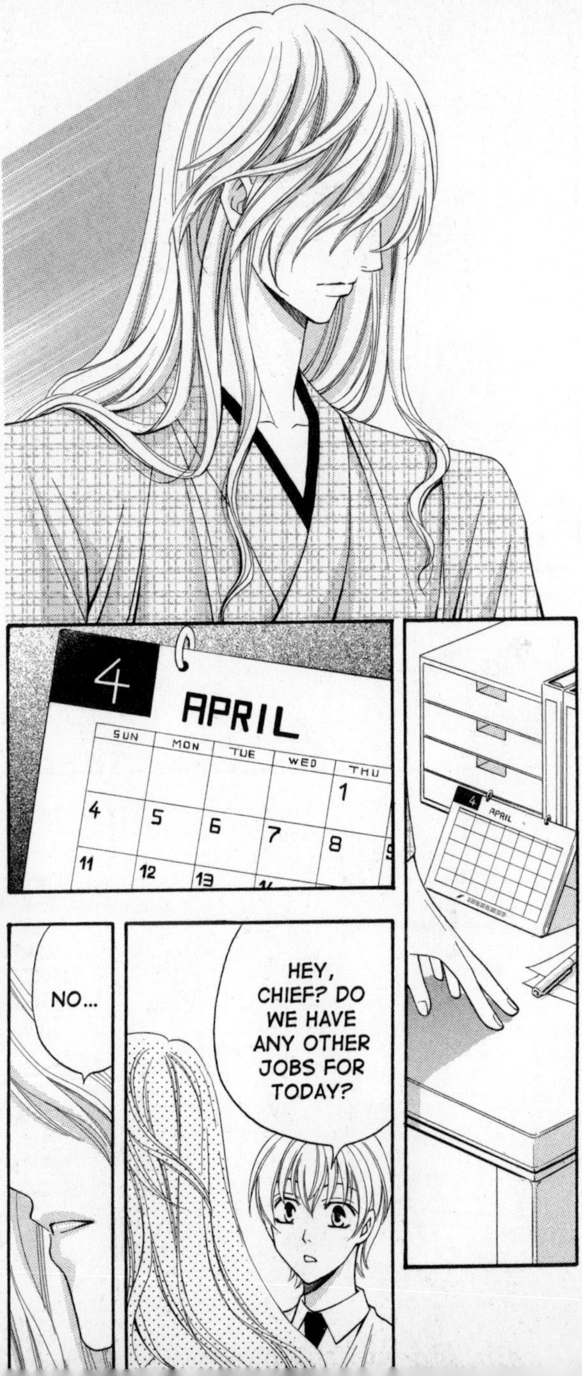
4
APRIL
SUN
MON
TUE
WED
THU
1
4
5
6
7
8
11
12
13
HEY, CHIEF? DO WE HAVE ANY OTHER JOBS FOR TODAY?
NO...

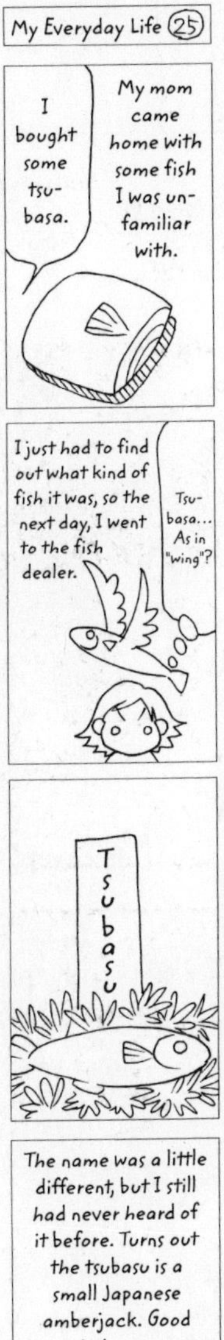
My Everyday Life 25
My mom came home with some fish I was unfamiliar with.
I bought some tsubasa.
Tsubasa... As in "wing"?
I just had to find out what kind of fish it was, so the next day, I went to the fish dealer.
Tsubasu
The name was a little different, but I still had never heard of it before. Turns out the tsubasu is a small Japanese amberjack. Good to know.
Ever-changing fish!

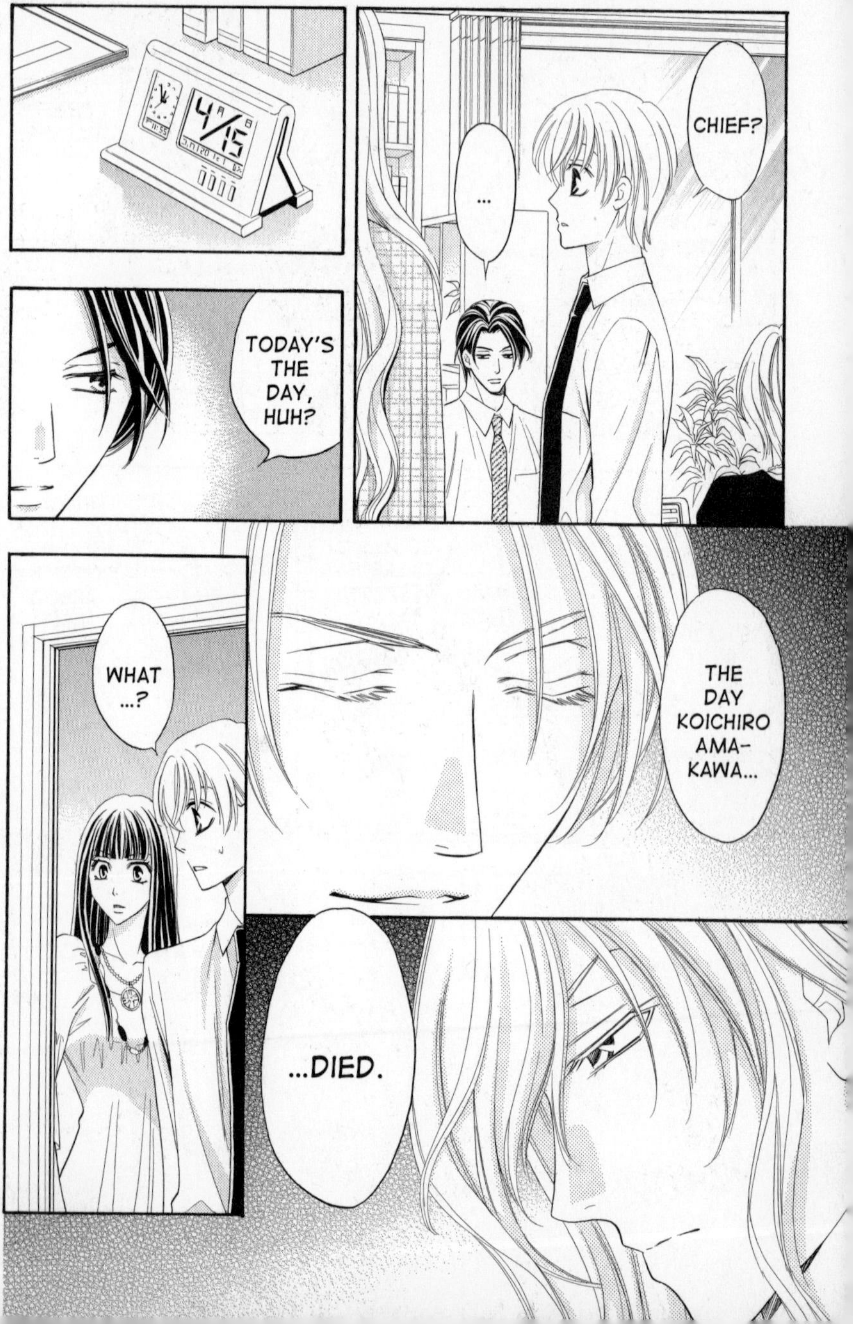
CHIEF?
...
TODAY'S THE DAY, HUH?
THE DAY KOICHIRO AMA-KAWA...
...DIED.
WHAT ...?

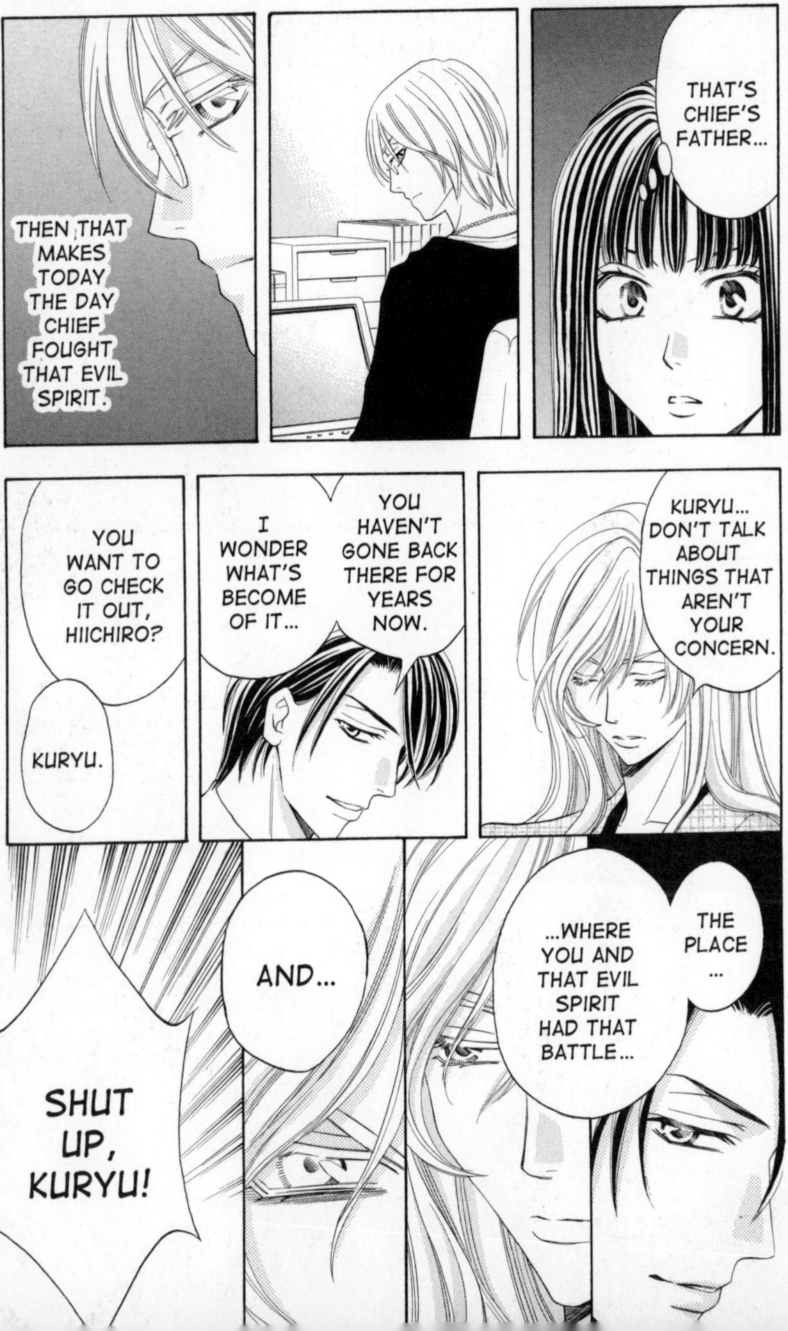
THAT'S CHIEF'S FATHER...
THEN THAT MAKES TODAY THE DAY CHIEF FOUGHT THAT EVIL SPIRIT.
KURYU... DON'T TALK ABOUT THINGS THAT AREN'T YOUR CONCERN.
YOU HAVEN'T GONE BACK THERE FOR YEARS NOW.
I WONDER WHAT'S BECOME OF IT...
YOU WANT TO GO CHECK IT OUT, HIICHIRO?
KURYU.
THE PLACE...
...WHERE YOU AND THAT EVIL SPIRIT HAD THAT BATTLE...
AND...
SHUT UP, KURYU!

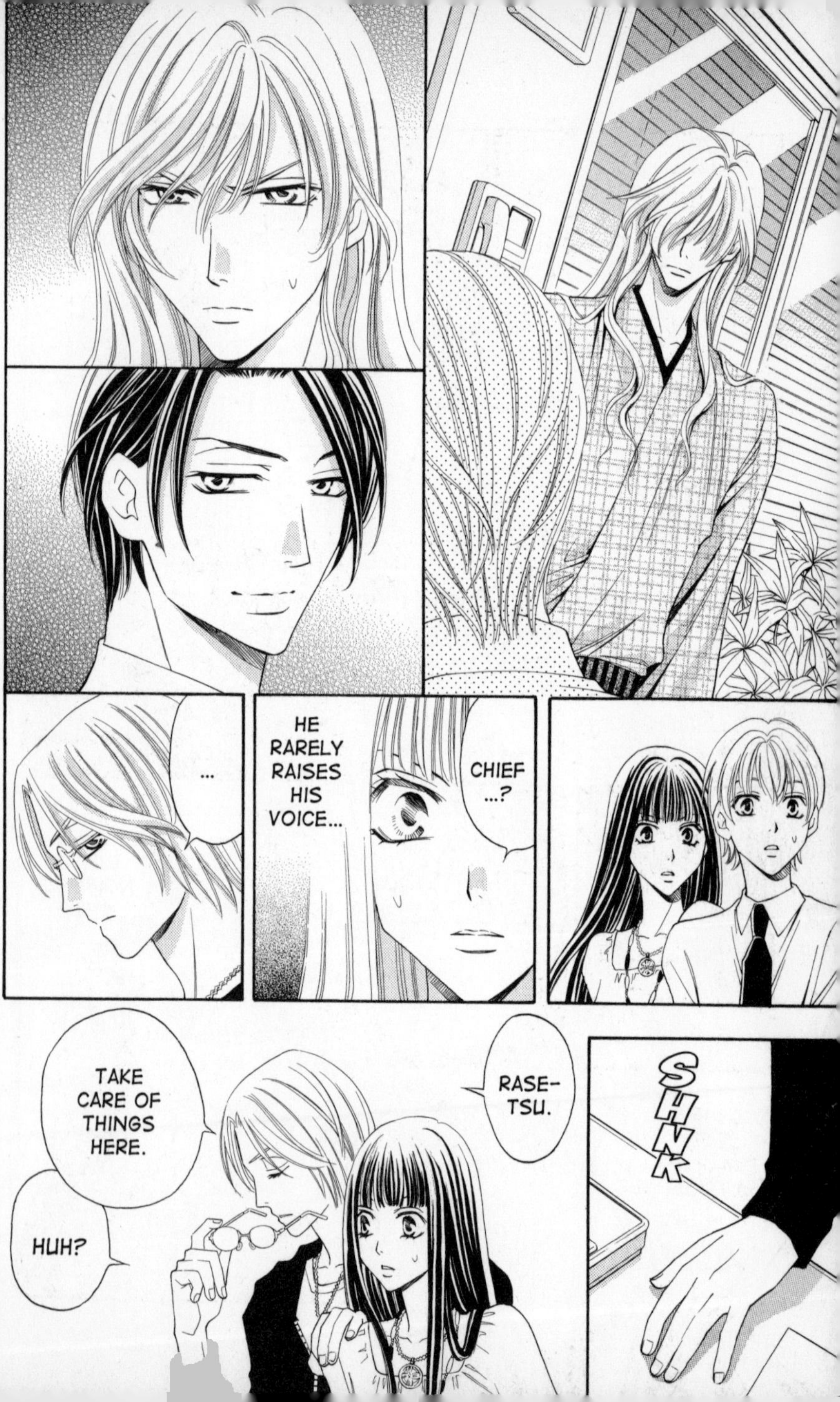
CHIEF ...?
HE RARELY RAISES HIS VOICE...
...
SHHNK
RASE-TSU.
TAKE CARE OF THINGS HERE.
HUH?

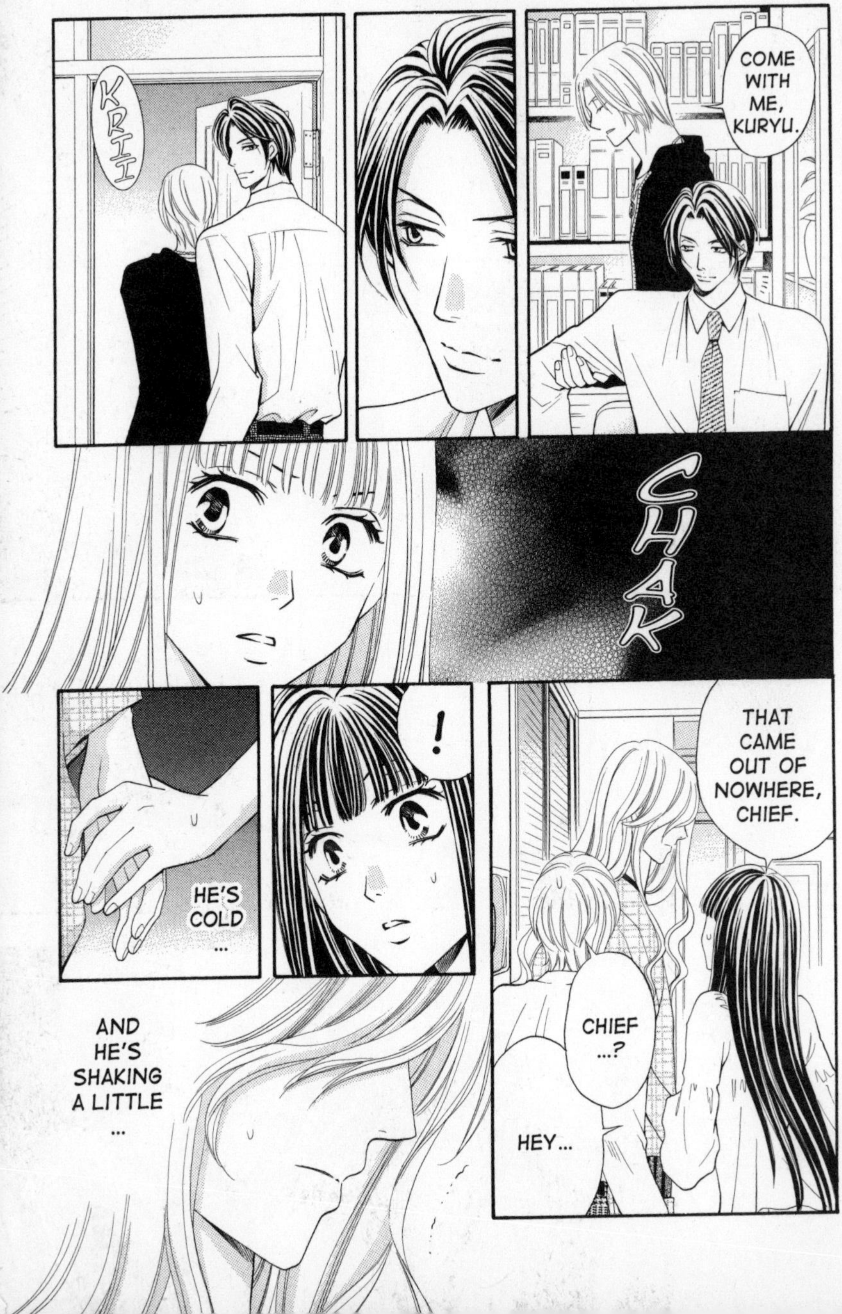
COME WITH ME, KURYU.
KRII
CHAK
THAT CAME OUT OF NOWHERE, CHIEF.
CHIEF ...?
HEY...
!
HE'S COLD ...
AND HE'S SHAKING A LITTLE ...

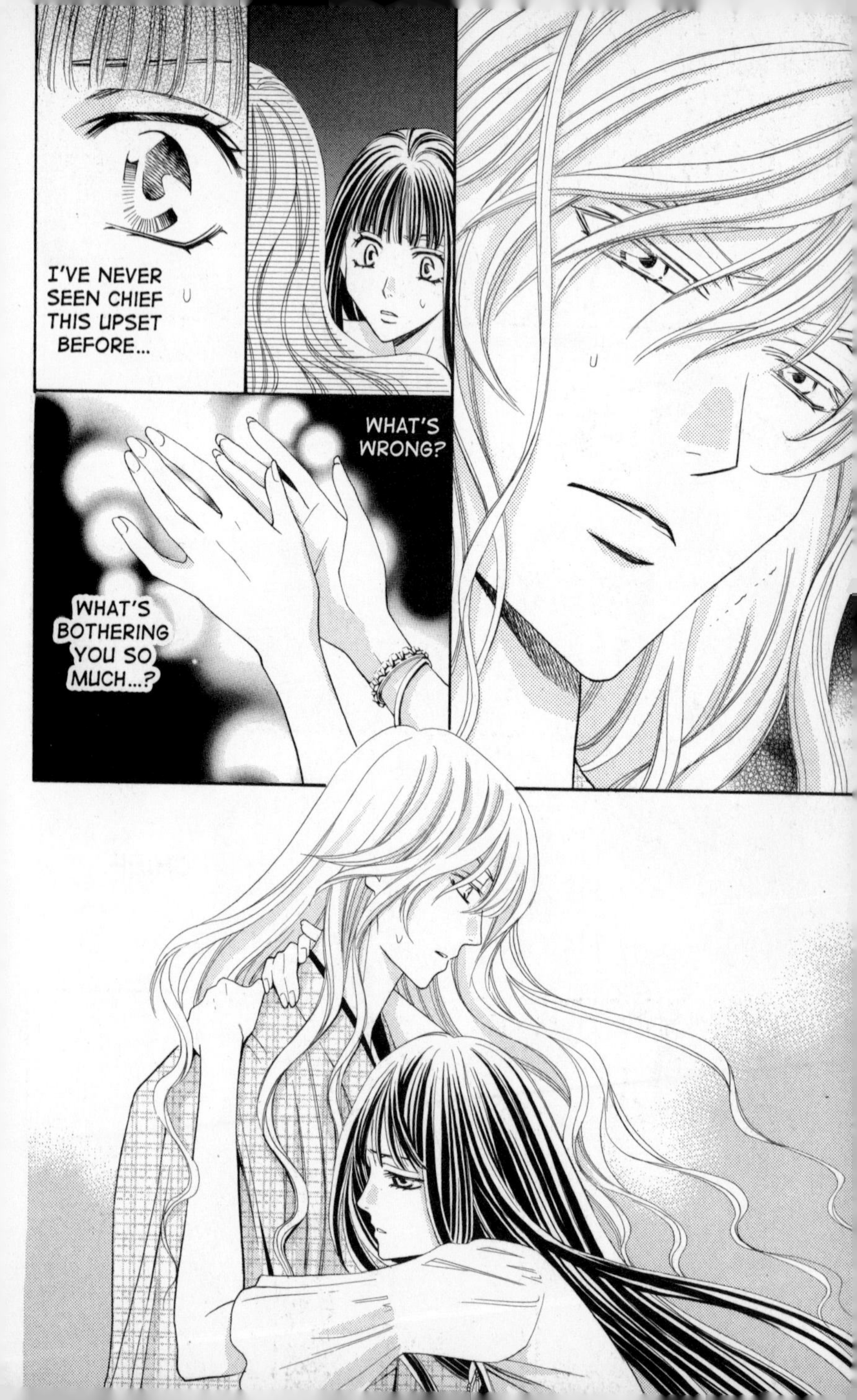
I'VE NEVER SEEN CHIEF THIS UPSET BEFORE...
WHAT'S WRONG?
WHAT'S BOTHERING YOU SO MUCH...?

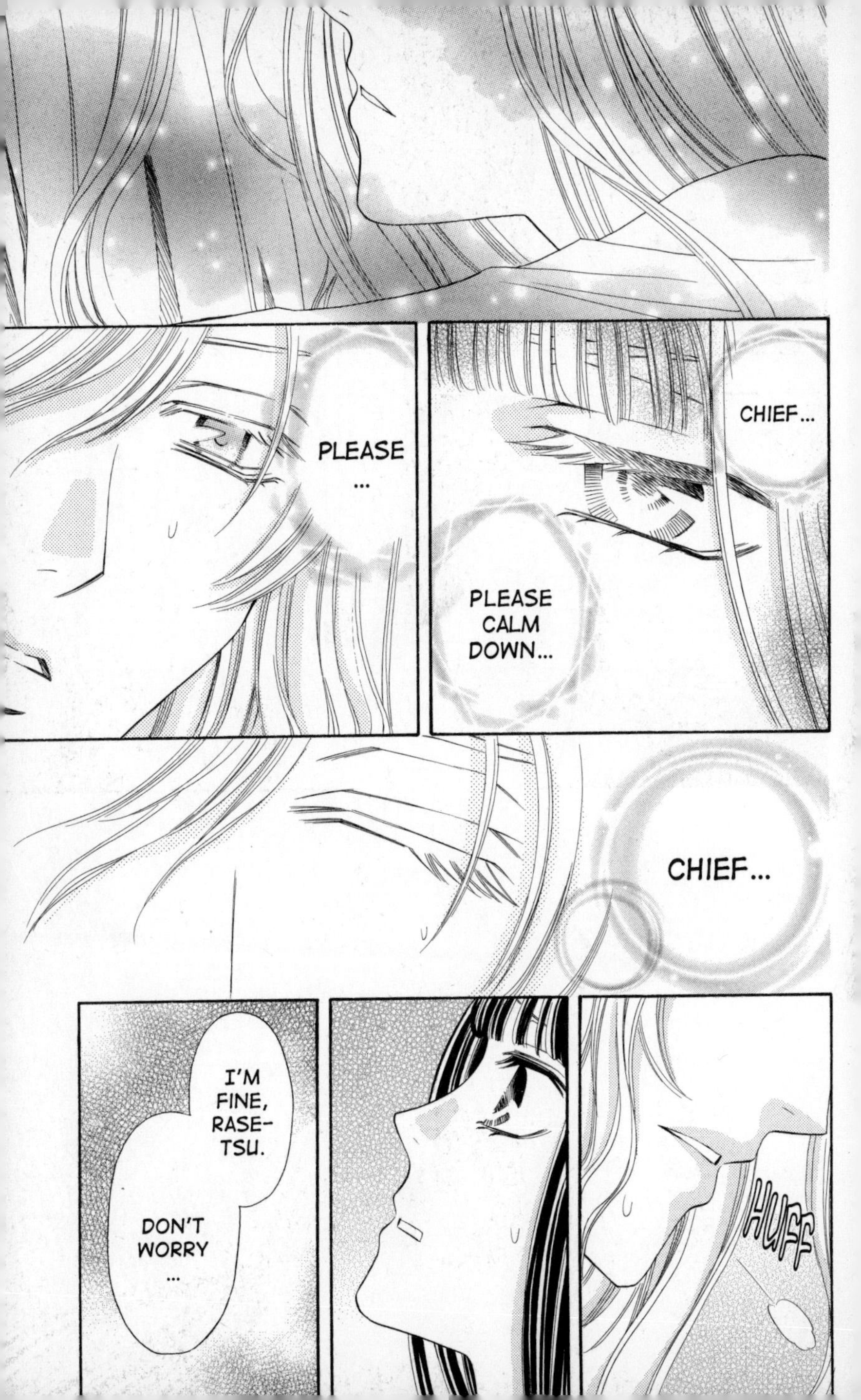
CHIEF...
PLEASE CALM DOWN...
PLEASE ...
CHIEF...
HUFF
I'M FINE, RASE-TSU.
DON'T WORRY ...

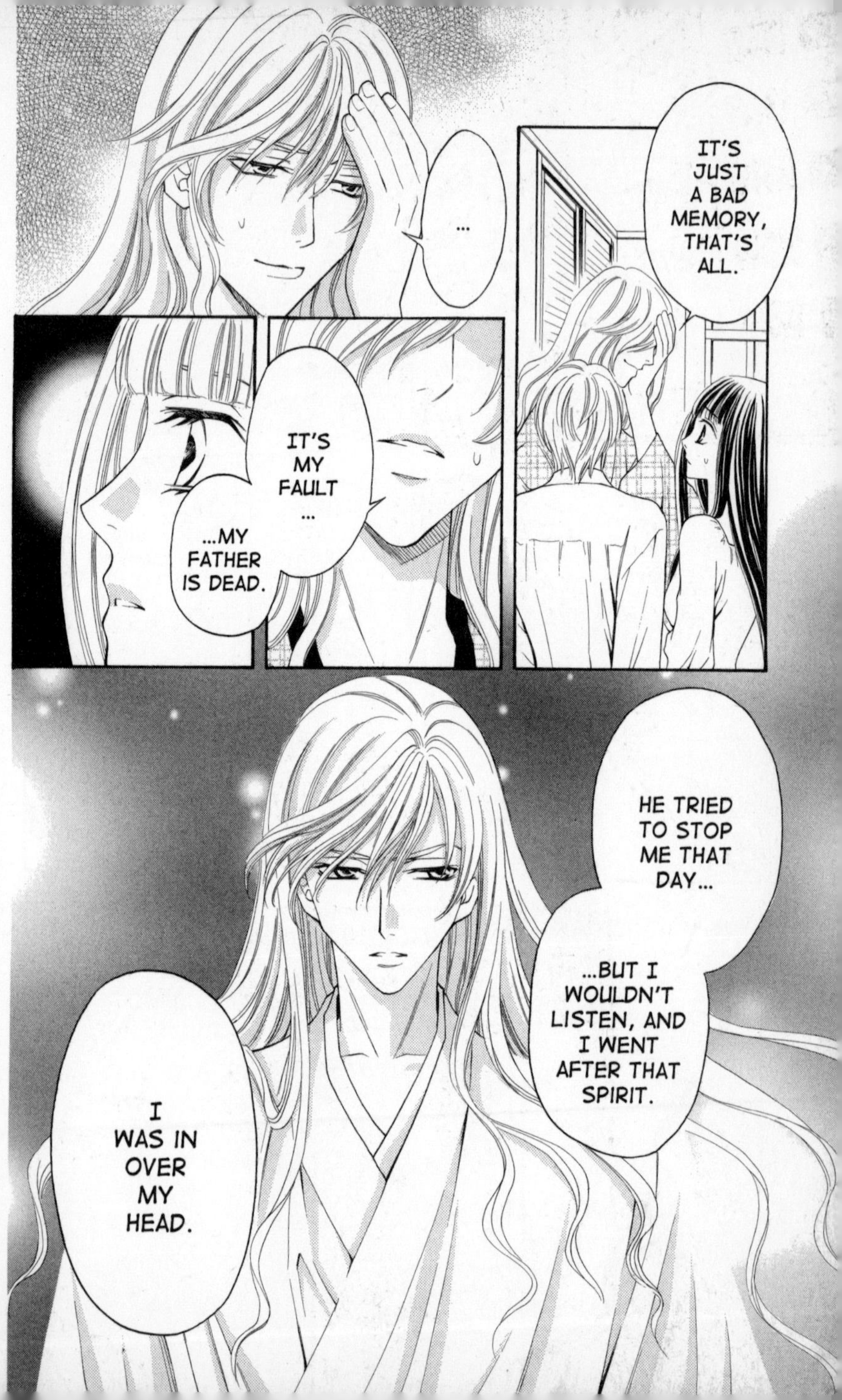
IT'S JUST A BAD MEMORY, THAT'S ALL.
...
IT'S MY FAULT ...
...MY FATHER IS DEAD.
HE TRIED TO STOP ME THAT DAY...
...BUT I WOULDN'T LISTEN, AND I WENT AFTER THAT SPIRIT.
I WAS IN OVER MY HEAD.

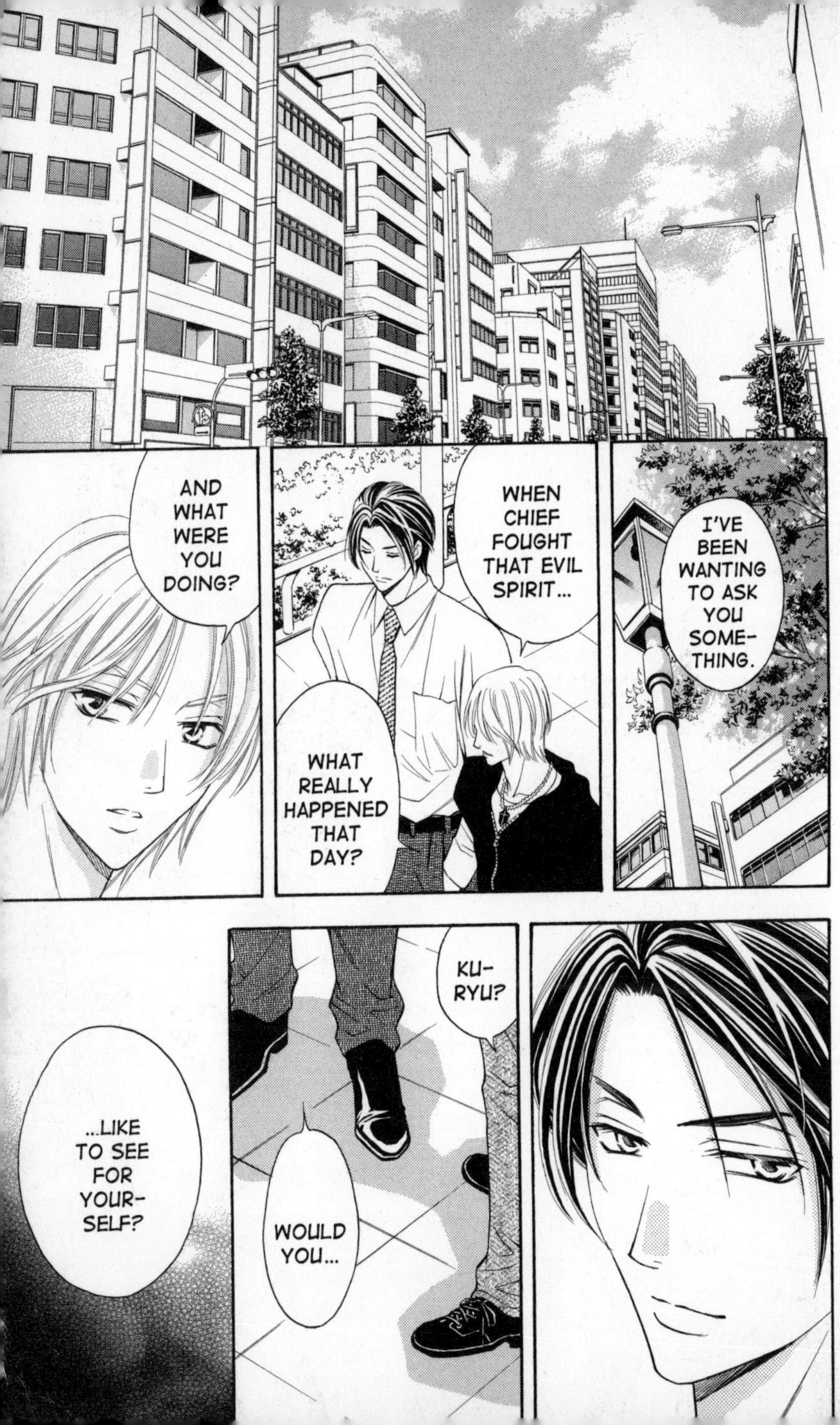
I'VE BEEN WANTING TO ASK YOU SOME-THING.
WHEN CHIEF FOUGHT THAT EVIL SPIRIT...
WHAT REALLY HAPPENED THAT DAY?
AND WHAT WERE YOU DOING?
KU-RYU?
WOULD YOU...
...LIKE TO SEE FOR YOUR-SELF?

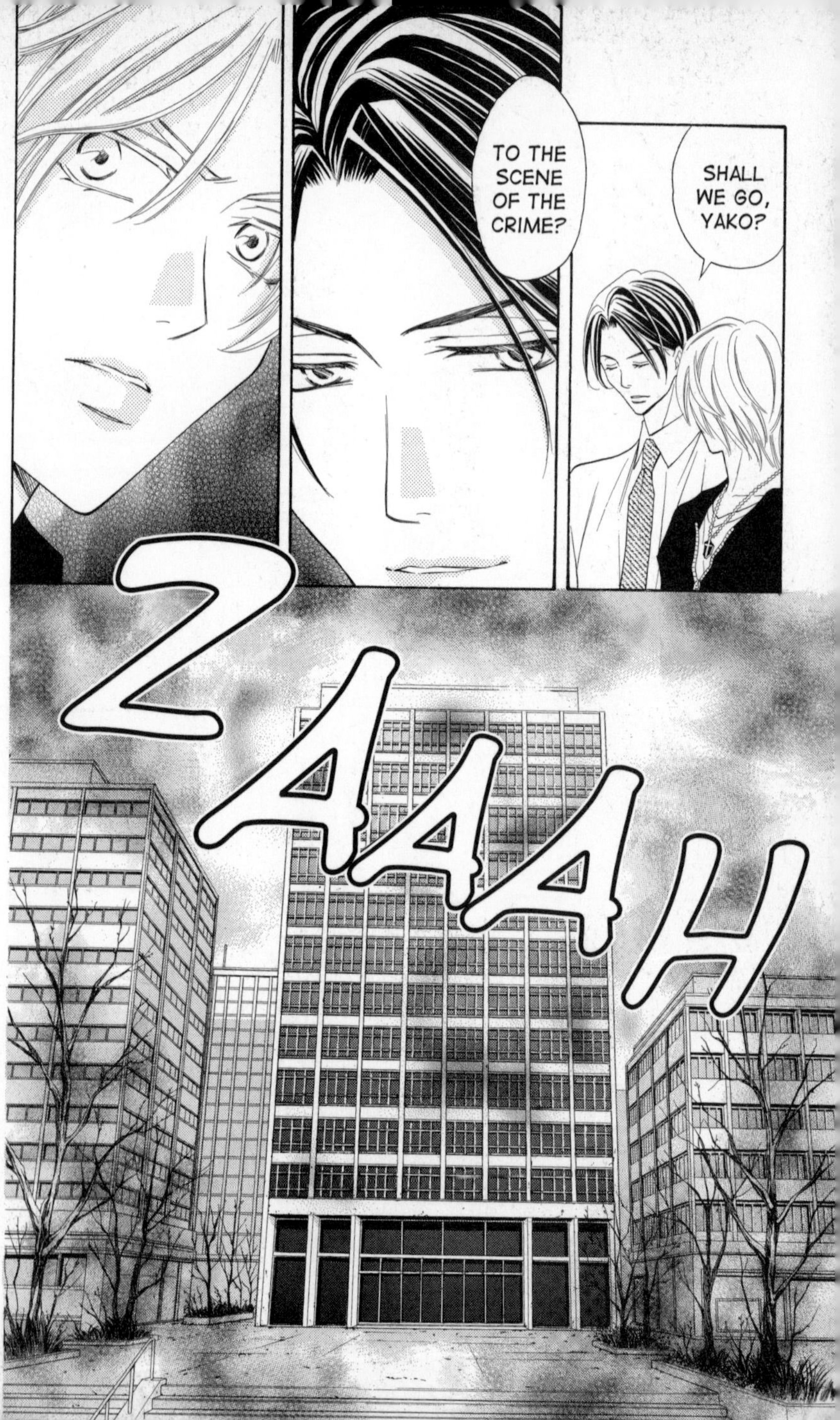
SHALL WE GO, YAKO?
TO THE SCENE OF THE CRIME?
ZAAAH

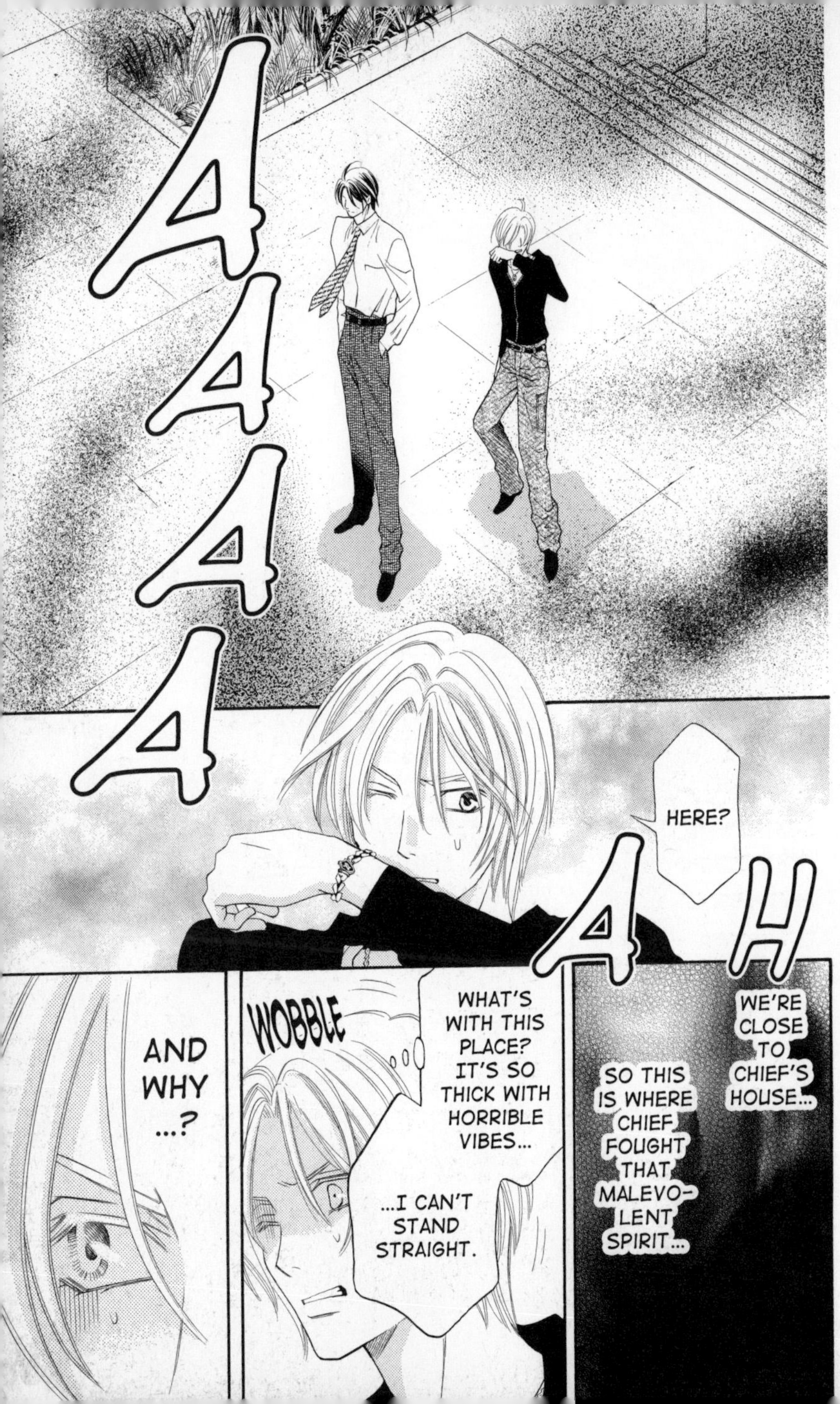
AAAA
HERE?
AH
WE'RE CLOSE TO CHIEF'S HOUSE...
SO THIS IS WHERE CHIEF FOUGHT THAT MALEVO-LENT SPIRIT...
WOBBLE
WHAT'S WITH THIS PLACE? IT'S SO THICK WITH HORRIBLE VIBES...
...I CAN'T STAND STRAIGHT.
AND WHY ...?

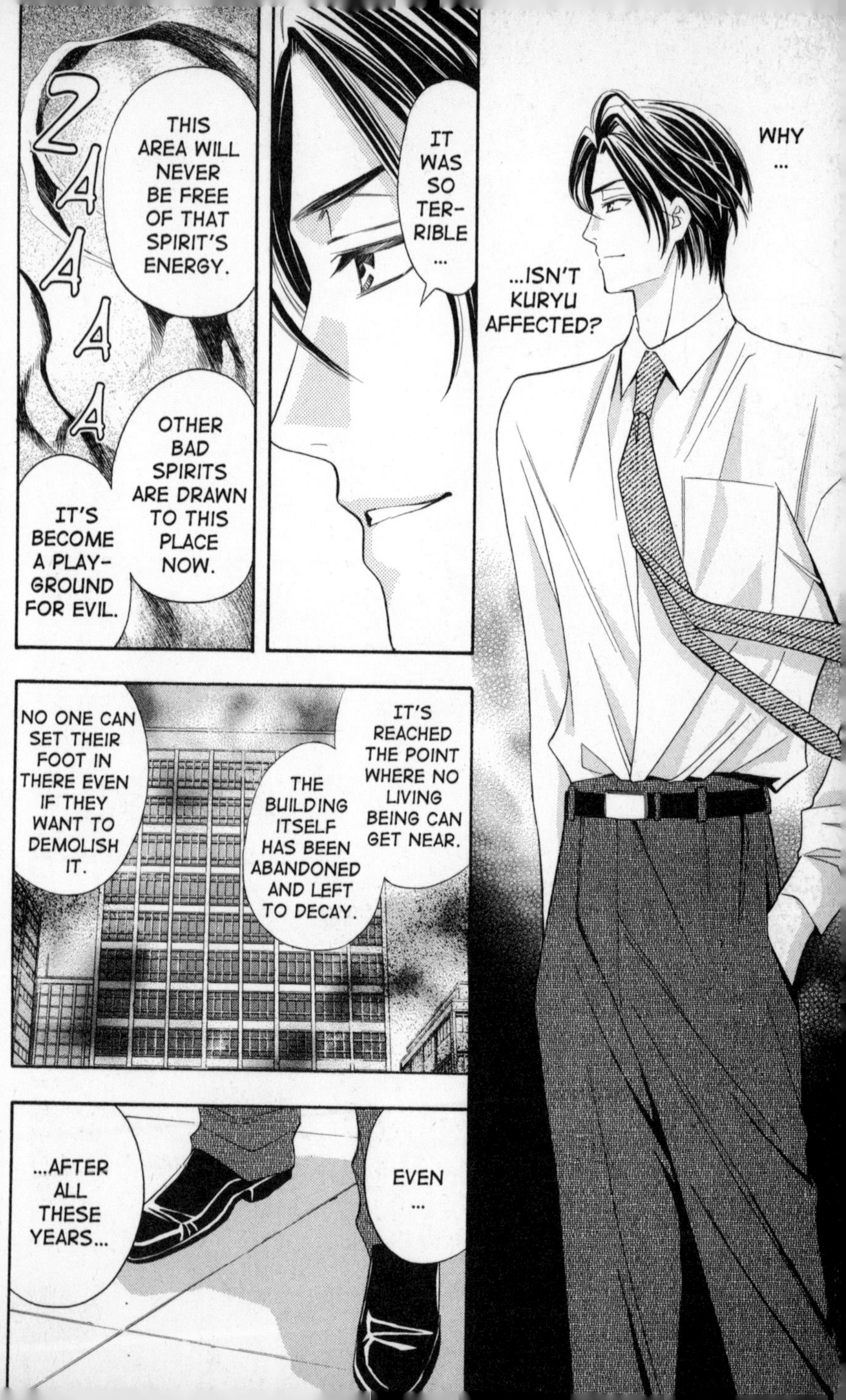
WHY ...
...ISN'T KURYU AFFECTED?
IT WAS SO TER-RIBLE ...
THIS AREA WILL NEVER BE FREE OF THAT SPIRIT'S ENERGY.
ZAAAA
OTHER BAD SPIRITS ARE DRAWN TO THIS PLACE NOW.
IT'S BECOME A PLAY-GROUND FOR EVIL.
IT'S REACHED THE POINT WHERE NO LIVING BEING CAN GET NEAR.
THE BUILDING ITSELF HAS BEEN ABANDONED AND LEFT TO DECAY.
NO ONE CAN SET THEIR FOOT IN THERE EVEN IF THEY WANT TO DEMOLISH IT.
EVEN ...
...AFTER ALL THESE YEARS...

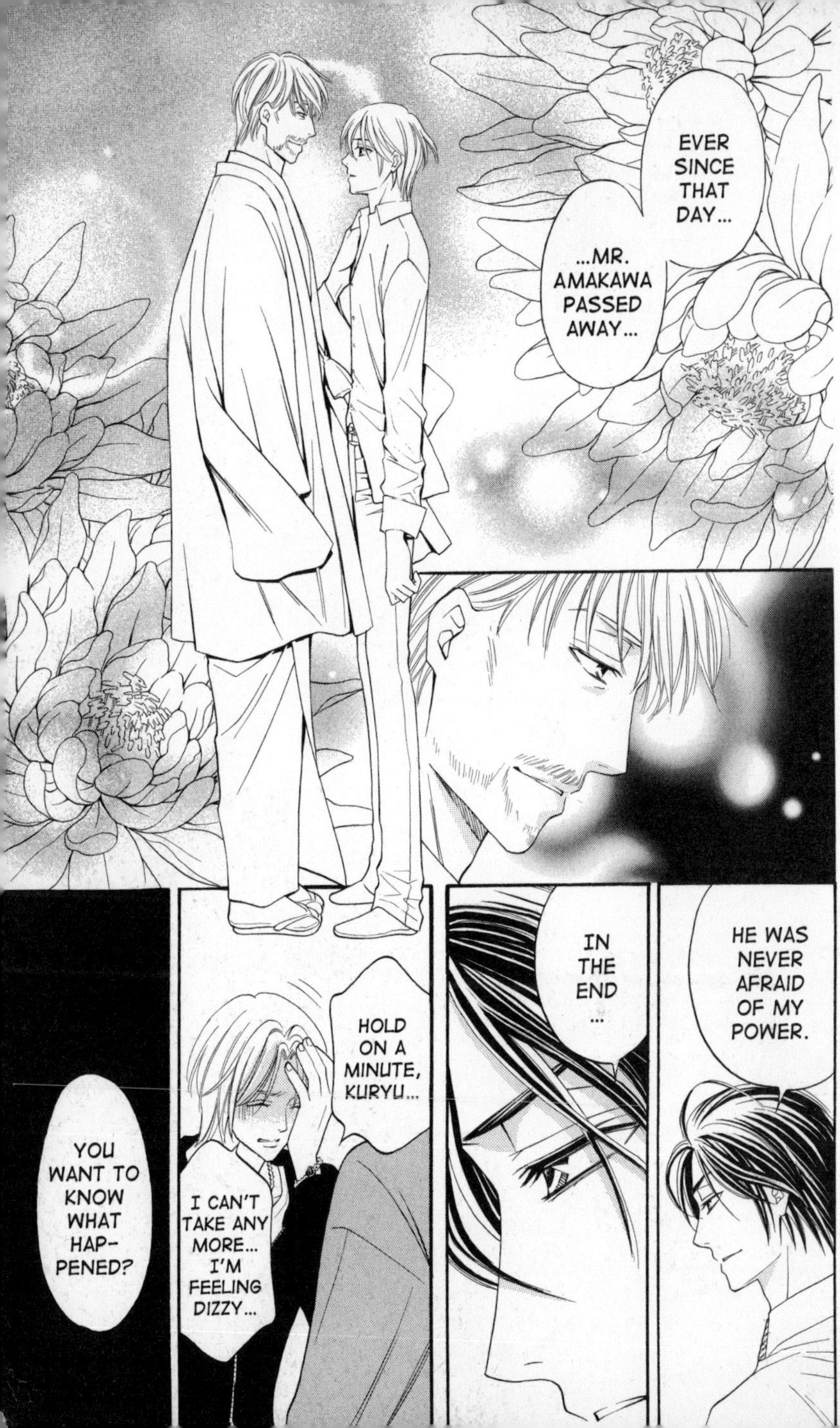
EVER SINCE THAT DAY...
...MR. AMAKAWA PASSED AWAY...
HE WAS NEVER AFRAID OF MY POWER.
IN THE END ...
HOLD ON A MINUTE, KURYU...
I CAN'T TAKE ANY MORE... I'M FEELING DIZZY...
YOU WANT TO KNOW WHAT HAP-PENED?

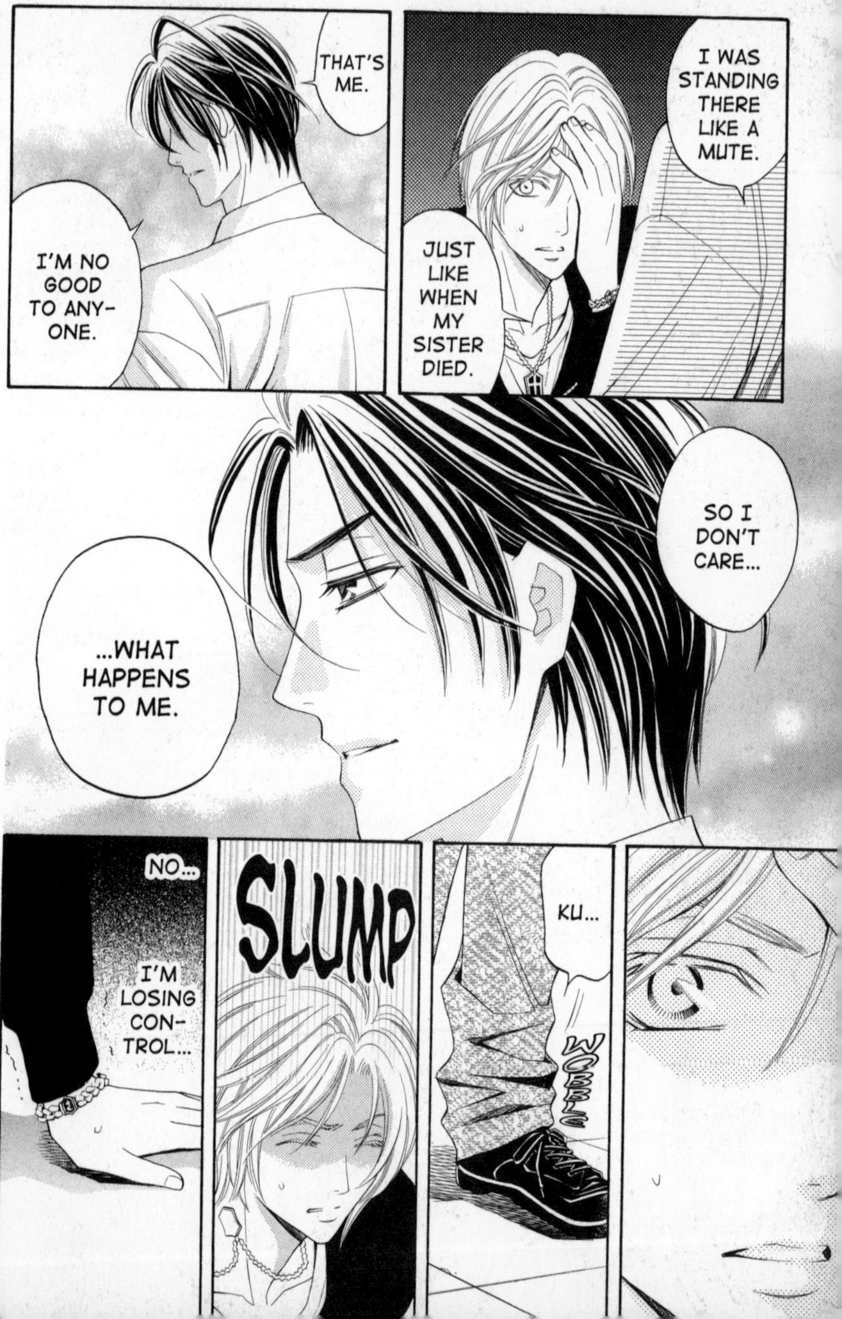
I WAS STANDING THERE LIKE A MUTE.
JUST LIKE WHEN MY SISTER DIED.
THAT'S ME.
I'M NO GOOD TO ANY-ONE.
SO I DON'T CARE...
...WHAT HAPPENS TO ME.
KU...
WOBBLE
SLUMP
NO...
I'M LOSING CON-TROL...

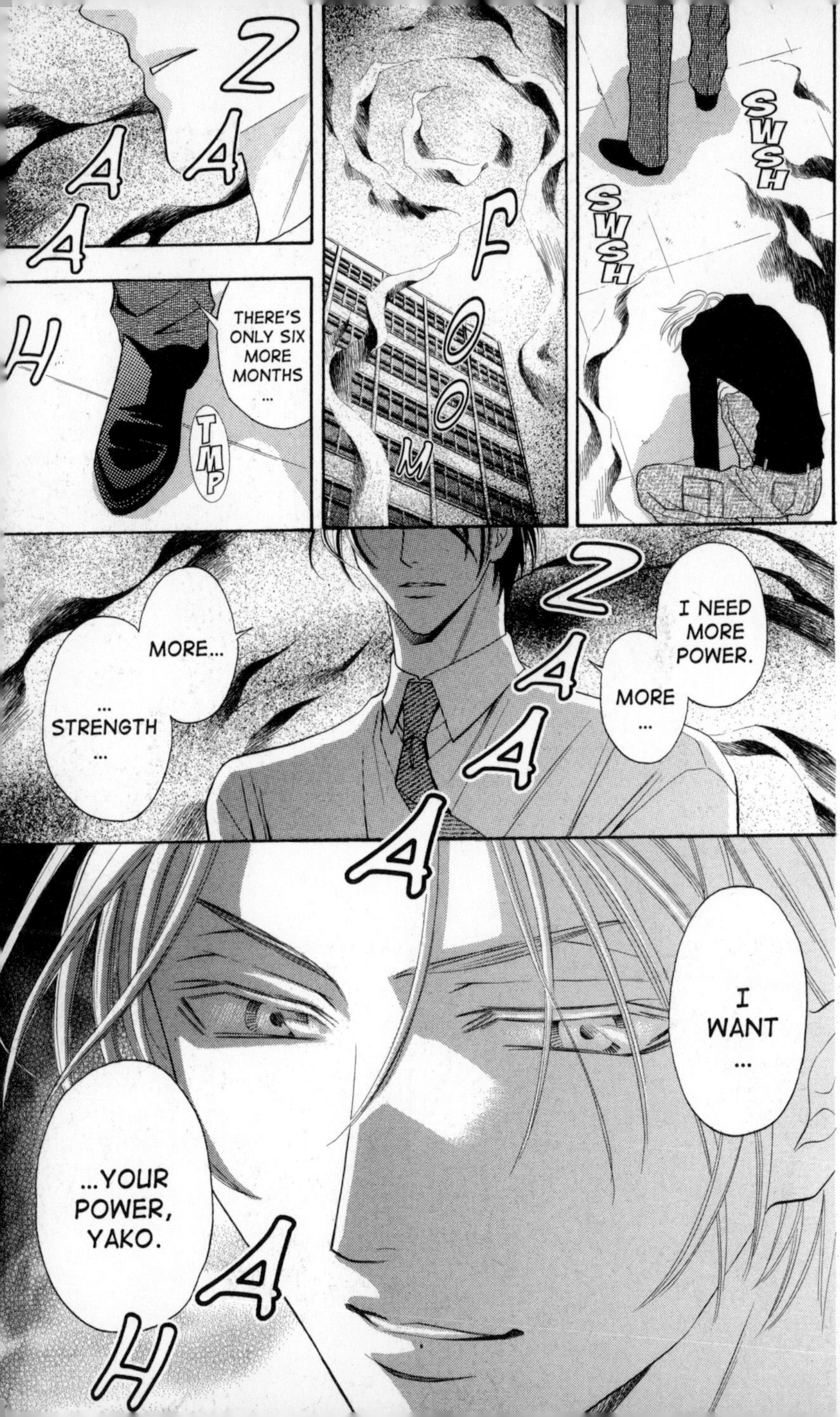
SWSH
SWSH
FOOOM
ZAAA
H
THERE'S ONLY SIX MORE MONTHS ...
TMP
I NEED MORE POWER.
MORE ...
MORE...
... STRENGTH ...
ZAAAA
I WANT ...
...YOUR POWER, YAKO.
AH

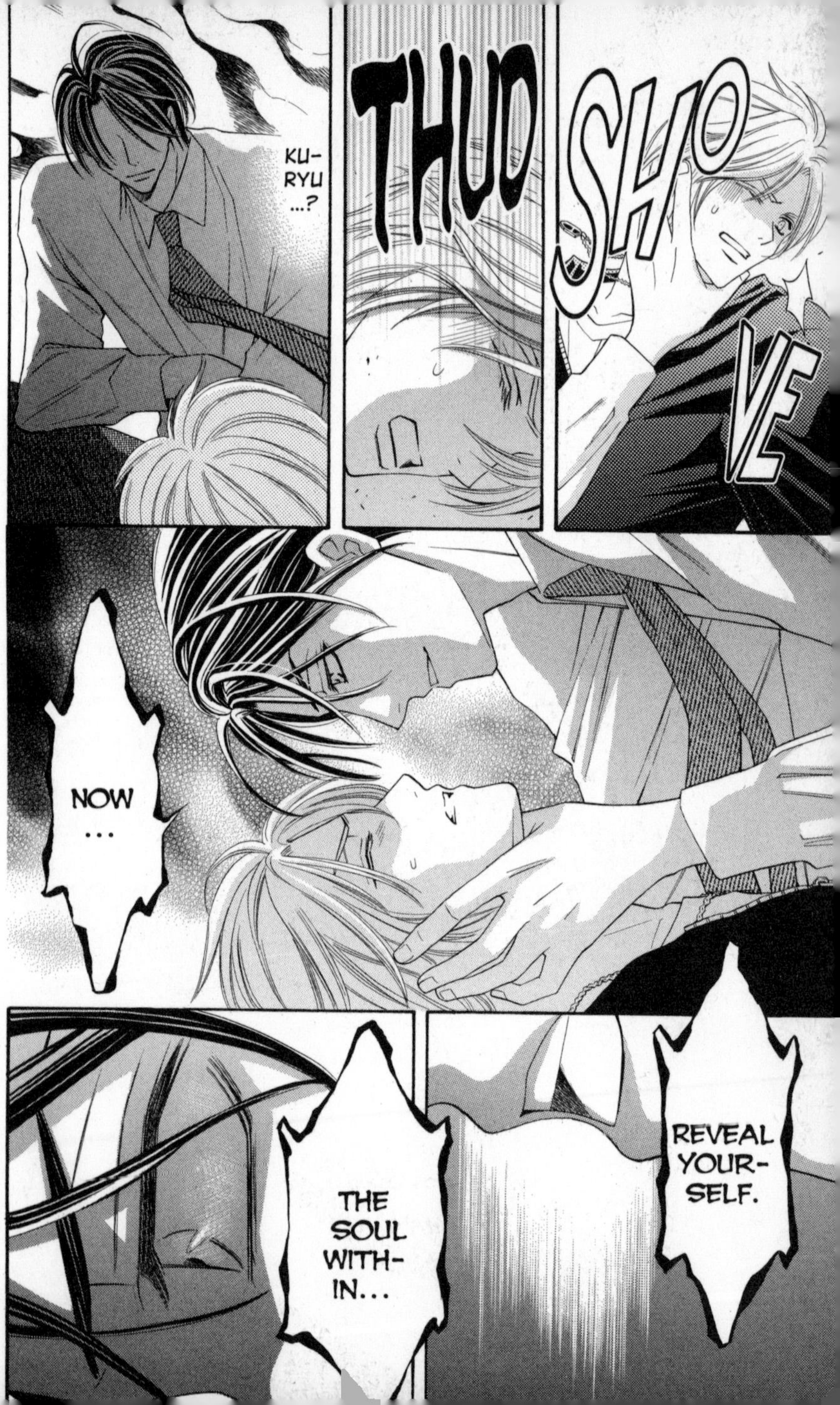
SHOVE
THUD
KU-RYU ...?
NOW ...
REVEAL YOUR-SELF.
THE SOUL WITH-IN...

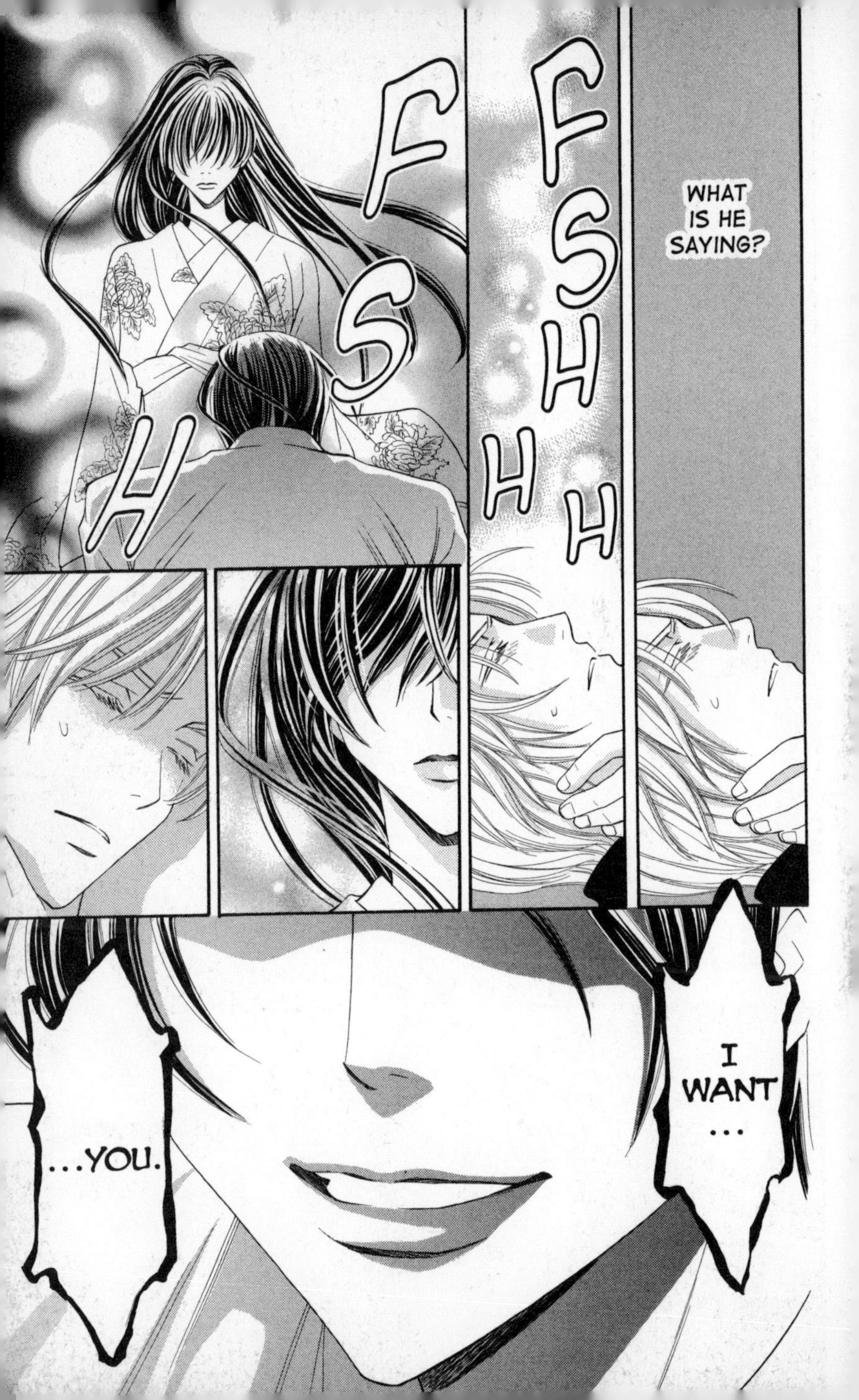
WHAT IS HE SAYING?
FSHHH
FSH
I WANT . . .
. . . YOU.

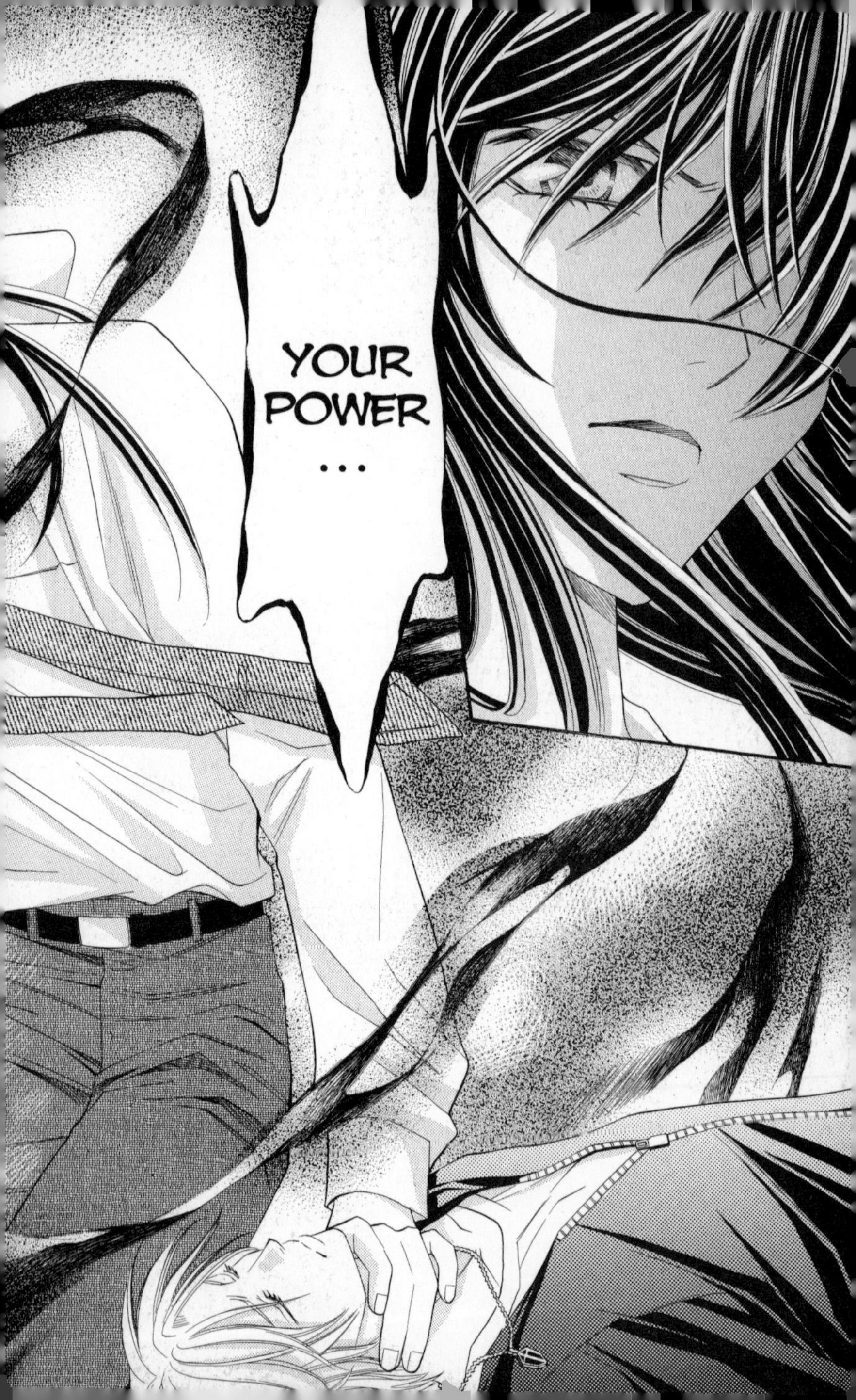
YOUR POWER
...

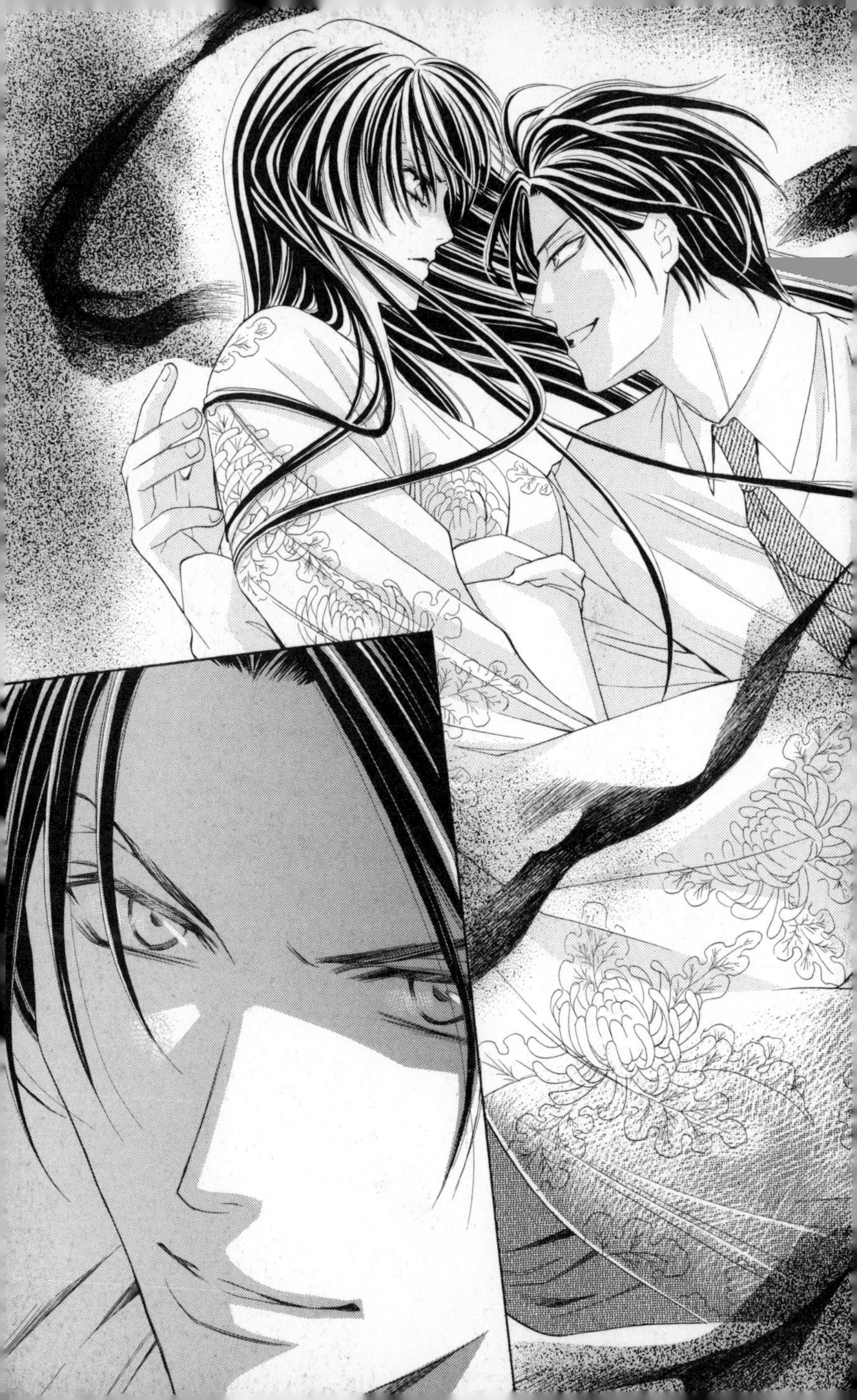

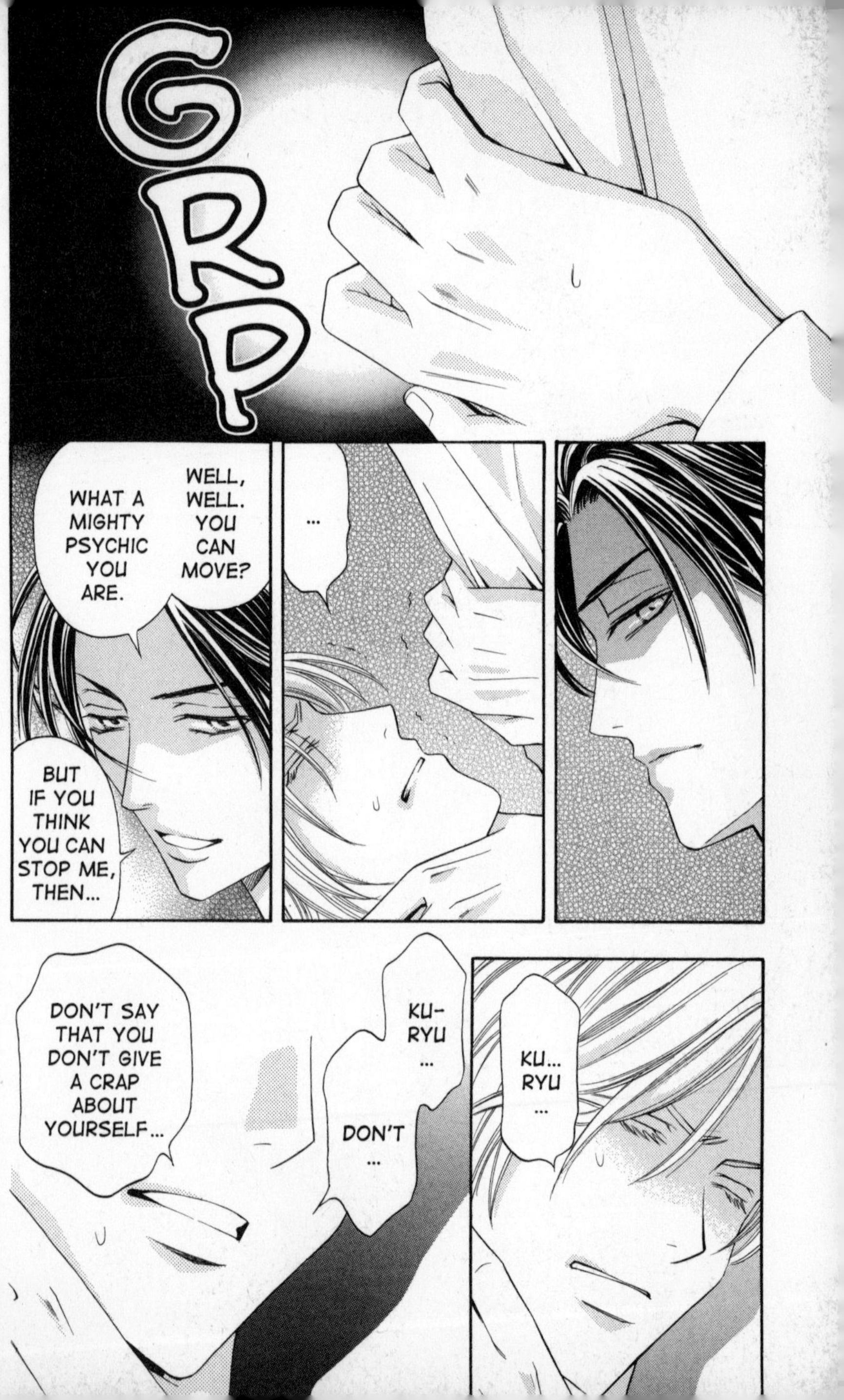
GRP
...
WELL, WELL. YOU CAN MOVE?
WHAT A MIGHTY PSYCHIC YOU ARE.
BUT IF YOU THINK YOU CAN STOP ME, THEN...
KU... RYU ...
KU-RYU ...
DON'T ...
DON'T SAY THAT YOU DON'T GIVE A CRAP ABOUT YOURSELF...

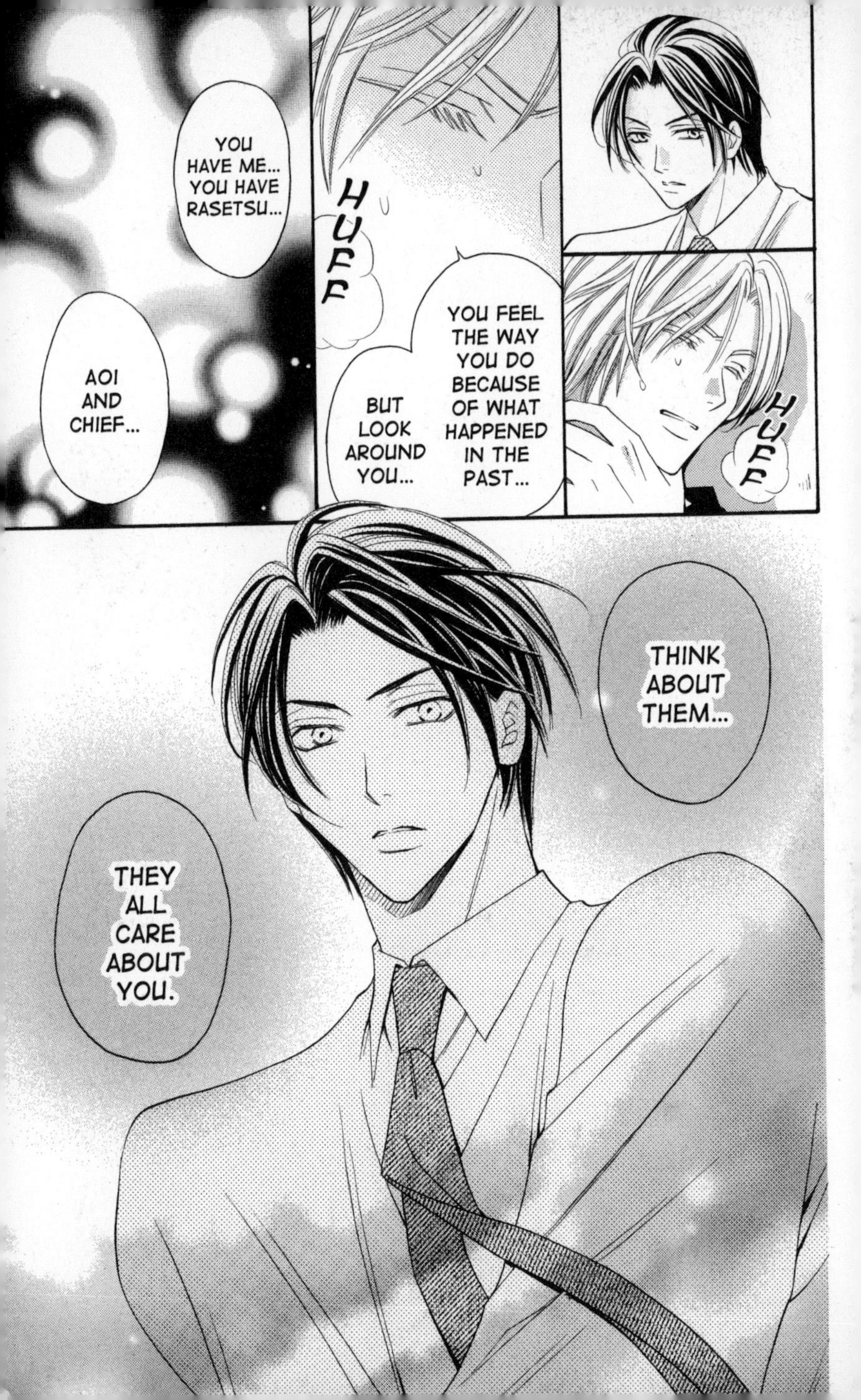
HUFF
YOU FEEL THE WAY YOU DO BECAUSE OF WHAT HAPPENED IN THE PAST...
HUFF
BUT LOOK AROUND YOU...
YOU HAVE ME... YOU HAVE RASETSU...
AOI AND CHIEF...
THINK ABOUT THEM...
THEY ALL CARE ABOUT YOU.

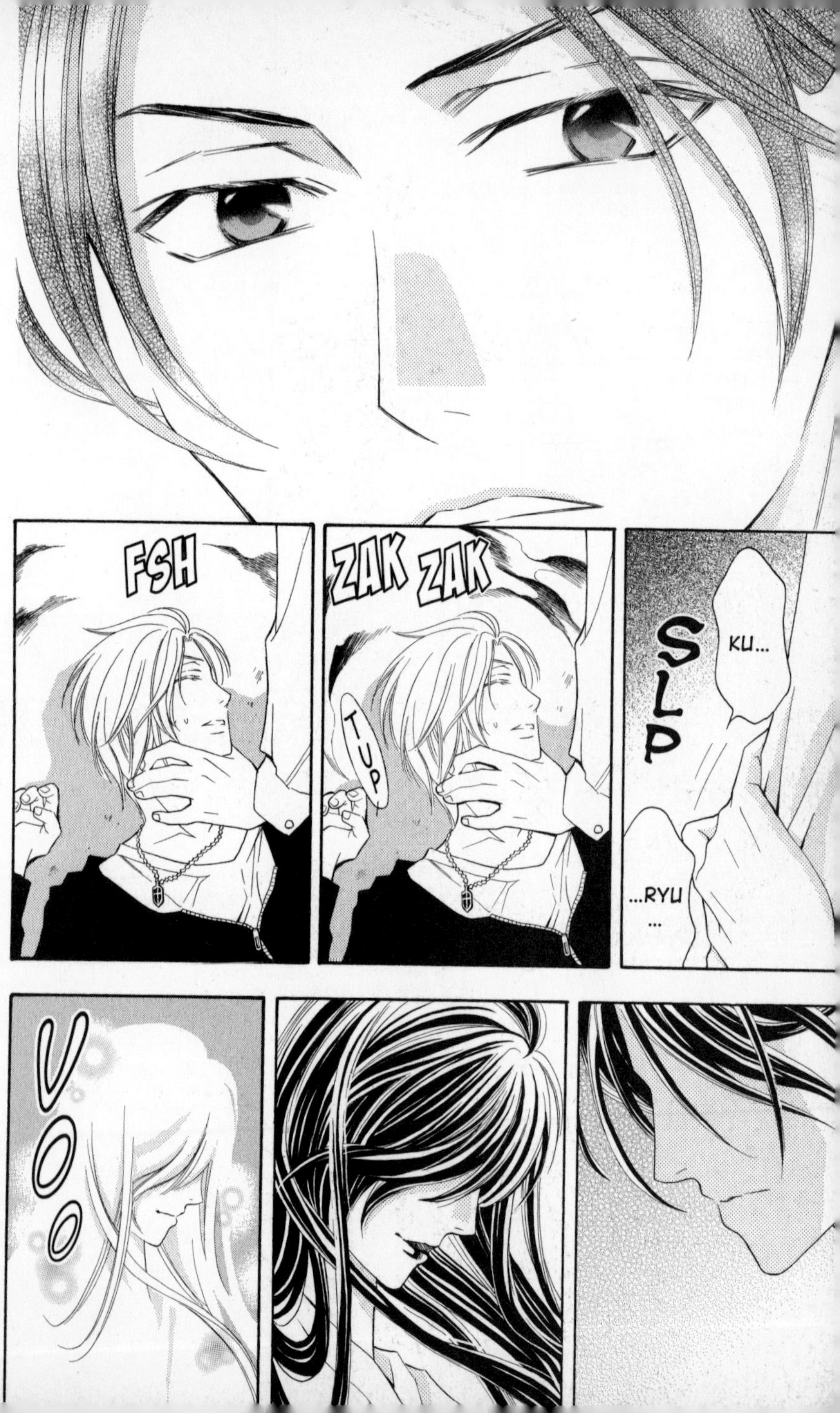
SLP
KU...
...RYU ...
ZAK ZAK
TUP
FSH
VOOO

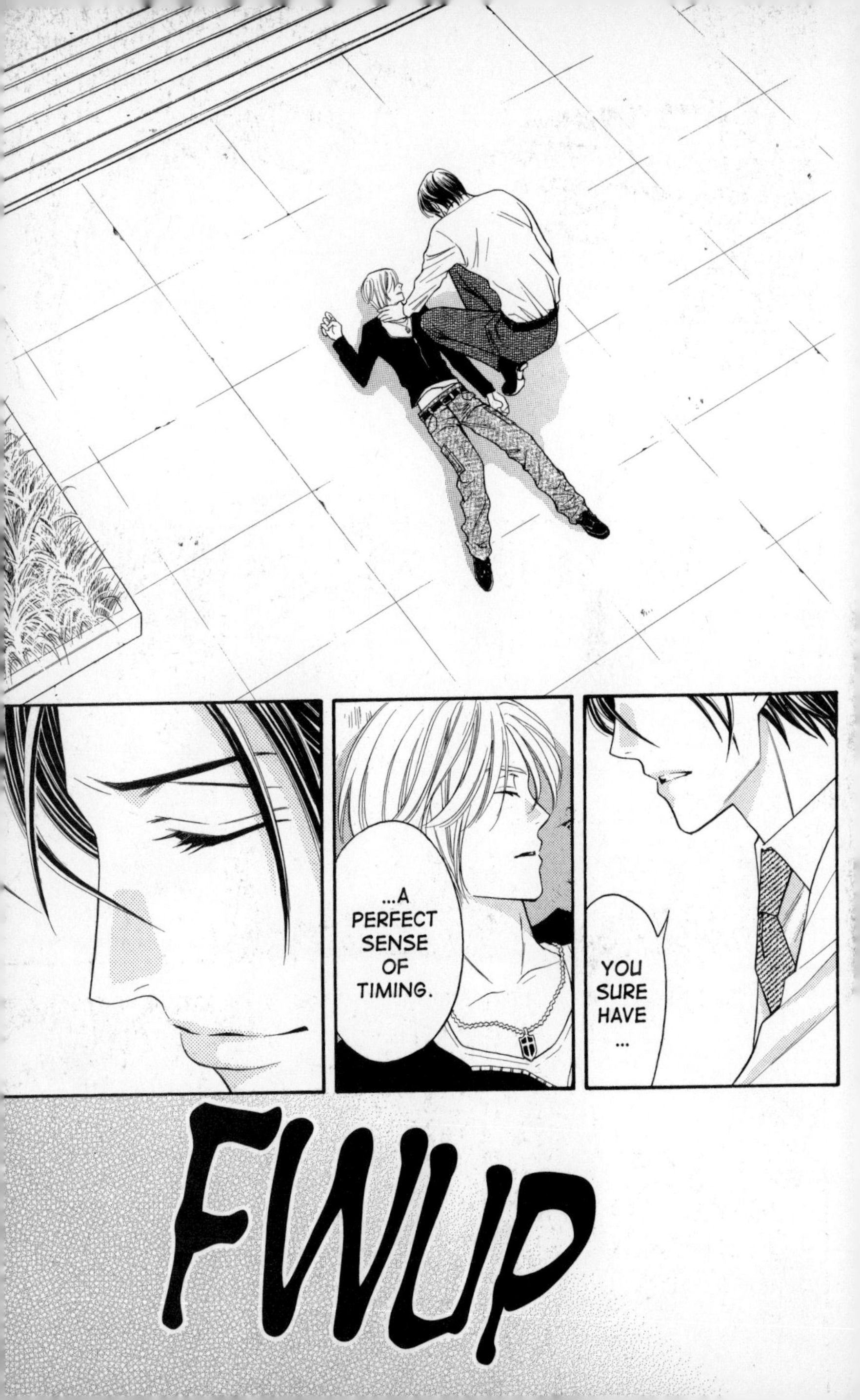
YOU SURE HAVE ...
...A PERFECT SENSE OF TIMING.
FWUP

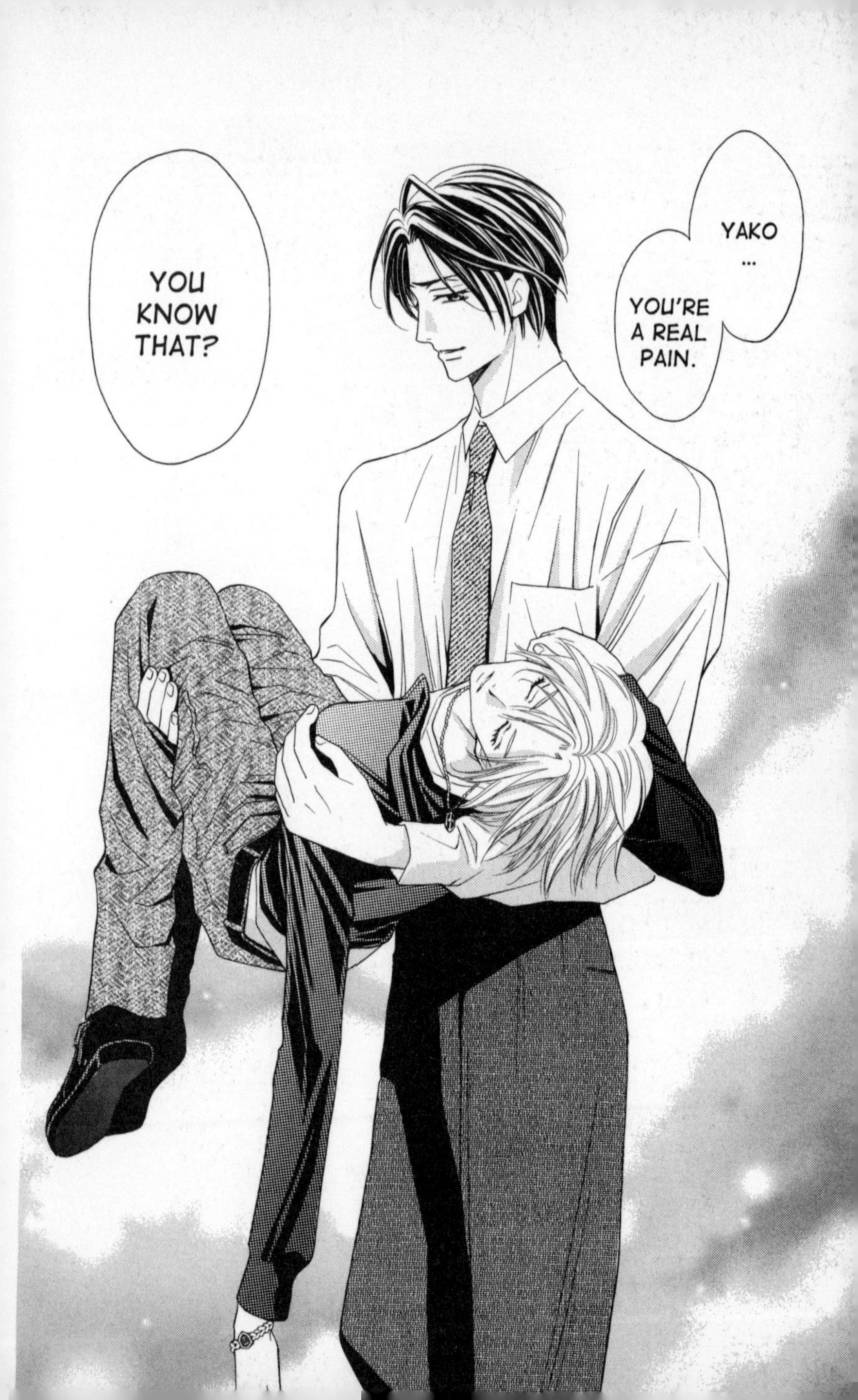
YAKO ... YOU'RE A REAL PAIN.
YOU KNOW THAT?

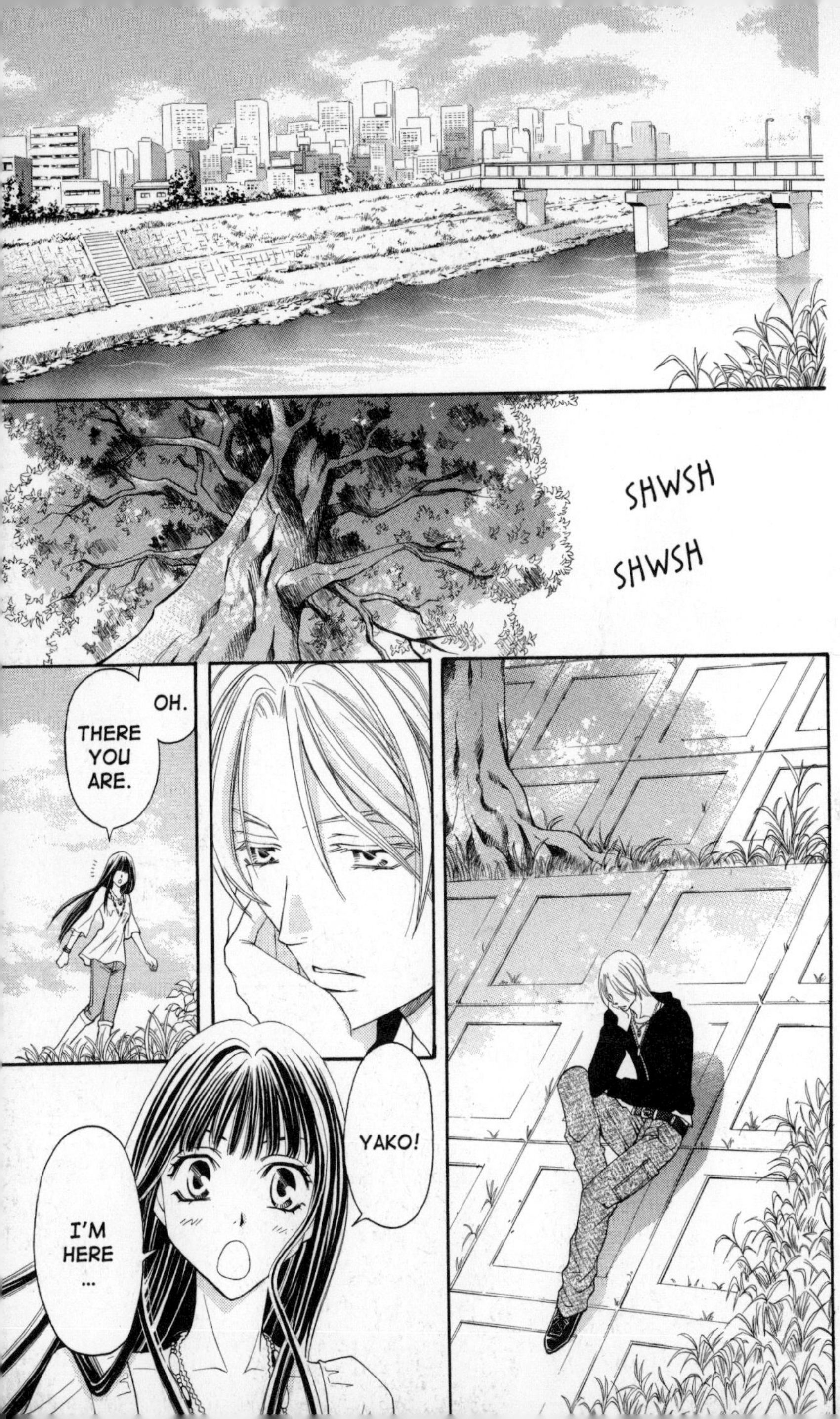
SHWSH
SHWSH
OH. THERE YOU ARE.
YAKO!
I'M HERE ...

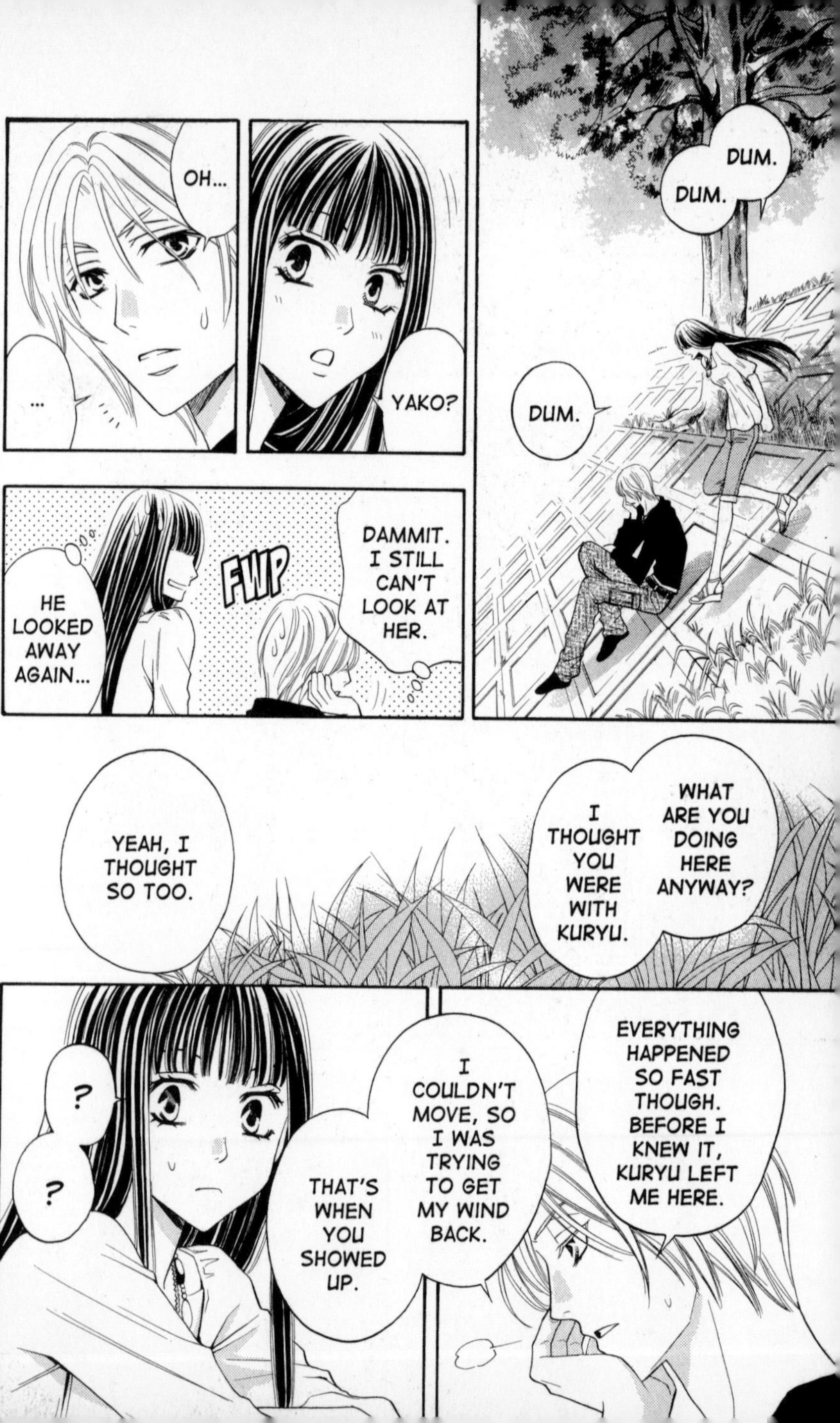
DUM.
DUM.
DUM.
YAKO?
OH...
...
DAMMIT. I STILL CAN'T LOOK AT HER.
FWP
HE LOOKED AWAY AGAIN...
WHAT ARE YOU DOING HERE ANYWAY?
I THOUGHT YOU WERE WITH KURYU.
YEAH, I THOUGHT SO TOO.
EVERYTHING HAPPENED SO FAST THOUGH. BEFORE I KNEW IT, KURYU LEFT ME HERE.
I COULDN'T MOVE, SO I WAS TRYING TO GET MY WIND BACK.
THAT'S WHEN YOU SHOWED UP.
?
?

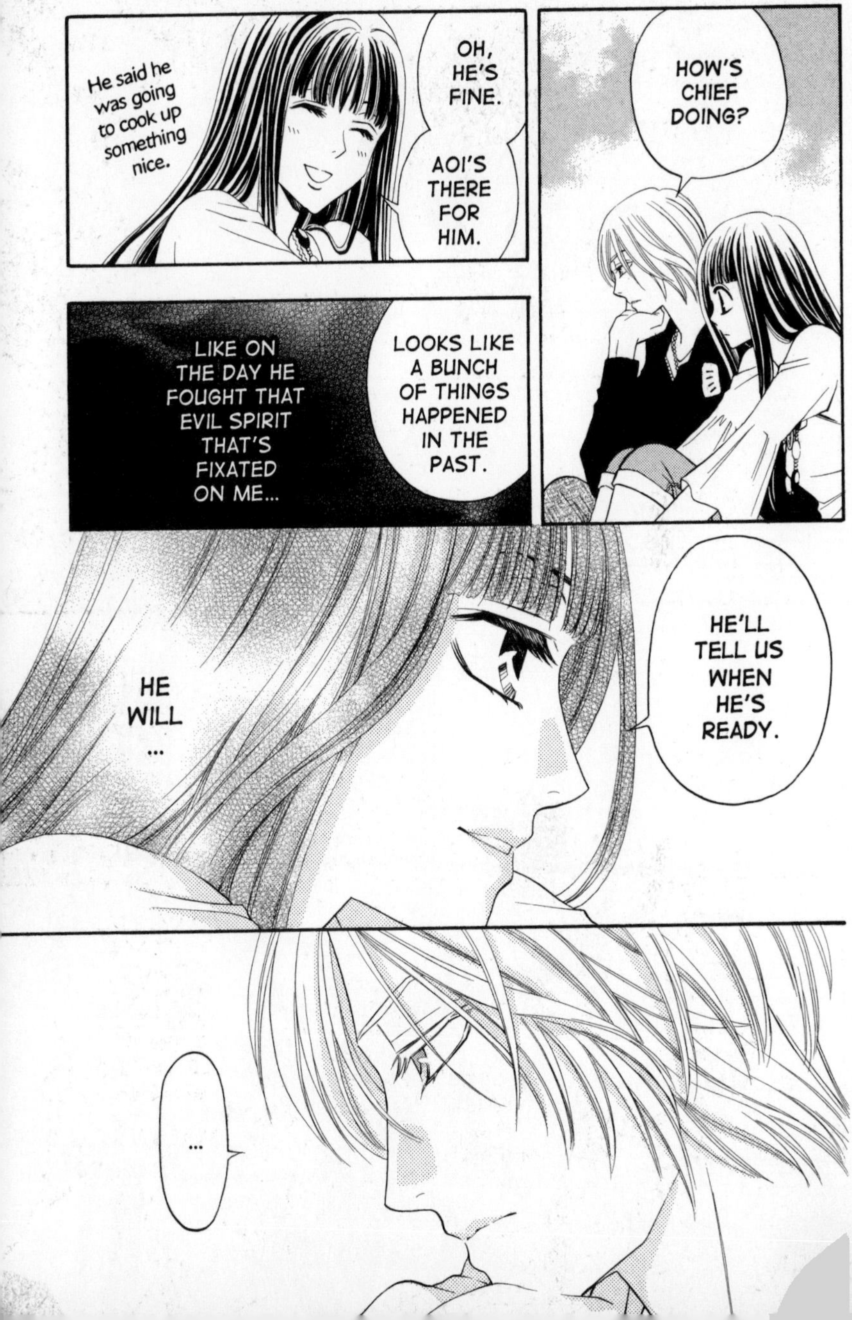
HOW'S CHIEF DOING?
OH, HE'S FINE.
AOI'S THERE FOR HIM.
He said he was going to cook up something nice.
LOOKS LIKE A BUNCH OF THINGS HAPPENED IN THE PAST.
LIKE ON THE DAY HE FOUGHT THAT EVIL SPIRIT THAT'S FIXATED ON ME...
HE'LL TELL US WHEN HE'S READY.
HE WILL ...
...

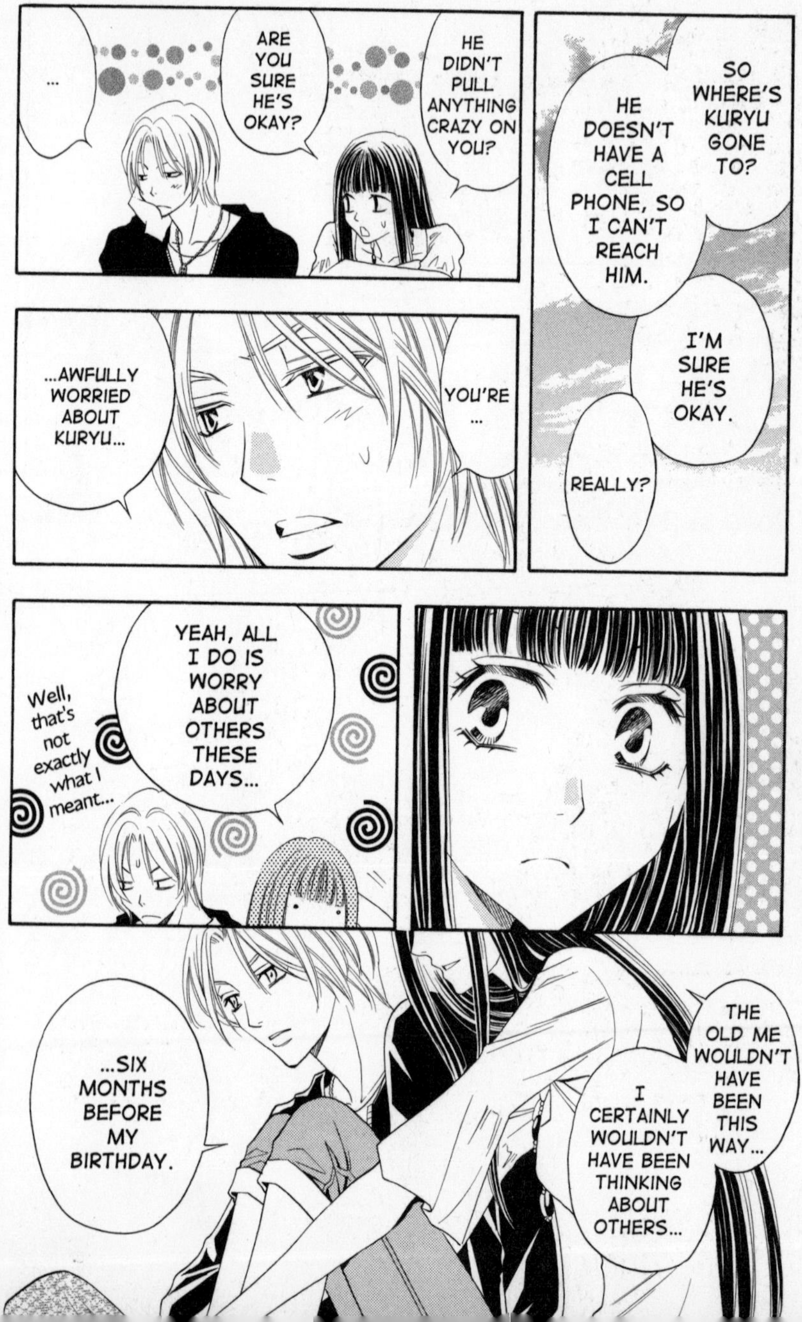
SO WHERE'S KURYU GONE TO?
HE DOESN'T HAVE A CELL PHONE, SO I CAN'T REACH HIM.
I'M SURE HE'S OKAY.
REALLY?
HE DIDN'T PULL ANYTHING CRAZY ON YOU?
ARE YOU SURE HE'S OKAY?
...
YOU'RE ...
...AWFULLY WORRIED ABOUT KURYU...
YEAH, ALL I DO IS WORRY ABOUT OTHERS THESE DAYS...
Well, that's not exactly what I meant...
THE OLD ME WOULDN'T HAVE BEEN THIS WAY...
I CERTAINLY WOULDN'T HAVE BEEN THINKING ABOUT OTHERS...
...SIX MONTHS BEFORE MY BIRTHDAY.

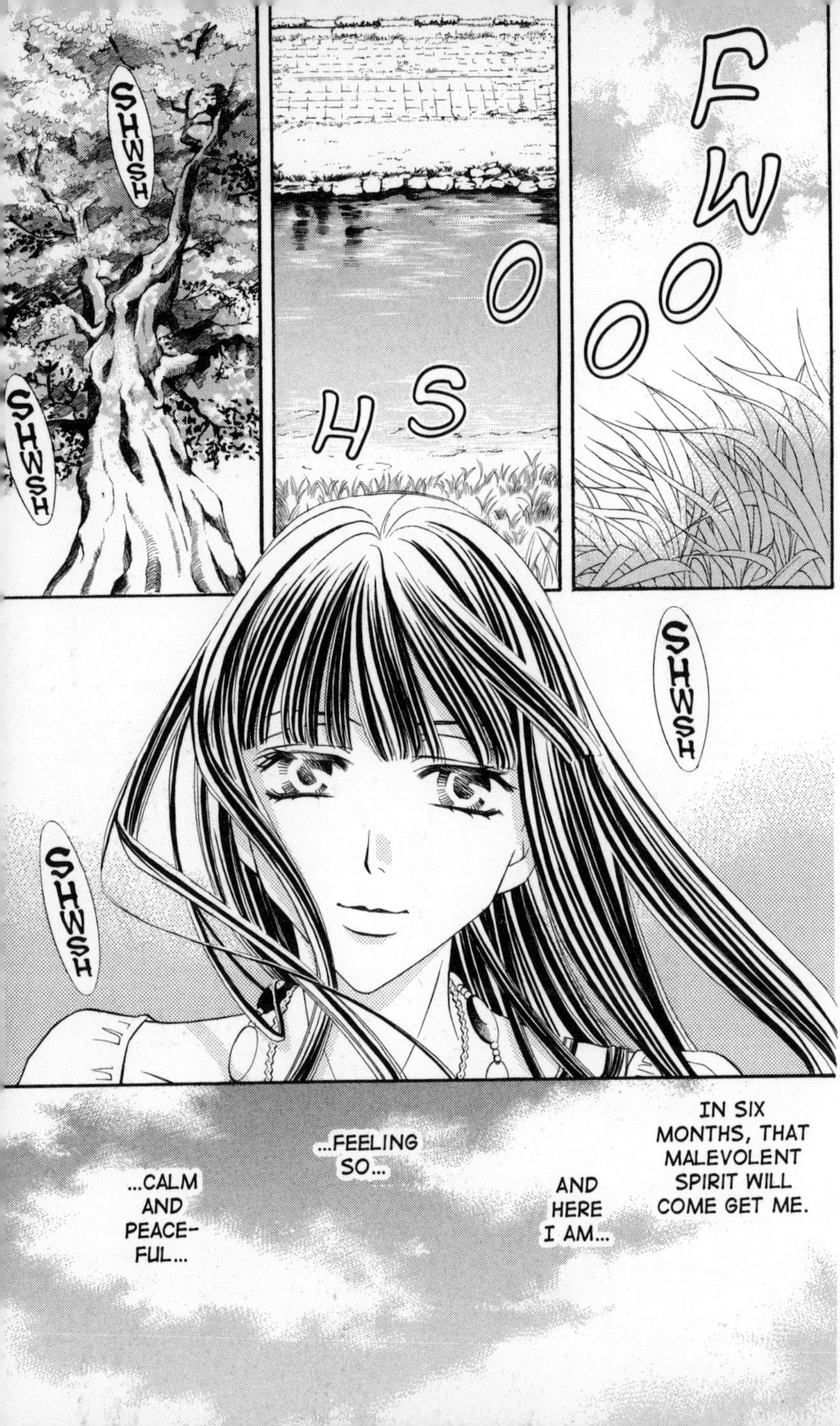
FWOOOSH
SHWSH
SHWSH
SHWSH
SHWSH
IN SIX MONTHS, THAT MALEVOLENT SPIRIT WILL COME GET ME.
AND HERE I AM...
...FEELING SO...
...CALM AND PEACE-FUL...

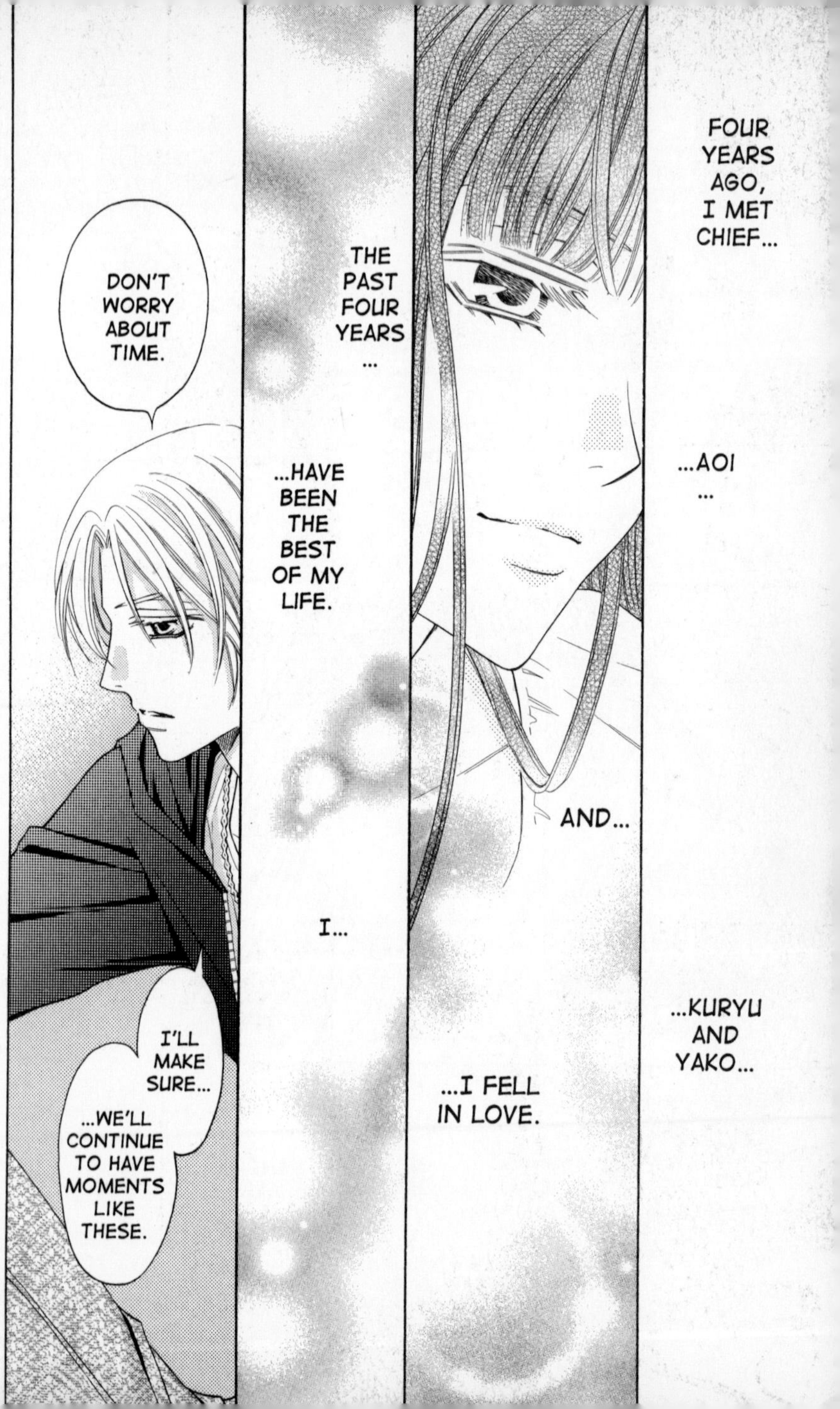
FOUR YEARS AGO, I MET CHIEF...
...AOI ...
...KURYU AND YAKO...
AND...
...I FELL IN LOVE.
THE PAST FOUR YEARS ...
...HAVE BEEN THE BEST OF MY LIFE.
I...
DON'T WORRY ABOUT TIME.
I'LL MAKE SURE...
...WE'LL CONTINUE TO HAVE MOMENTS LIKE THESE.

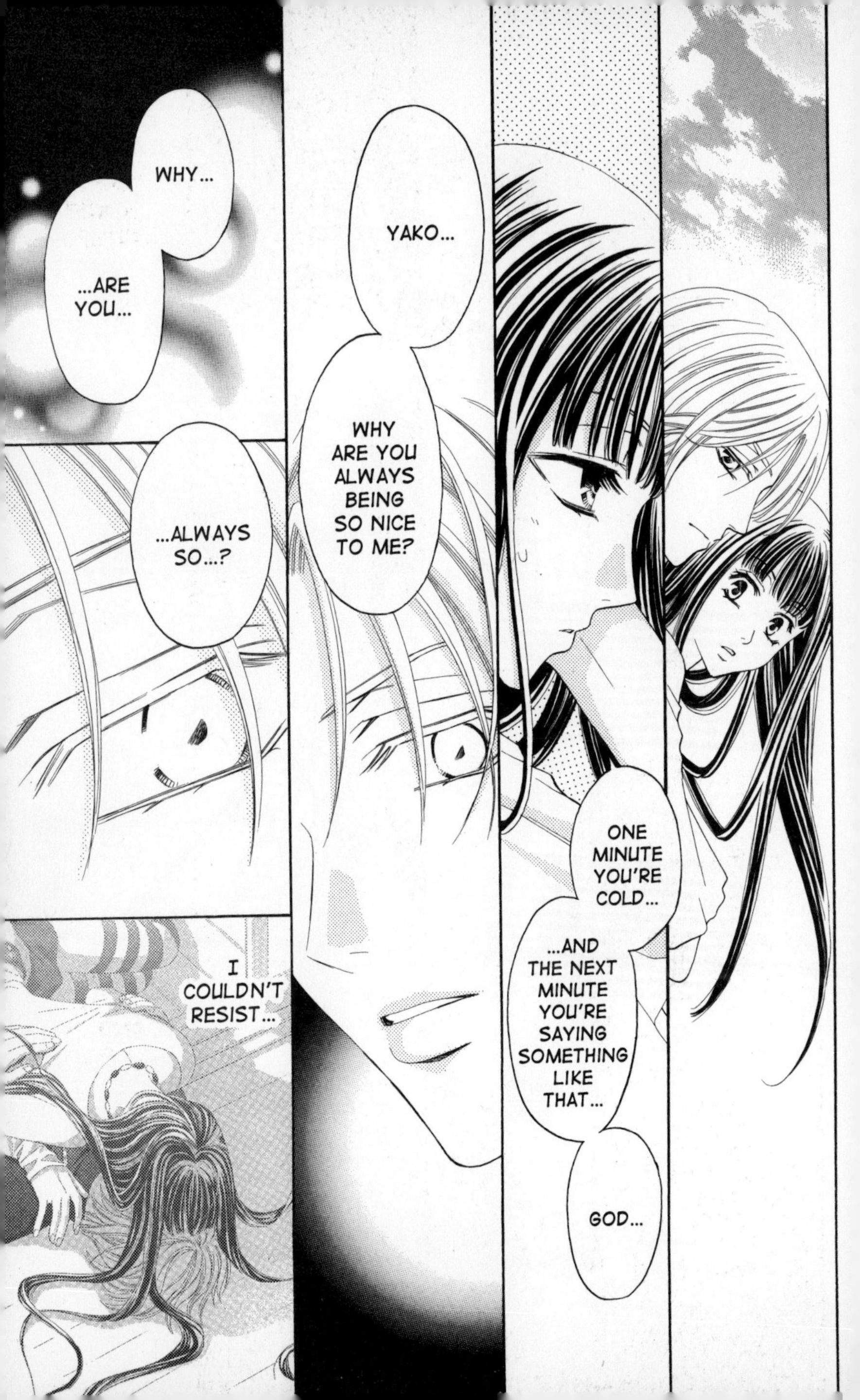
ONE MINUTE YOU'RE COLD...
...AND THE NEXT MINUTE YOU'RE SAYING SOMETHING LIKE THAT...
GOD...
YAKO...
WHY ARE YOU ALWAYS BEING SO NICE TO ME?
WHY...
...ARE YOU...
...ALWAYS SO...?
I COULDN'T RESIST...

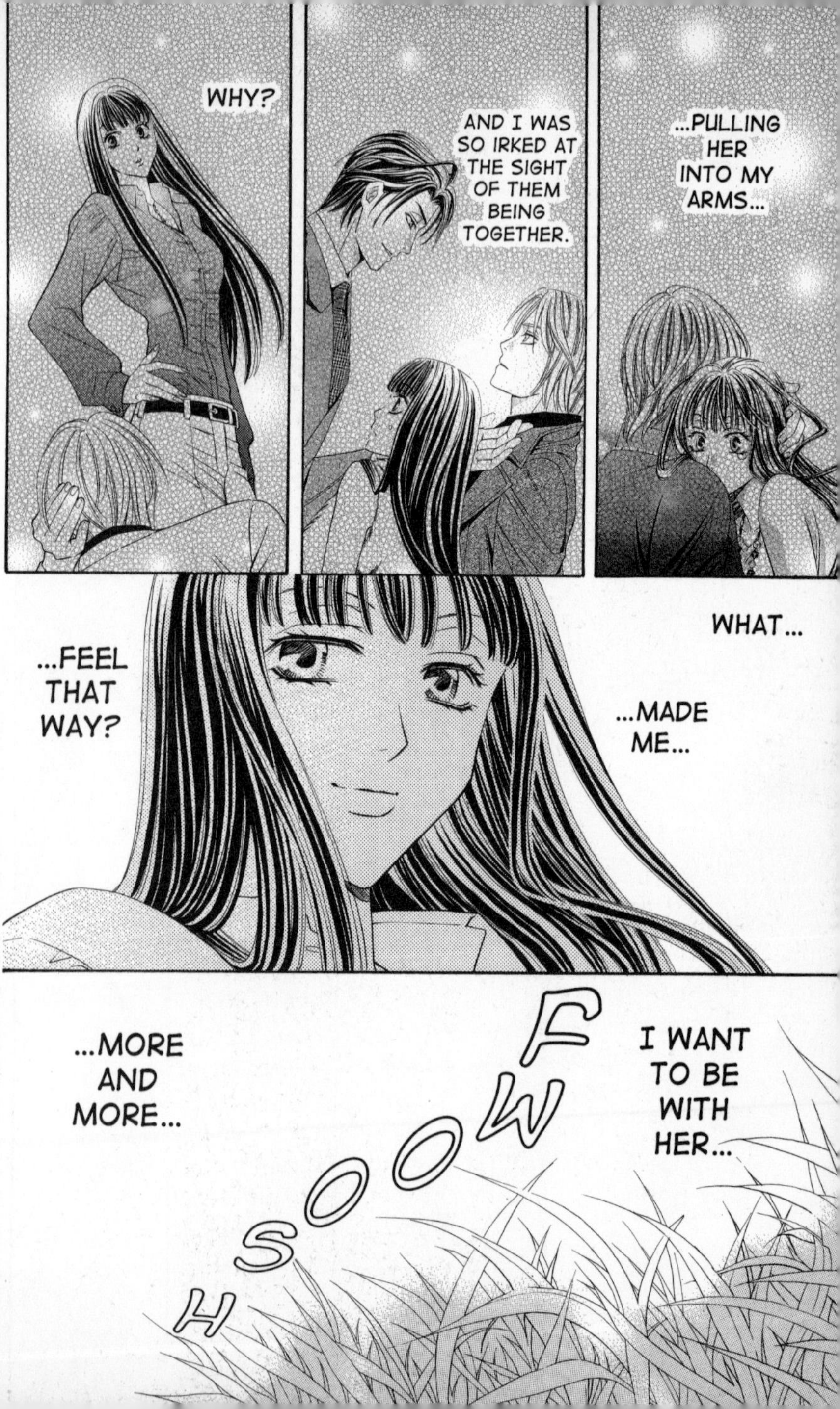
...PULLING HER INTO MY ARMS...
AND I WAS SO IRKED AT THE SIGHT OF THEM BEING TOGETHER.
WHY?
WHAT...
...MADE ME...
...FEEL THAT WAY?
I WANT TO BE WITH HER...
FWOOSH
...MORE AND MORE...

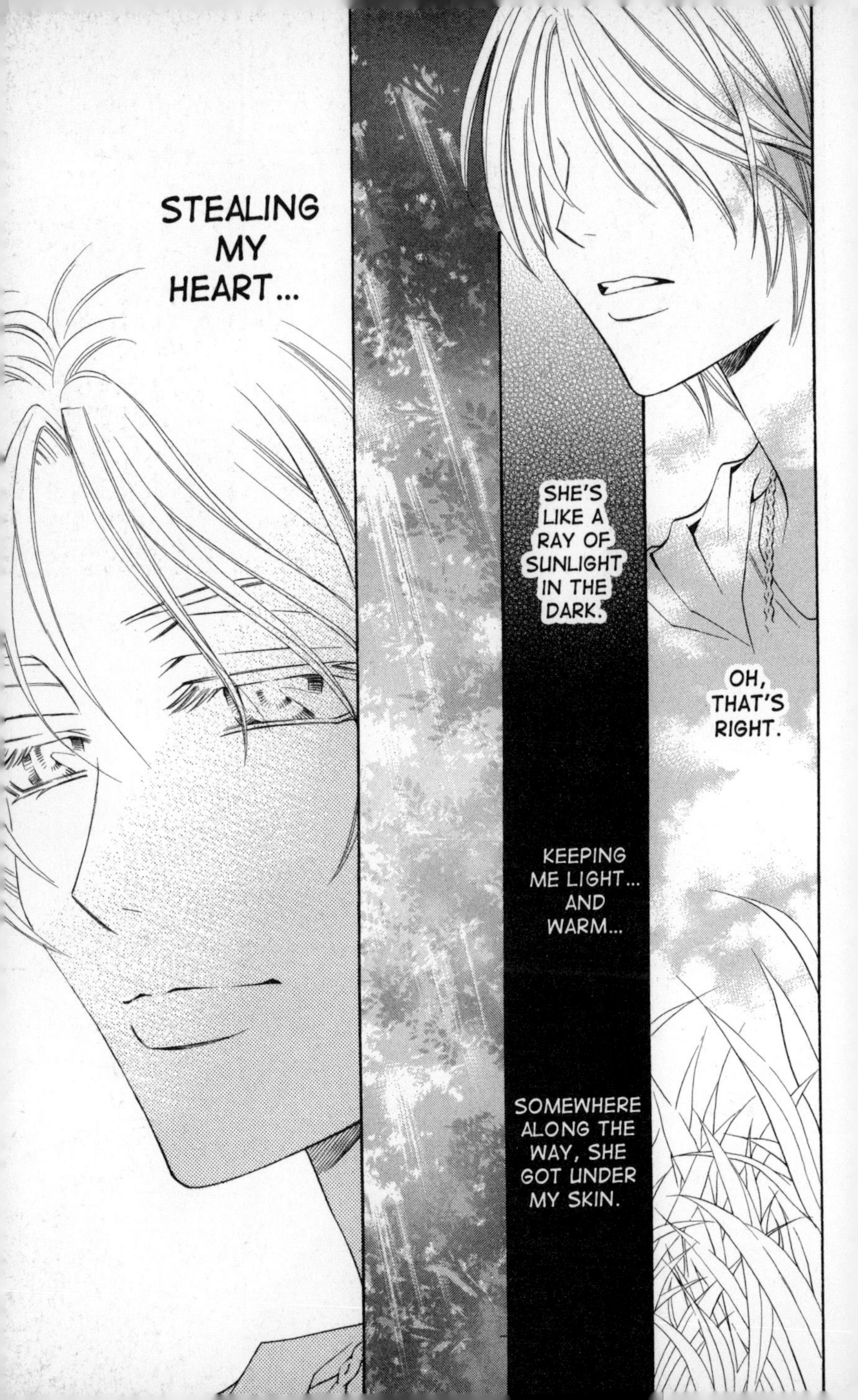
OH, THAT'S RIGHT.
SHE'S LIKE A RAY OF SUNLIGHT IN THE DARK.
KEEPING ME LIGHT... AND WARM...
SOMEWHERE ALONG THE WAY, SHE GOT UNDER MY SKIN.
STEALING MY HEART...

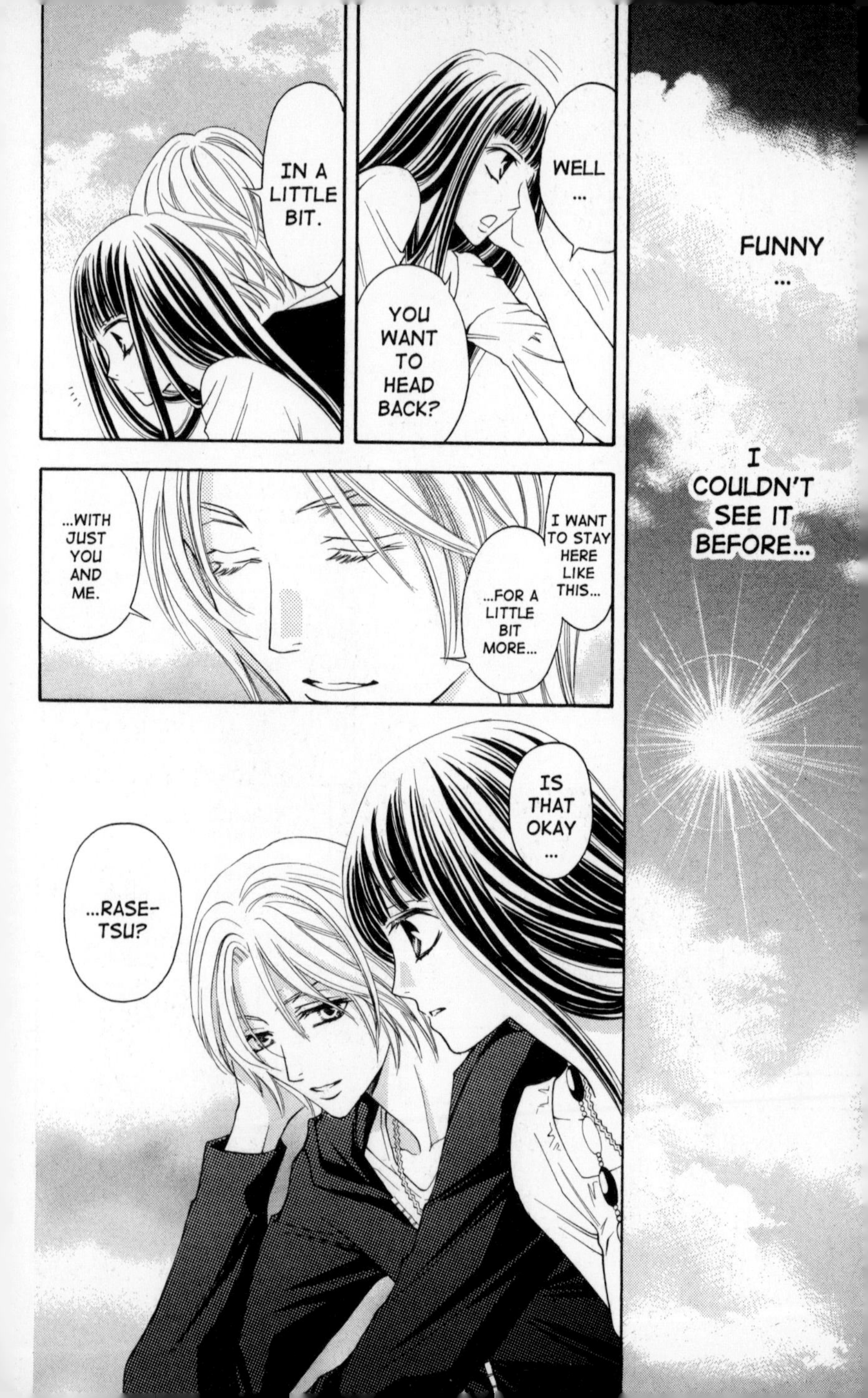
FUNNY ...
I COULDN'T SEE IT BEFORE...
WELL ...
YOU WANT TO HEAD BACK?
IN A LITTLE BIT.
I WANT TO STAY HERE LIKE THIS...
...FOR A LITTLE BIT MORE...
...WITH JUST YOU AND ME.
IS THAT OKAY ...
...RASE-TSU?

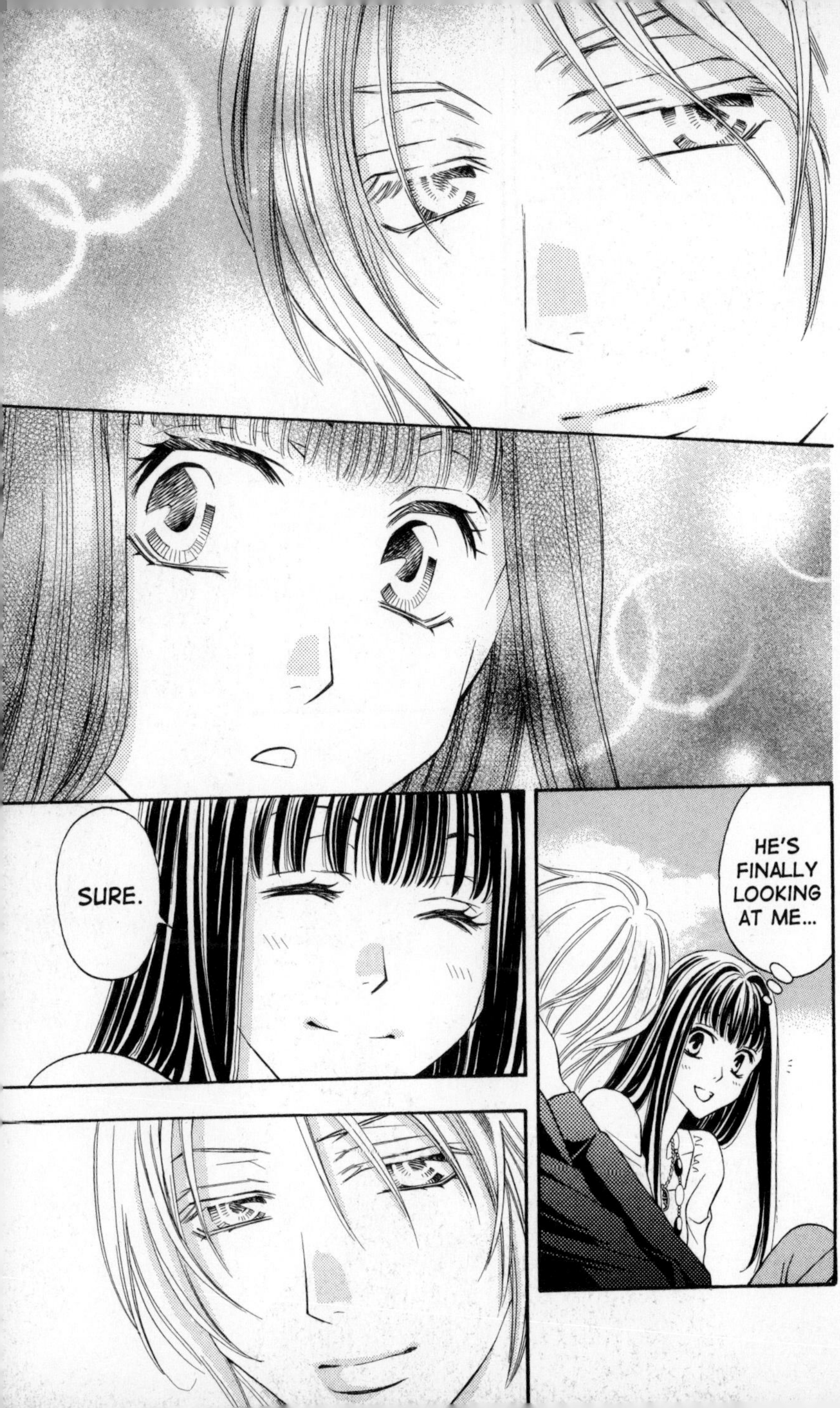
HE'S FINALLY LOOKING AT ME...
SURE.

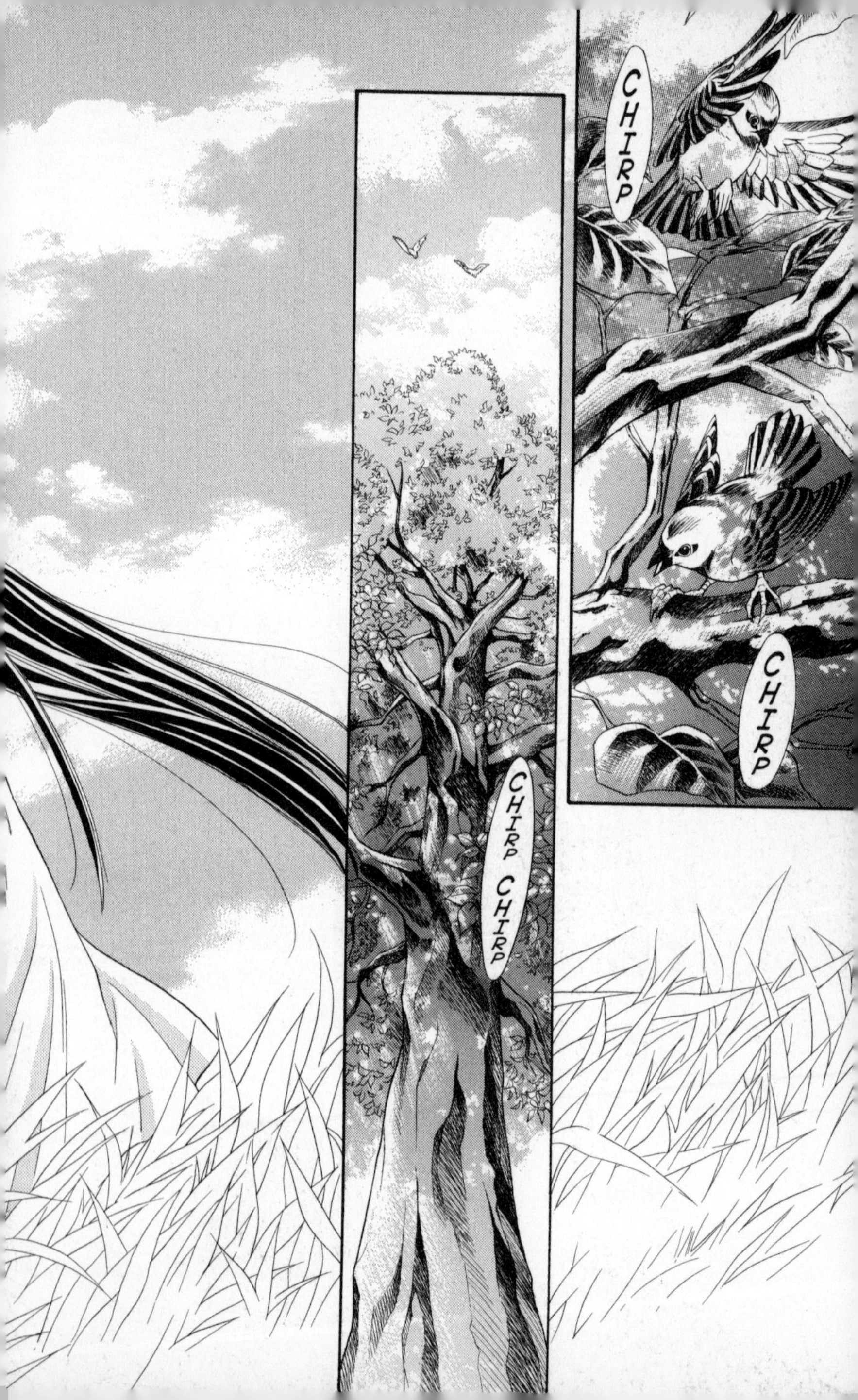
CHIRP
CHIRP
CHIRP CHIRP

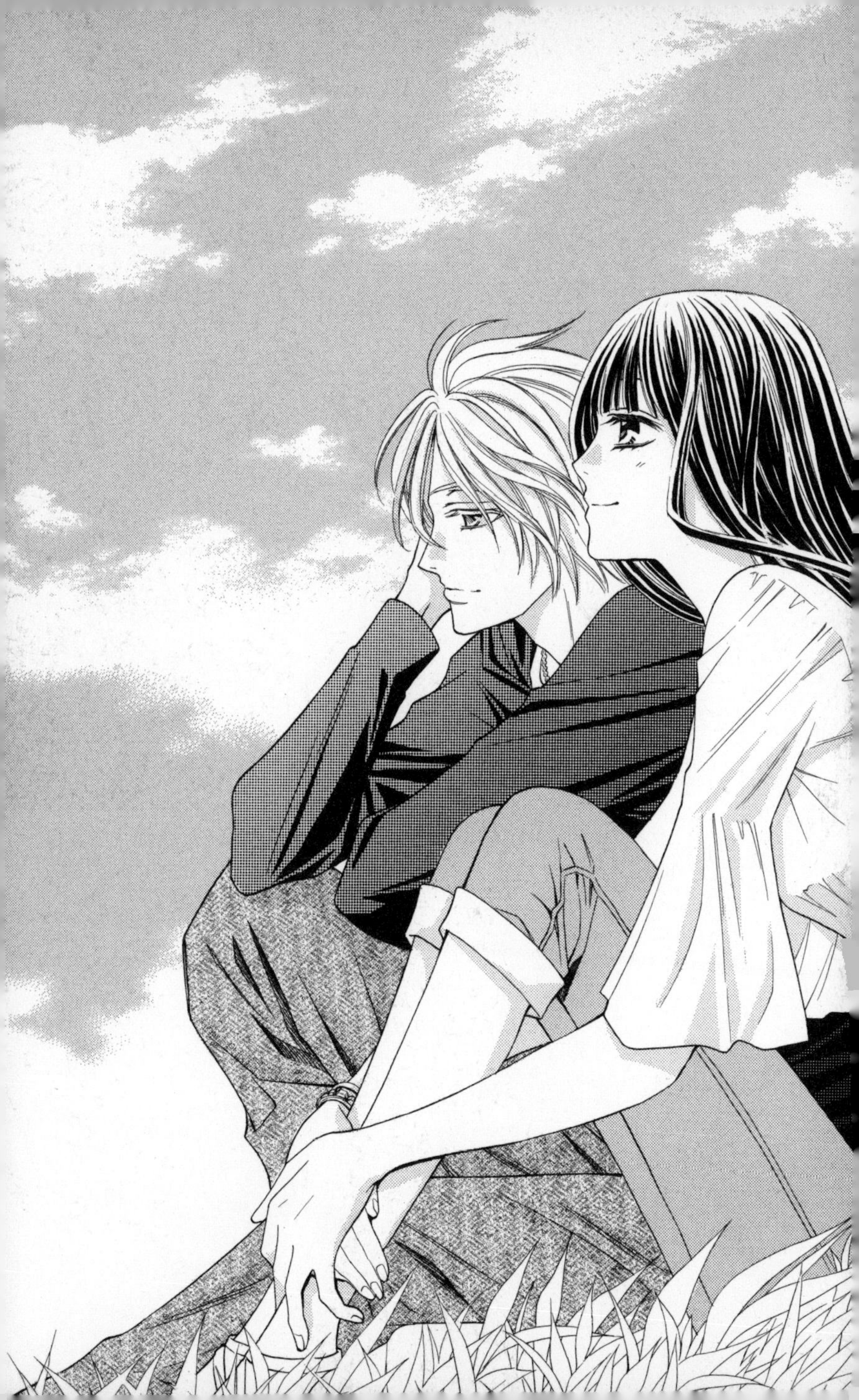

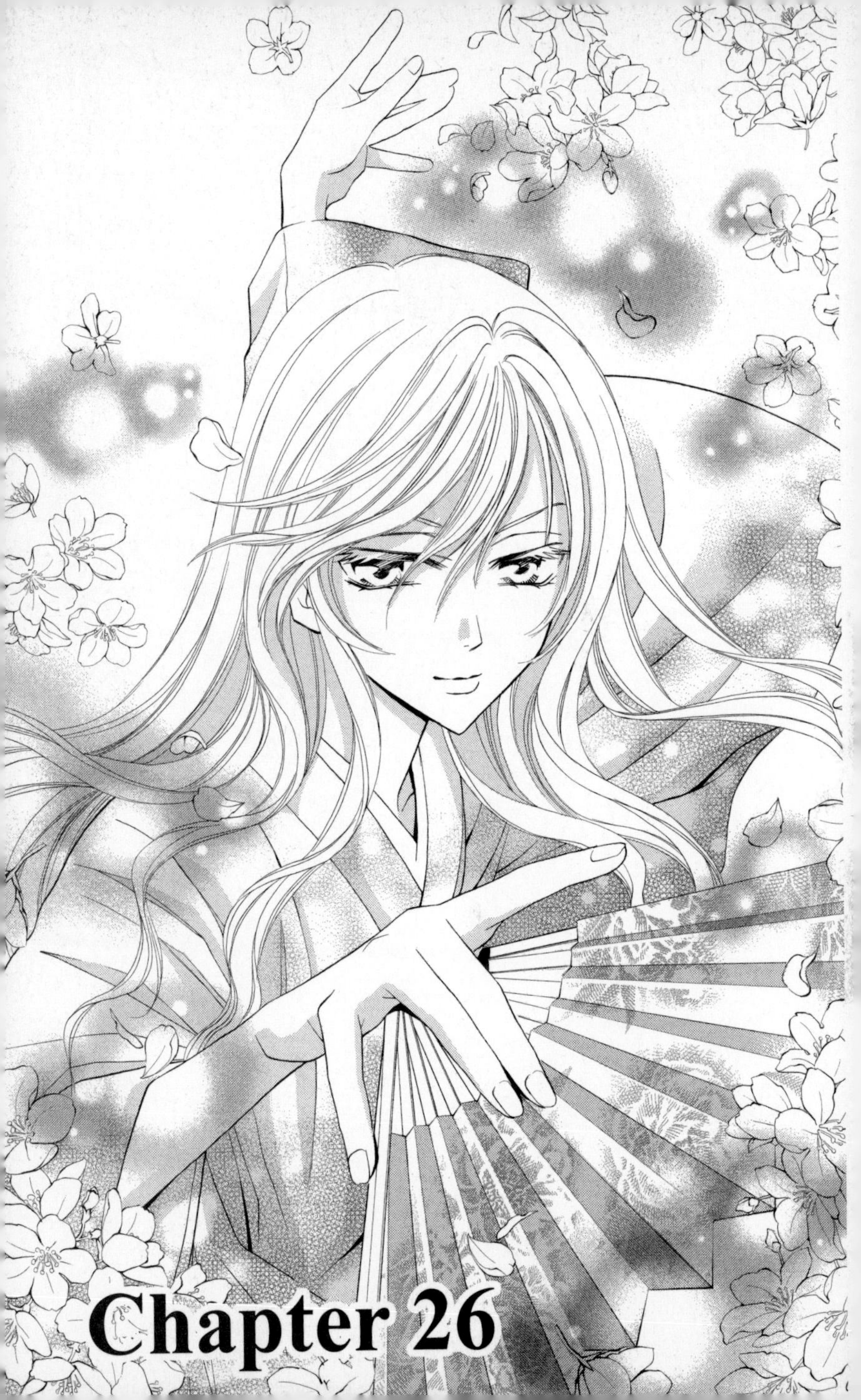
Chapter 26

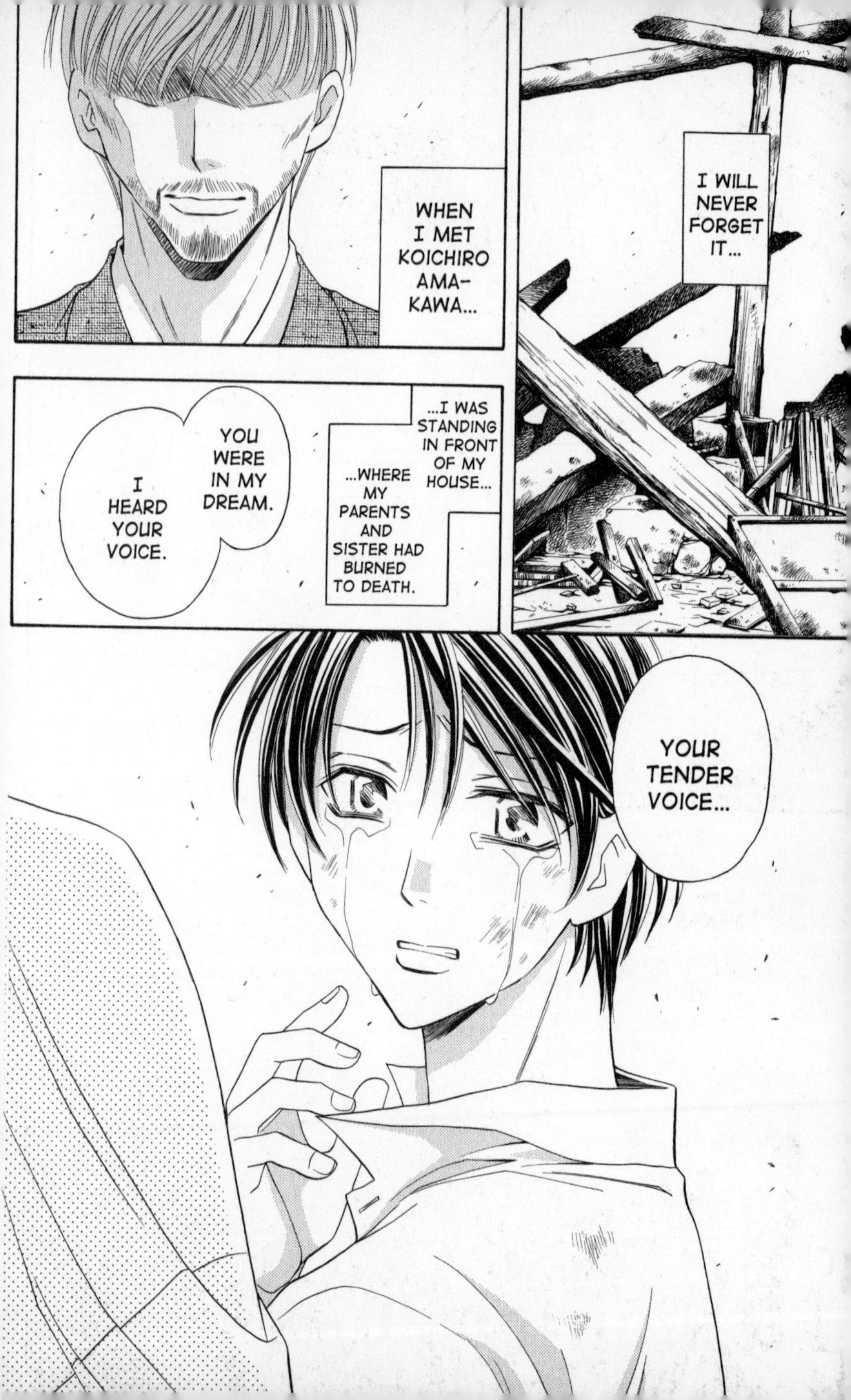
I WILL NEVER FORGET IT...
WHEN I MET KOICHIRO AMA-KAWA...
...I WAS STANDING IN FRONT OF MY HOUSE...
...WHERE MY PARENTS AND SISTER HAD BURNED TO DEATH.
YOU WERE IN MY DREAM.
I HEARD YOUR VOICE.
YOUR TENDER VOICE...

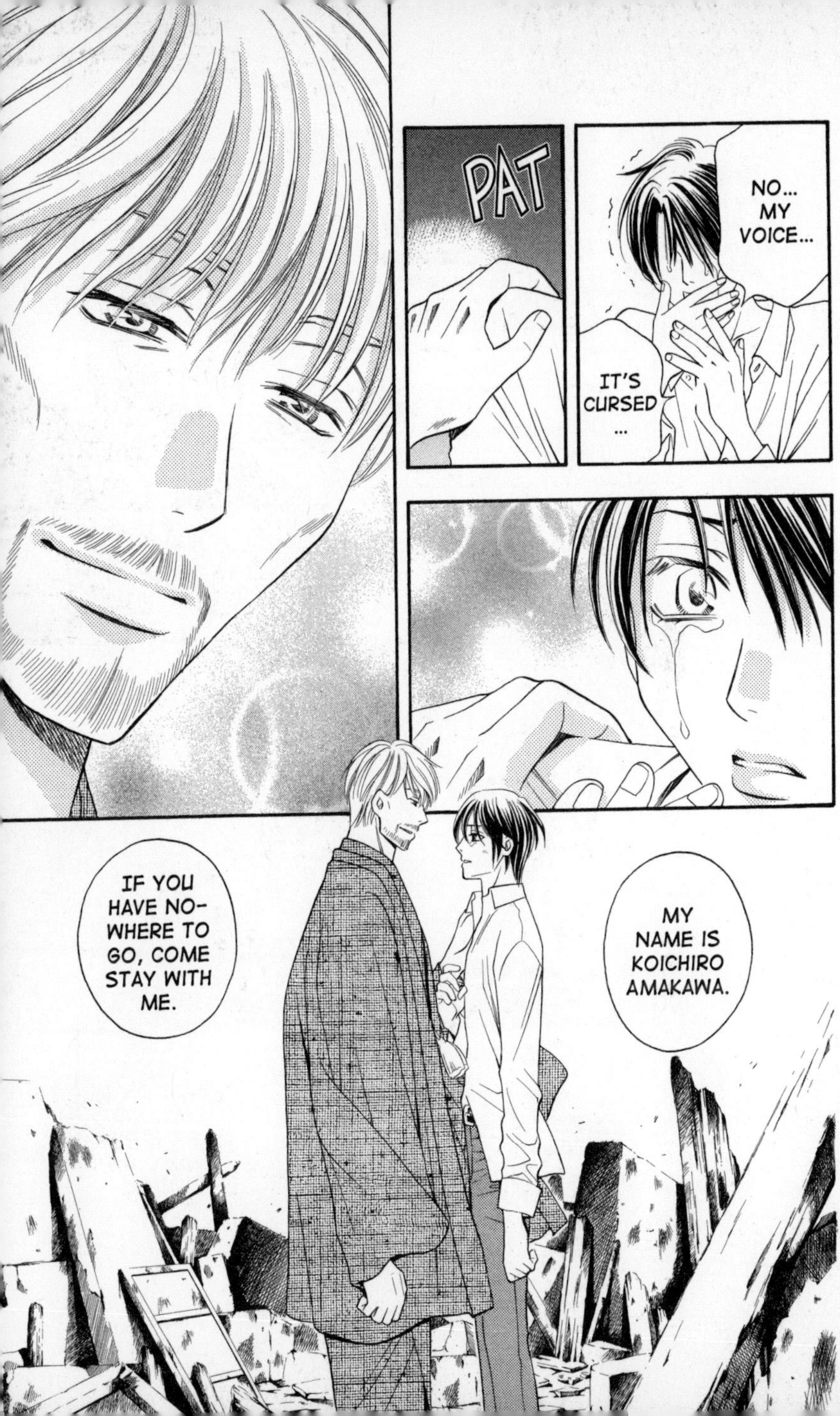
NO... MY VOICE...
IT'S CURSED ...
PAT
MY NAME IS KOICHIRO AMAKAWA.
IF YOU HAVE NO-WHERE TO GO, COME STAY WITH ME.

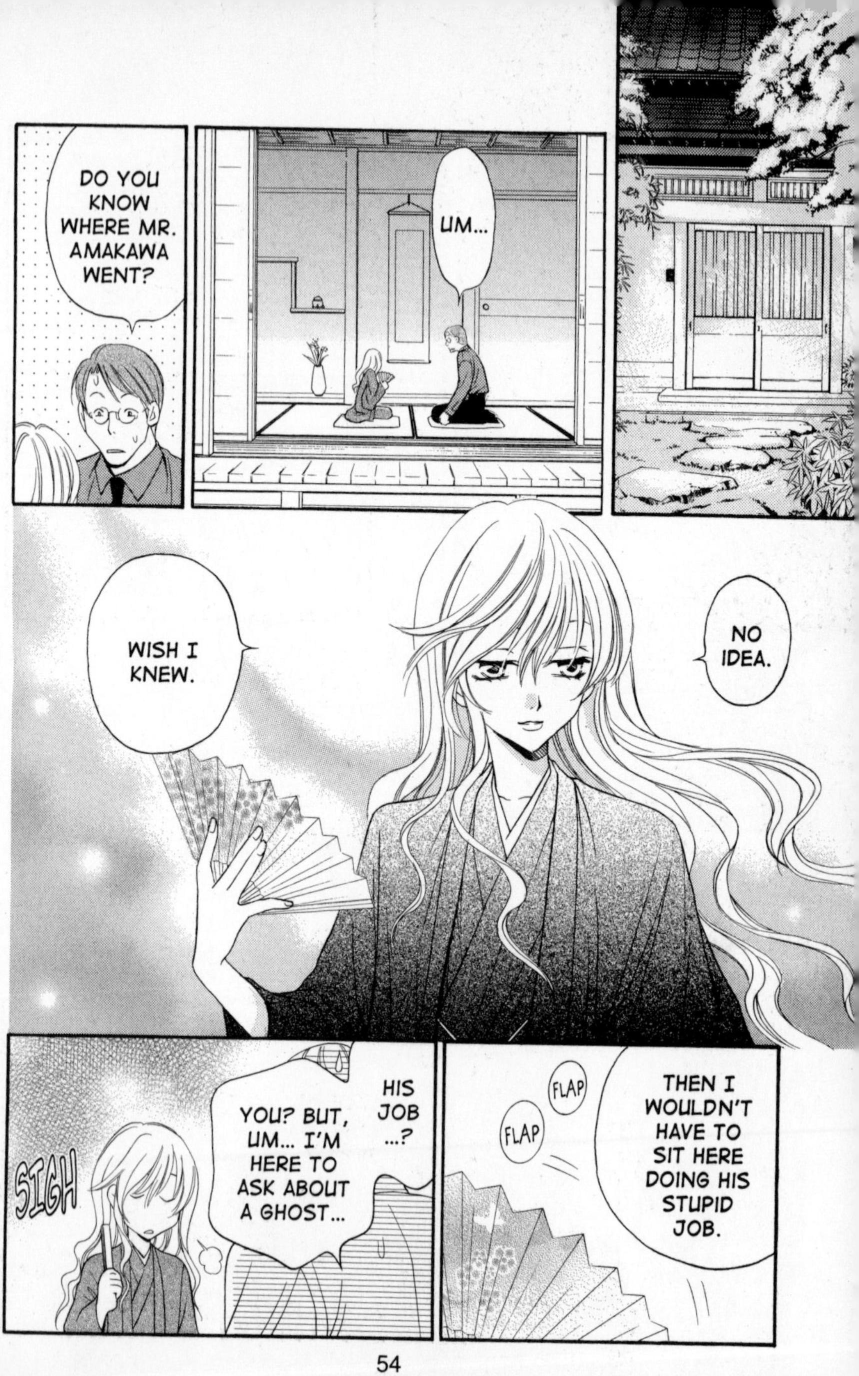
UM...
DO YOU KNOW WHERE MR. AMAKAWA WENT?
NO IDEA.
WISH I KNEW.
THEN I WOULDN'T HAVE TO SIT HERE DOING HIS STUPID JOB.
FLAP
FLAP
HIS JOB ...?
YOU? BUT, UM... I'M HERE TO ASK ABOUT A GHOST...
SIGH

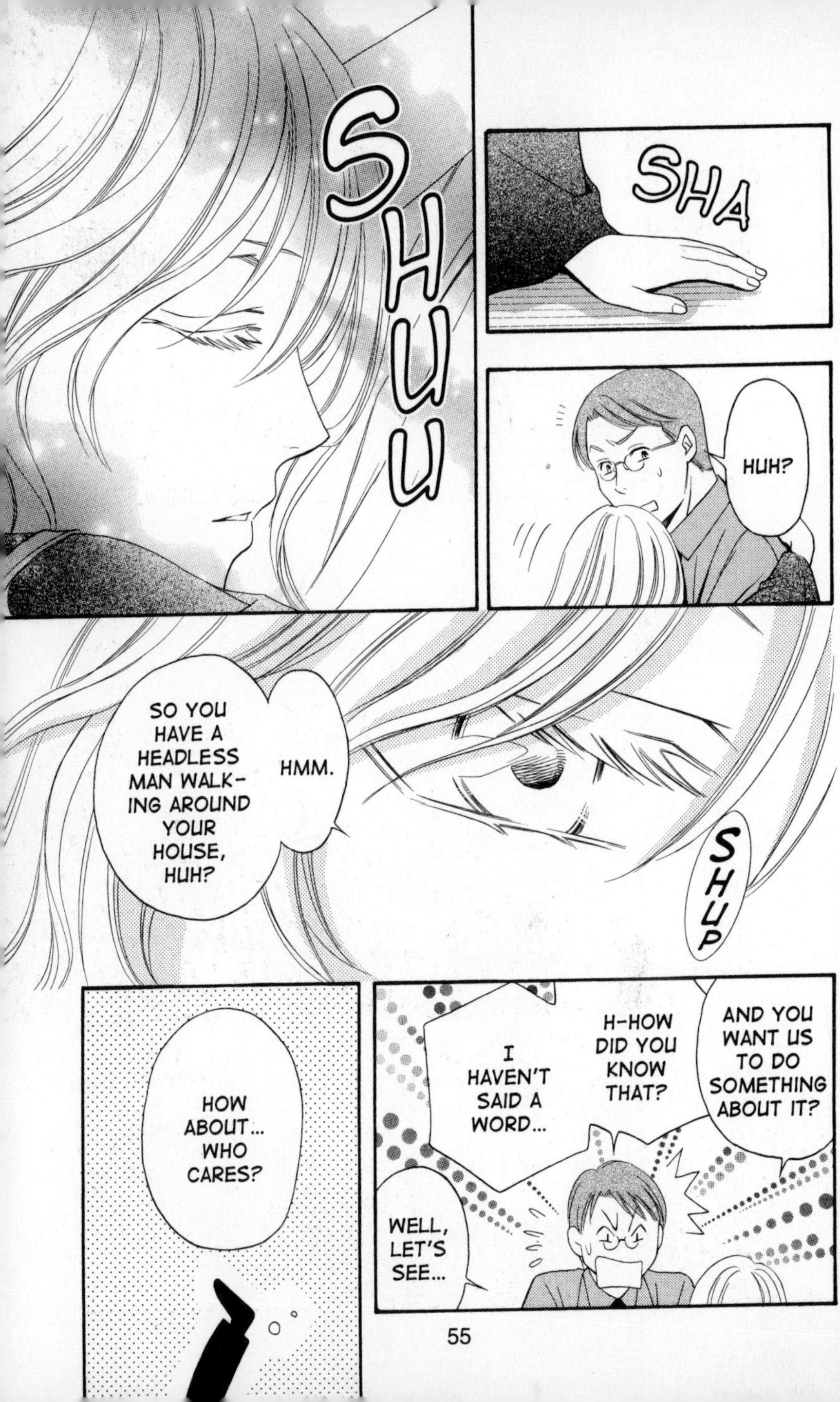
SHA
HUH?
SHUUU
SHUP
HMM.
SO YOU HAVE A HEADLESS MAN WALKING AROUND YOUR HOUSE, HUH?
AND YOU WANT US TO DO SOMETHING ABOUT IT?
H-HOW DID YOU KNOW THAT?
I HAVEN'T SAID A WORD...
WELL, LET'S SEE...
HOW ABOUT... WHO CARES?

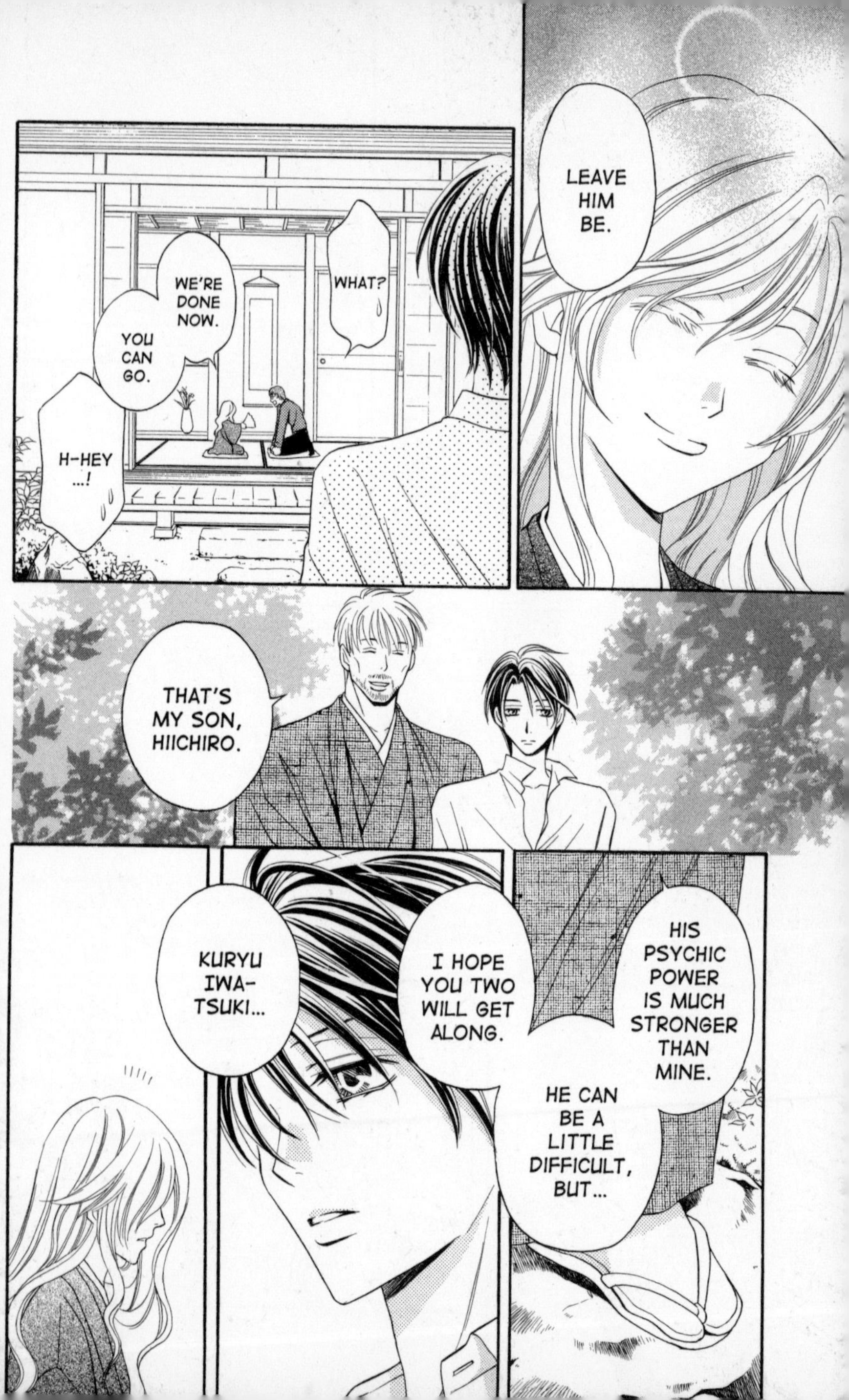
LEAVE HIM BE.
WHAT?
WE'RE DONE NOW.
YOU CAN GO.
H-HEY ...!
THAT'S MY SON, HIICHIRO.
HIS PSYCHIC POWER IS MUCH STRONGER THAN MINE.
HE CAN BE A LITTLE DIFFICULT, BUT...
I HOPE YOU TWO WILL GET ALONG.
KURYU IWA-TSUKI...

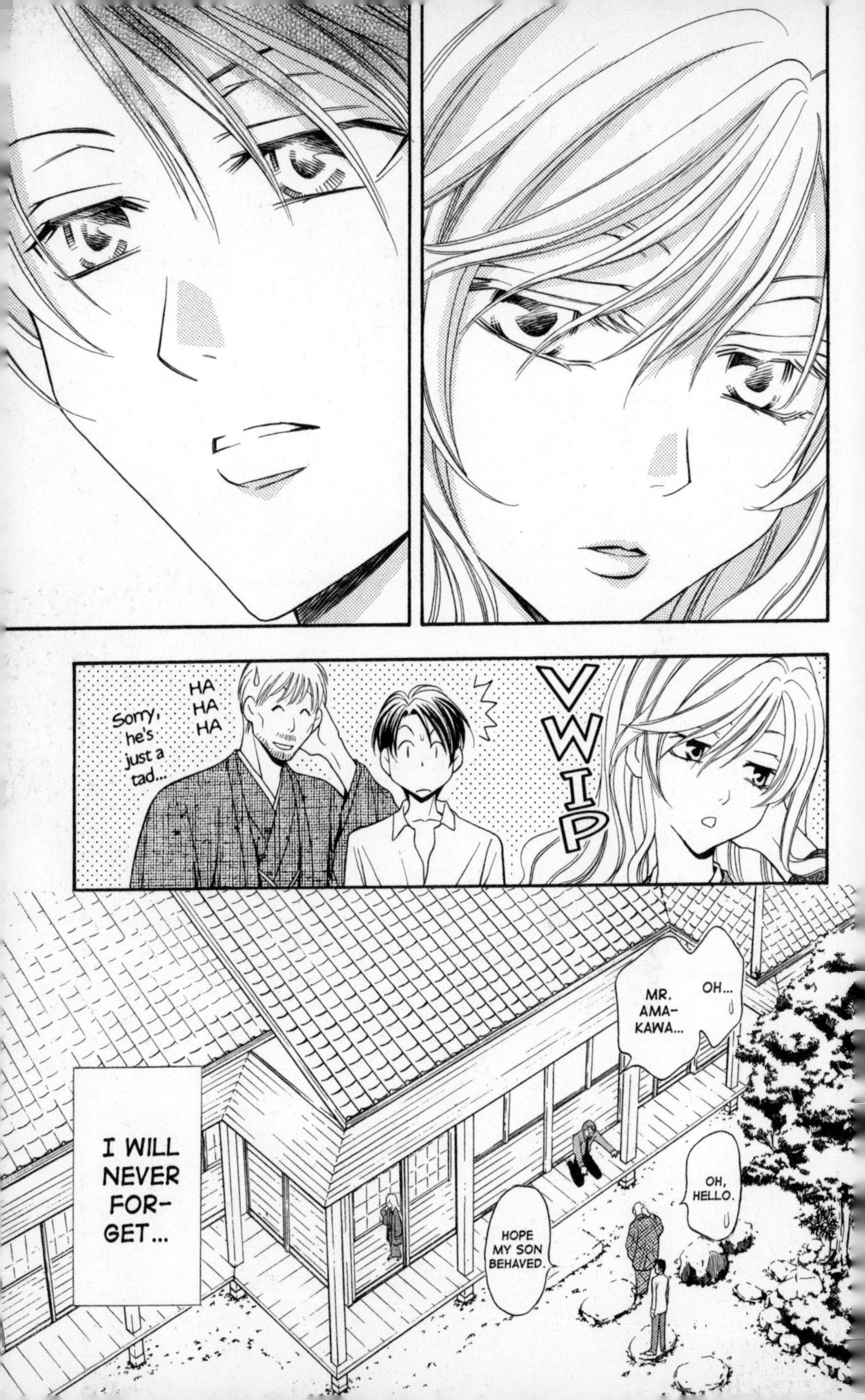
VWIP
HA HA HA
Sorry, he's just a tad...
OH... MR. AMA-KAWA...
OH, HELLO.
HOPE MY SON BEHAVED.
I WILL NEVER FOR-GET...

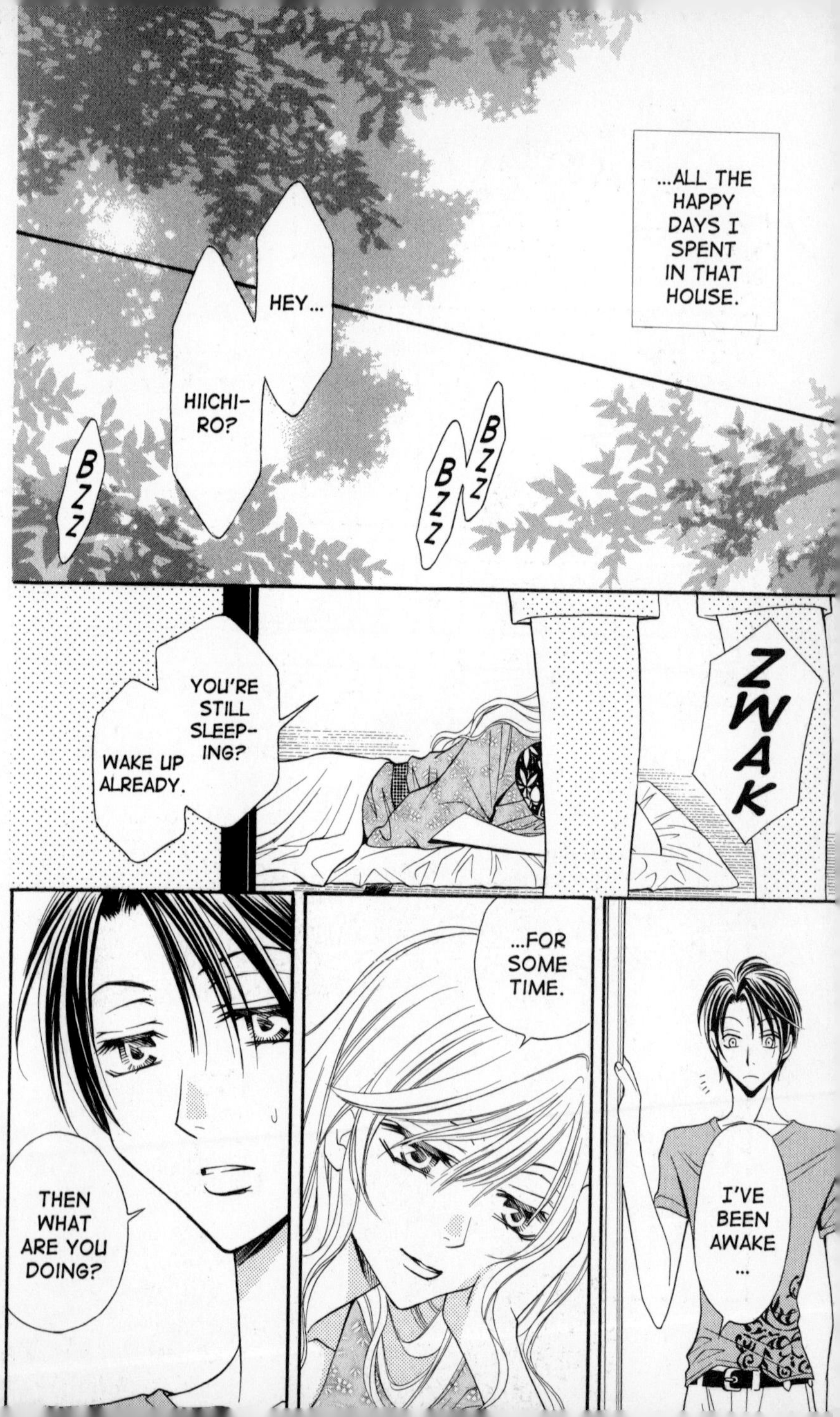
...ALL THE HAPPY DAYS I SPENT IN THAT HOUSE.
BZZ
BZZ
HEY... HIICHIRO?
BZZ
ZWAK
YOU'RE STILL SLEEPING? WAKE UP ALREADY.
I'VE BEEN AWAKE...
...FOR SOME TIME.
THEN WHAT ARE YOU DOING?

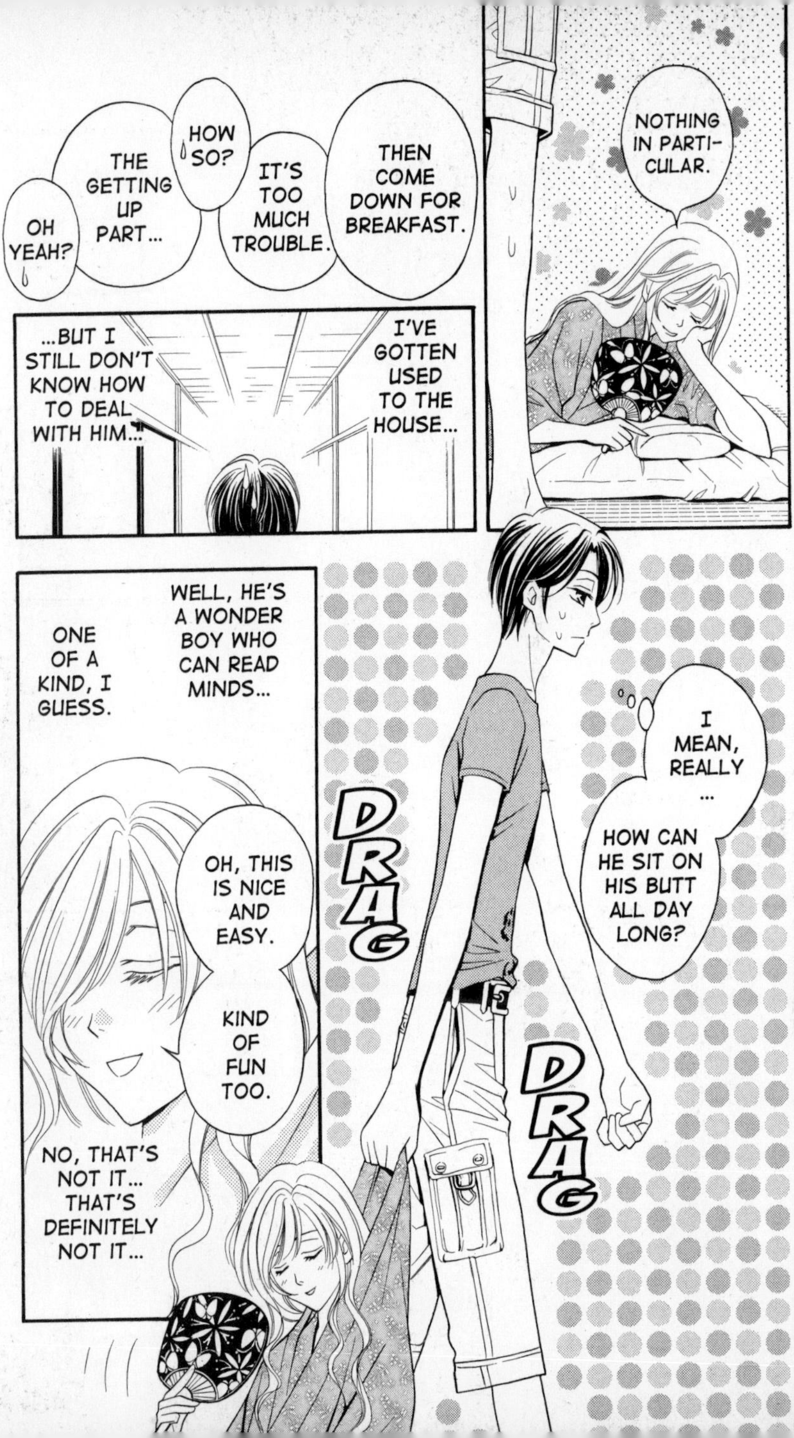
NOTHING IN PARTICULAR.
THEN COME DOWN FOR BREAKFAST.
IT'S TOO MUCH TROUBLE.
HOW SO?
THE GETTING UP PART...
OH YEAH?
I'VE GOTTEN USED TO THE HOUSE...
...BUT I STILL DON'T KNOW HOW TO DEAL WITH HIM...
I MEAN, REALLY ...
HOW CAN HE SIT ON HIS BUTT ALL DAY LONG?
DRAG
DRAG
WELL, HE'S A WONDER BOY WHO CAN READ MINDS...
ONE OF A KIND, I GUESS.
OH, THIS IS NICE AND EASY.
KIND OF FUN TOO.
NO, THAT'S NOT IT... THAT'S DEFINITELY NOT IT...

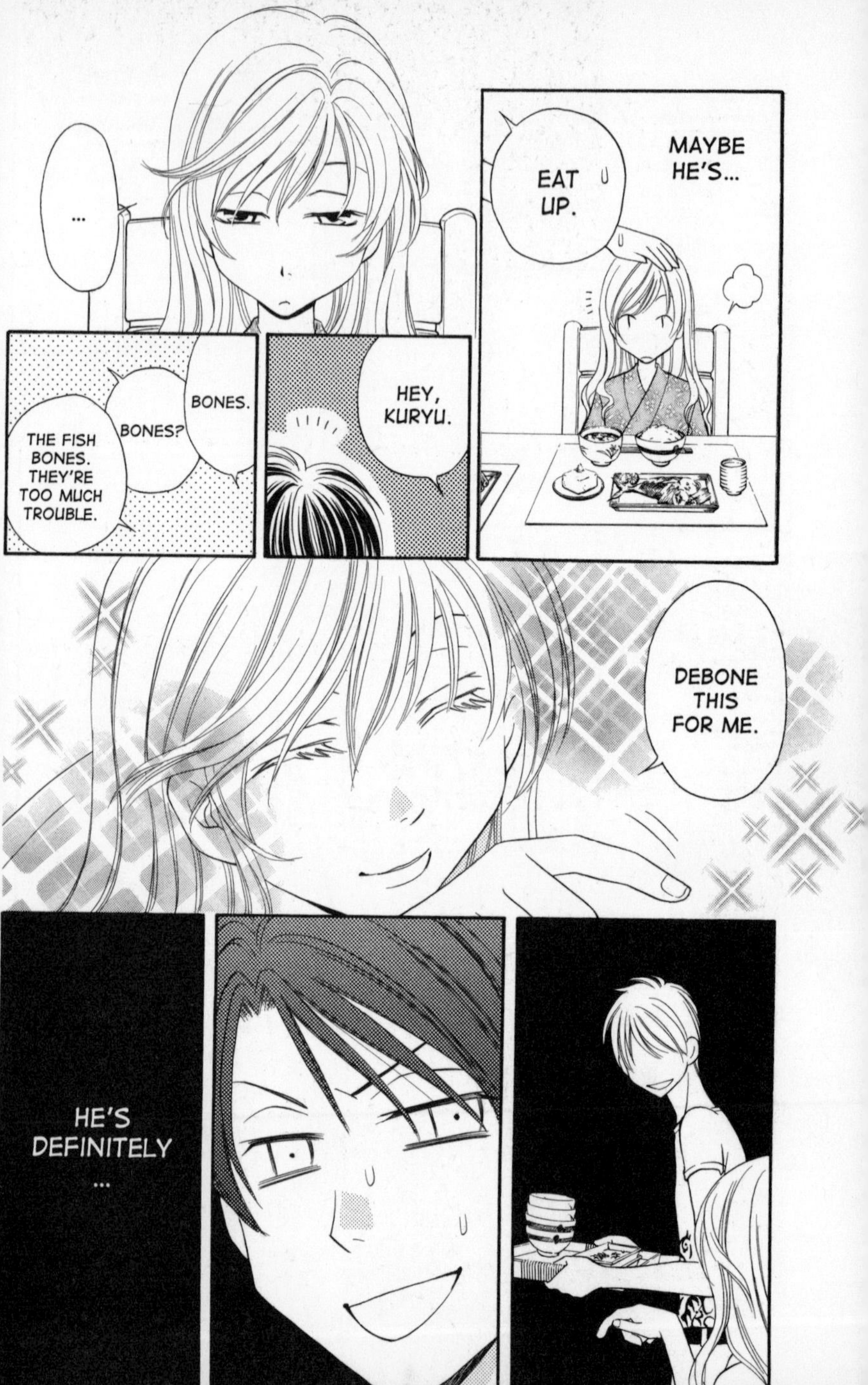
MAYBE HE'S...
EAT UP.
...
HEY, KURYU.
BONES.
BONES?
THE FISH BONES. THEY'RE TOO MUCH TROUBLE.
DEBONE THIS FOR ME.
HE'S DEFINITELY ...

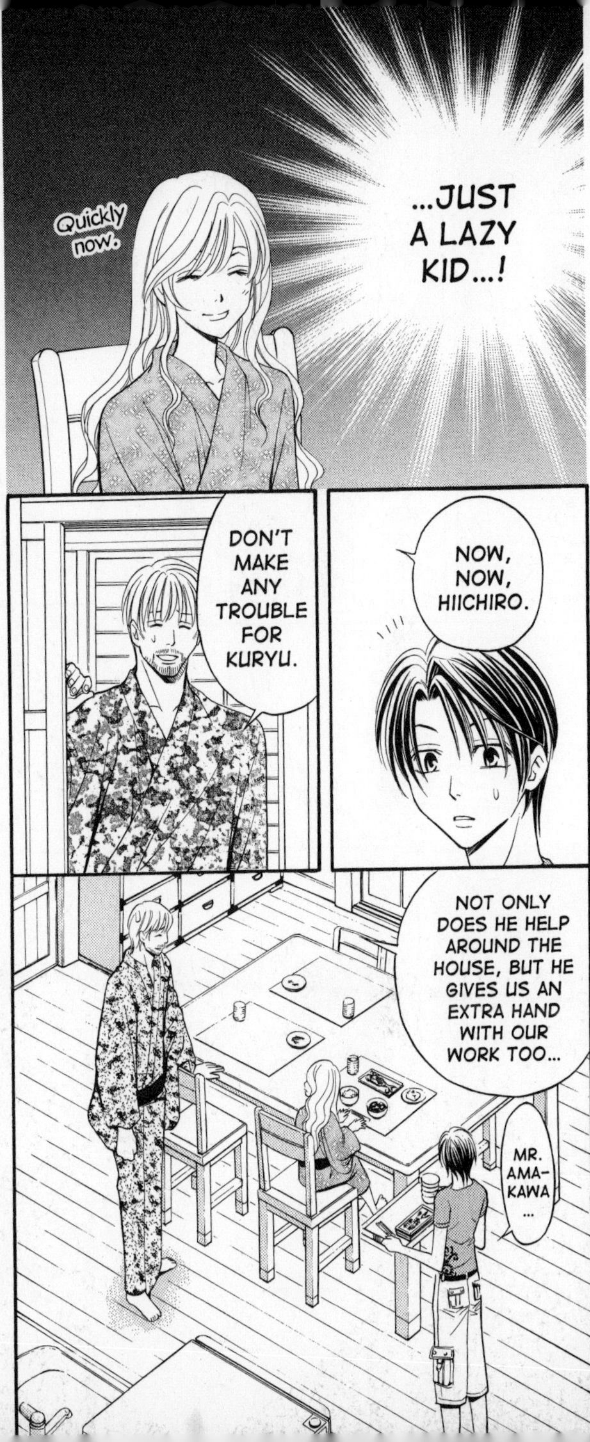
...JUST A LAZY KID...!
Quickly now.
NOW, NOW, HIICHIRO.
DON'T MAKE ANY TROUBLE FOR KURYU.
NOT ONLY DOES HE HELP AROUND THE HOUSE, BUT HE GIVES US AN EXTRA HAND WITH OUR WORK TOO...
MR. AMAKAWA...

My Everyday Life 26

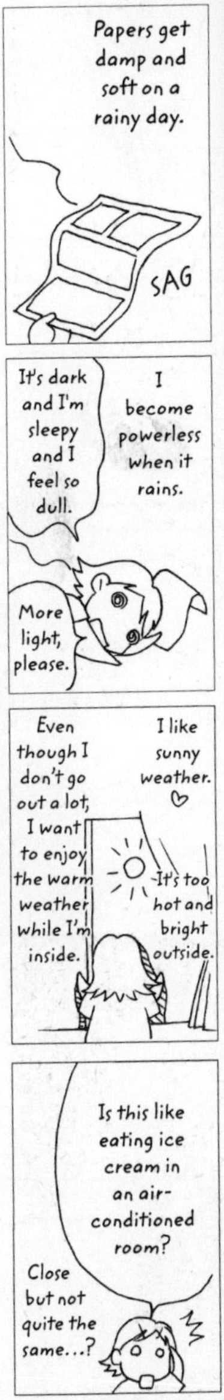
Papers get damp and soft on a rainy day.
SAG
It's dark and I'm sleepy and I feel so dull.
I become powerless when it rains.
More light, please.
Even though I don't go out a lot, I want to enjoy the warm weather while I'm inside.
I like sunny weather. ♡
It's too hot and bright outside.
Is this like eating ice cream in an air-conditioned room?
Close but not quite the same...?

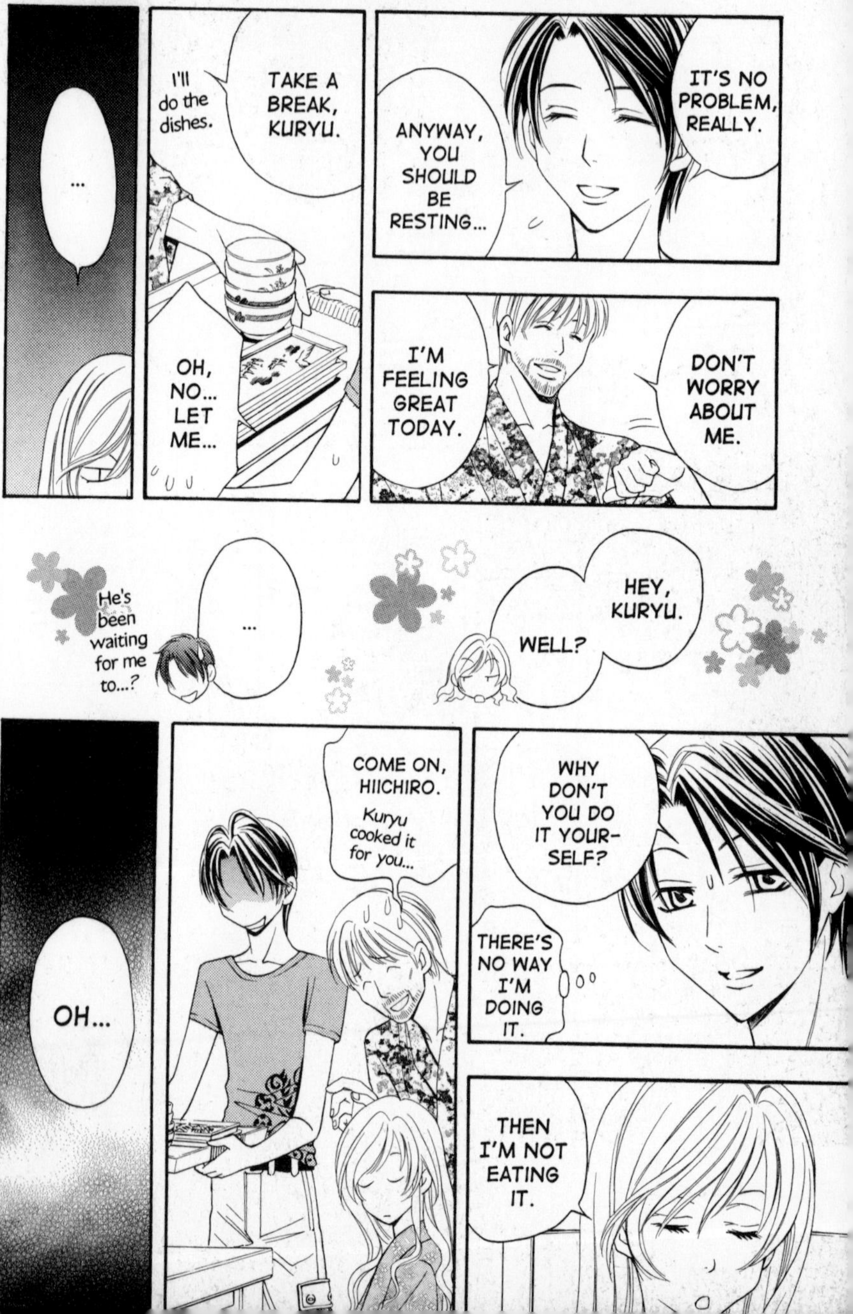
IT'S NO PROBLEM, REALLY.
ANYWAY, YOU SHOULD BE RESTING...
DON'T WORRY ABOUT ME.
I'M FEELING GREAT TODAY.
TAKE A BREAK, KURYU.
I'll do the dishes.
OH, NO... LET ME...
...
HEY, KURYU.
WELL?
...
He's been waiting for me to...?
WHY DON'T YOU DO IT YOURSELF?
THERE'S NO WAY I'M DOING IT.
THEN I'M NOT EATING IT.
COME ON, HIICHIRO.
Kuryu cooked it for you...
OH...

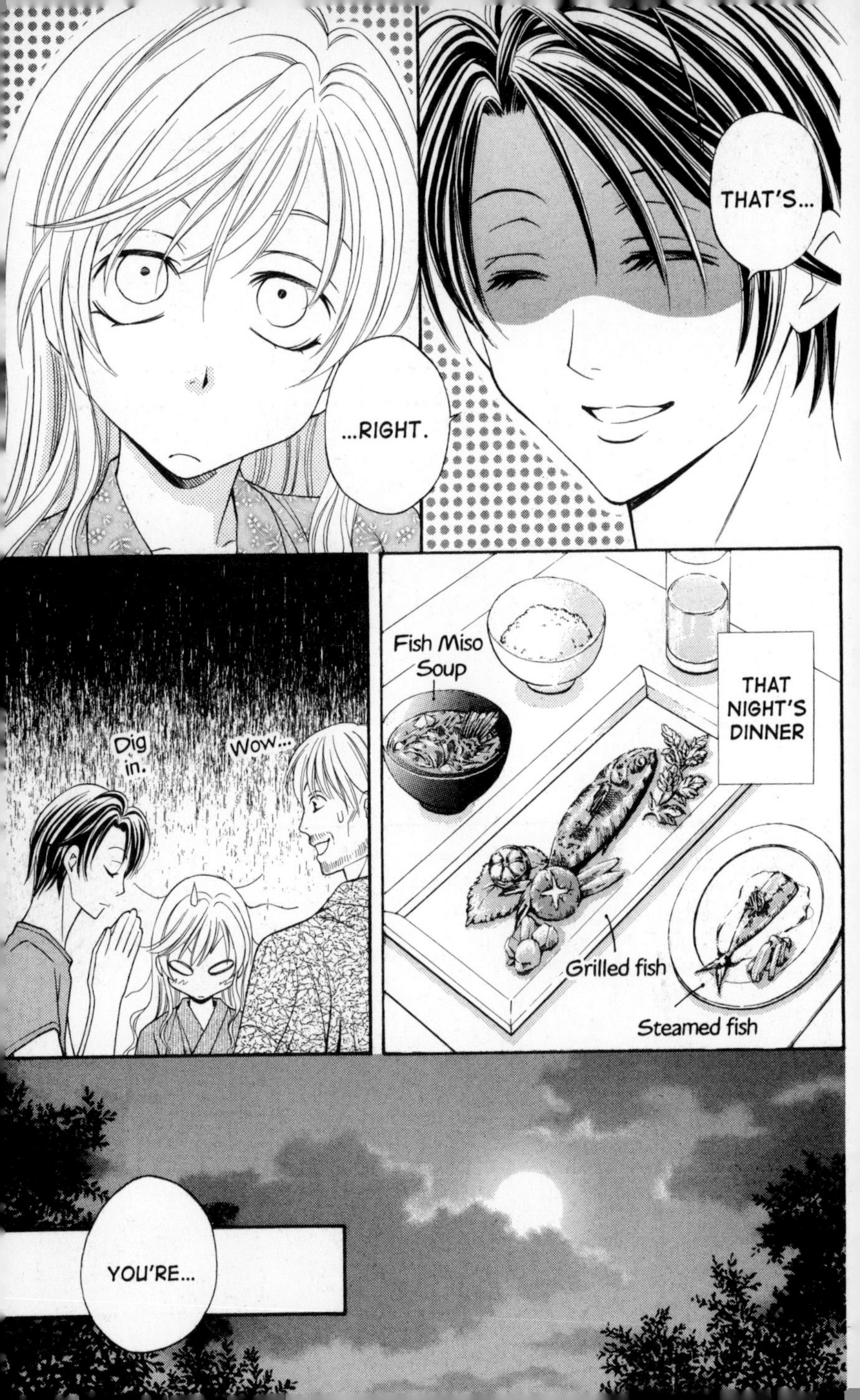
THAT'S...
...RIGHT.
THAT NIGHT'S DINNER
Fish Miso Soup
Grilled fish
Steamed fish
Wow...
Dig in.
YOU'RE...

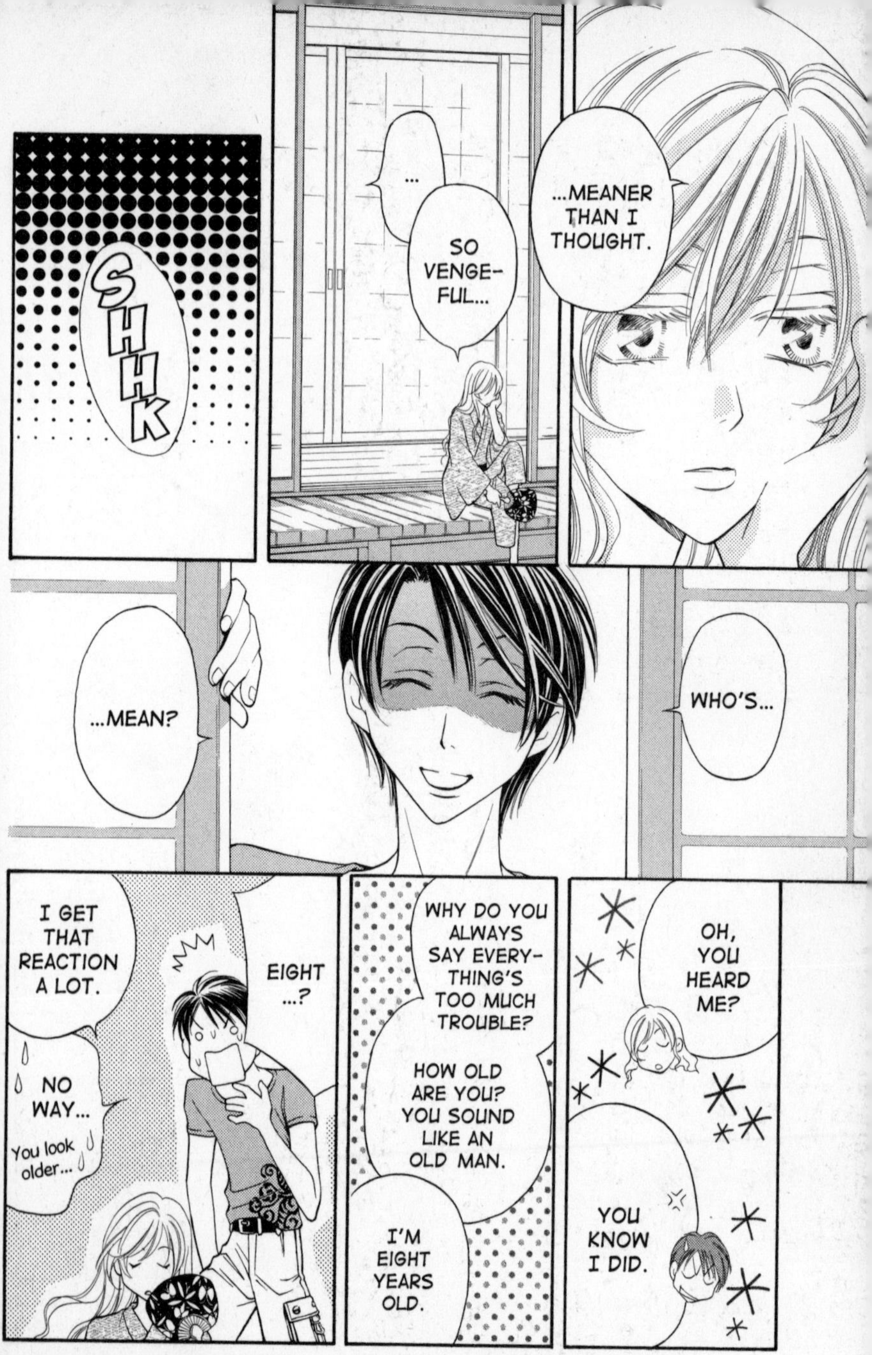
...MEANER THAN I THOUGHT.
...
SO VENGE-FUL...
SHHK
WHO'S...
...MEAN?
OH, YOU HEARD ME?
YOU KNOW I DID.
WHY DO YOU ALWAYS SAY EVERY-THING'S TOO MUCH TROUBLE?
HOW OLD ARE YOU? YOU SOUND LIKE AN OLD MAN.
I'M EIGHT YEARS OLD.
EIGHT ...?
I GET THAT REACTION A LOT.
NO WAY...
You look older...

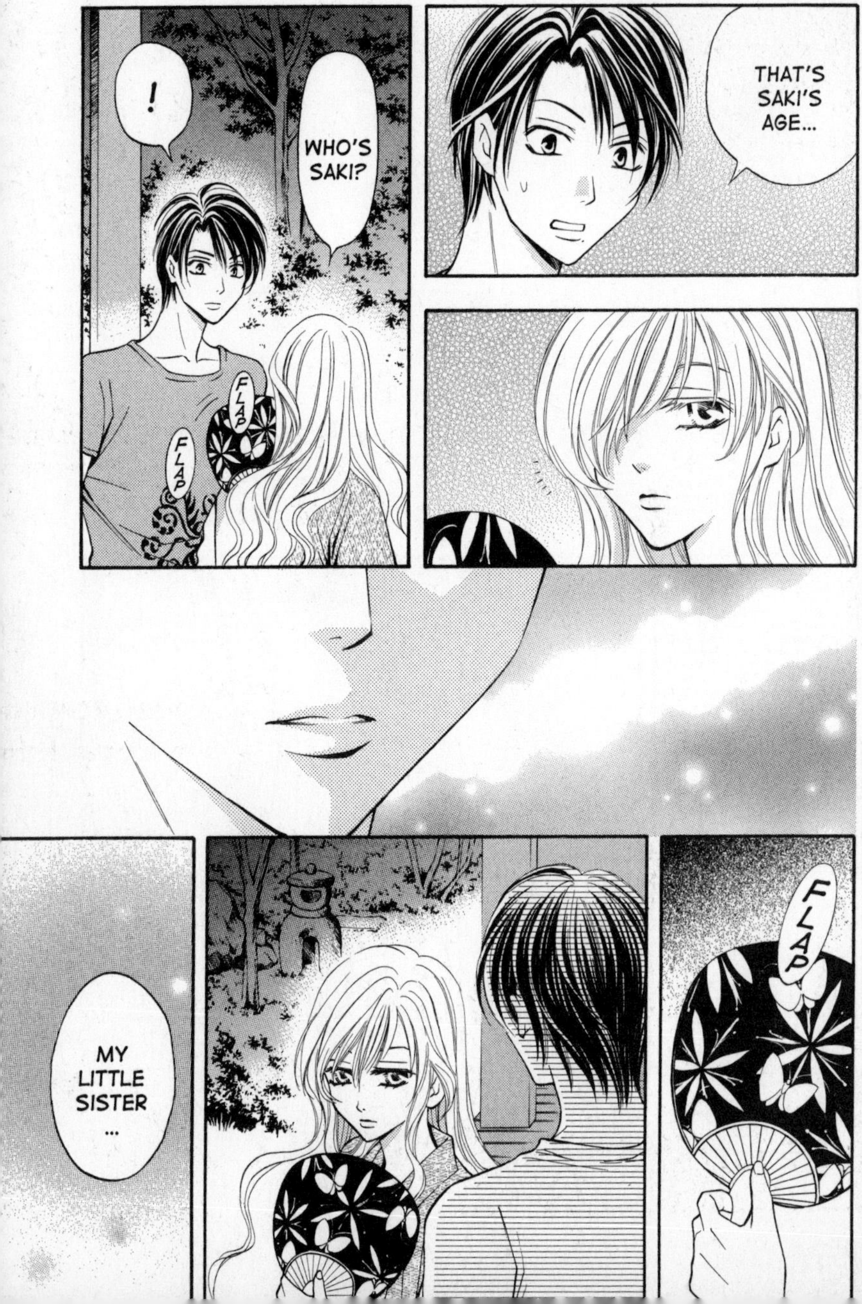
THAT'S SAKI'S AGE...
WHO'S SAKI?
!
FLAP
FLAP
FLAP
MY LITTLE SISTER ...

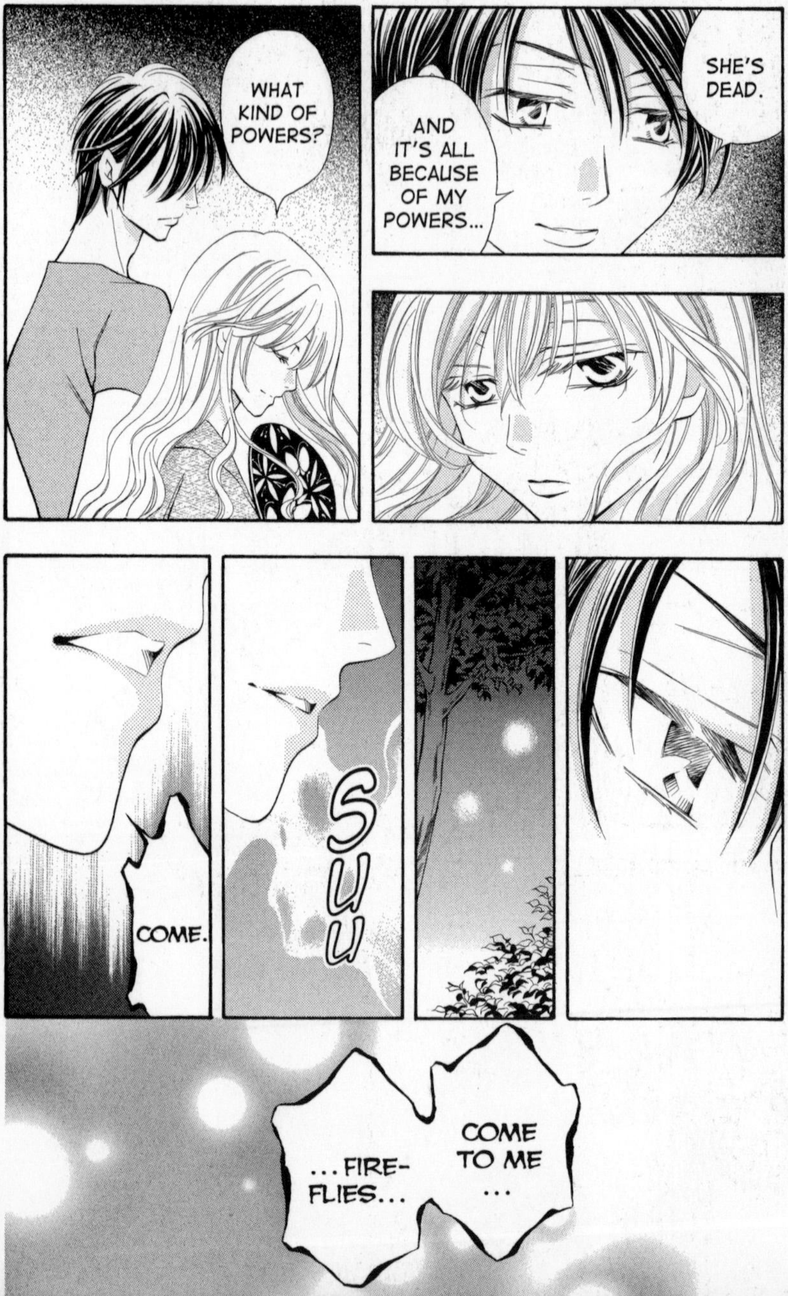
SHE'S DEAD.
AND IT'S ALL BECAUSE OF MY POWERS...
WHAT KIND OF POWERS?
SUUU
COME.
COME TO ME ...
...FIRE-FLIES...

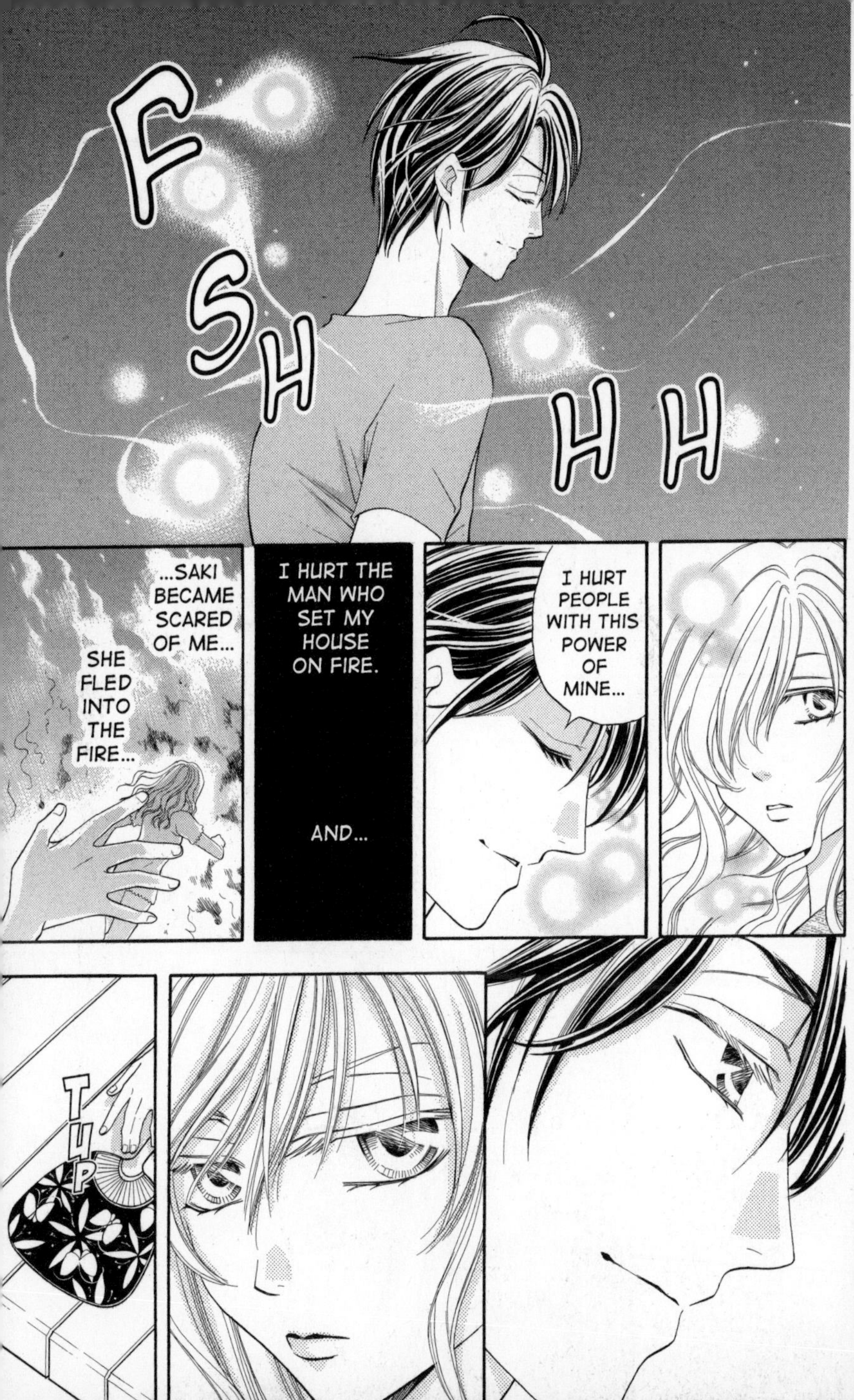
FSHHHH
I HURT PEOPLE WITH THIS POWER OF MINE...
I HURT THE MAN WHO SET MY HOUSE ON FIRE.
AND...
...SAKI BECAME SCARED OF ME...
SHE FLED INTO THE FIRE...
TUP

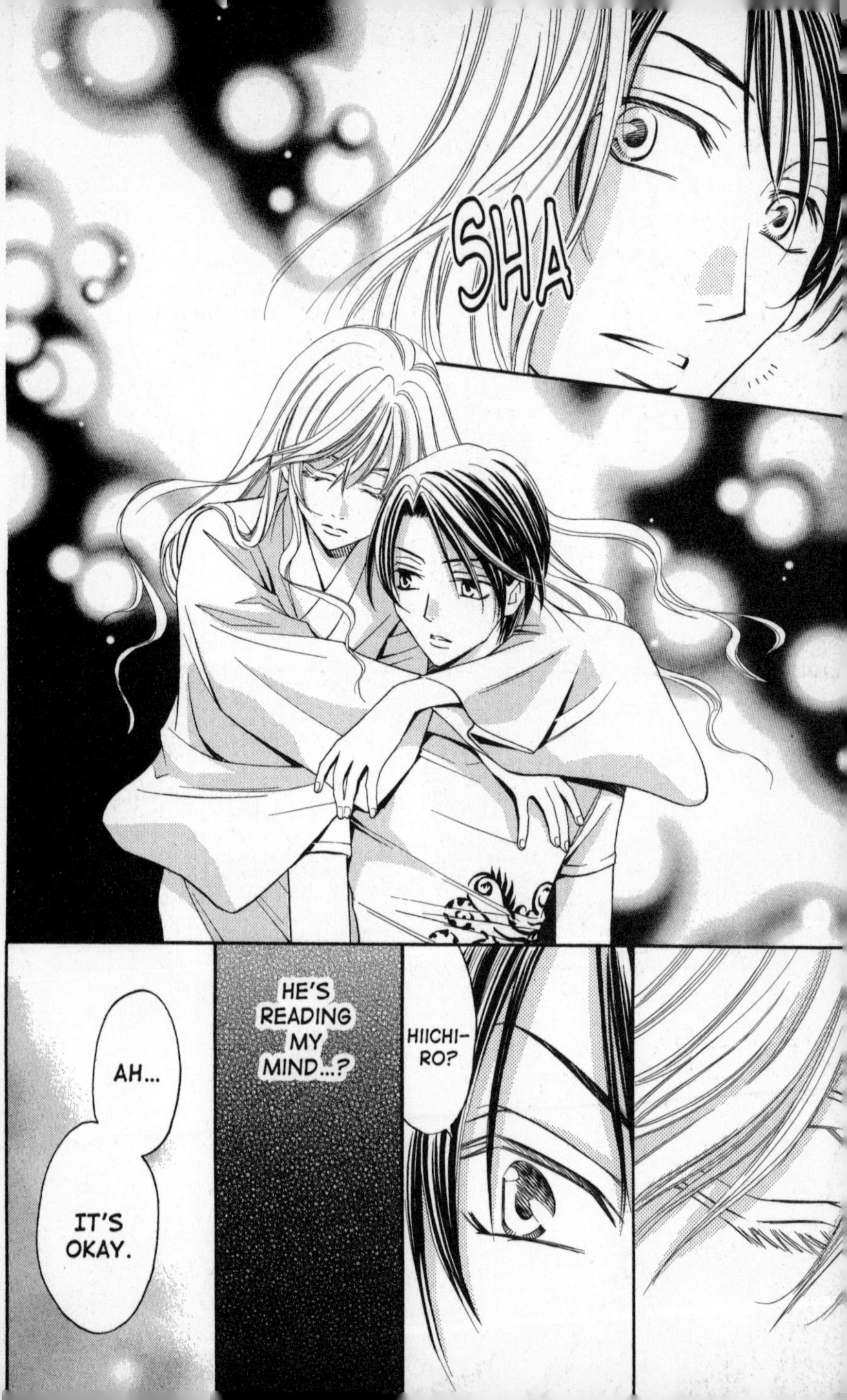
SHA
HIICHI-RO?
HE'S READING MY MIND...?
AH...
IT'S OKAY.

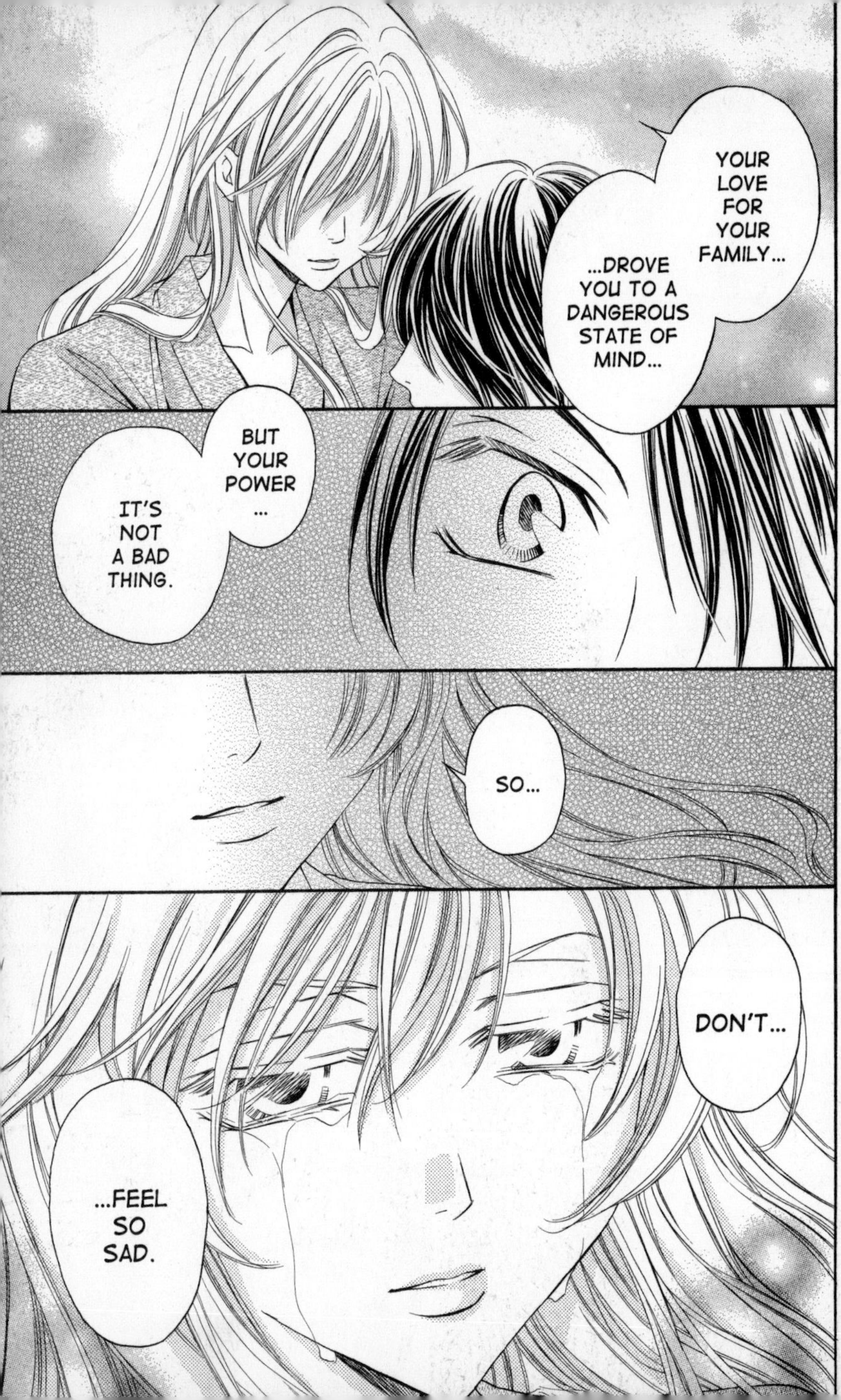
YOUR LOVE FOR YOUR FAMILY...
...DROVE YOU TO A DANGEROUS STATE OF MIND...
BUT YOUR POWER ...
IT'S NOT A BAD THING.
SO...
DON'T...
...FEEL SO SAD.

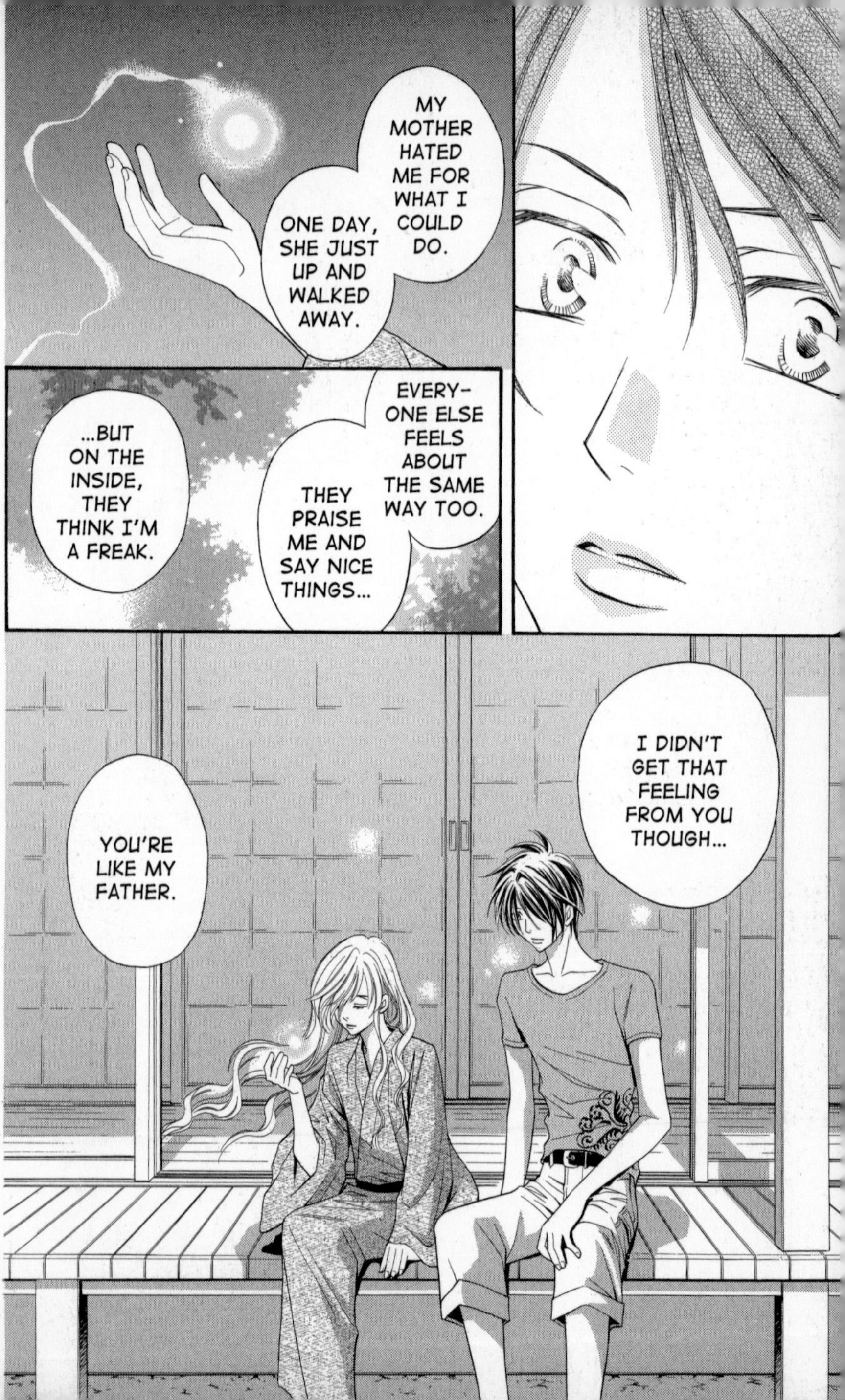
MY MOTHER HATED ME FOR WHAT I COULD DO.
ONE DAY, SHE JUST UP AND WALKED AWAY.
EVERY-ONE ELSE FEELS ABOUT THE SAME WAY TOO.
THEY PRAISE ME AND SAY NICE THINGS...
...BUT ON THE INSIDE, THEY THINK I'M A FREAK.
I DIDN'T GET THAT FEELING FROM YOU THOUGH...
YOU'RE LIKE MY FATHER.

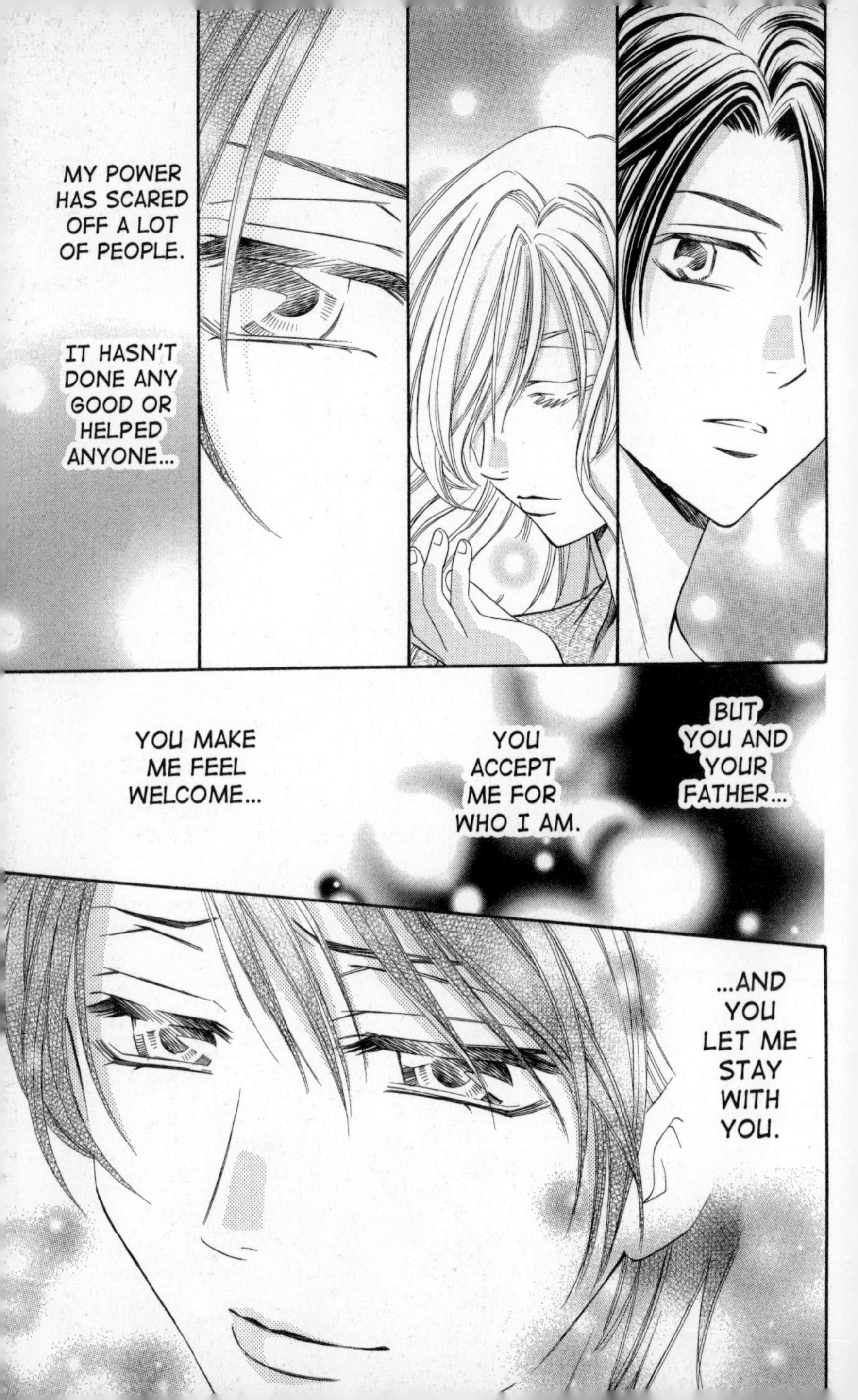
MY POWER HAS SCARED OFF A LOT OF PEOPLE.
IT HASN'T DONE ANY GOOD OR HELPED ANYONE...
BUT YOU AND YOUR FATHER...
YOU ACCEPT ME FOR WHO I AM.
YOU MAKE ME FEEL WELCOME...
...AND YOU LET ME STAY WITH YOU.

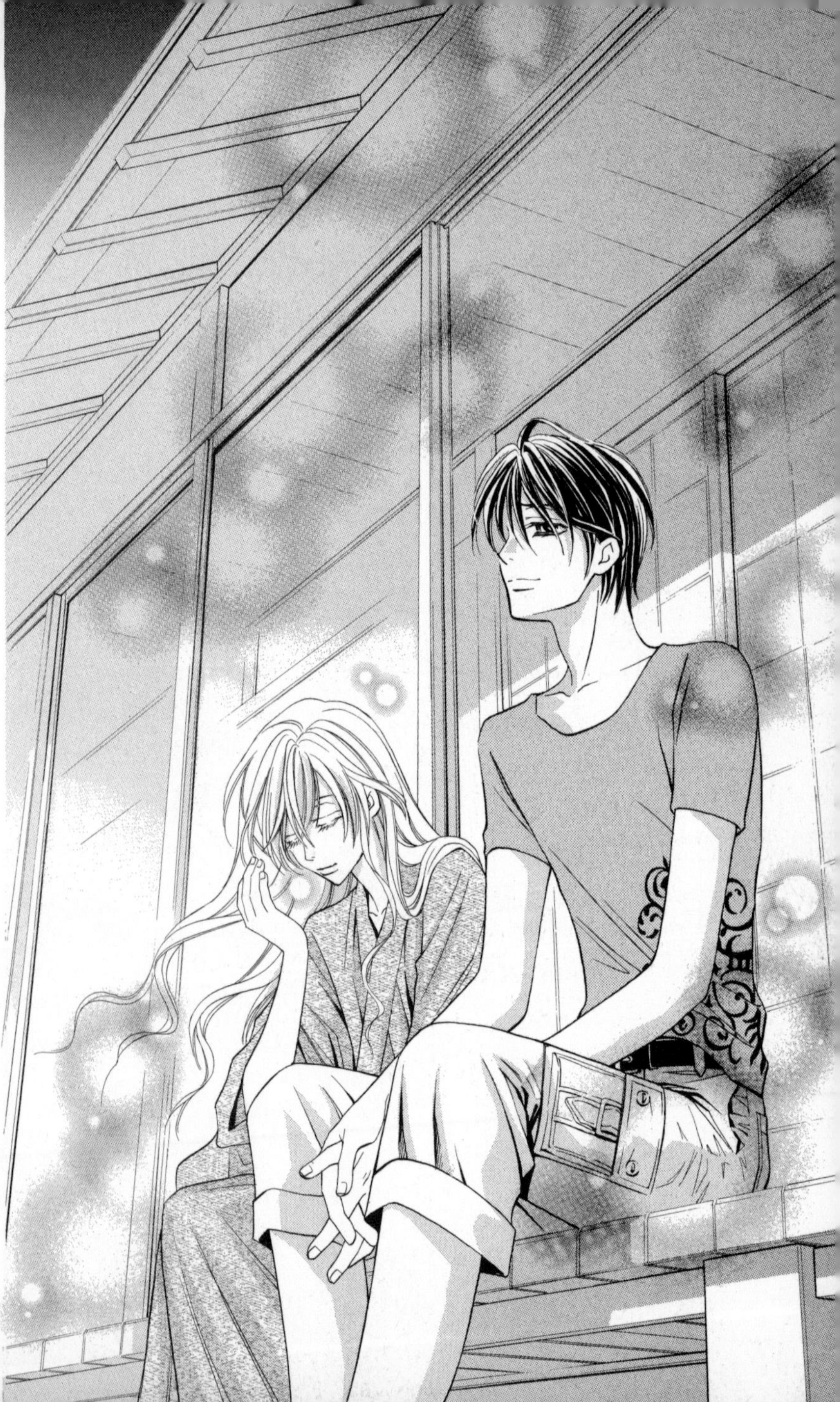

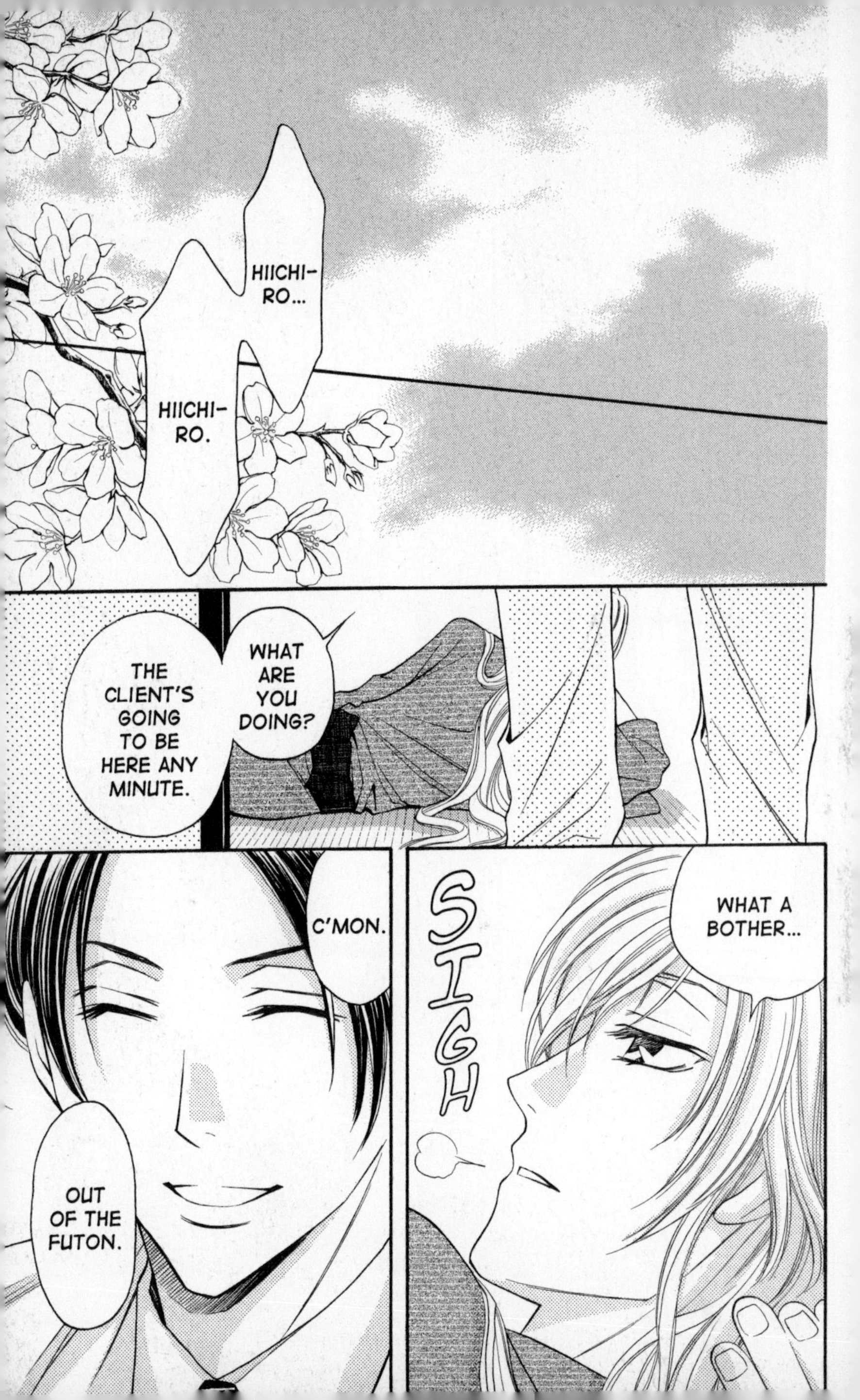
HIICHI-RO...
HIICHI-RO.
WHAT ARE YOU DOING?
THE CLIENT'S GOING TO BE HERE ANY MINUTE.
WHAT A BOTHER...
SIGH
C'MON.
OUT OF THE FUTON.

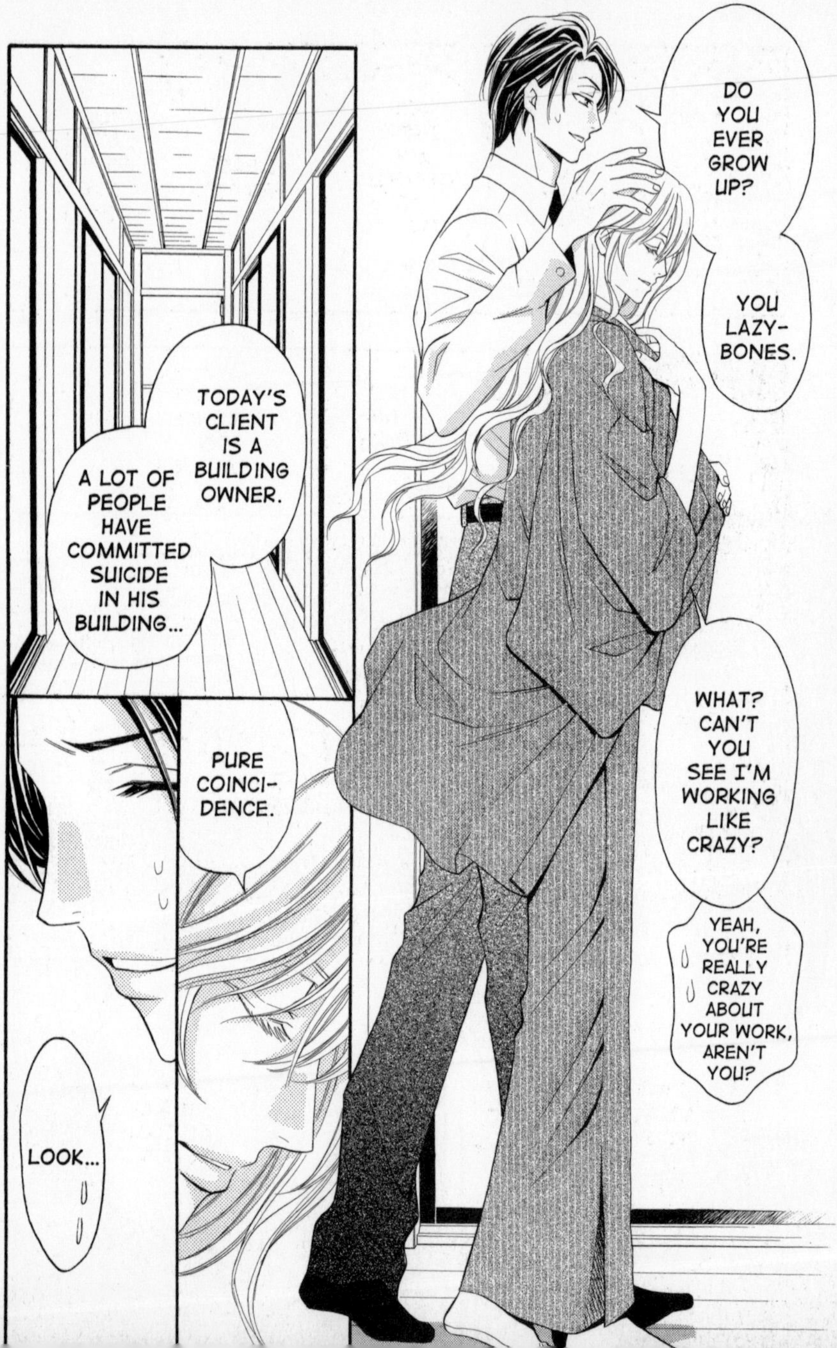
DO YOU EVER GROW UP?
YOU LAZY-BONES.
WHAT? CAN'T YOU SEE I'M WORKING LIKE CRAZY?
YEAH, YOU'RE REALLY CRAZY ABOUT YOUR WORK, AREN'T YOU?
TODAY'S CLIENT IS A BUILDING OWNER.
A LOT OF PEOPLE HAVE COMMITTED SUICIDE IN HIS BUILDING...
PURE COINCI-DENCE.
LOOK...

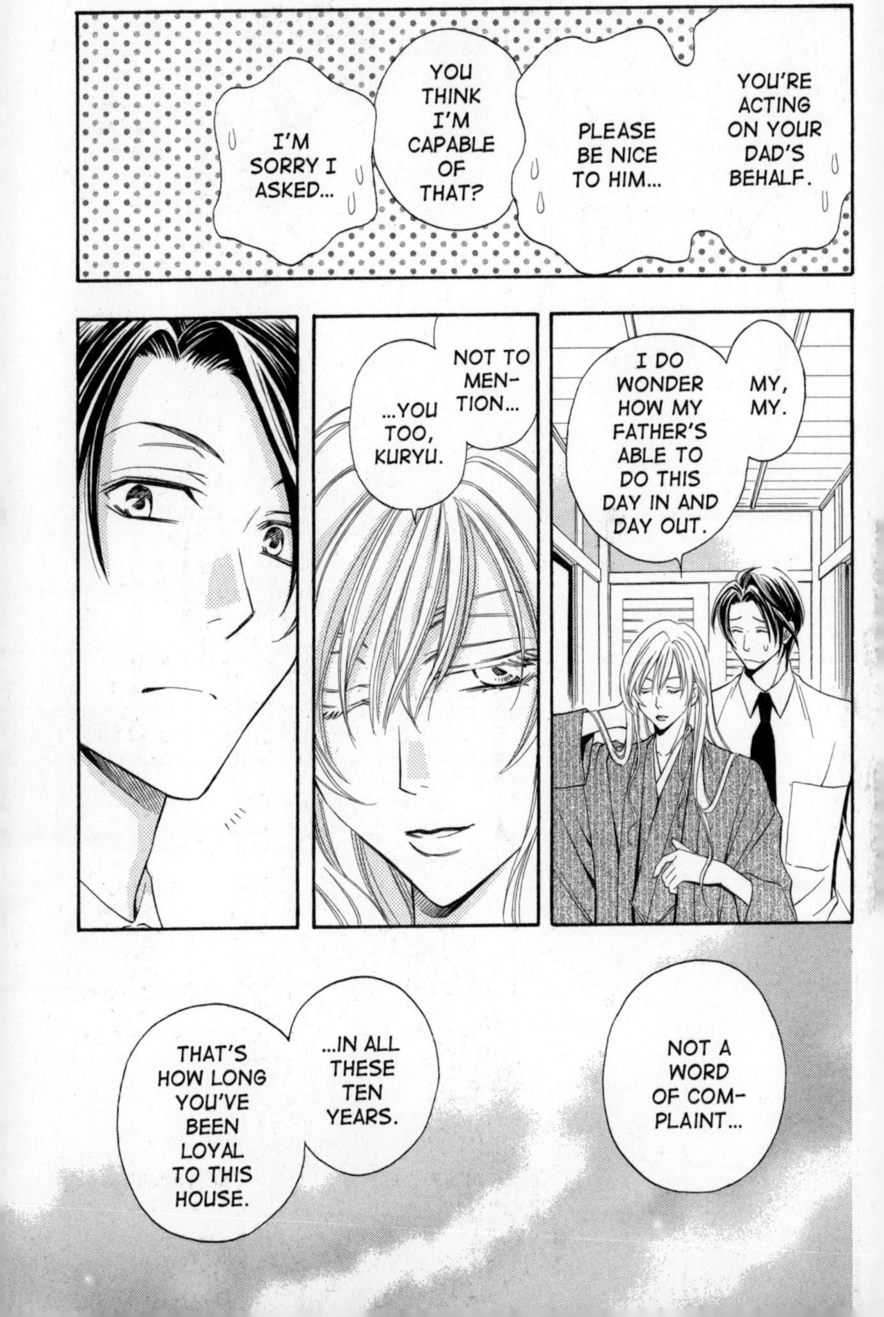
YOU'RE ACTING ON YOUR DAD'S BEHALF.
PLEASE BE NICE TO HIM...
YOU THINK I'M CAPABLE OF THAT?
I'M SORRY I ASKED...
MY, MY.
I DO WONDER HOW MY FATHER'S ABLE TO DO THIS DAY IN AND DAY OUT.
NOT TO MEN-TION...
...YOU TOO, KURYU.
NOT A WORD OF COM-PLAINT...
...IN ALL THESE TEN YEARS.
THAT'S HOW LONG YOU'VE BEEN LOYAL TO THIS HOUSE.

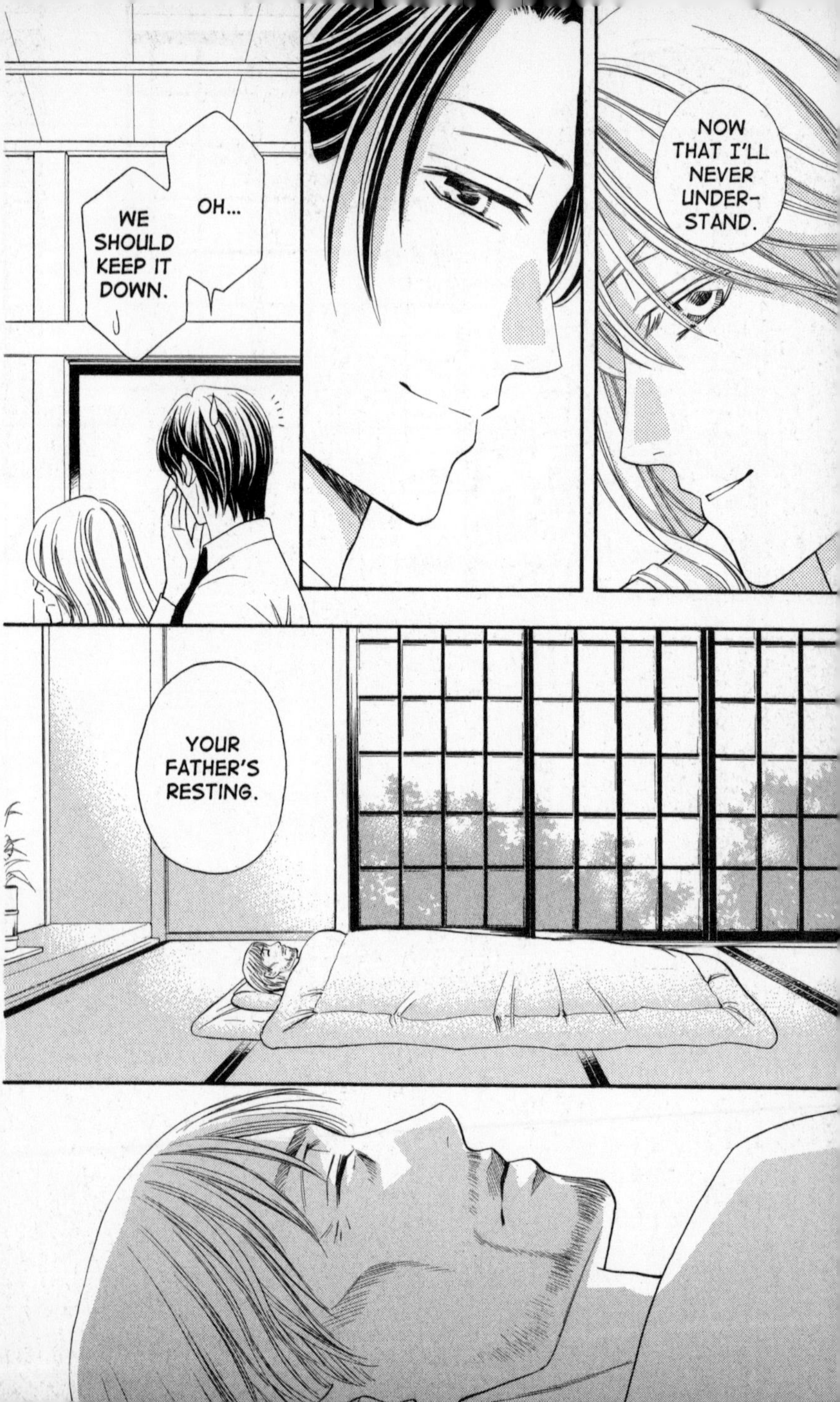
NOW THAT I'LL NEVER UNDER-STAND.
OH...
WE SHOULD KEEP IT DOWN.
YOUR FATHER'S RESTING.

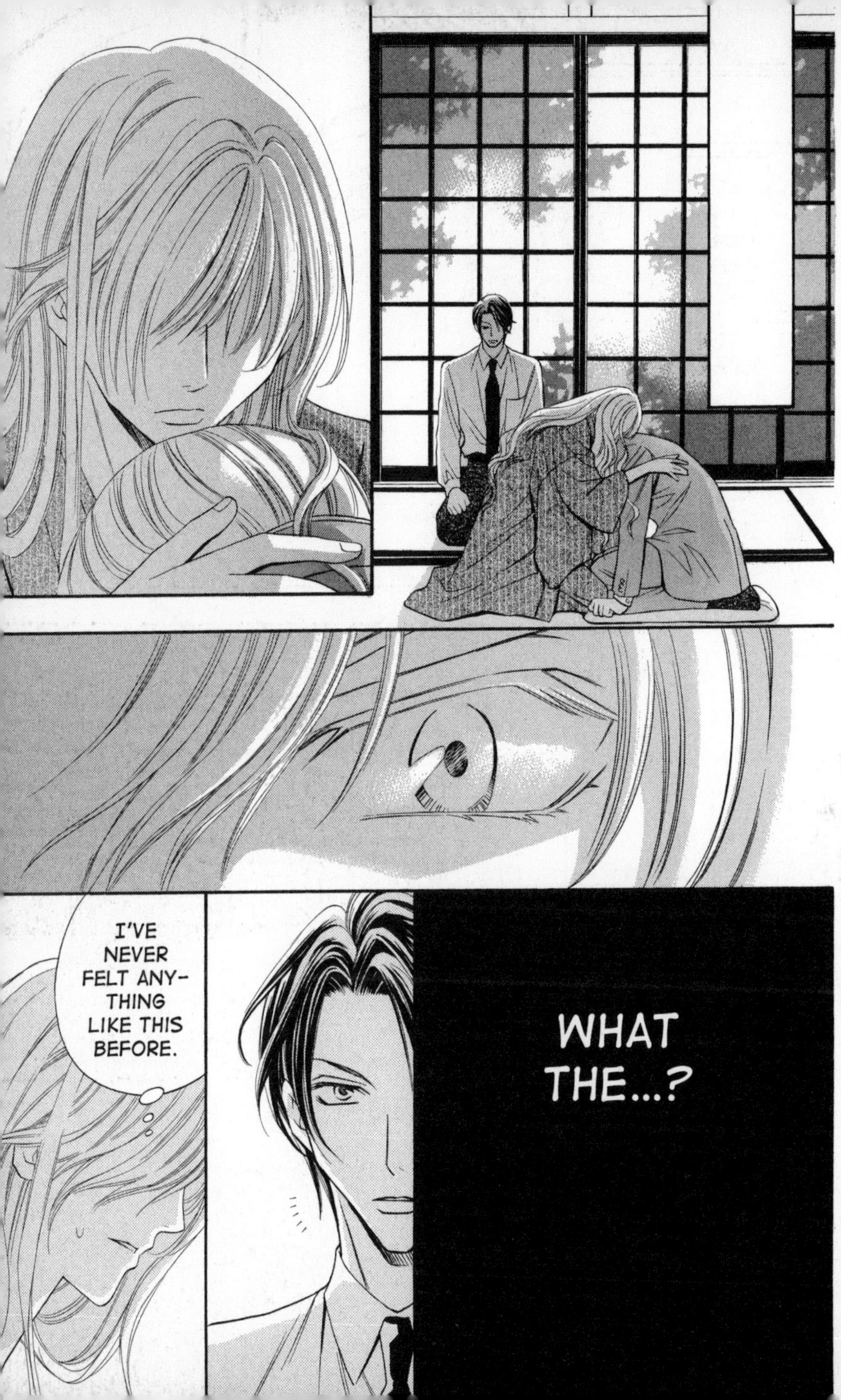
WHAT THE...?
I'VE NEVER FELT ANY-THING LIKE THIS BEFORE.

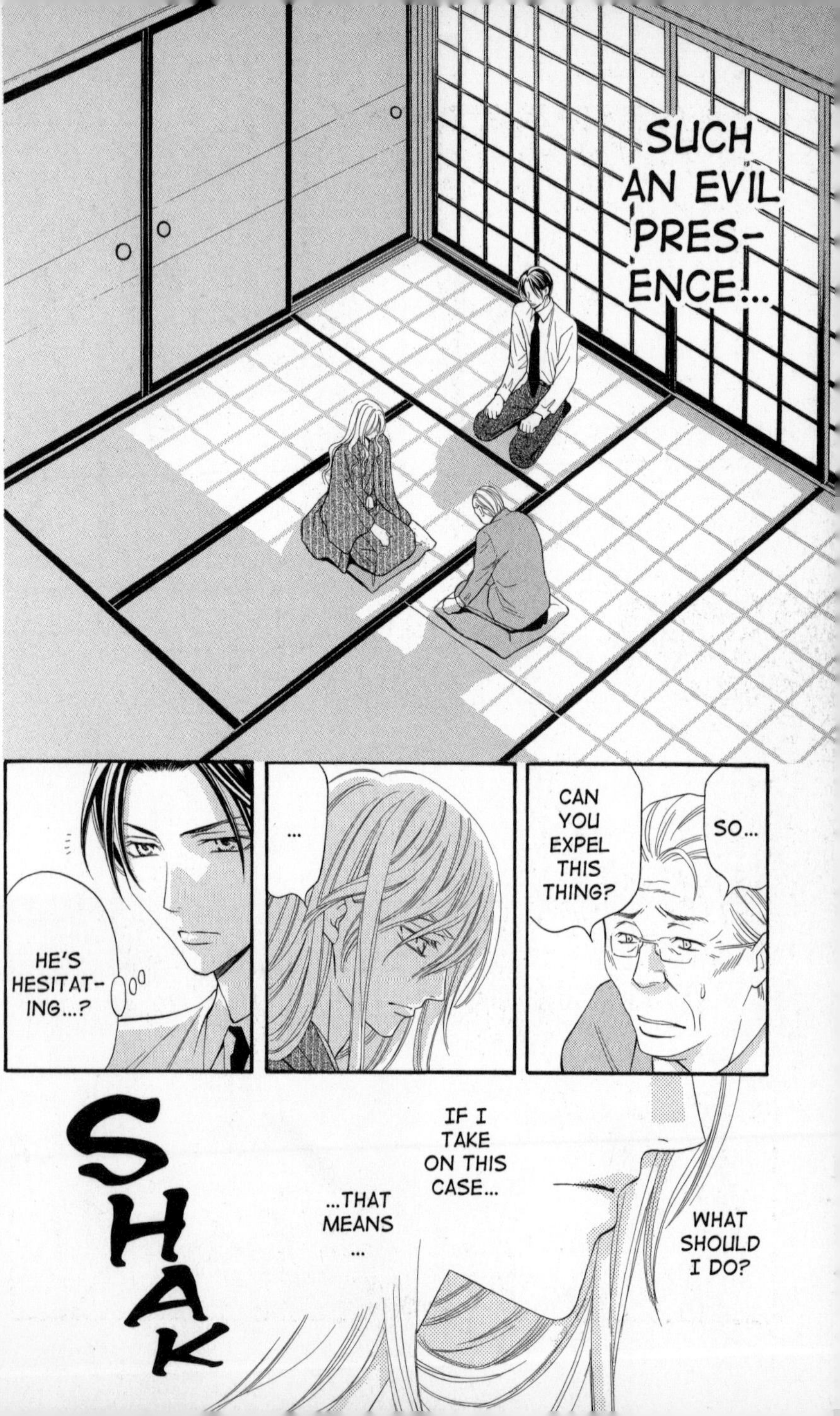
SUCH AN EVIL PRES-ENCE...
SO...
CAN YOU EXPEL THIS THING?
...
HE'S HESITAT-ING...?
WHAT SHOULD I DO?
IF I TAKE ON THIS CASE...
...THAT MEANS ...
SHAK

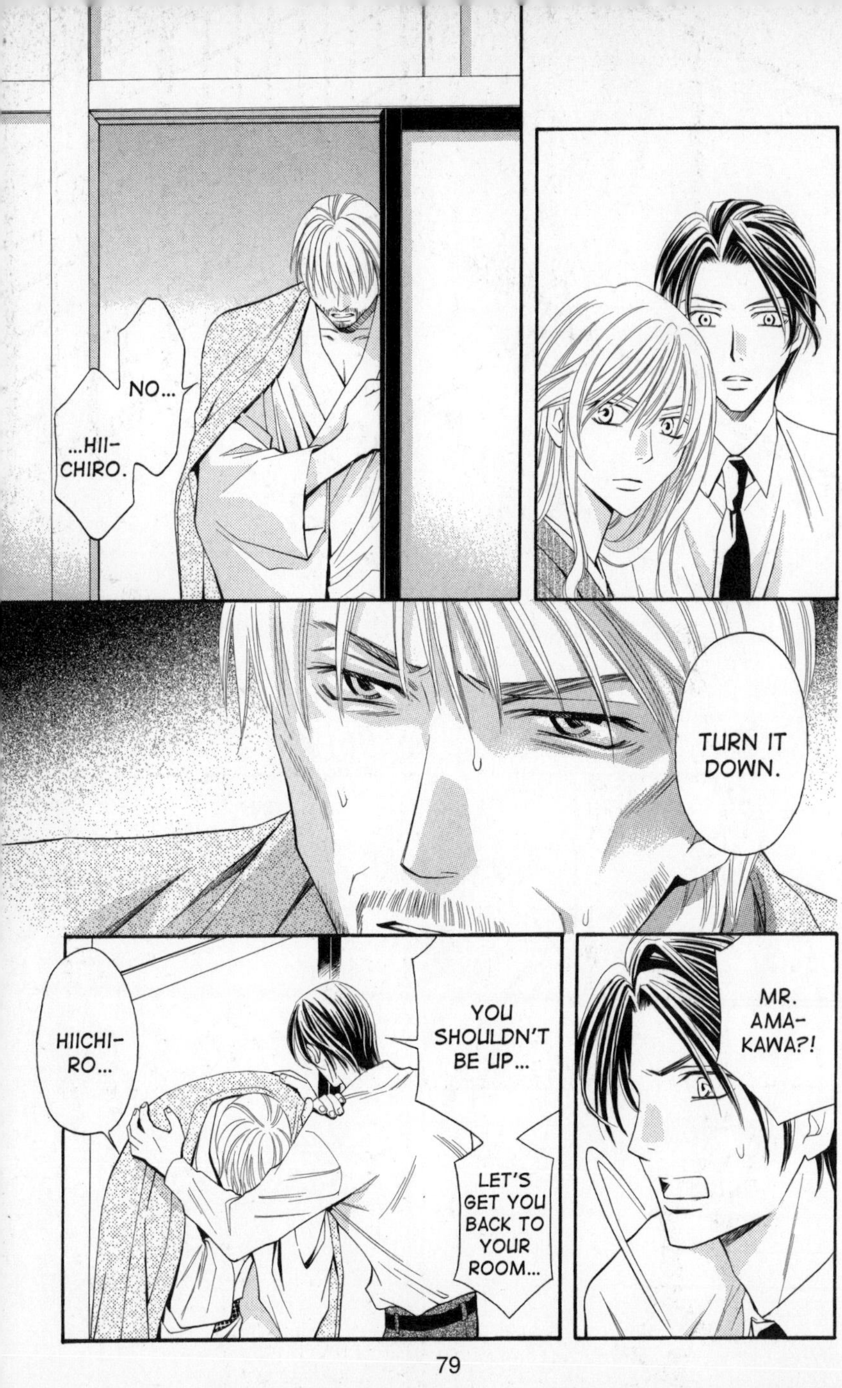
NO...
...HII-CHIRO.
TURN IT DOWN.
MR. AMA-KAWA?!
YOU SHOULDN'T BE UP...
HIICHI-RO...
LET'S GET YOU BACK TO YOUR ROOM...

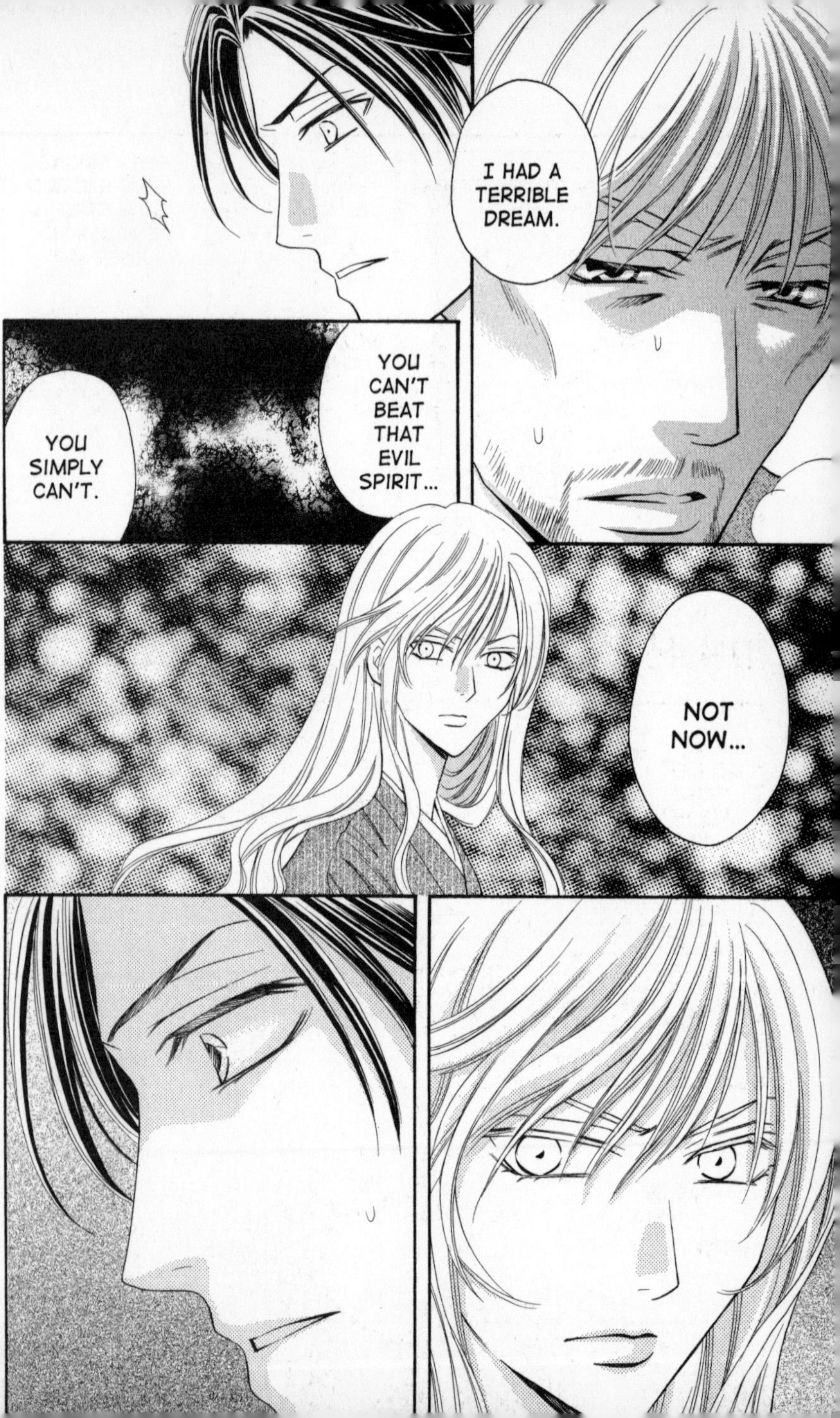
I HAD A TERRIBLE DREAM.
YOU CAN'T BEAT THAT EVIL SPIRIT...
YOU SIMPLY CAN'T.
NOT NOW...

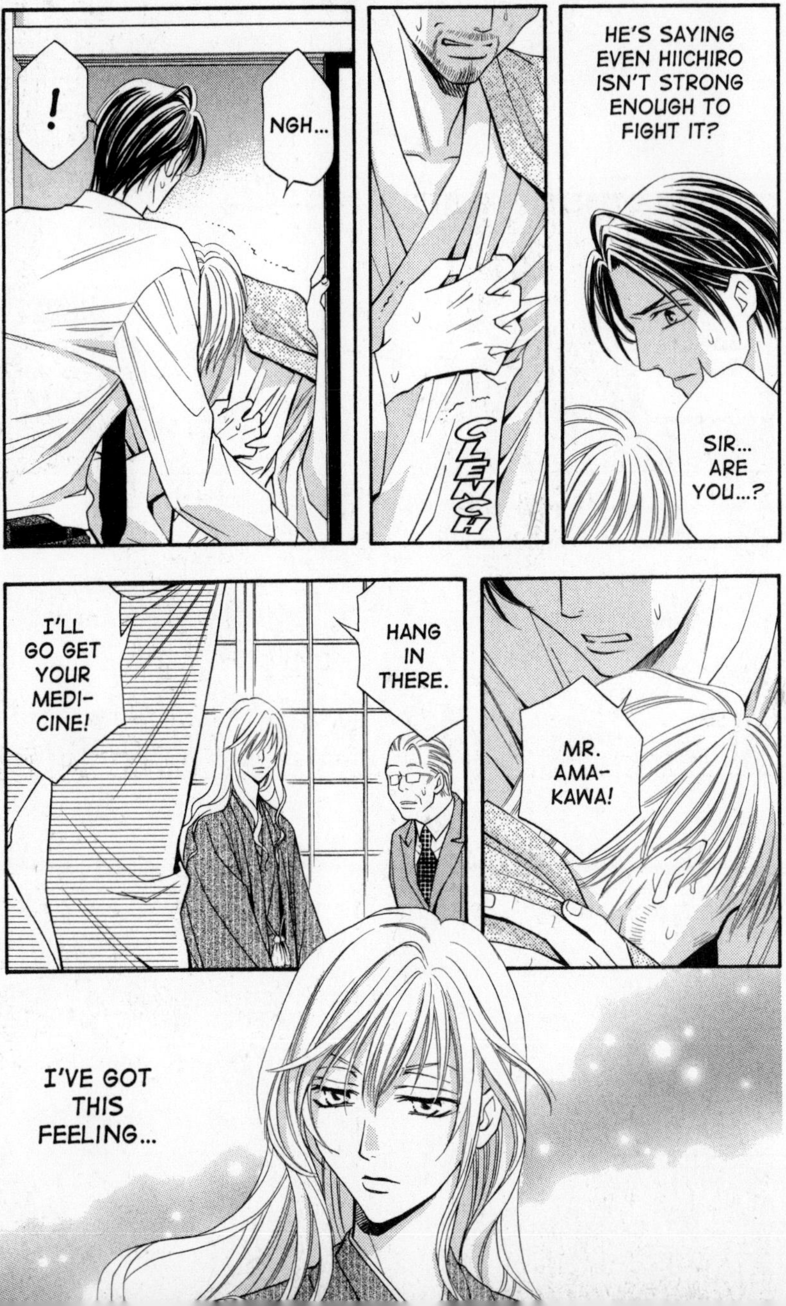
HE'S SAYING EVEN HIICHIRO ISN'T STRONG ENOUGH TO FIGHT IT?
SIR... ARE YOU...?
CLENCH
NGH...
!
MR. AMA-KAWA!
HANG IN THERE.
I'LL GO GET YOUR MEDI-CINE!
I'VE GOT THIS FEELING...

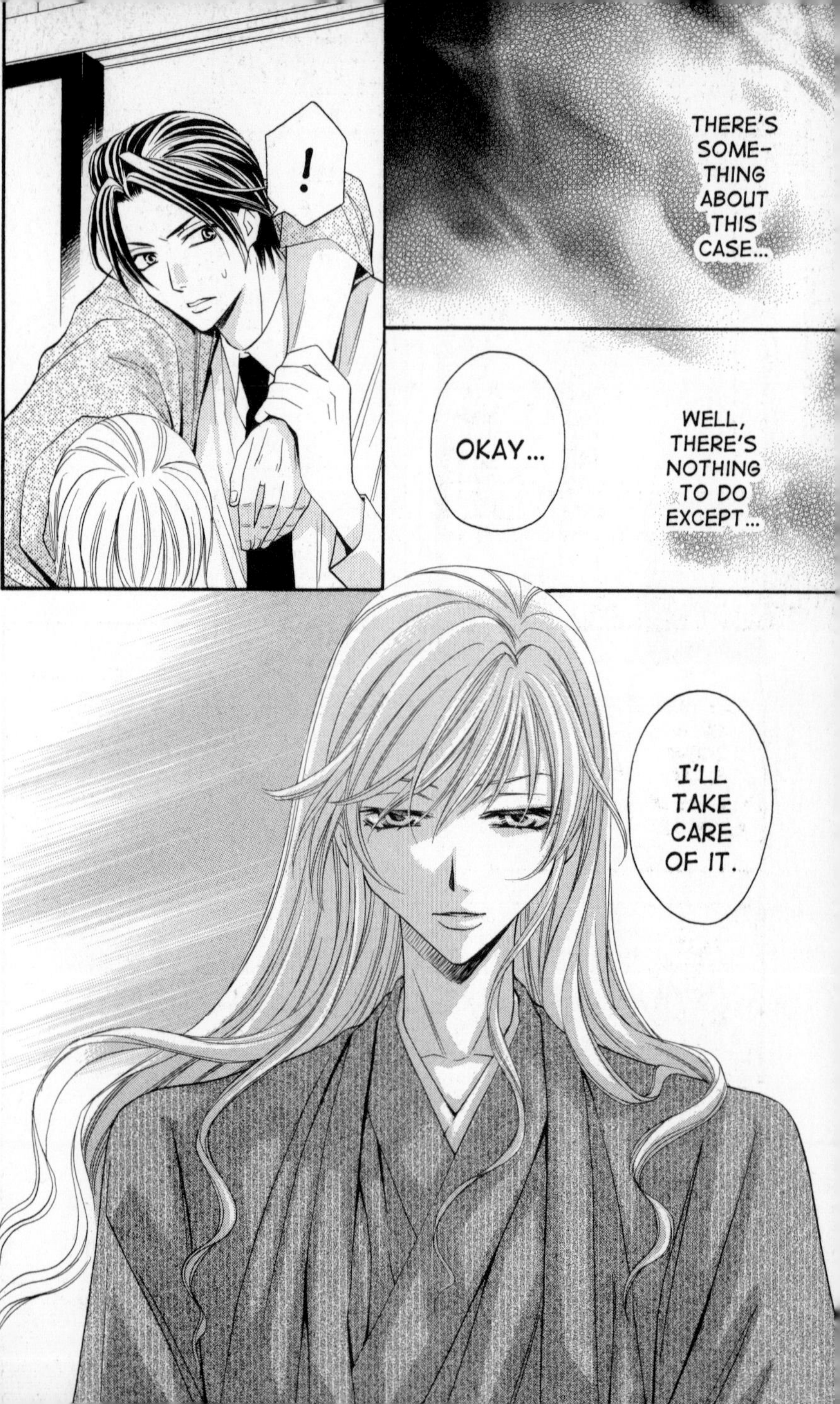
THERE'S SOME-THING ABOUT THIS CASE...
WELL, THERE'S NOTHING TO DO EXCEPT...
OKAY...
!
I'LL TAKE CARE OF IT.

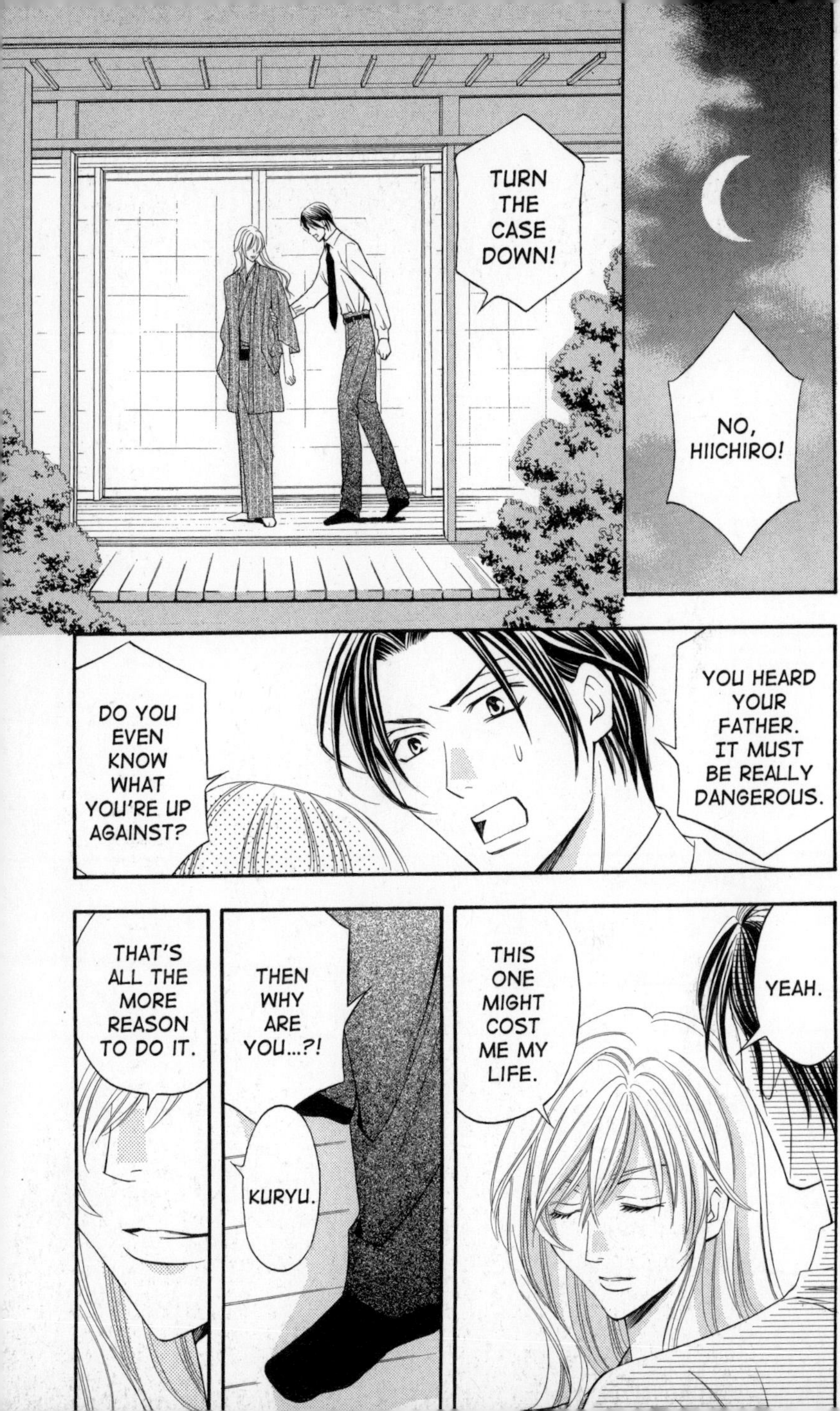
NO, HIICHIRO!
TURN THE CASE DOWN!
YOU HEARD YOUR FATHER. IT MUST BE REALLY DANGEROUS.
DO YOU EVEN KNOW WHAT YOU'RE UP AGAINST?
YEAH.
THIS ONE MIGHT COST ME MY LIFE.
THEN WHY ARE YOU...?!
KURYU.
THAT'S ALL THE MORE REASON TO DO IT.

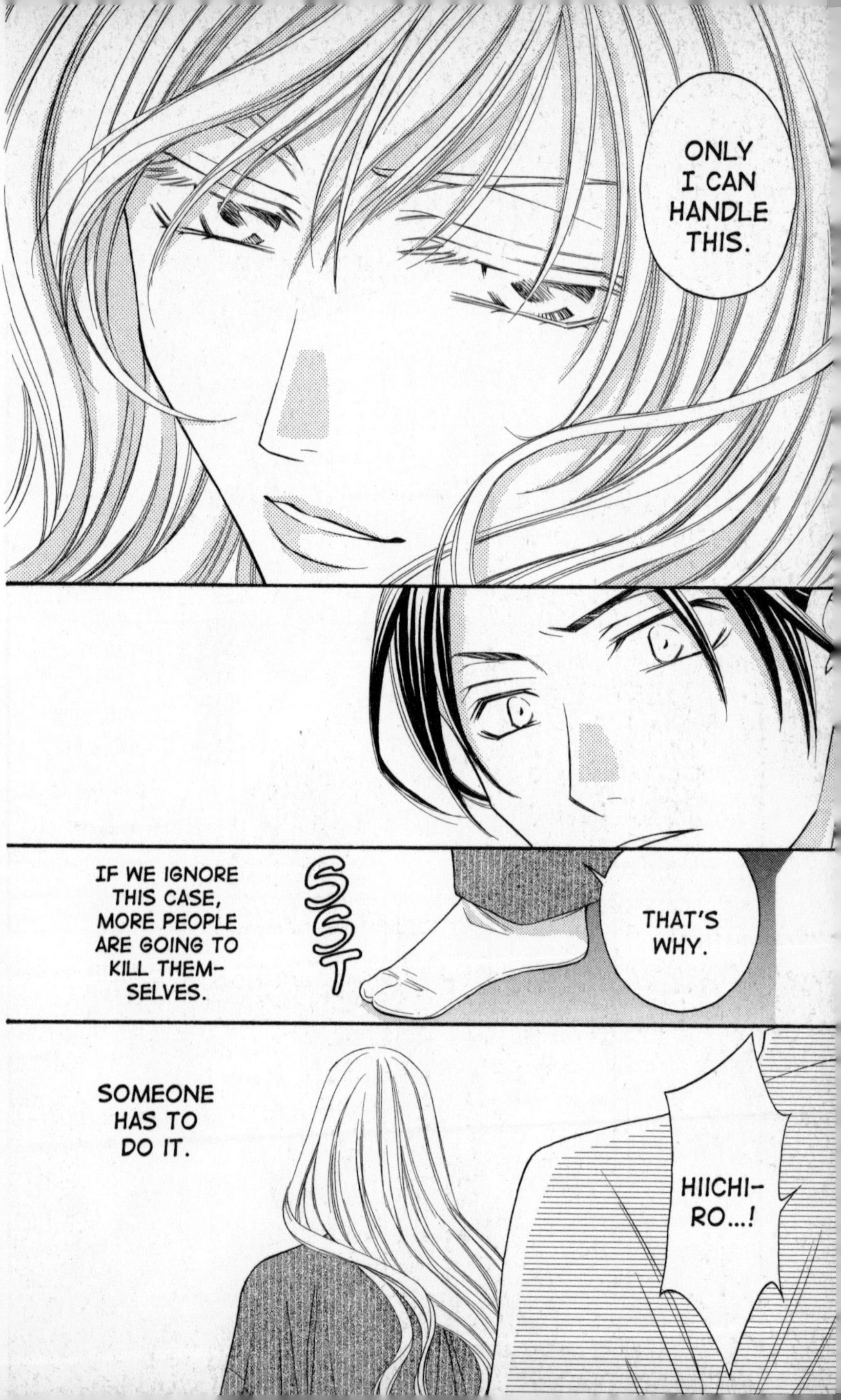
ONLY I CAN HANDLE THIS.
THAT'S WHY.
SST
IF WE IGNORE THIS CASE, MORE PEOPLE ARE GOING TO KILL THEM-SELVES.
HIICHI-RO...!
SOMEONE HAS TO DO IT.

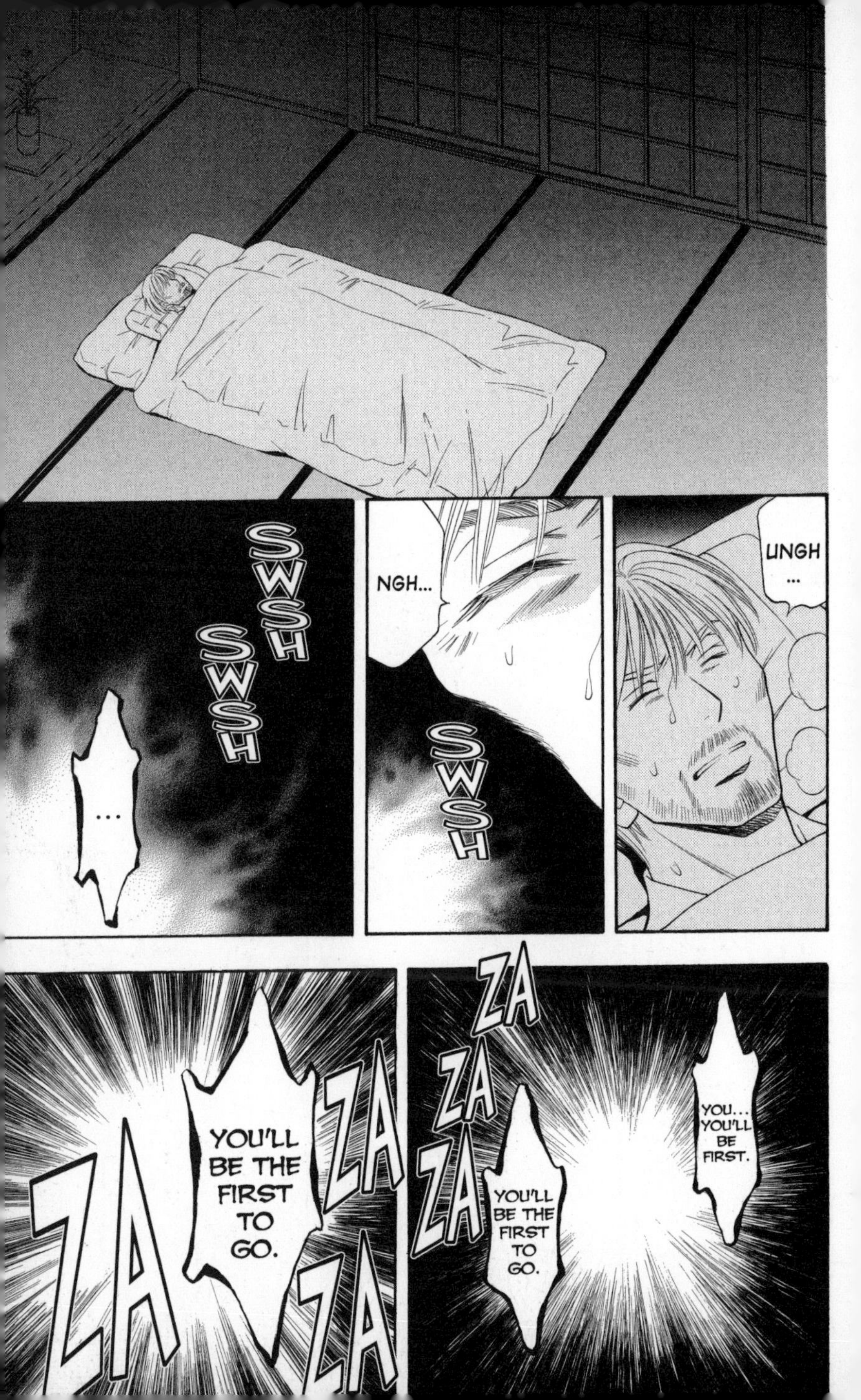
UNGH ...
NGH...
SWSH
SWSH
SWSH
...
ZA
ZA
ZA
YOU... YOU'LL BE FIRST.
YOU'LL BE THE FIRST TO GO.
ZA
YOU'LL BE THE FIRST TO GO.
ZA
ZA

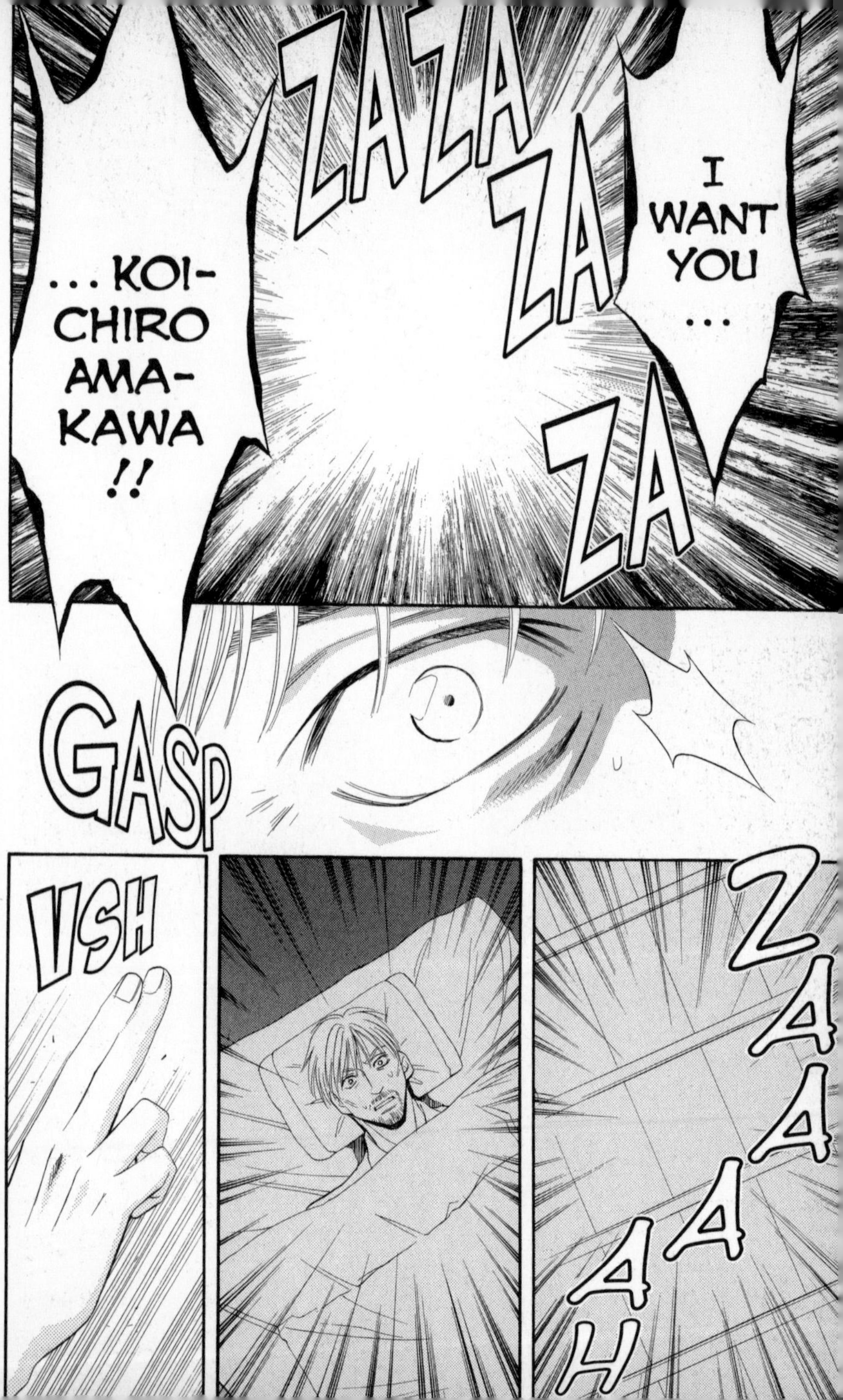
I WANT YOU ...
ZAZAZAZAZA
... KOI-CHIRO AMA-KAWA !!
GASP
ZAAAAAH
VSH

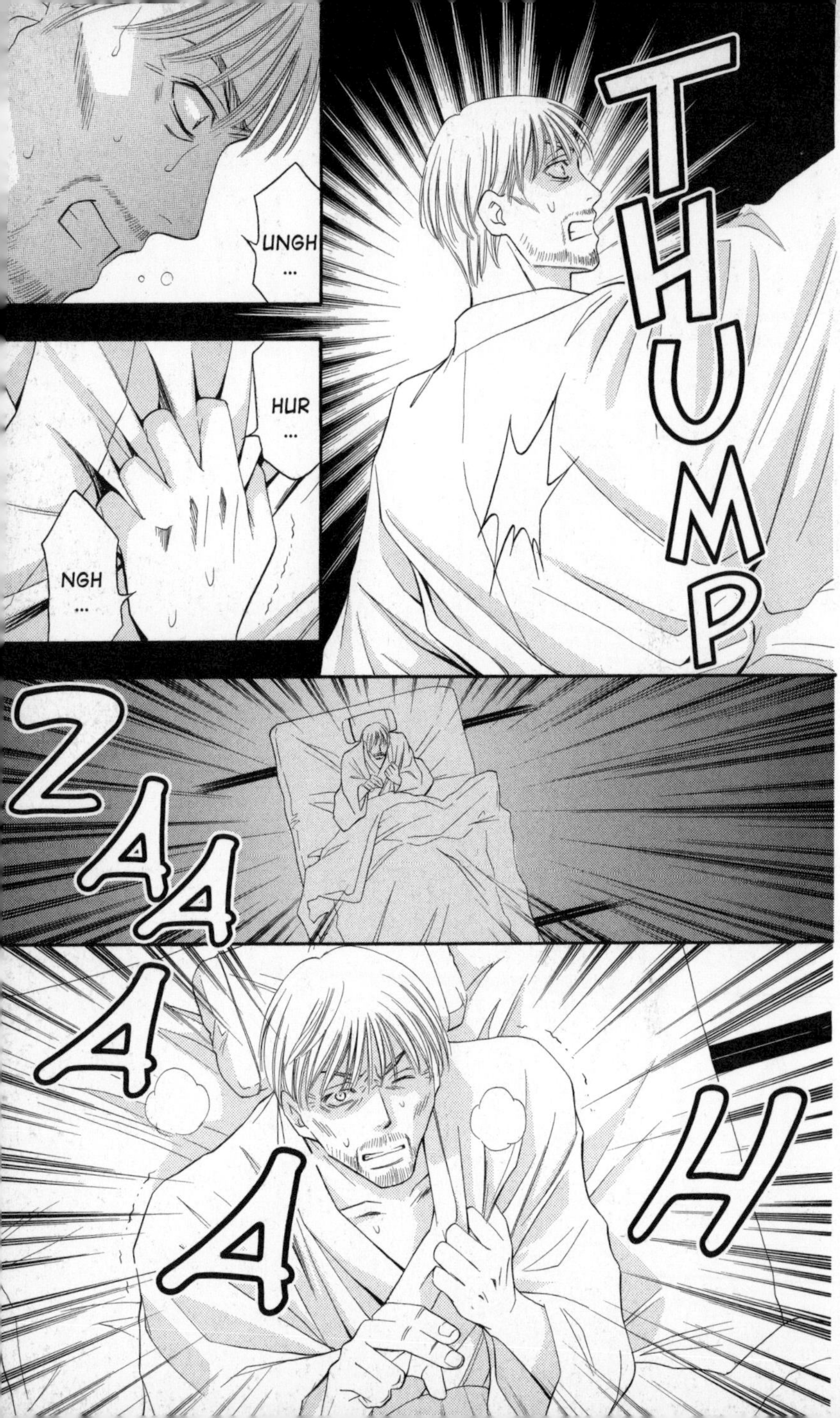
THUMP
UNGH ...
HUR ...
NGH ...
ZAAAAH

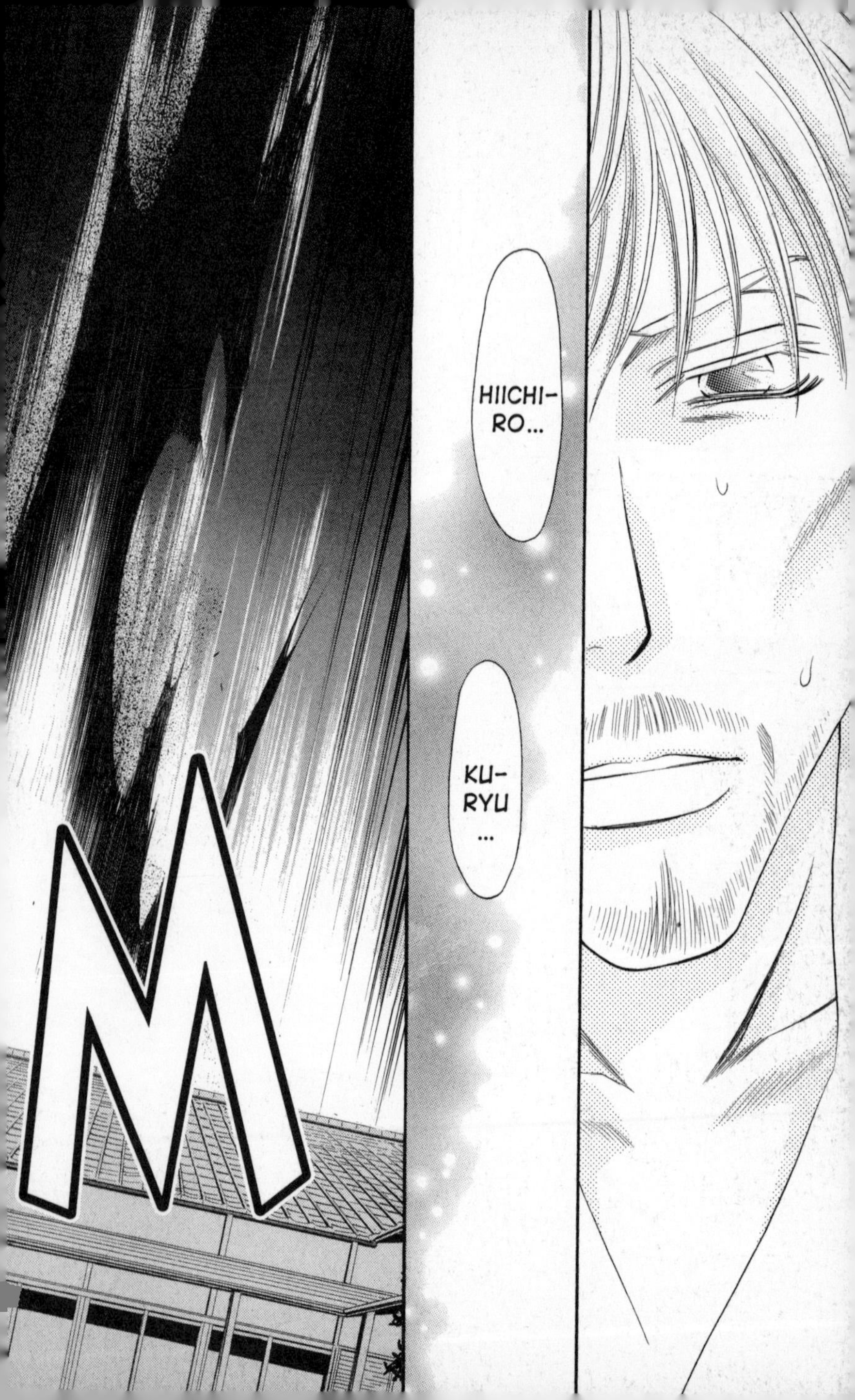
HIICHI-RO...
KU-RYU ...
M

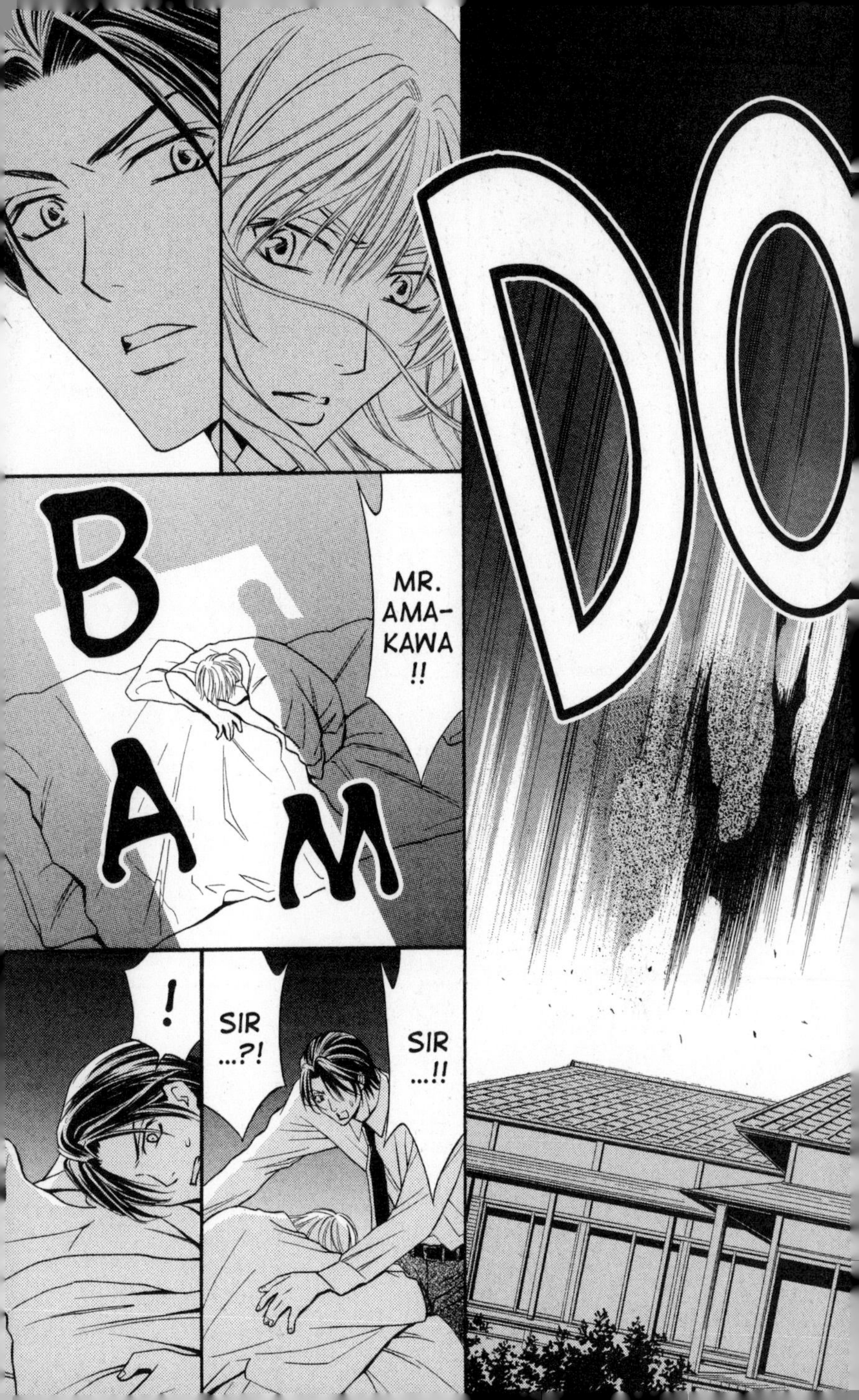

DO
MR. AMA-KAWA!!
BAM
SIR ...!!
SIR ...?!
!

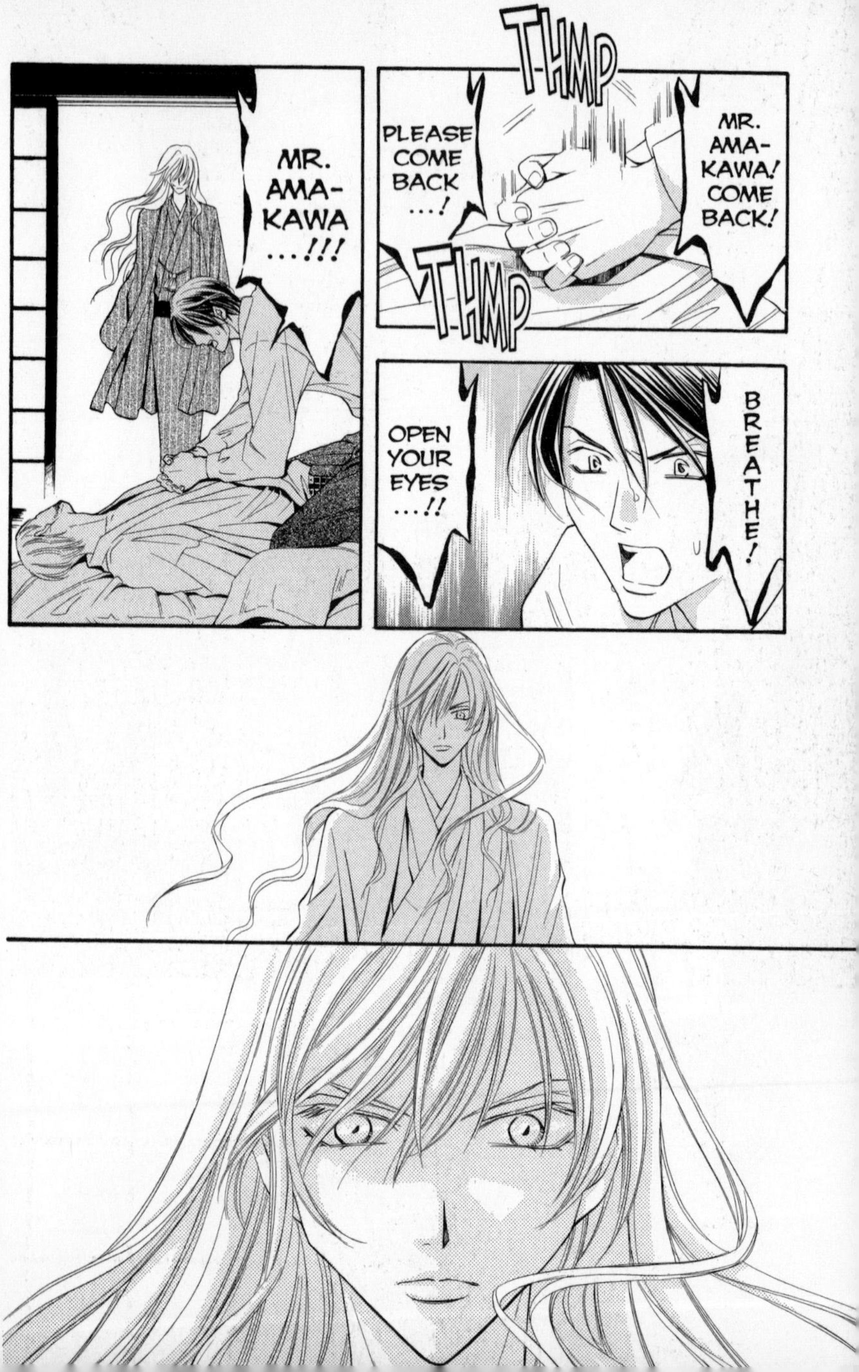
THMP
MR. AMA-KAWA! COME BACK!
PLEASE COME BACK ...!
THMP
BREATHE!
OPEN YOUR EYES ...!!
MR. AMA-KAWA ...!!!

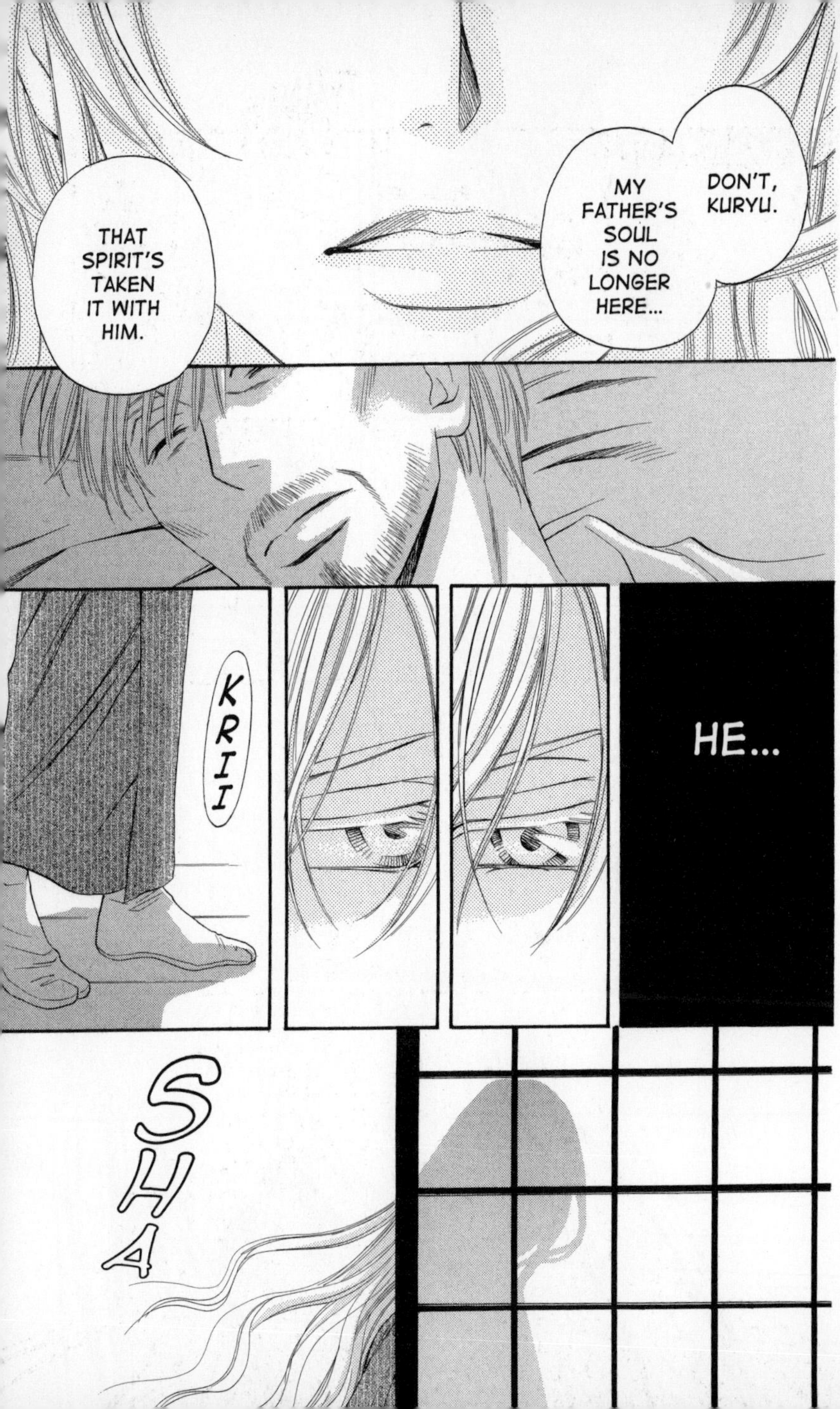
DON'T, KURYU.
MY FATHER'S SOUL IS NO LONGER HERE...
THAT SPIRIT'S TAKEN IT WITH HIM.
HE...
KRII
SHA

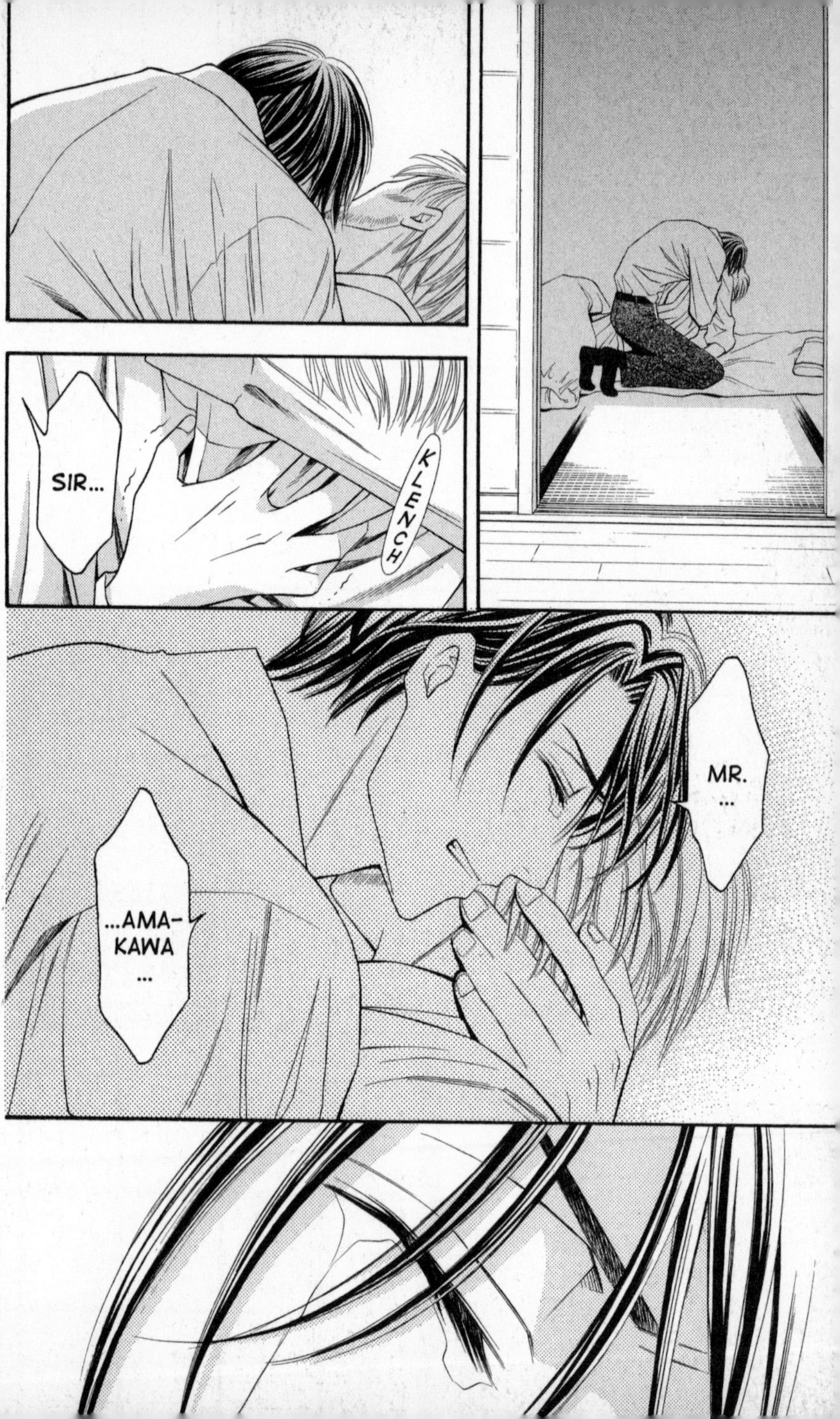
KLENCH
SIR...
MR. ...
...AMA-KAWA ...

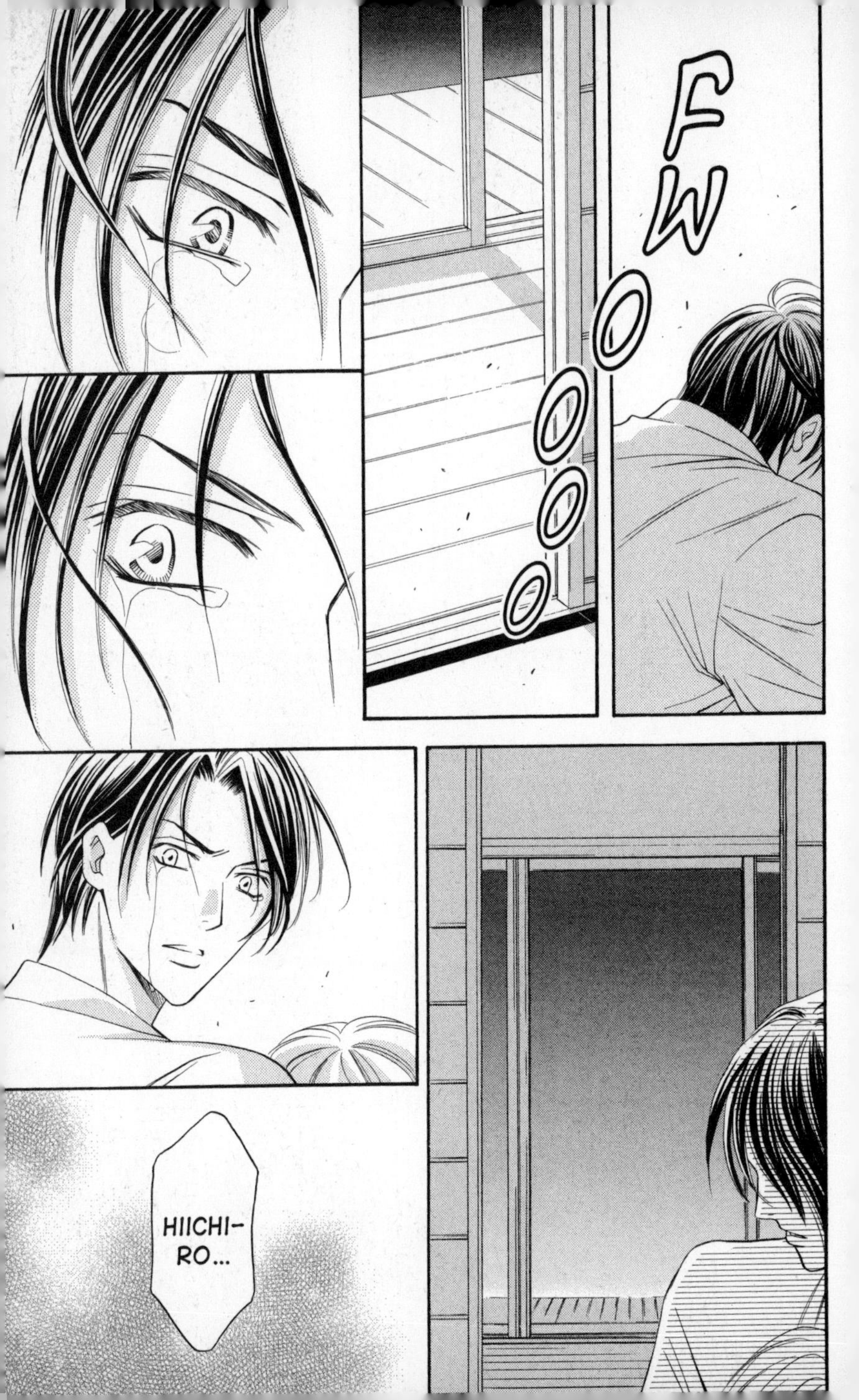
FWOOOOO
HIICHI-
RO...

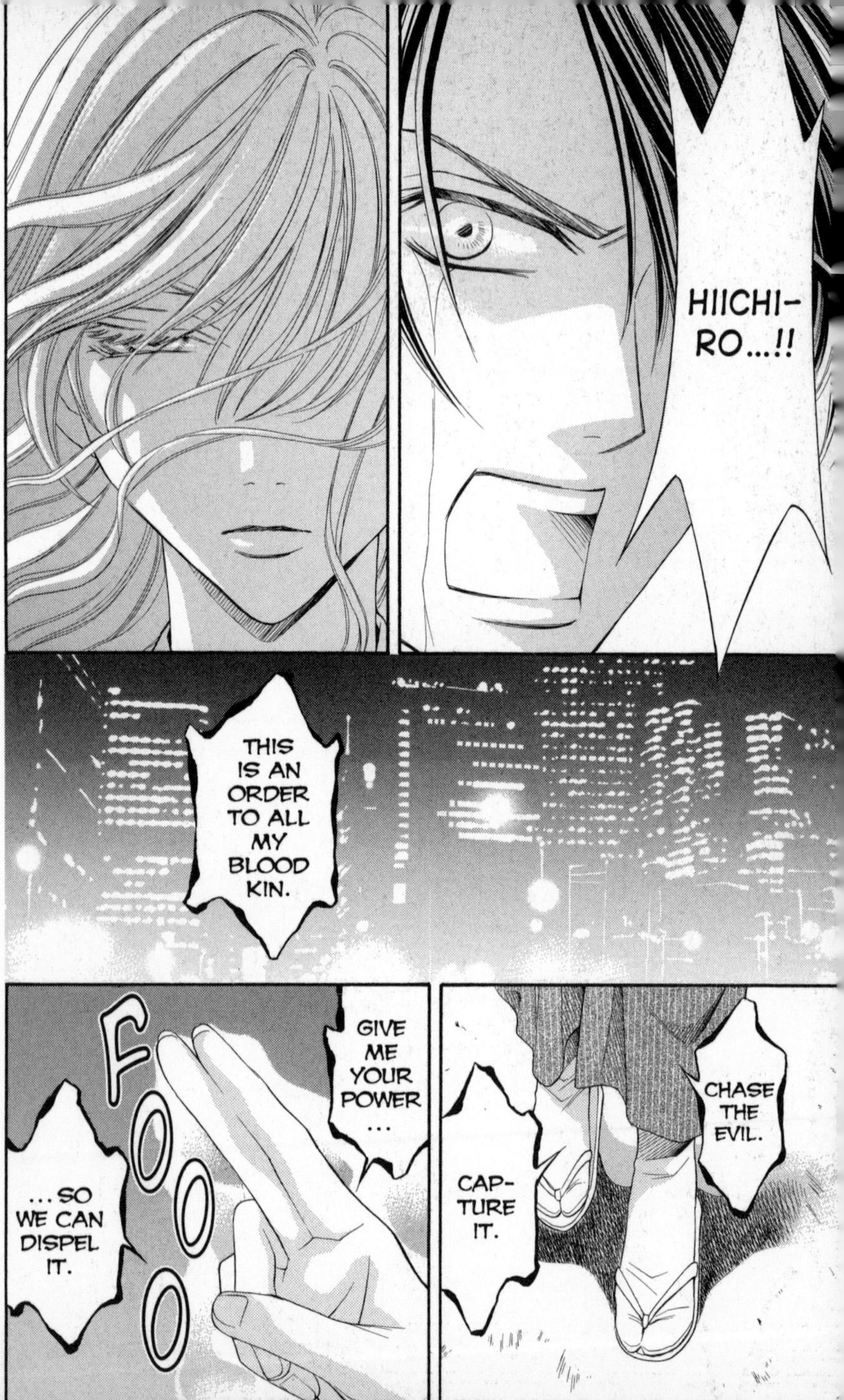
HIICHI-RO...!!
THIS IS AN ORDER TO ALL MY BLOOD KIN.
CHASE THE EVIL.
CAP-TURE IT.
GIVE ME YOUR POWER...
FOOOO
...SO WE CAN DISPEL IT.

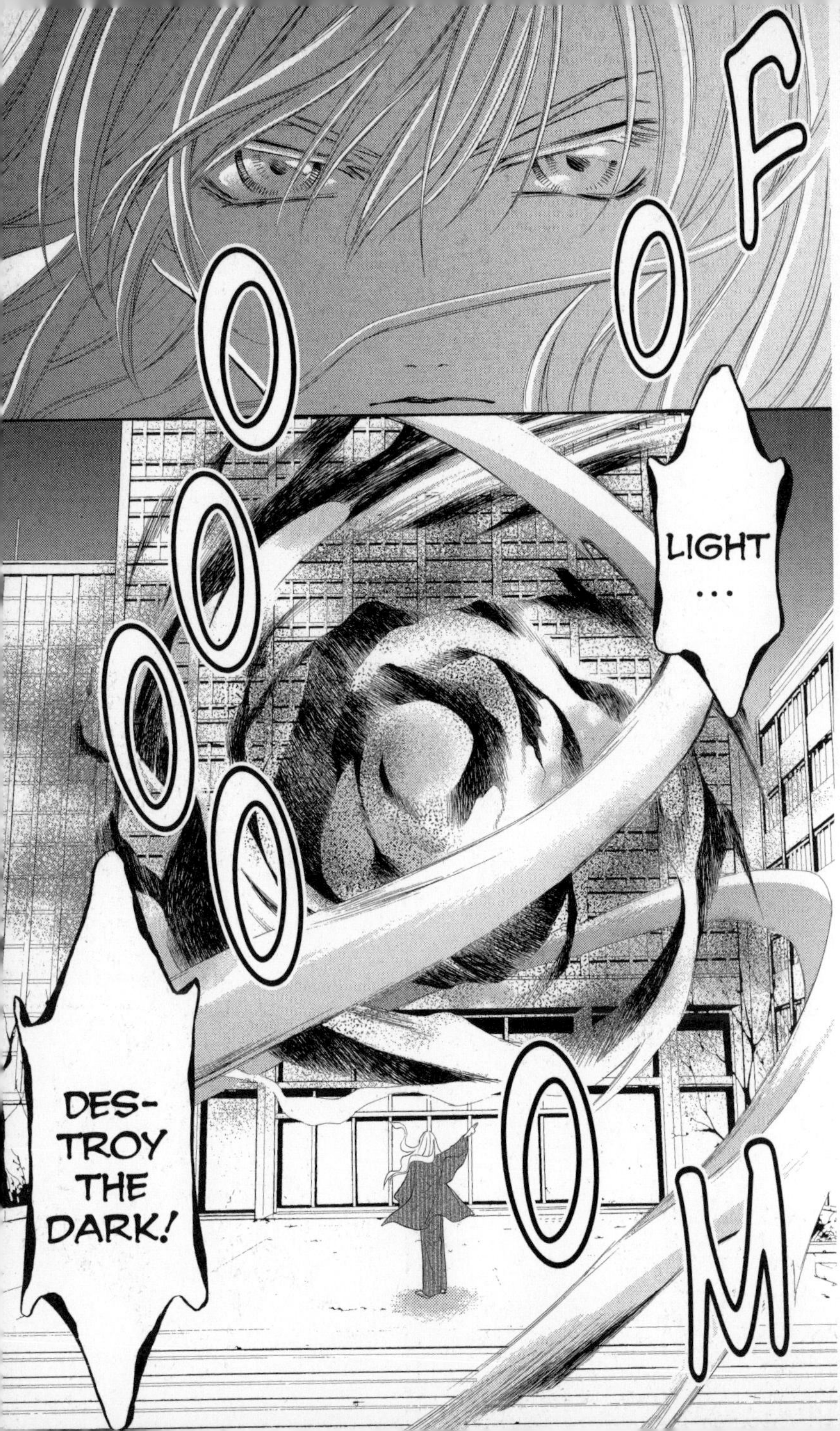
FOOOOOOM
LIGHT...
DES-
TROY
THE
DARK!

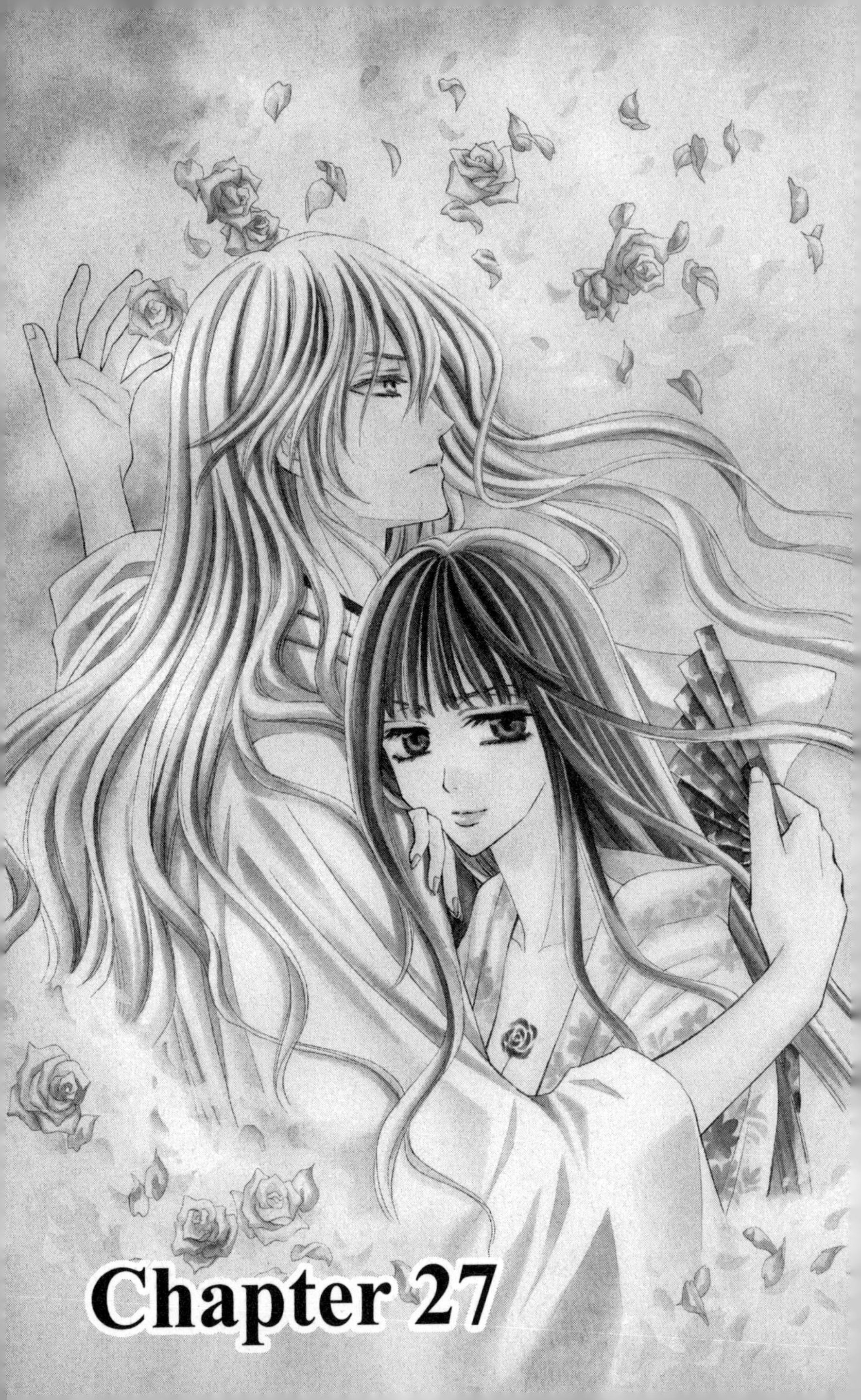

Chapter 27

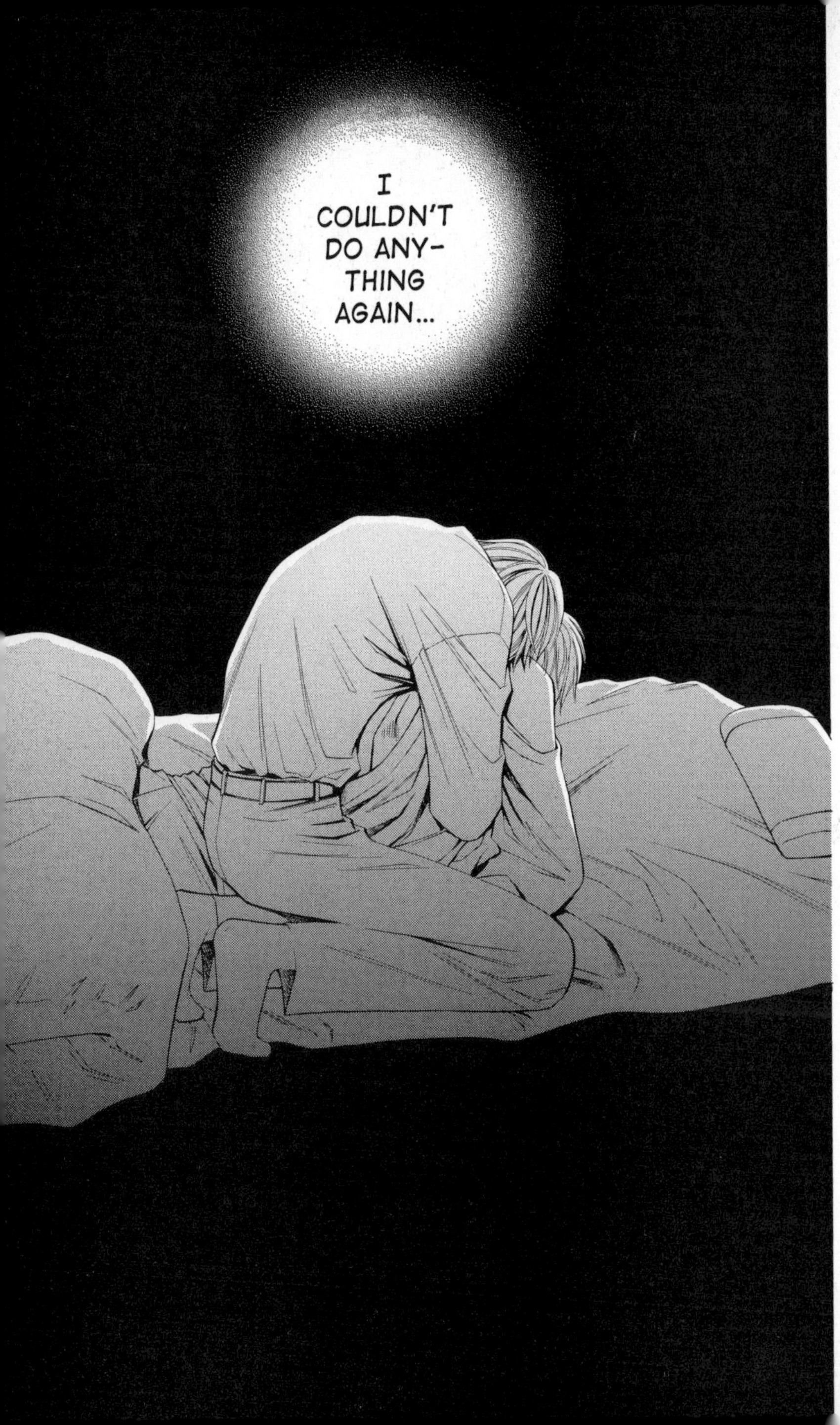
I COULDN'T DO ANY-THING AGAIN...

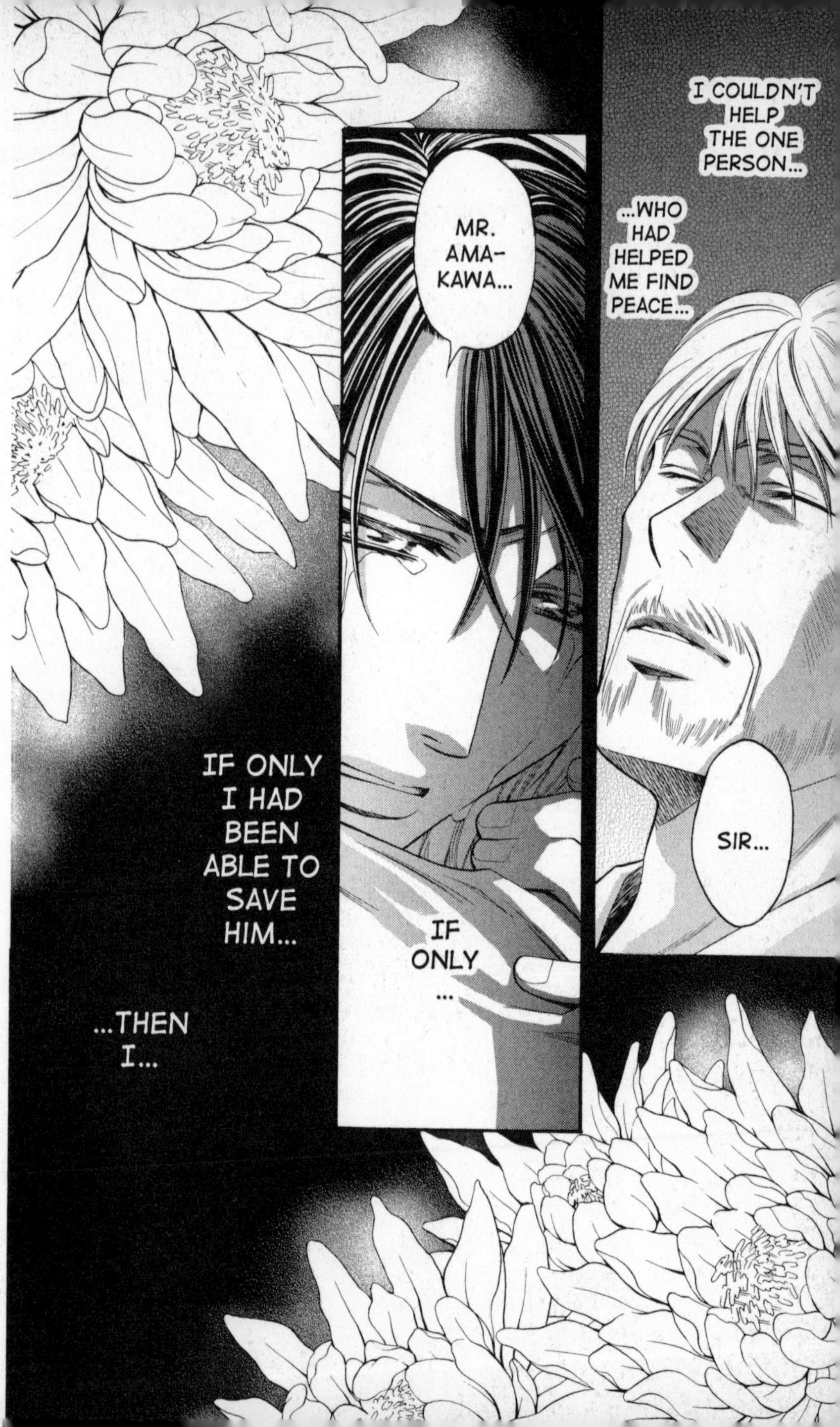
I COULDN'T HELP THE ONE PERSON...
...WHO HAD HELPED ME FIND PEACE...
SIR...
MR. AMA-KAWA...
IF ONLY...
IF ONLY I HAD BEEN ABLE TO SAVE HIM...
...THEN I...

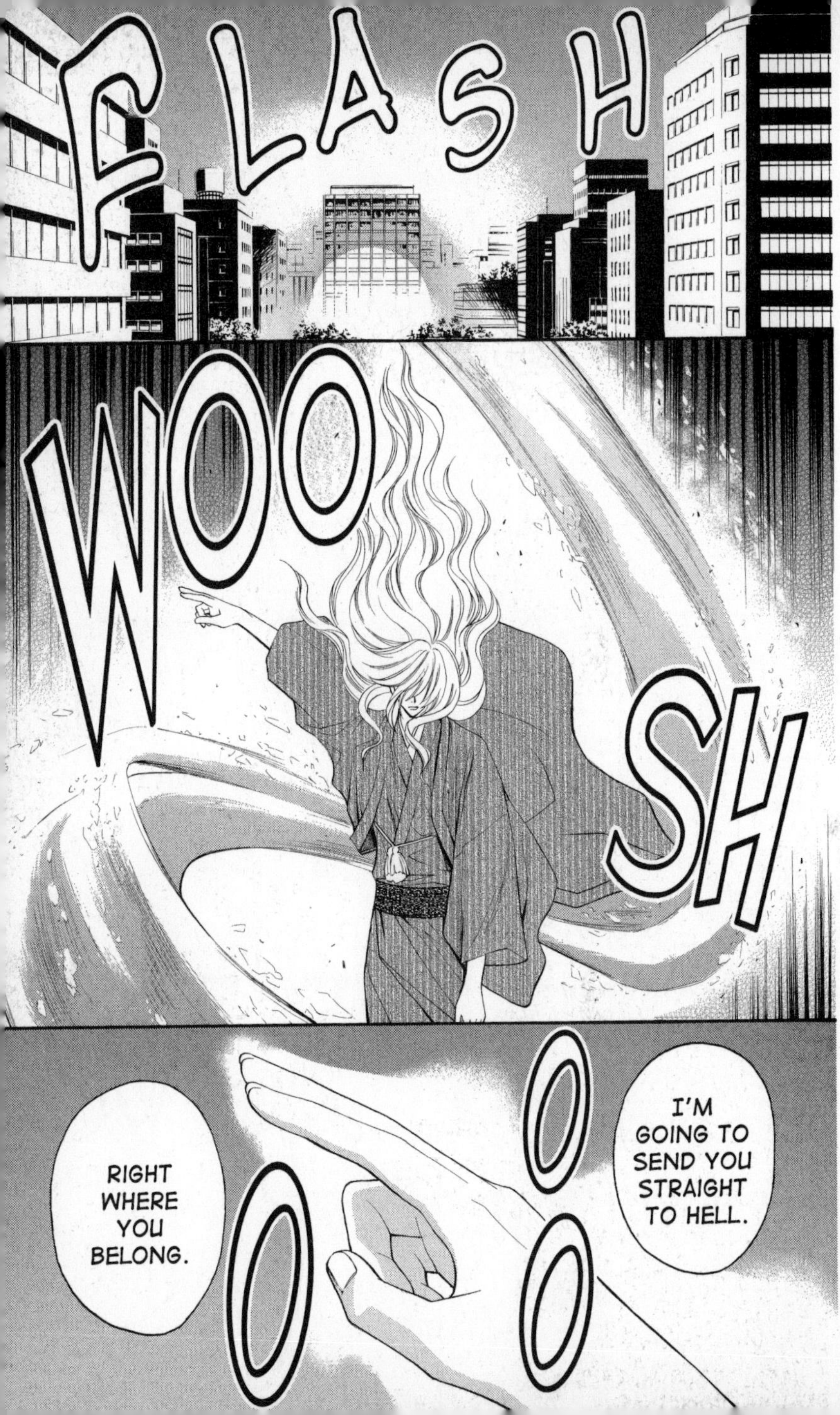
FLASH
WOO
SH
I'M GOING TO SEND YOU STRAIGHT TO HELL.
OOOO
RIGHT WHERE YOU BELONG.

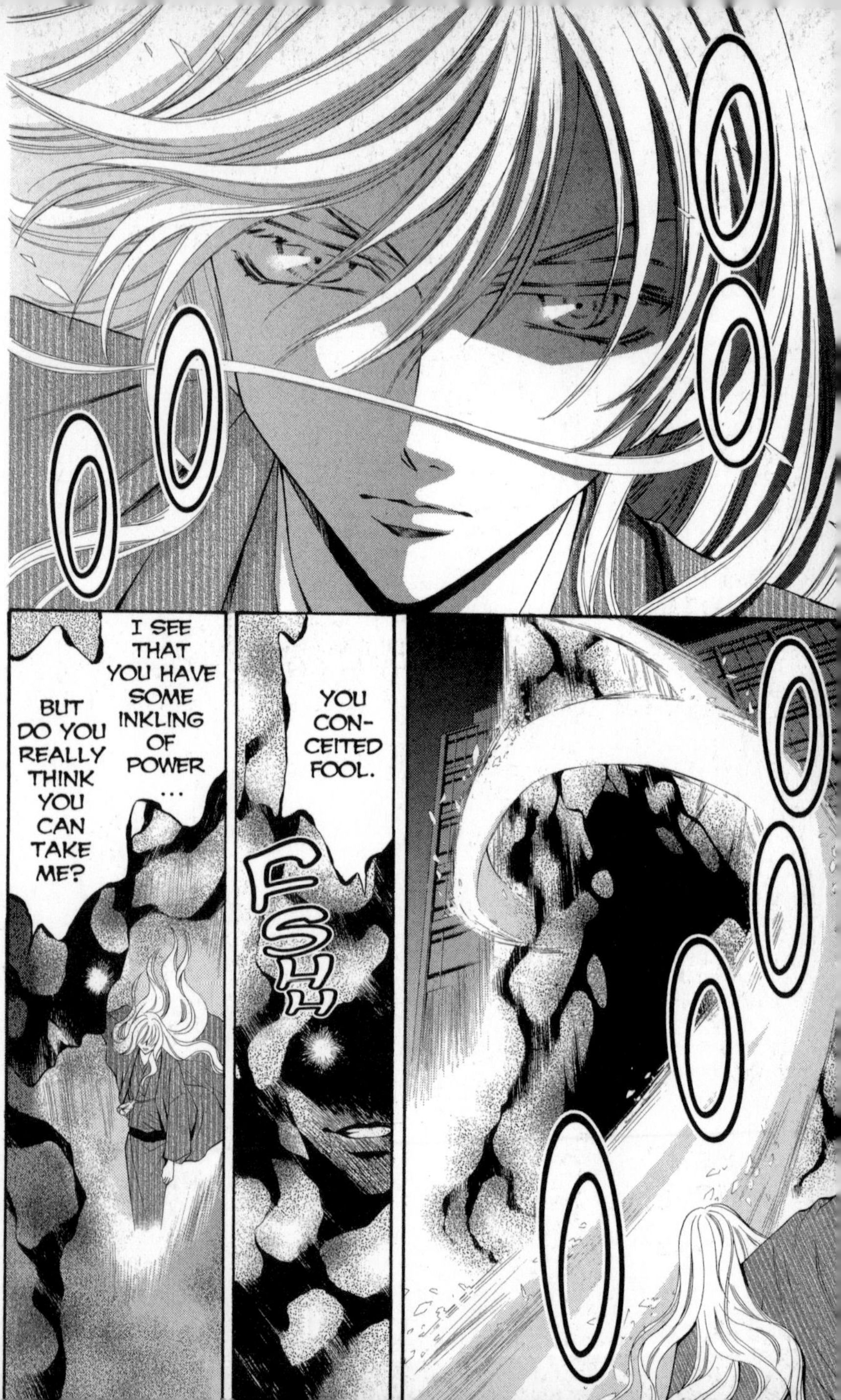
YOU CON-CEITED FOOL.
FSHH
I SEE THAT YOU HAVE SOME INKLING OF POWER...
BUT DO YOU REALLY THINK YOU CAN TAKE ME?

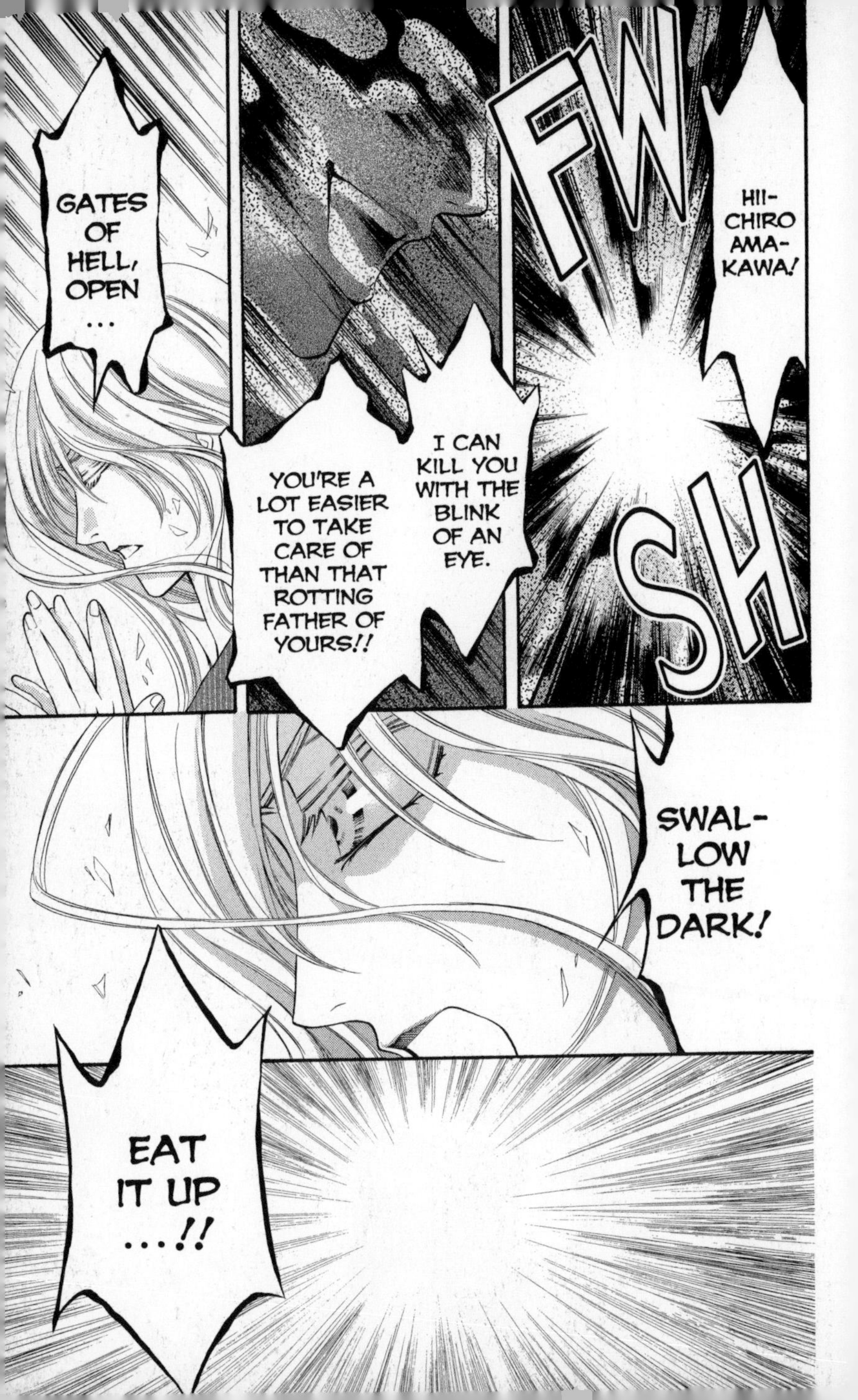

FW
HII-CHIRO AMAKAWA!
SH
I CAN KILL YOU WITH THE BLINK OF AN EYE.
YOU'RE A LOT EASIER TO TAKE CARE OF THAN THAT ROTTING FATHER OF YOURS!!
GATES OF HELL, OPEN ...
SWAL-LOW THE DARK!
EAT IT UP ...!!

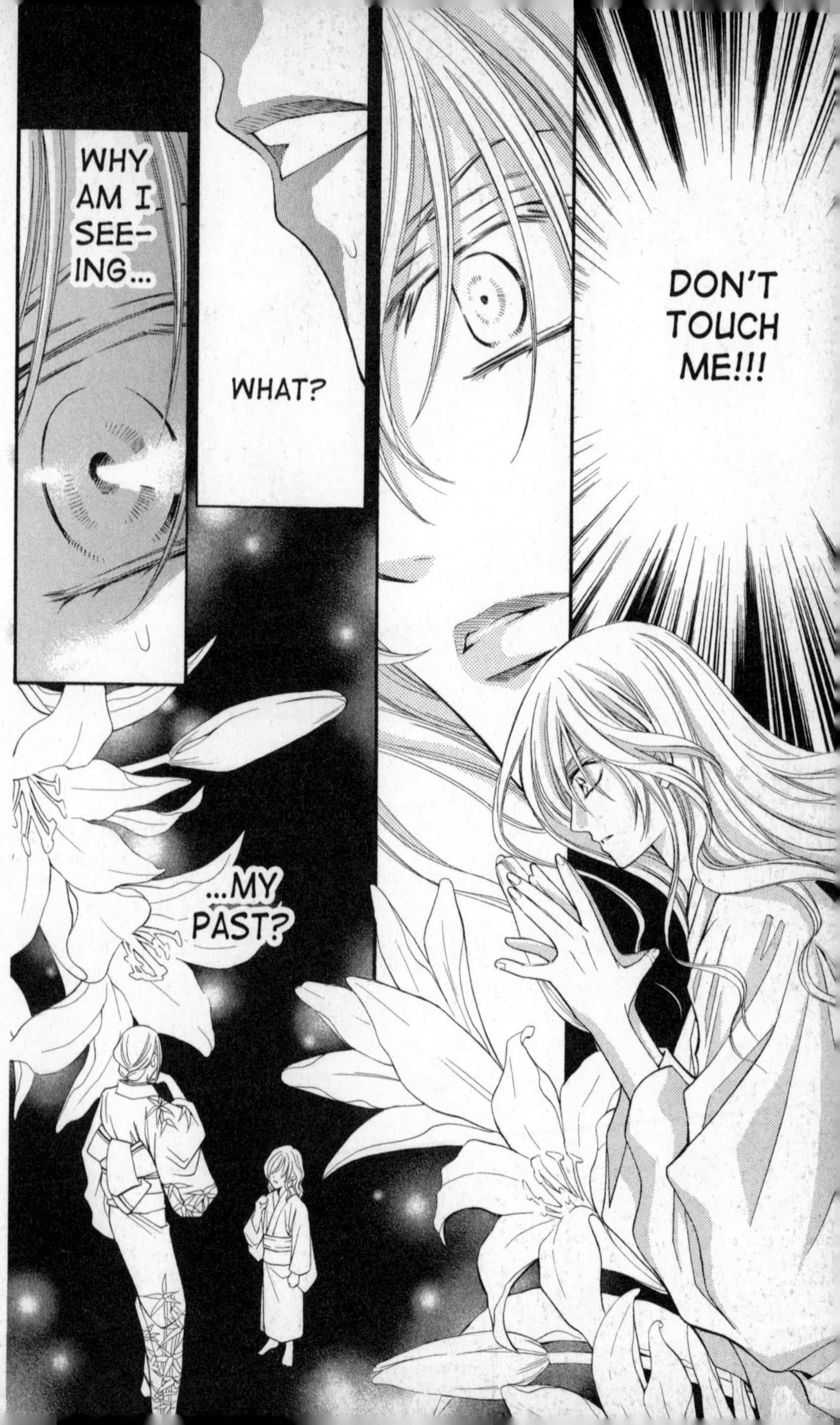

DON'T TOUCH ME!!!
WHAT?
WHY AM I SEE-ING...
...MY PAST?

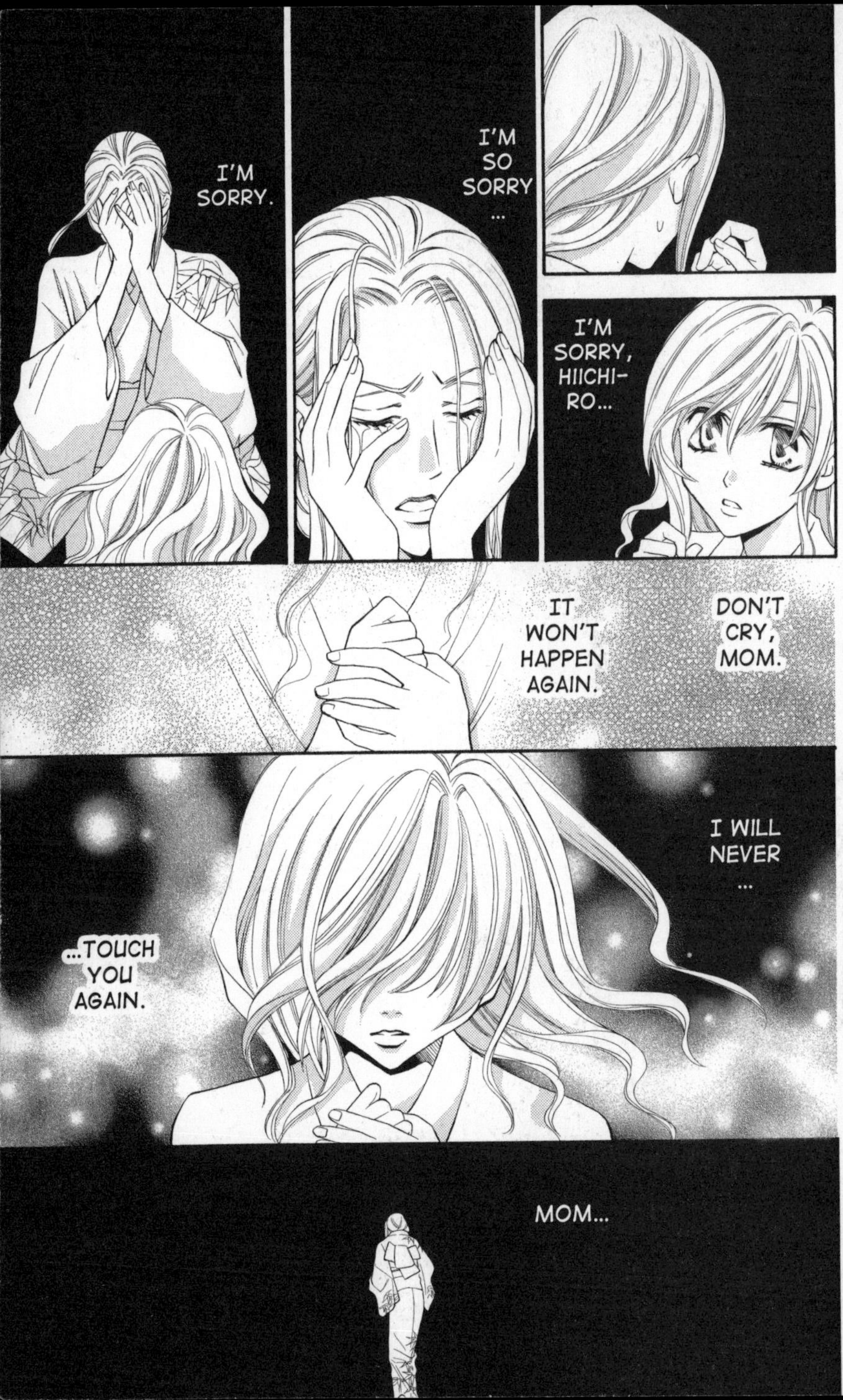
I'M SORRY, HIICHIRO...
I'M SO SORRY ...
I'M SORRY.
DON'T CRY, MOM.
IT WON'T HAPPEN AGAIN.
I WILL NEVER ...
...TOUCH YOU AGAIN.
MOM...

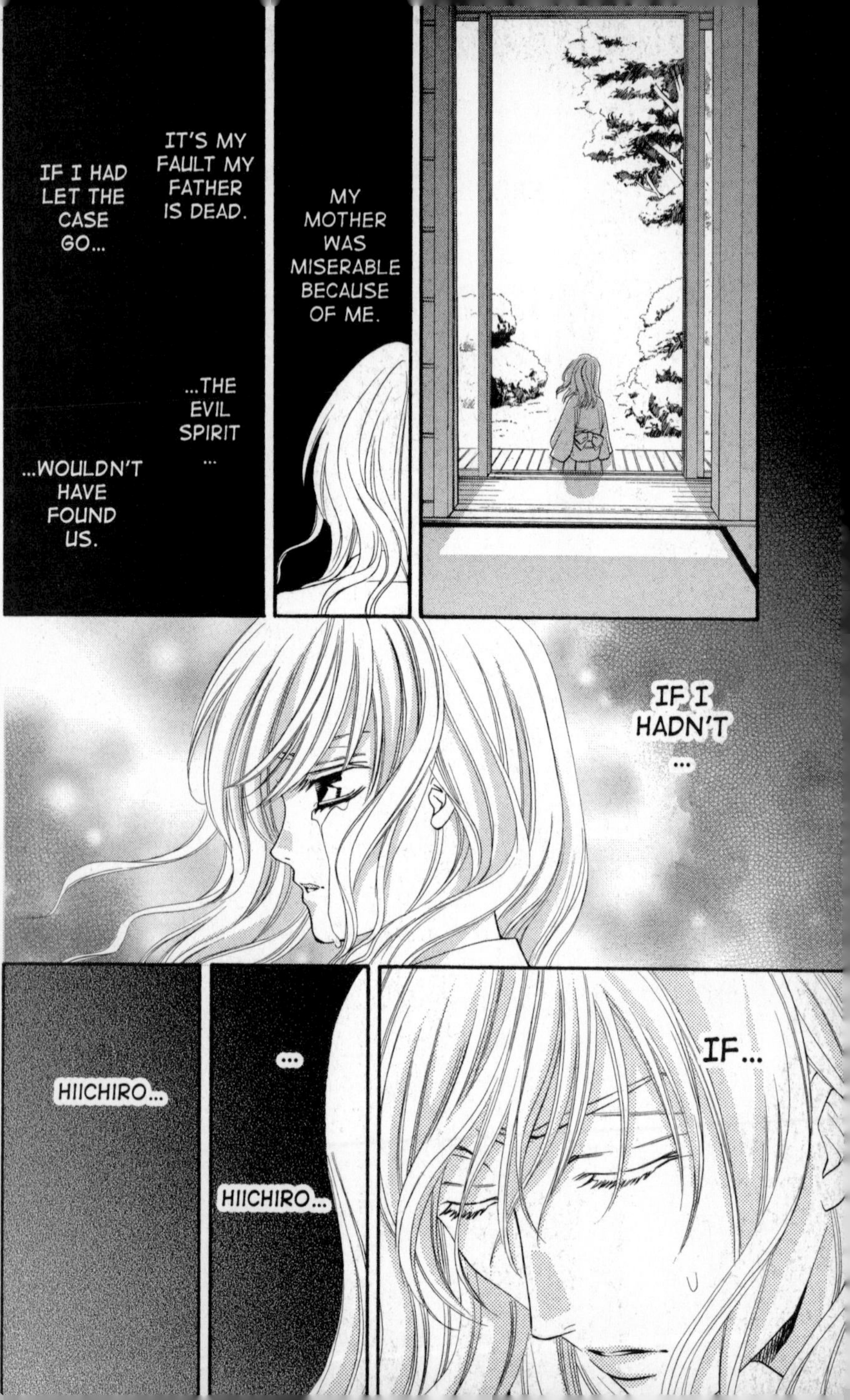
MY MOTHER WAS MISERABLE BECAUSE OF ME.
IT'S MY FAULT MY FATHER IS DEAD.
IF I HAD LET THE CASE GO...
...THE EVIL SPIRIT ...
...WOULDN'T HAVE FOUND US.
IF I HADN'T ...
IF...
...
HIICHIRO...
HIICHIRO...

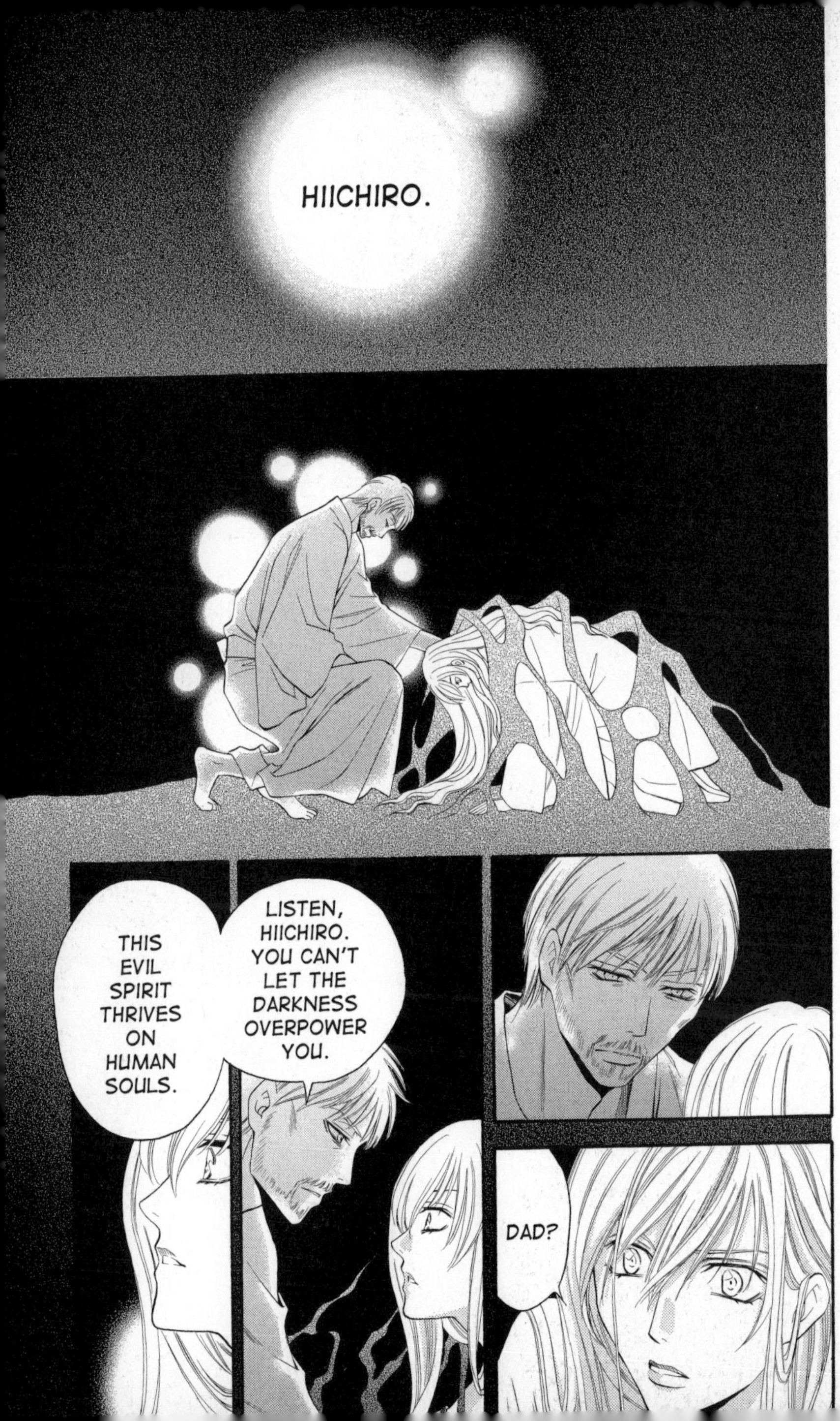
HIICHIRO.
DAD?
LISTEN, HIICHIRO. YOU CAN'T LET THE DARKNESS OVERPOWER YOU.
THIS EVIL SPIRIT THRIVES ON HUMAN SOULS.

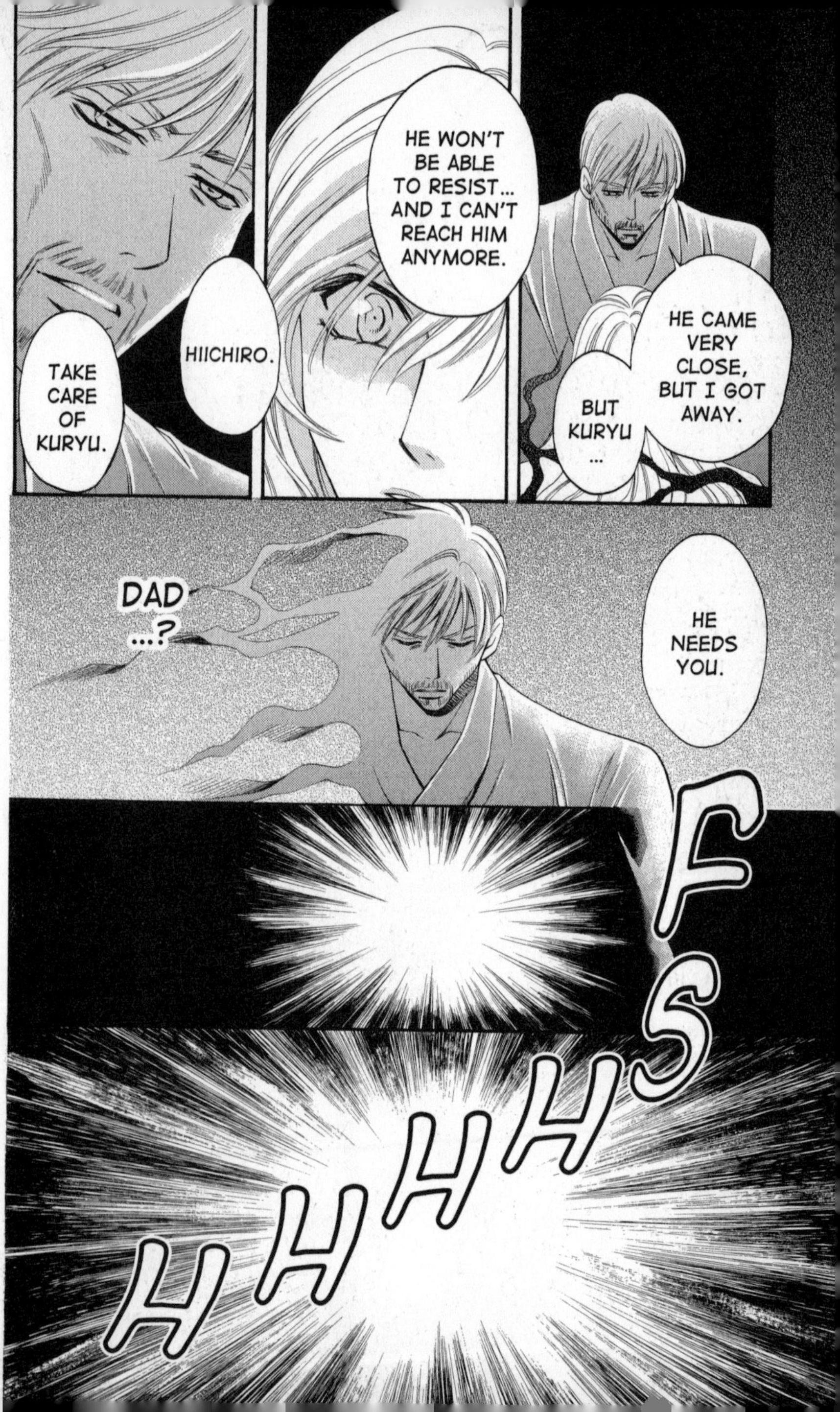
HE CAME VERY CLOSE, BUT I GOT AWAY.
BUT KURYU ...
HE WON'T BE ABLE TO RESIST... AND I CAN'T REACH HIM ANYMORE.
HIICHIRO.
TAKE CARE OF KURYU.
HE NEEDS YOU.
DAD ...?
FSHHHHH

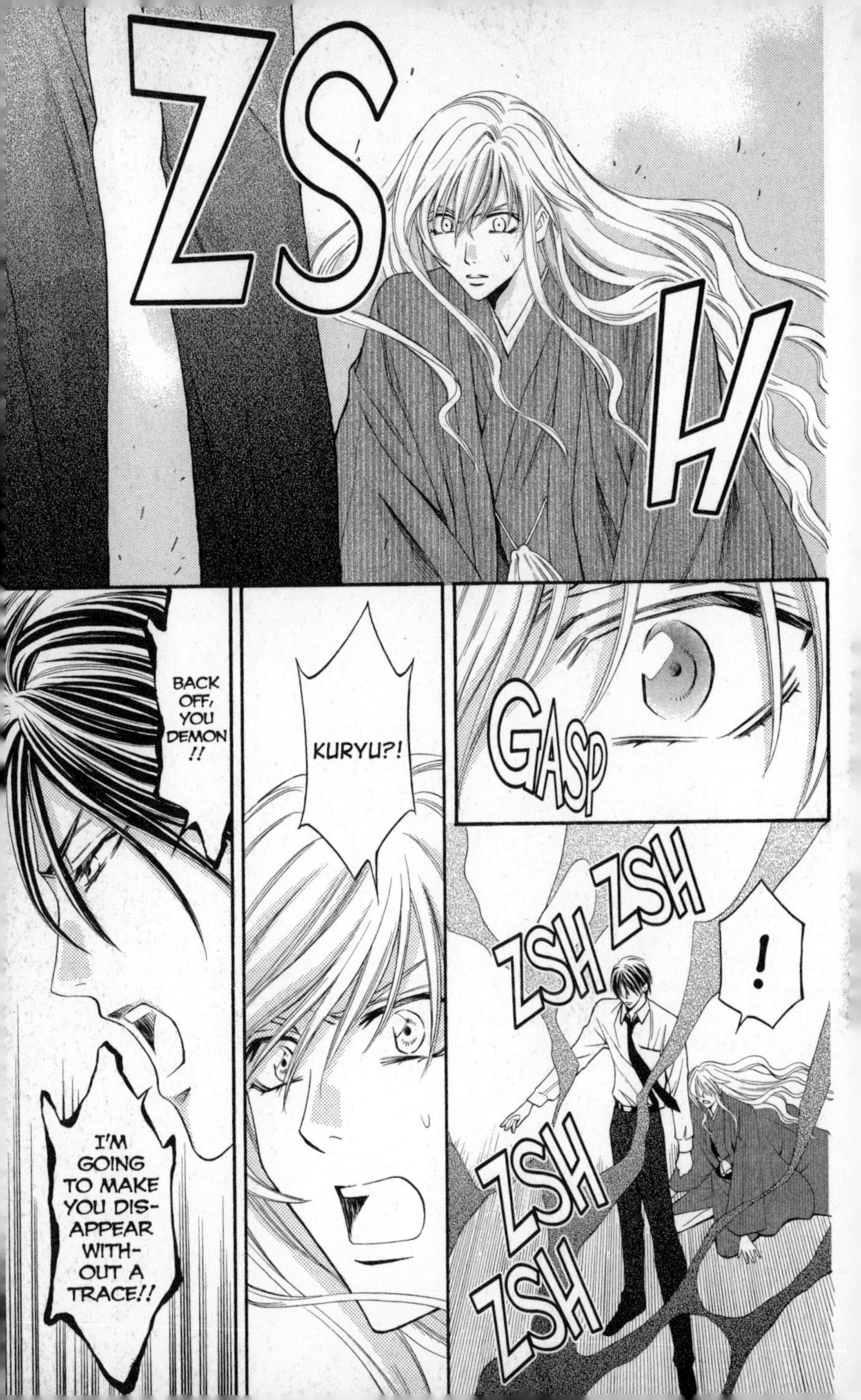
ZSH
GASP
ZSH ZSH
!
ZSH
ZSH
KURYU?!
BACK OFF, YOU DEMON!!
I'M GOING TO MAKE YOU DIS-APPEAR WITH-OUT A TRACE!!

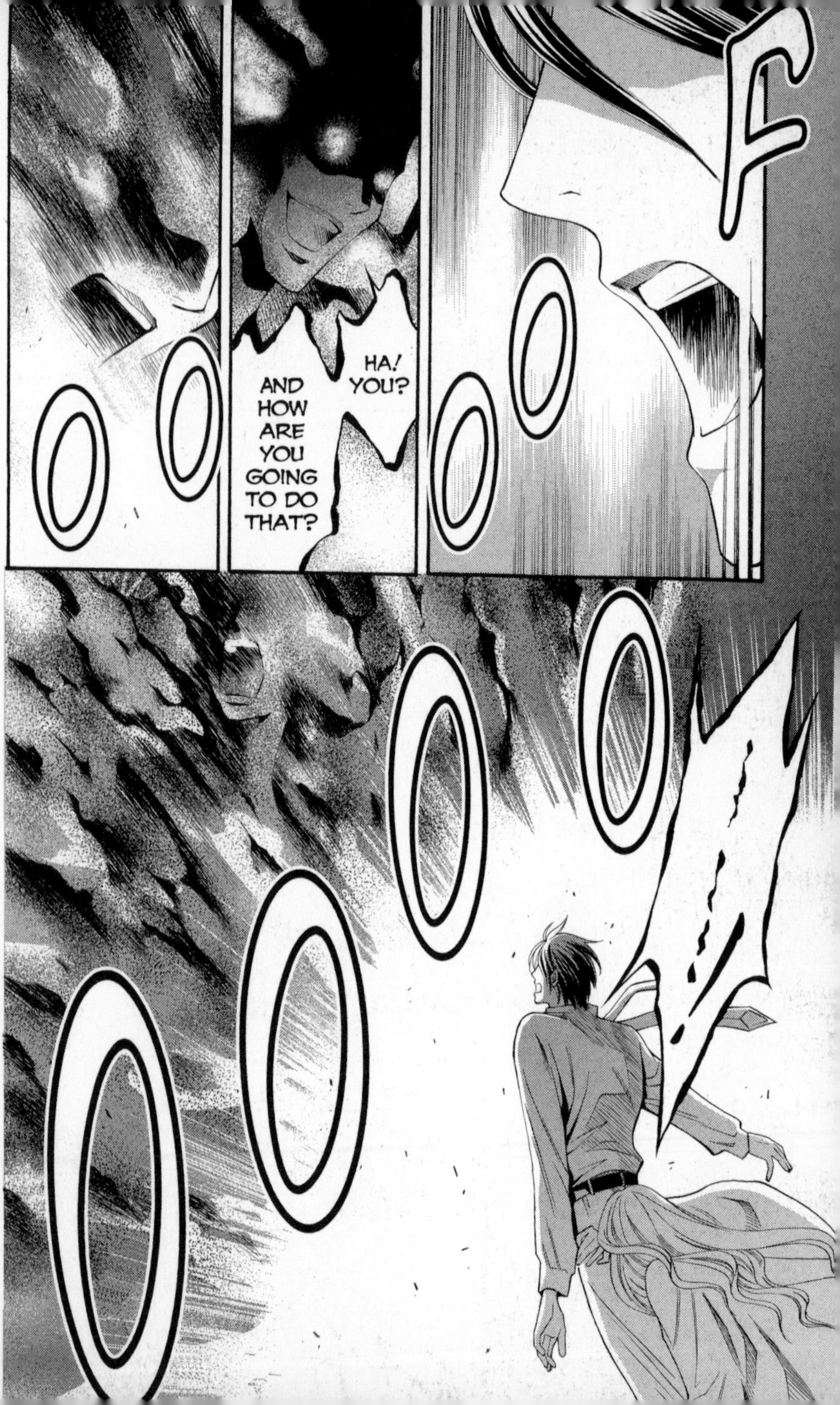

F
HA! YOU?
AND HOW ARE YOU GOING TO DO THAT?

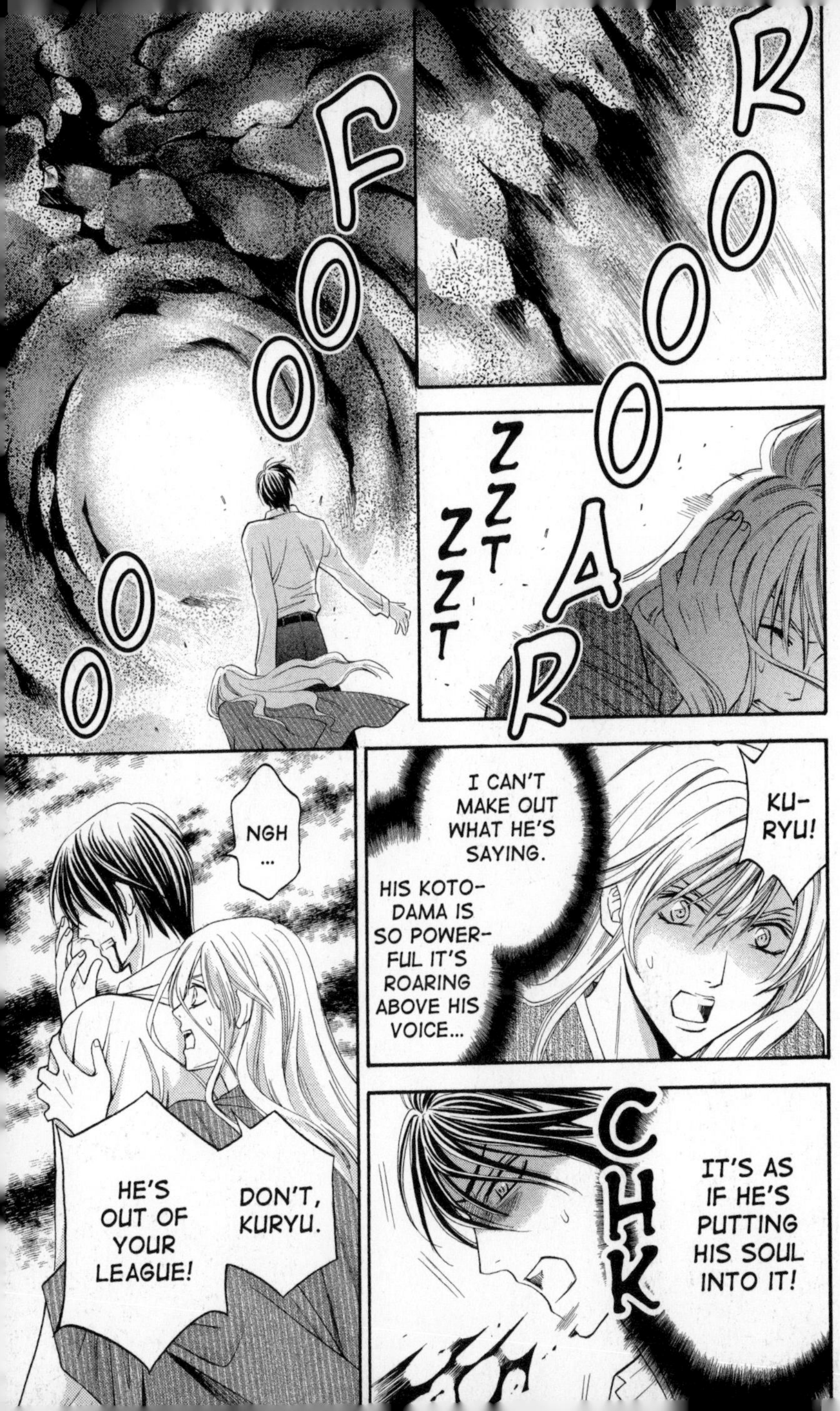
ROOOAR
ZZT
ZZT
FOOOOO
KU-RYU!
I CAN'T MAKE OUT WHAT HE'S SAYING.
HIS KOTO-DAMA IS SO POWER-FUL IT'S ROARING ABOVE HIS VOICE...
NGH...
DON'T, KURYU.
HE'S OUT OF YOUR LEAGUE!
CHK
IT'S AS IF HE'S PUTTING HIS SOUL INTO IT!

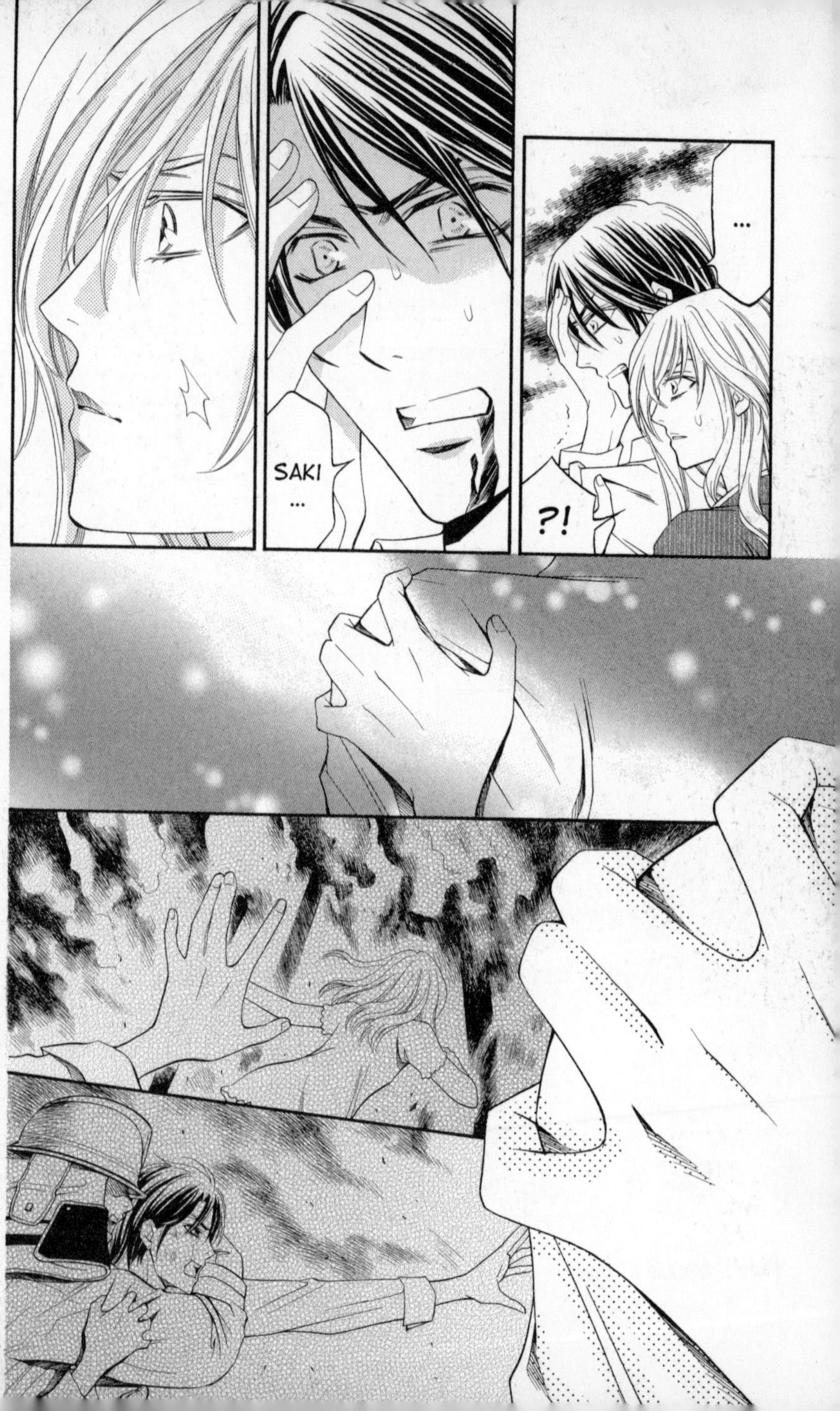
...
?!
SAKI ...

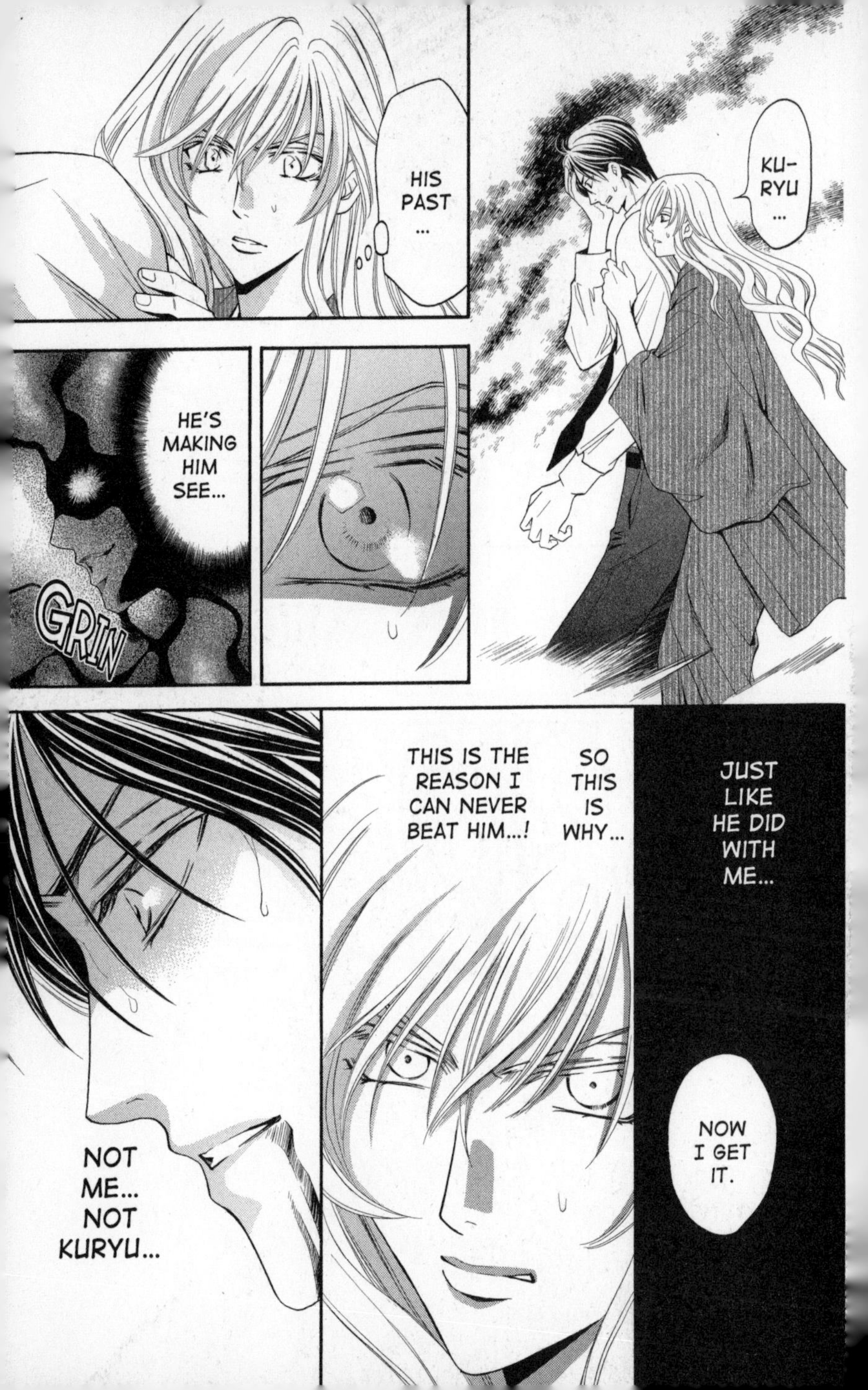
KU-RYU...
HIS PAST...
HE'S MAKING HIM SEE...
GRIN
JUST LIKE HE DID WITH ME...
NOW I GET IT.
SO THIS IS WHY...
THIS IS THE REASON I CAN NEVER BEAT HIM...!
NOT ME... NOT KURYU...

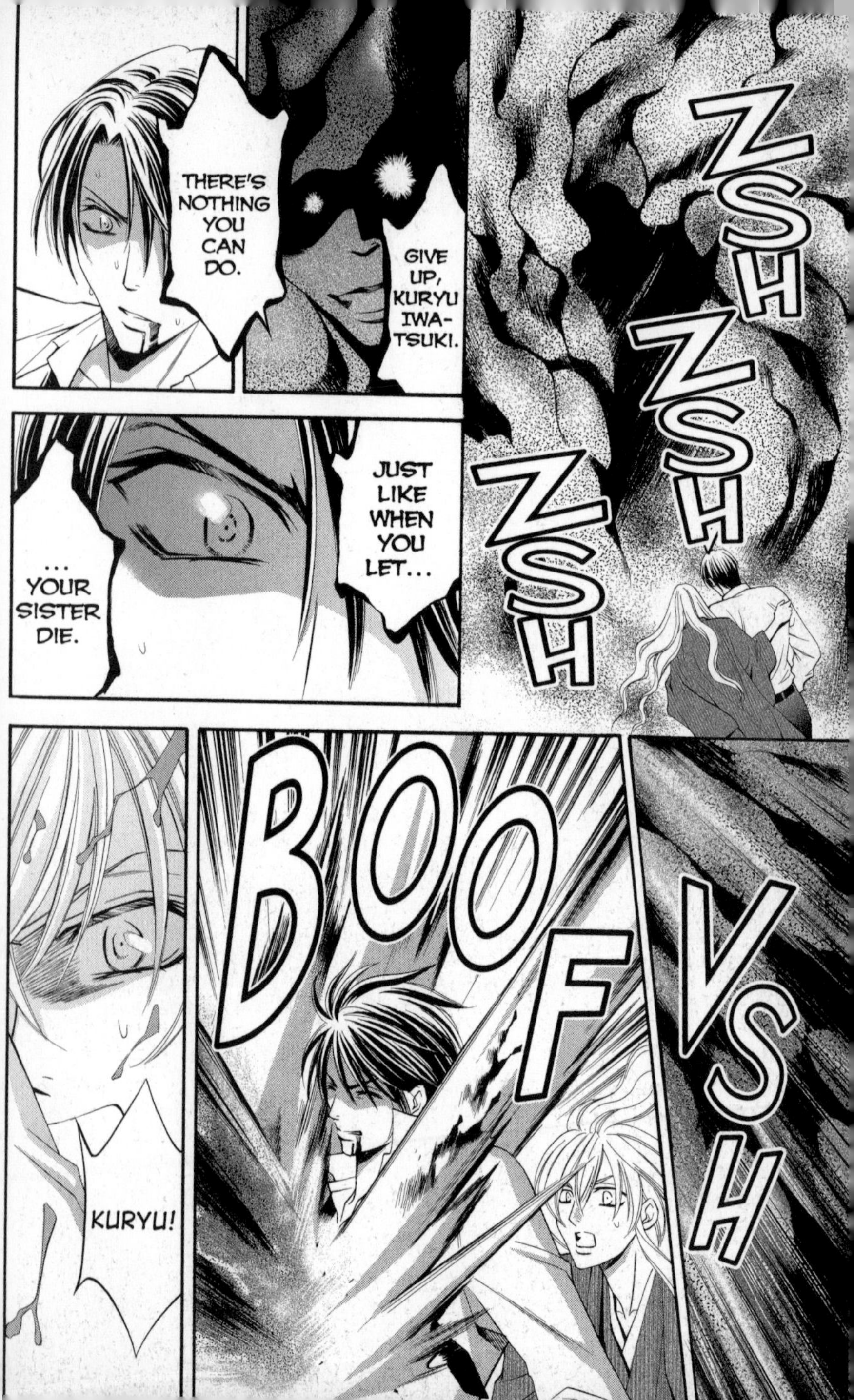
ZSHH
ZSHH
ZSHH
GIVE UP, KURYU IWATSUKI.
THERE'S NOTHING YOU CAN DO.
JUST LIKE WHEN YOU LET...
...YOUR SISTER DIE.
VSHH
BOOF
KURYU!

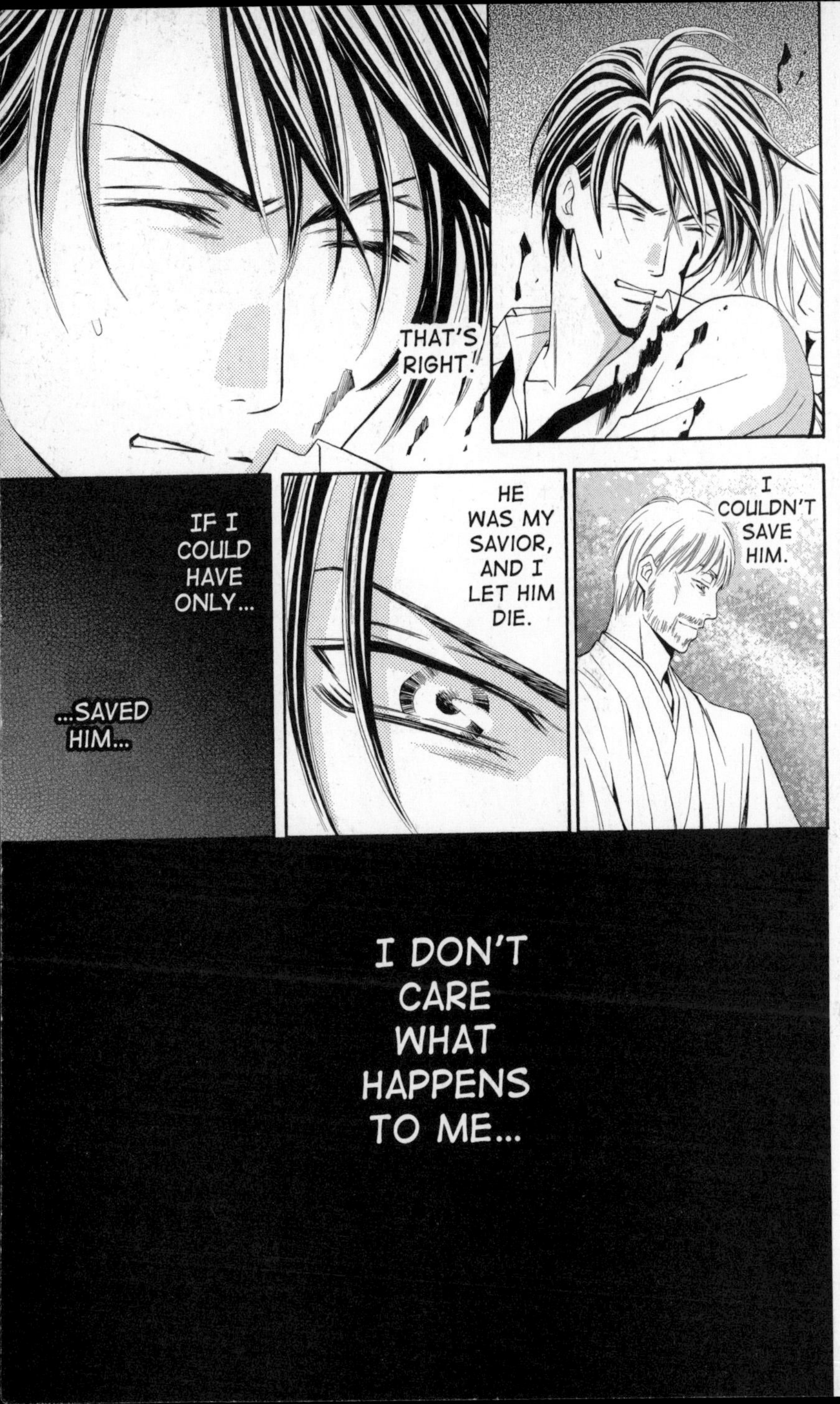
THAT'S RIGHT!
I COULDN'T SAVE HIM.
HE WAS MY SAVIOR, AND I LET HIM DIE.
IF I COULD HAVE ONLY...
...SAVED HIM...
I DON'T CARE WHAT HAPPENS TO ME...

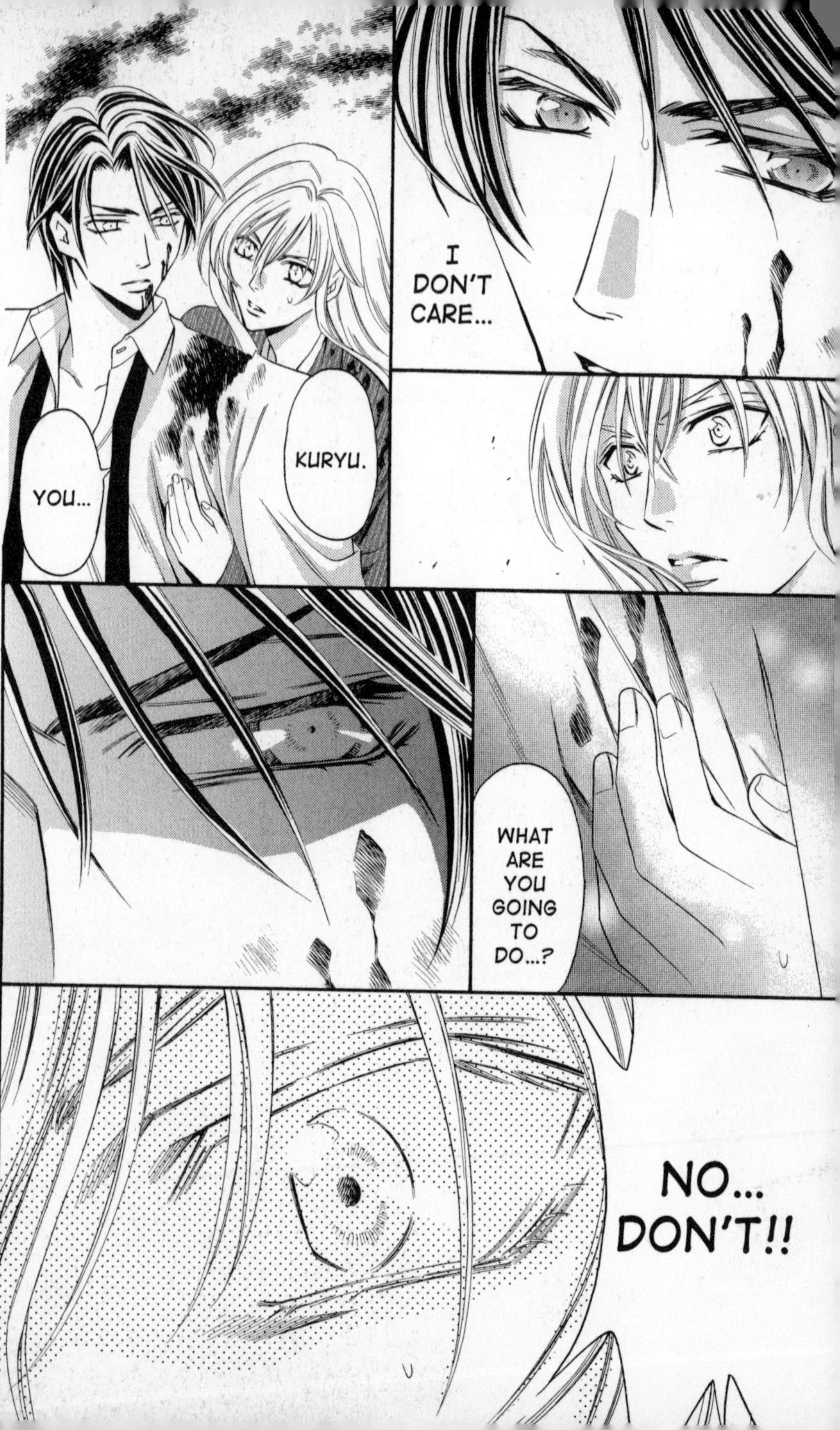
I DON'T CARE...
KURYU.
YOU...
WHAT ARE YOU GOING TO DO...?
NO... DON'T!!

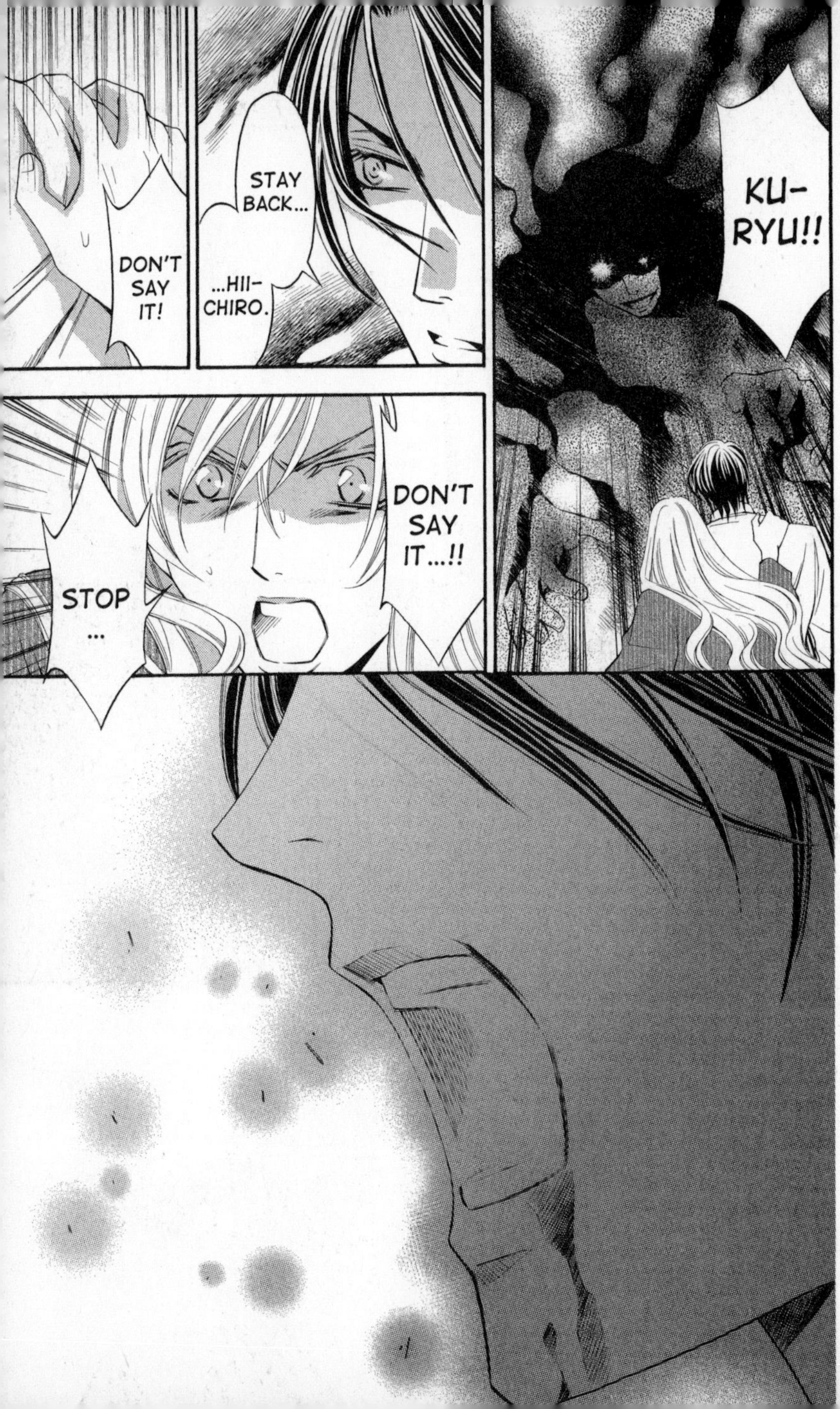
KU-RYU!!
STAY BACK...
...HII-CHIRO.
DON'T SAY IT!
DON'T SAY IT...!!
STOP ...

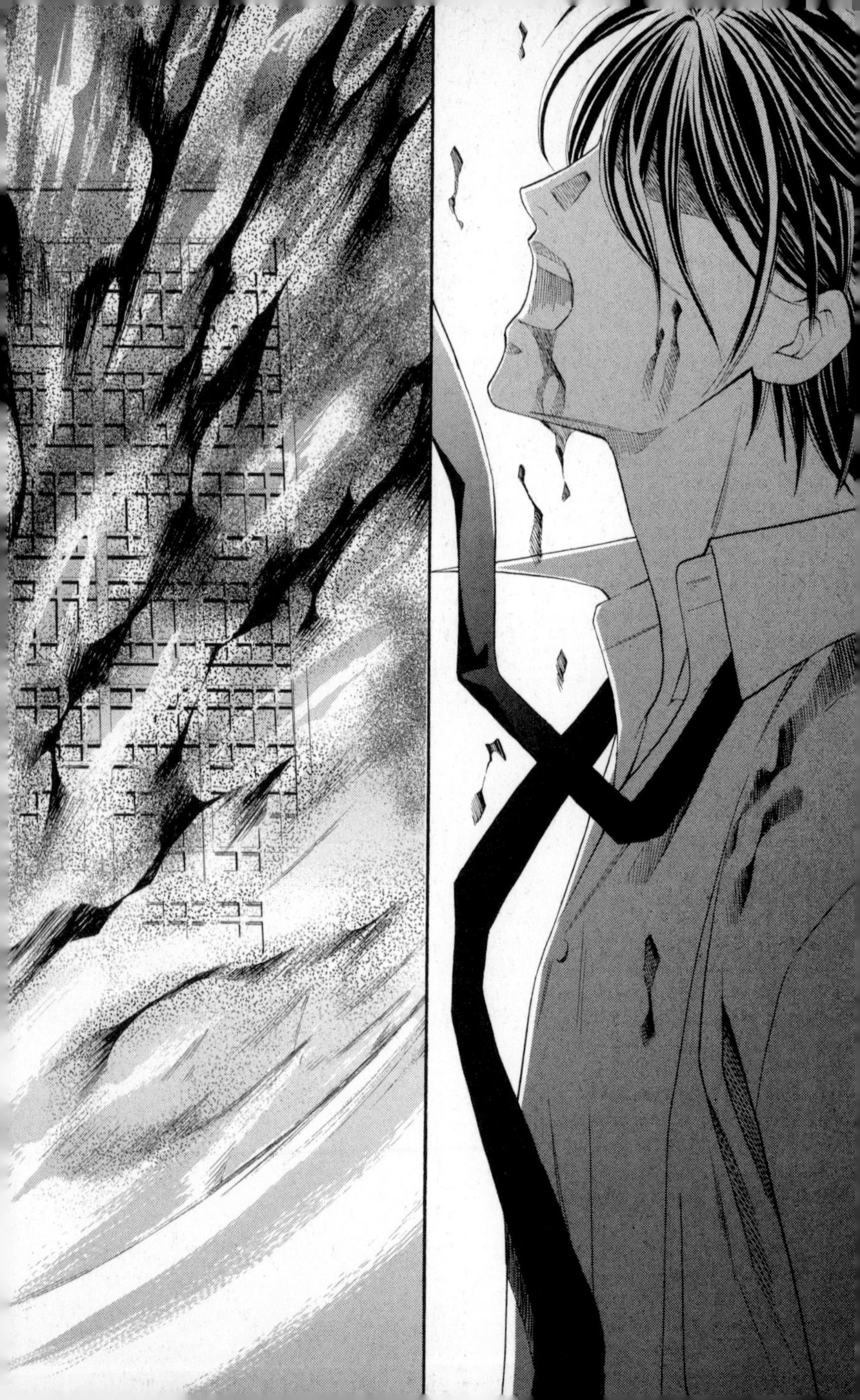

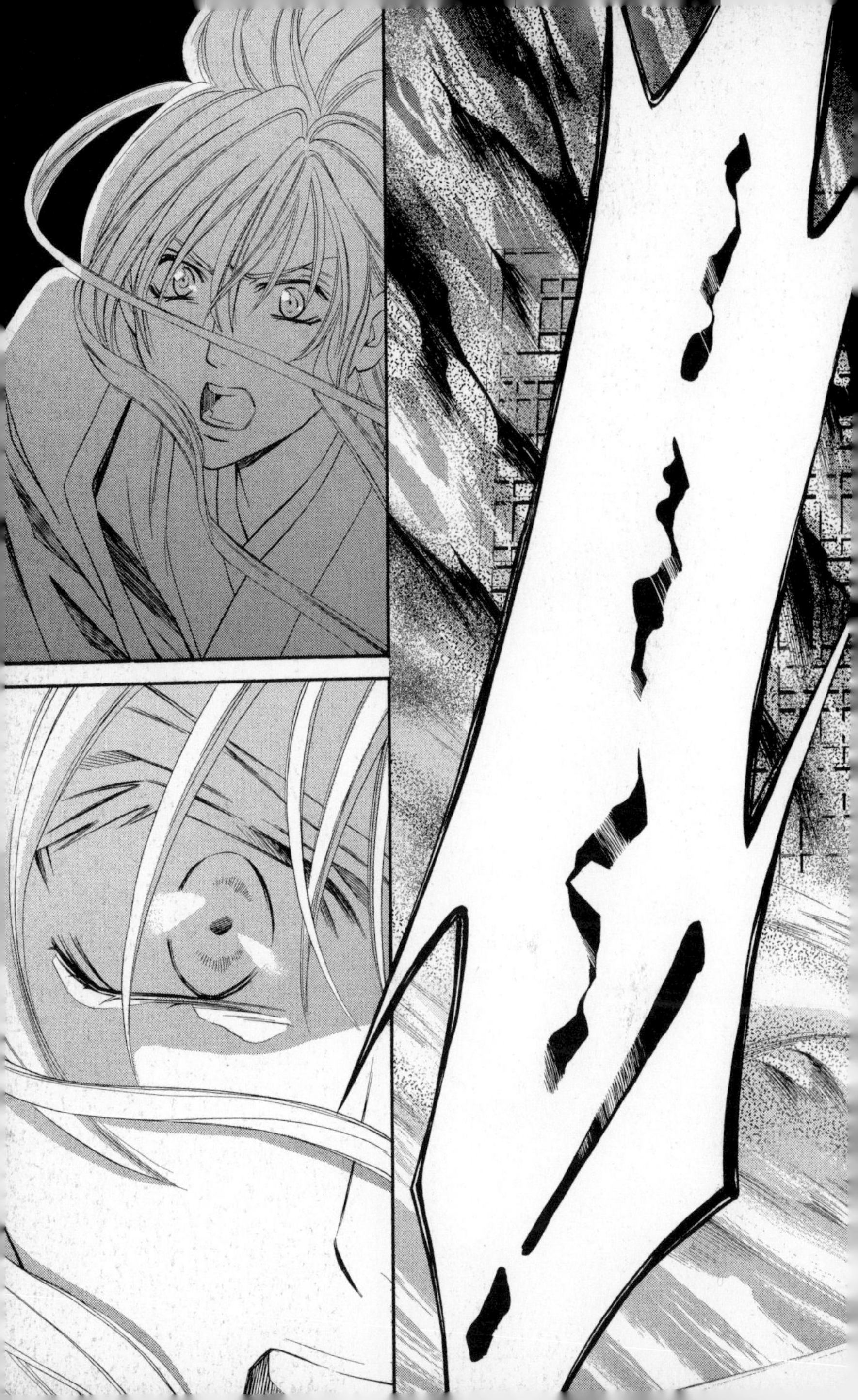

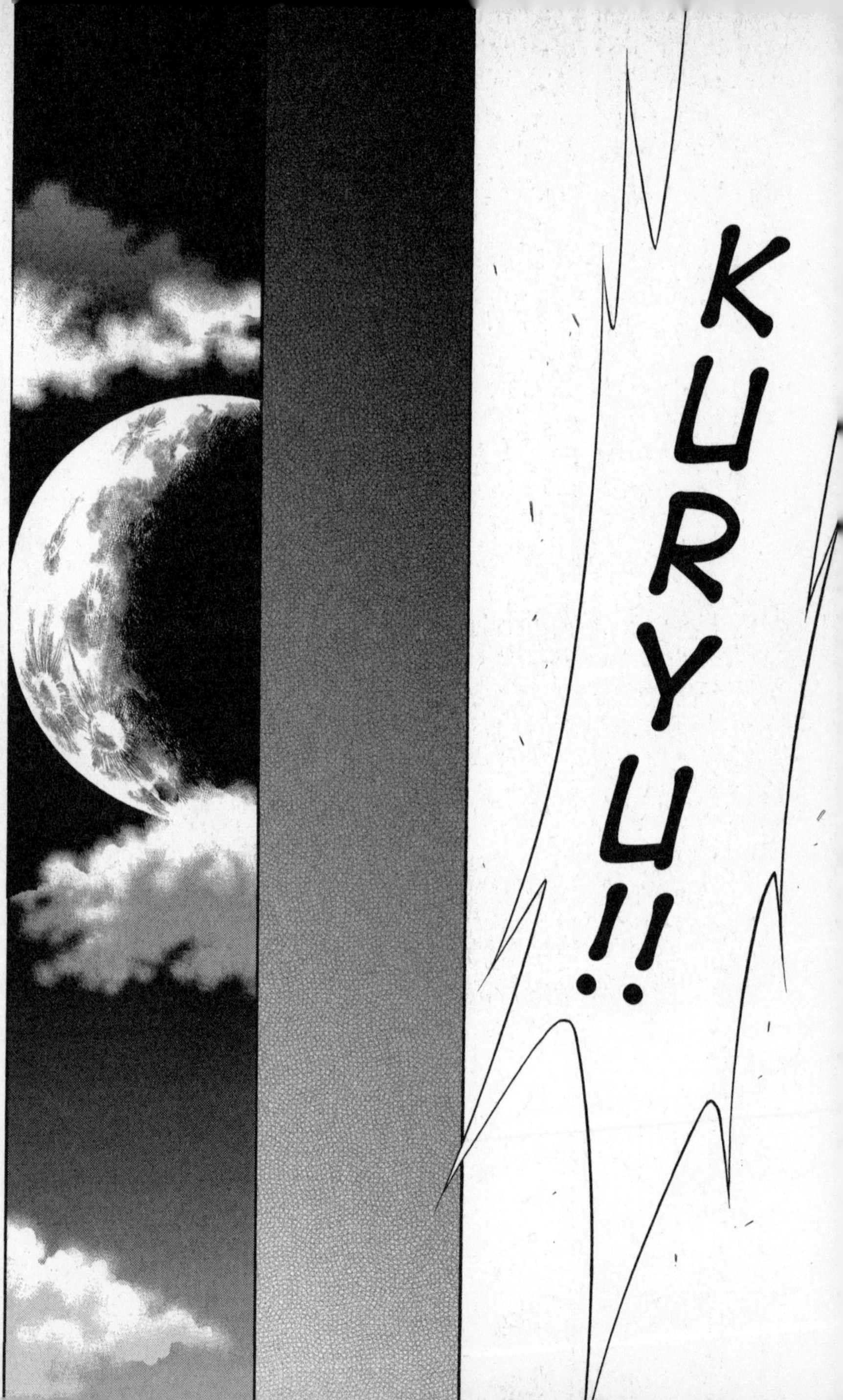
KURYU!!

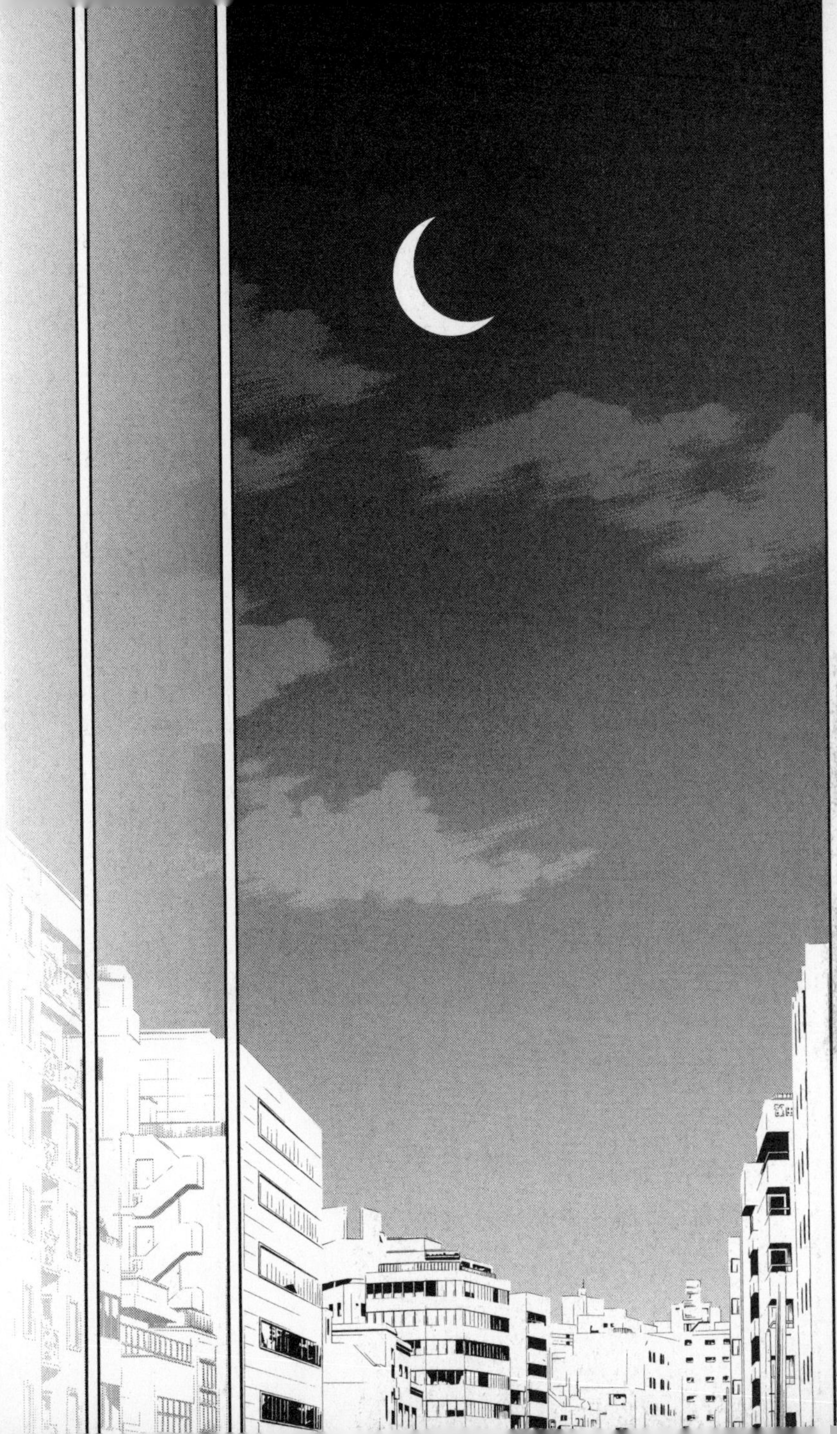

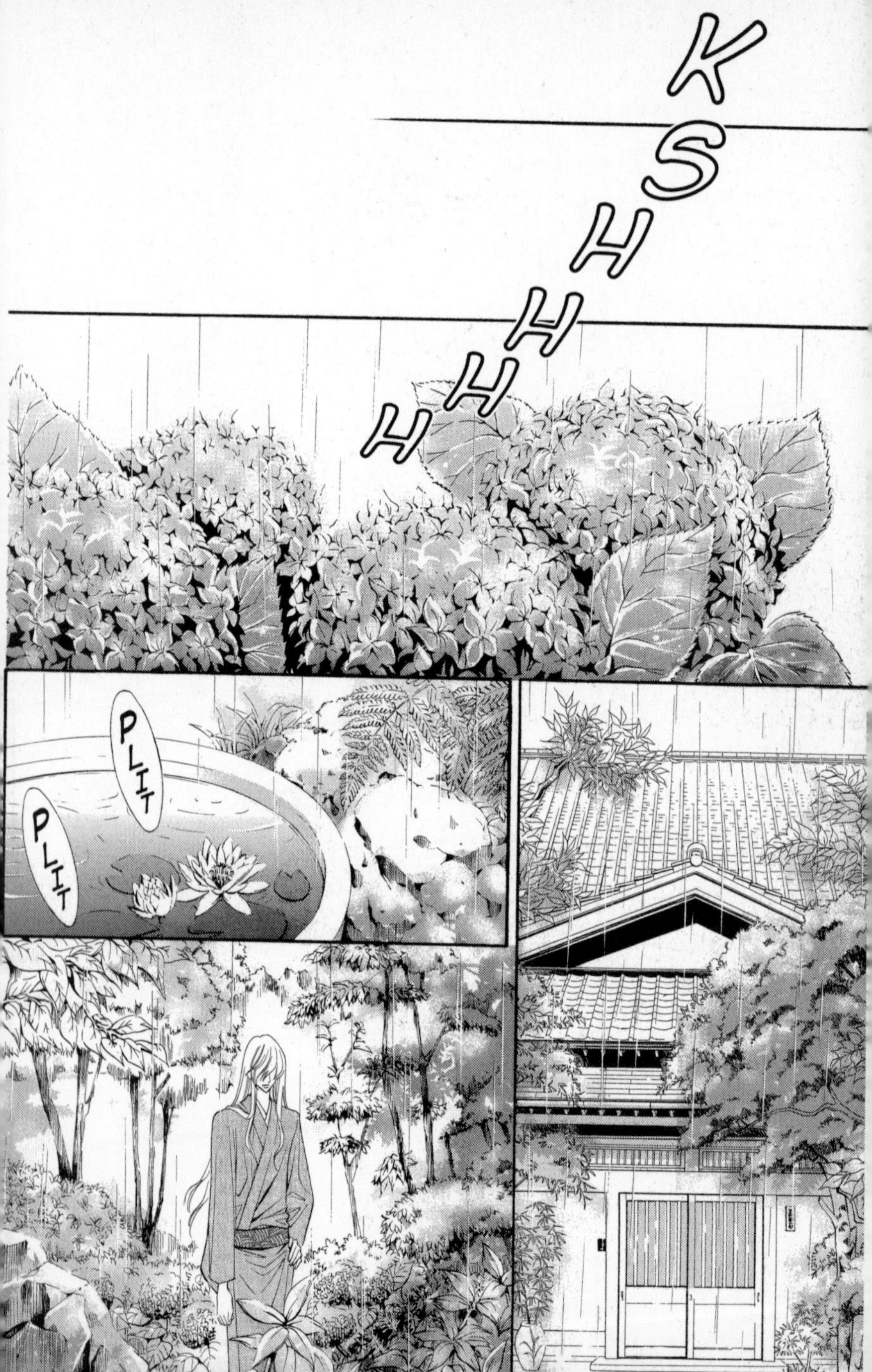
KSHHHH
PLIT
PLIT

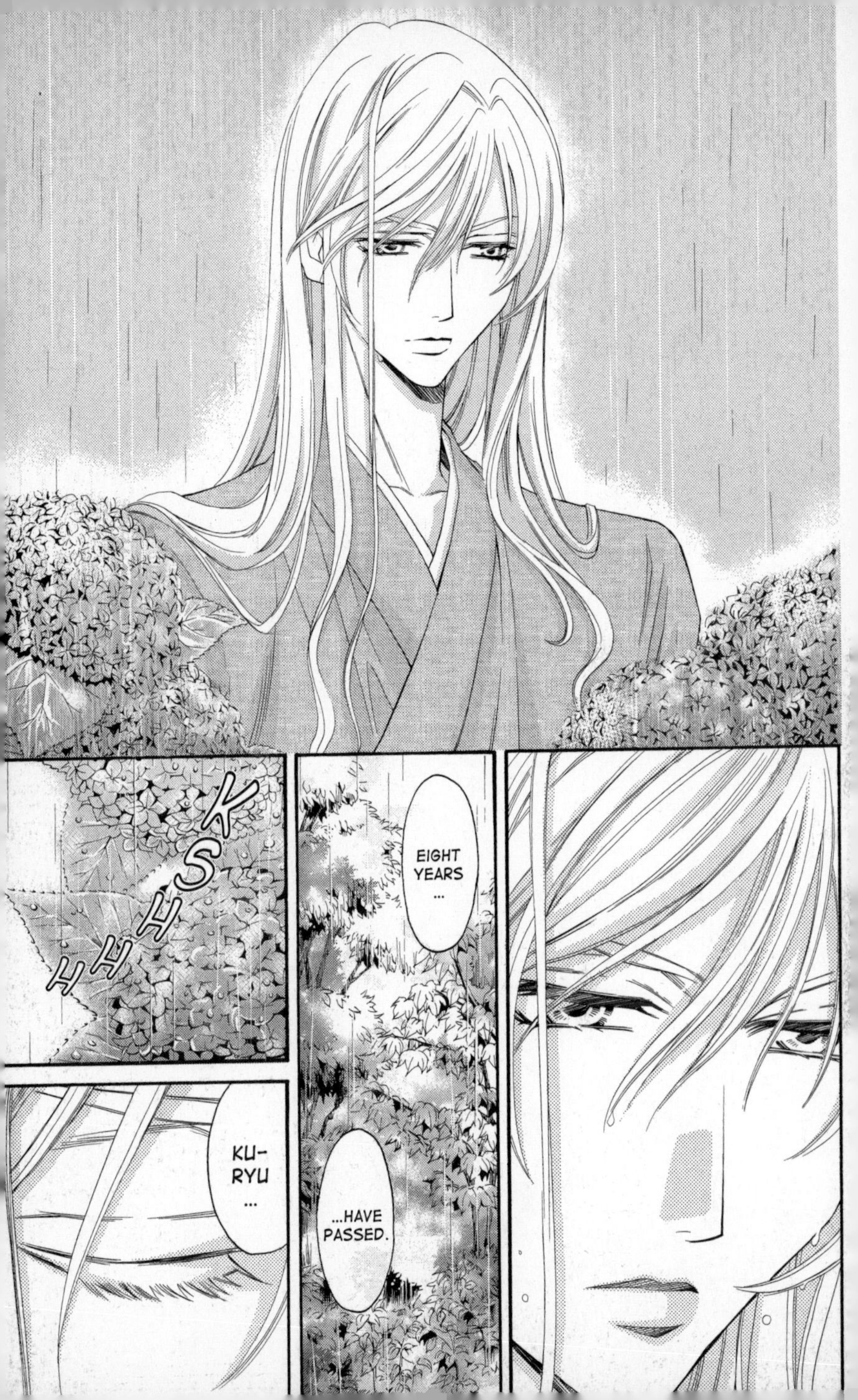
EIGHT YEARS ...
...HAVE PASSED.
KSHHH
KU-RYU ...

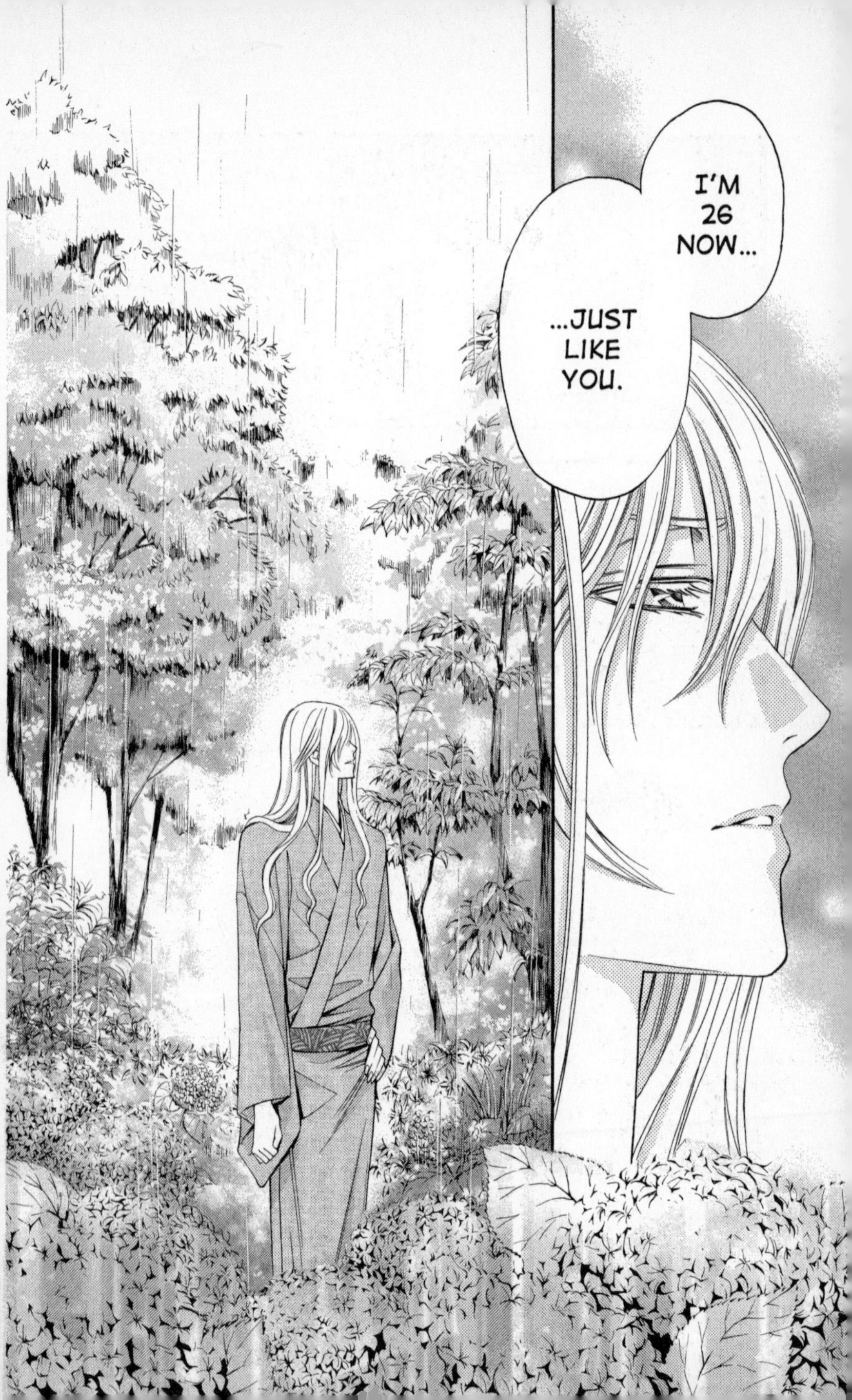
I'M 26 NOW...
...JUST LIKE YOU.

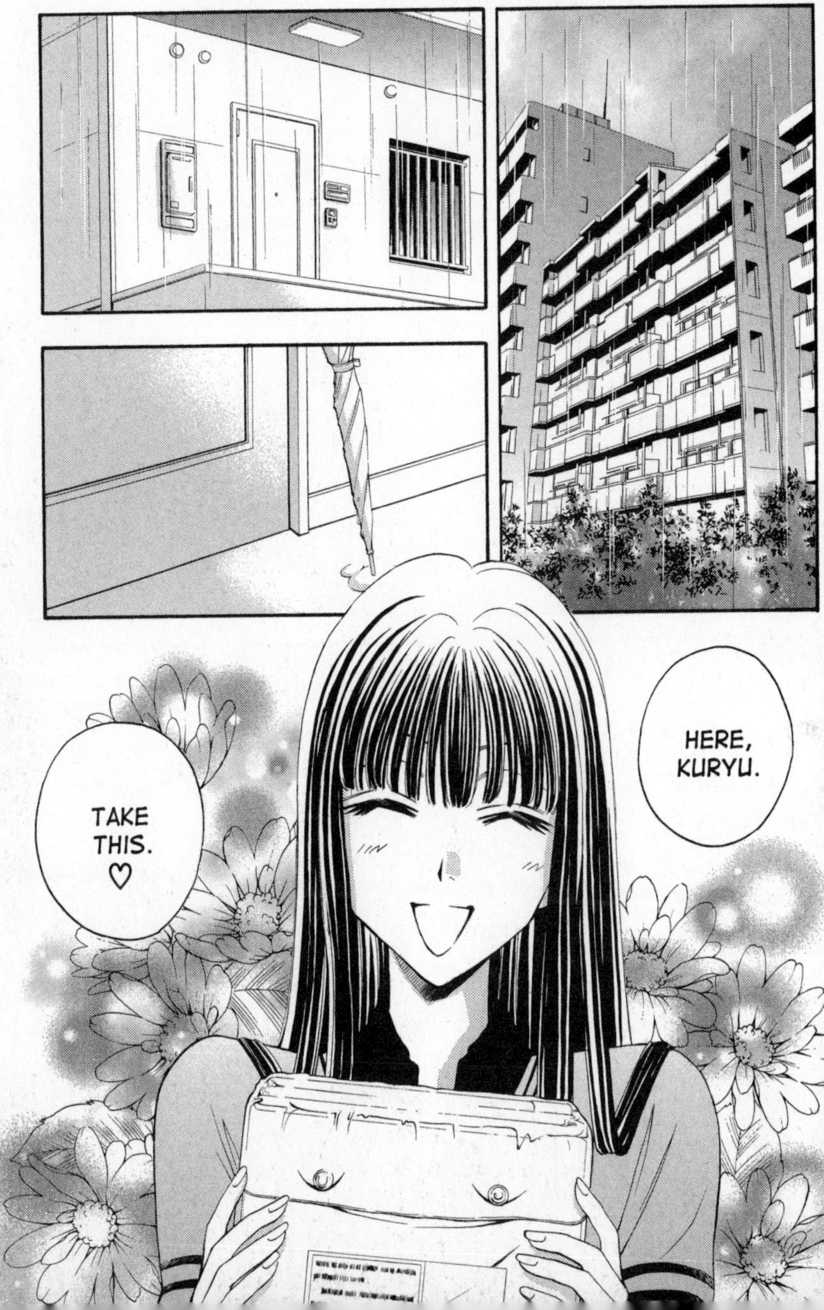
HERE, KURYU.
TAKE THIS. ♡

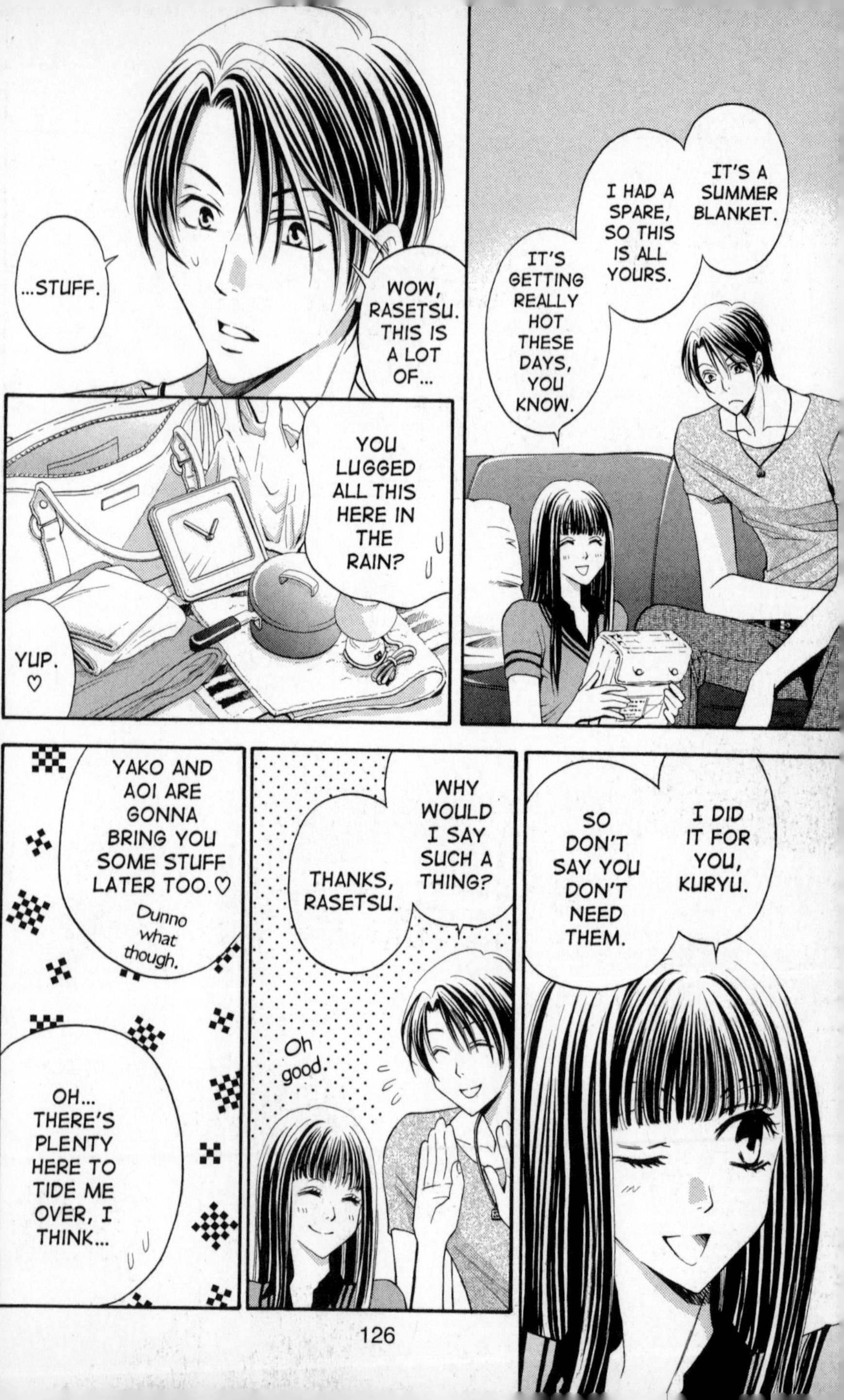
IT'S A SUMMER BLANKET.
I HAD A SPARE, SO THIS IS ALL YOURS.
IT'S GETTING REALLY HOT THESE DAYS, YOU KNOW.
WOW, RASETSU. THIS IS A LOT OF...
...STUFF.
YOU LUGGED ALL THIS HERE IN THE RAIN?
YUP. ♡
I DID IT FOR YOU, KURYU.
SO DON'T SAY YOU DON'T NEED THEM.
WHY WOULD I SAY SUCH A THING?
THANKS, RASETSU.
Oh good.
YAKO AND AOI ARE GONNA BRING YOU SOME STUFF LATER TOO.♡
Dunno what though.
OH... THERE'S PLENTY HERE TO TIDE ME OVER, I THINK...

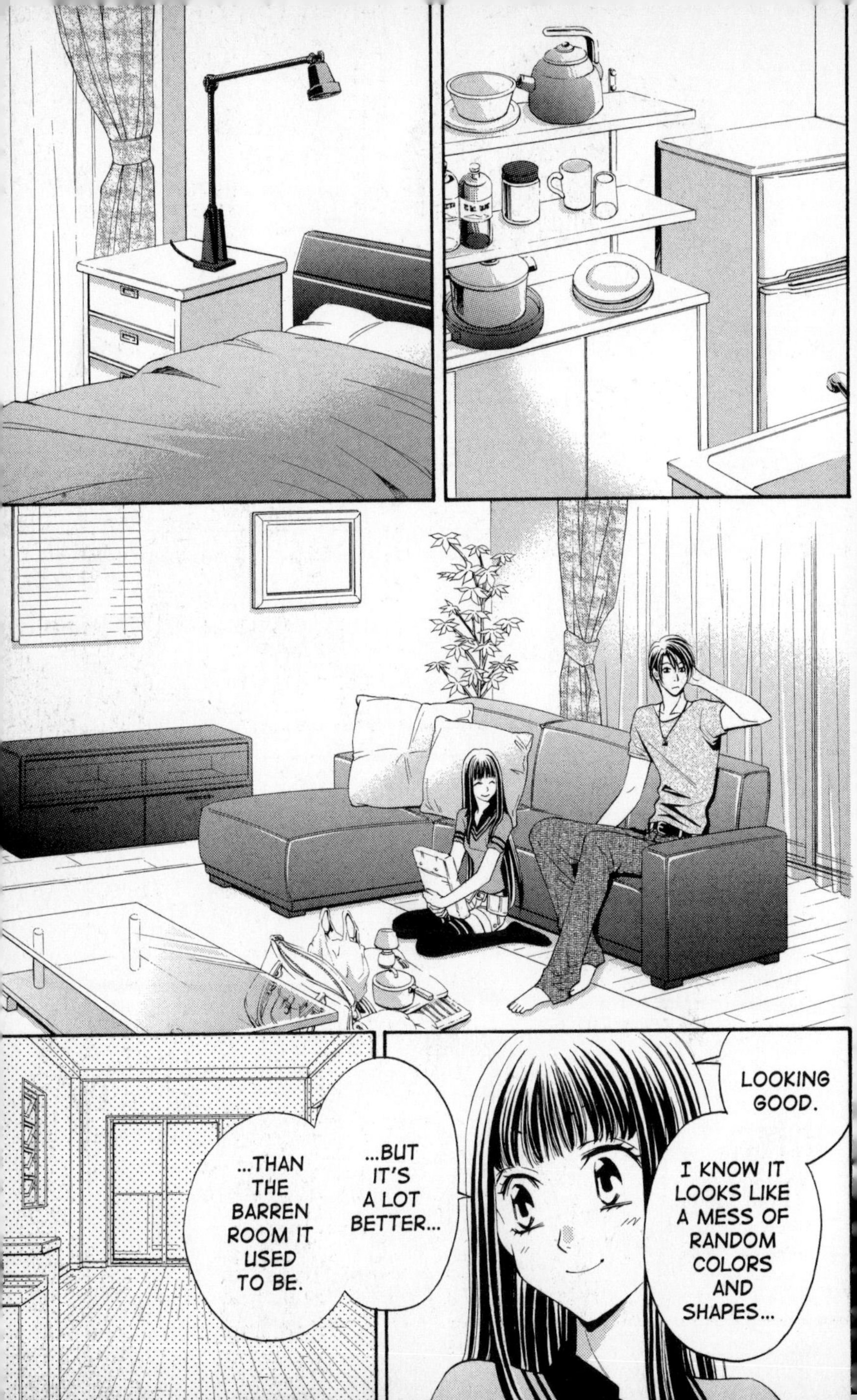
LOOKING GOOD.
I KNOW IT LOOKS LIKE A MESS OF RANDOM COLORS AND SHAPES...
...BUT IT'S A LOT BETTER...
...THAN THE BARREN ROOM IT USED TO BE.

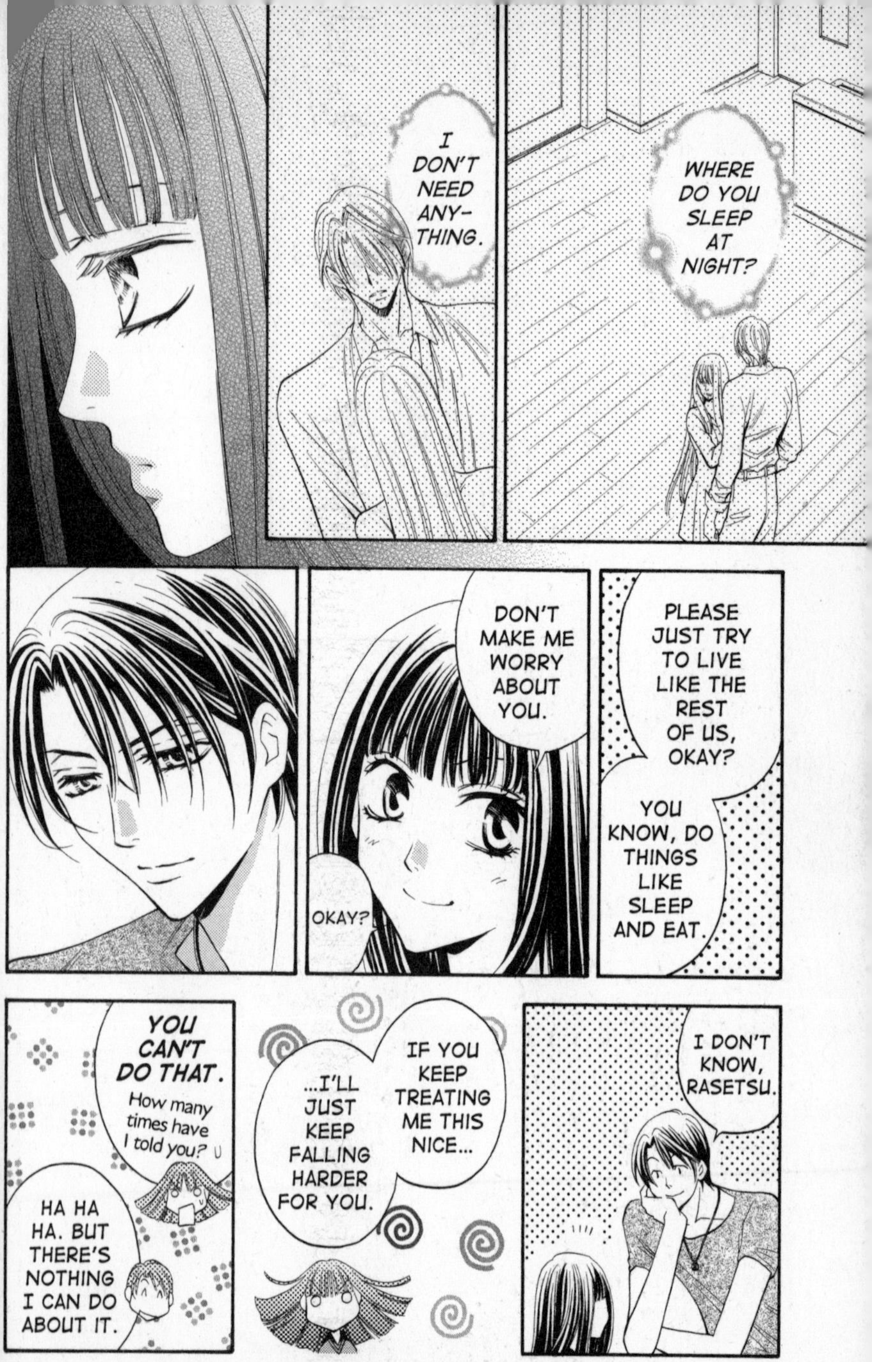
WHERE DO YOU SLEEP AT NIGHT?
I DON'T NEED ANYTHING.
PLEASE JUST TRY TO LIVE LIKE THE REST OF US, OKAY?
YOU KNOW, DO THINGS LIKE SLEEP AND EAT.
DON'T MAKE ME WORRY ABOUT YOU.
OKAY?
I DON'T KNOW, RASETSU.
IF YOU KEEP TREATING ME THIS NICE...
...I'LL JUST KEEP FALLING HARDER FOR YOU.
YOU CAN'T DO THAT. How many times have I told you?
HA HA HA. BUT THERE'S NOTHING I CAN DO ABOUT IT.

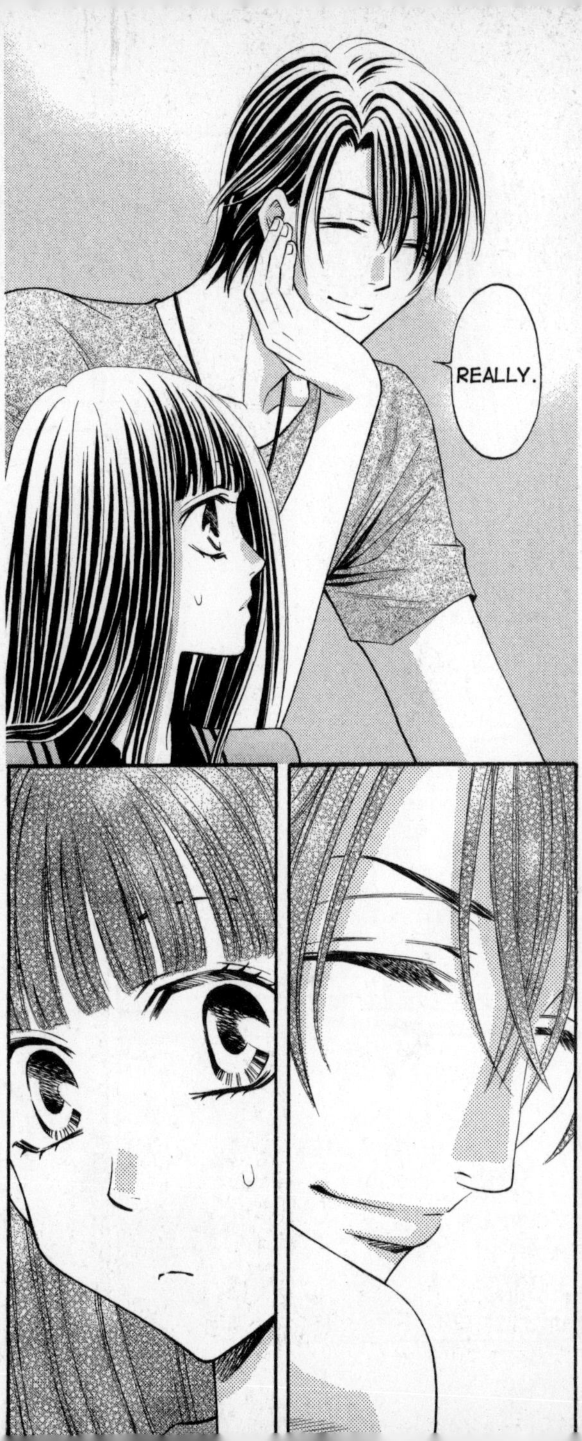
REALLY.

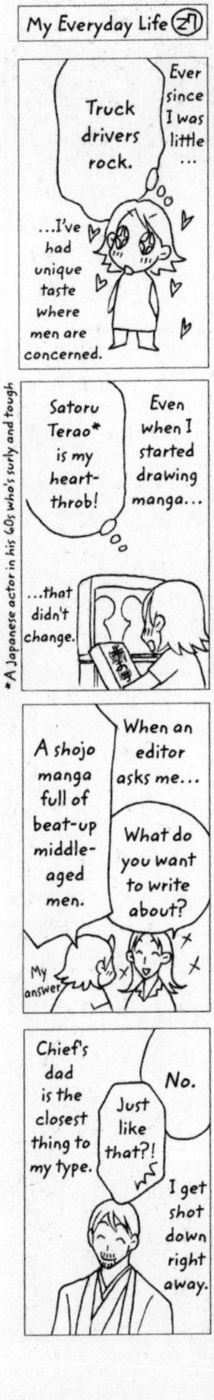
My Everyday Life 27
Ever since I was little...
Truck drivers rock.
...I've had unique taste where men are concerned.
Even when I started drawing manga...
Satoru Terao* is my heart-throb!
...that didn't change.
*A Japanese actor in his 60s who's surly and tough
When an editor asks me...
What do you want to write about?
A shojo manga full of beat-up middle-aged men.
My answer
Chief's dad is the closest thing to my type.
No.
Just like that?!
I get shot down right away.

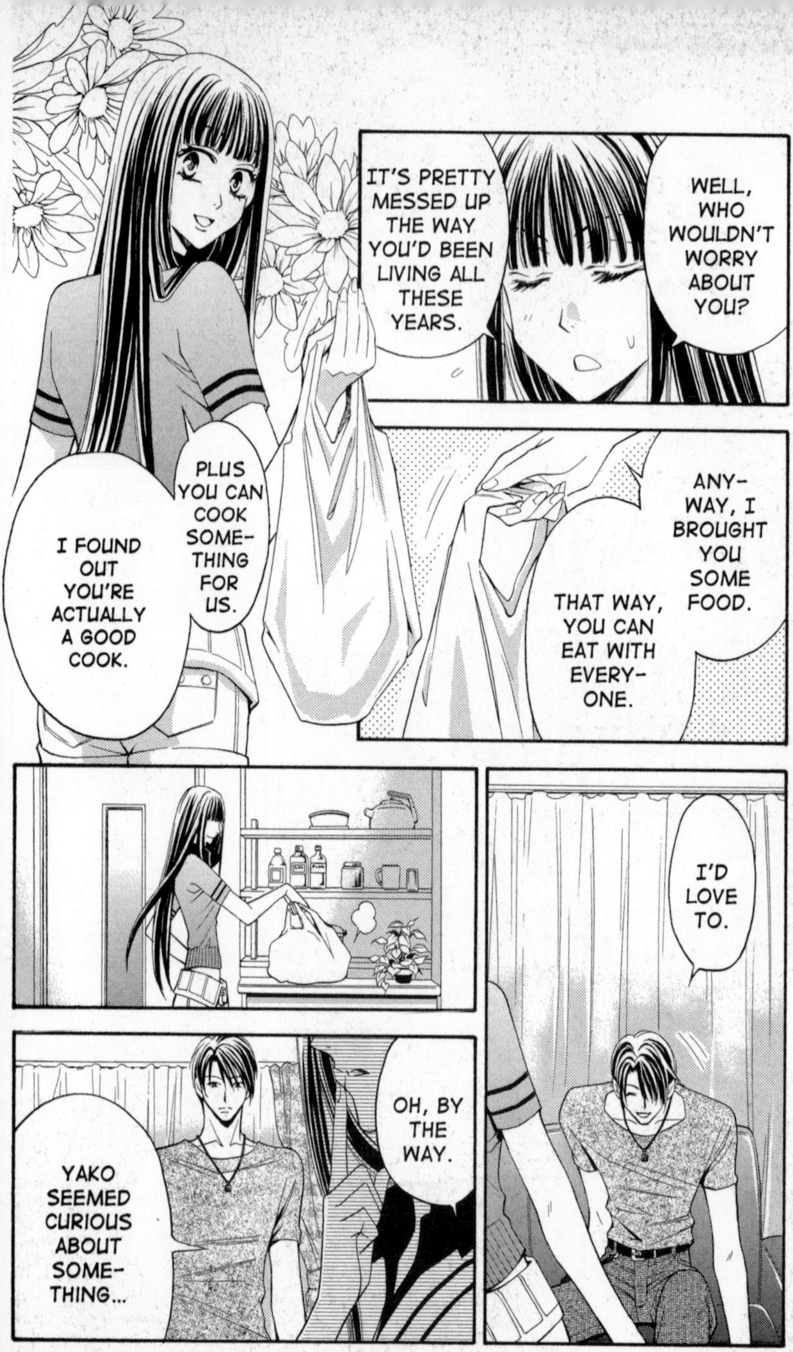
WELL, WHO WOULDN'T WORRY ABOUT YOU?
IT'S PRETTY MESSED UP THE WAY YOU'D BEEN LIVING ALL THESE YEARS.
ANY-WAY, I BROUGHT YOU SOME FOOD.
THAT WAY, YOU CAN EAT WITH EVERY-ONE.
PLUS YOU CAN COOK SOME-THING FOR US.
I FOUND OUT YOU'RE ACTUALLY A GOOD COOK.
I'D LOVE TO.
OH, BY THE WAY.
YAKO SEEMED CURIOUS ABOUT SOME-THING...

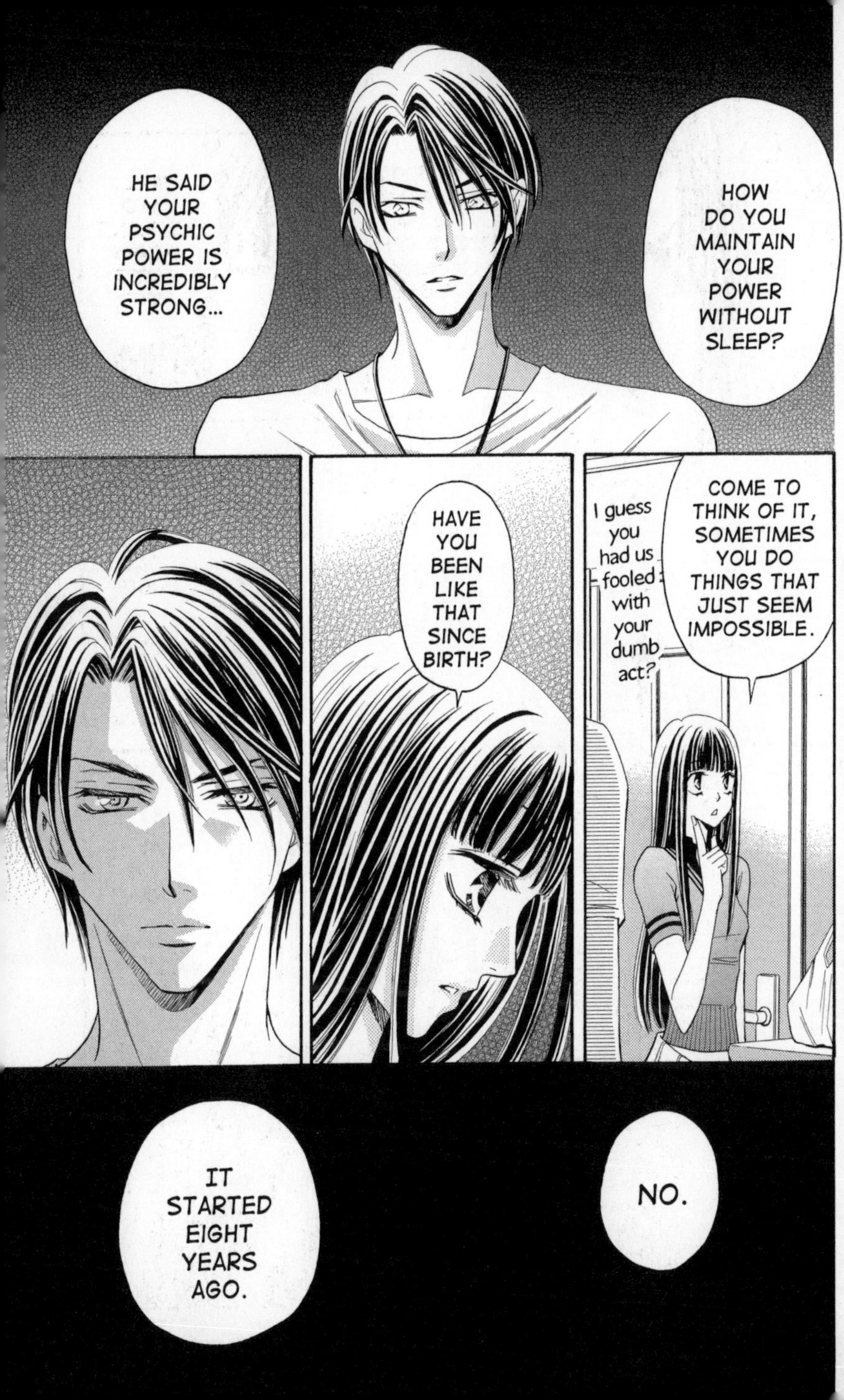
HOW DO YOU MAINTAIN YOUR POWER WITHOUT SLEEP?
HE SAID YOUR PSYCHIC POWER IS INCREDIBLY STRONG...
COME TO THINK OF IT, SOMETIMES YOU DO THINGS THAT JUST SEEM IMPOSSIBLE.
I guess you had us fooled with your dumb act?
HAVE YOU BEEN LIKE THAT SINCE BIRTH?
NO.
IT STARTED EIGHT YEARS AGO.

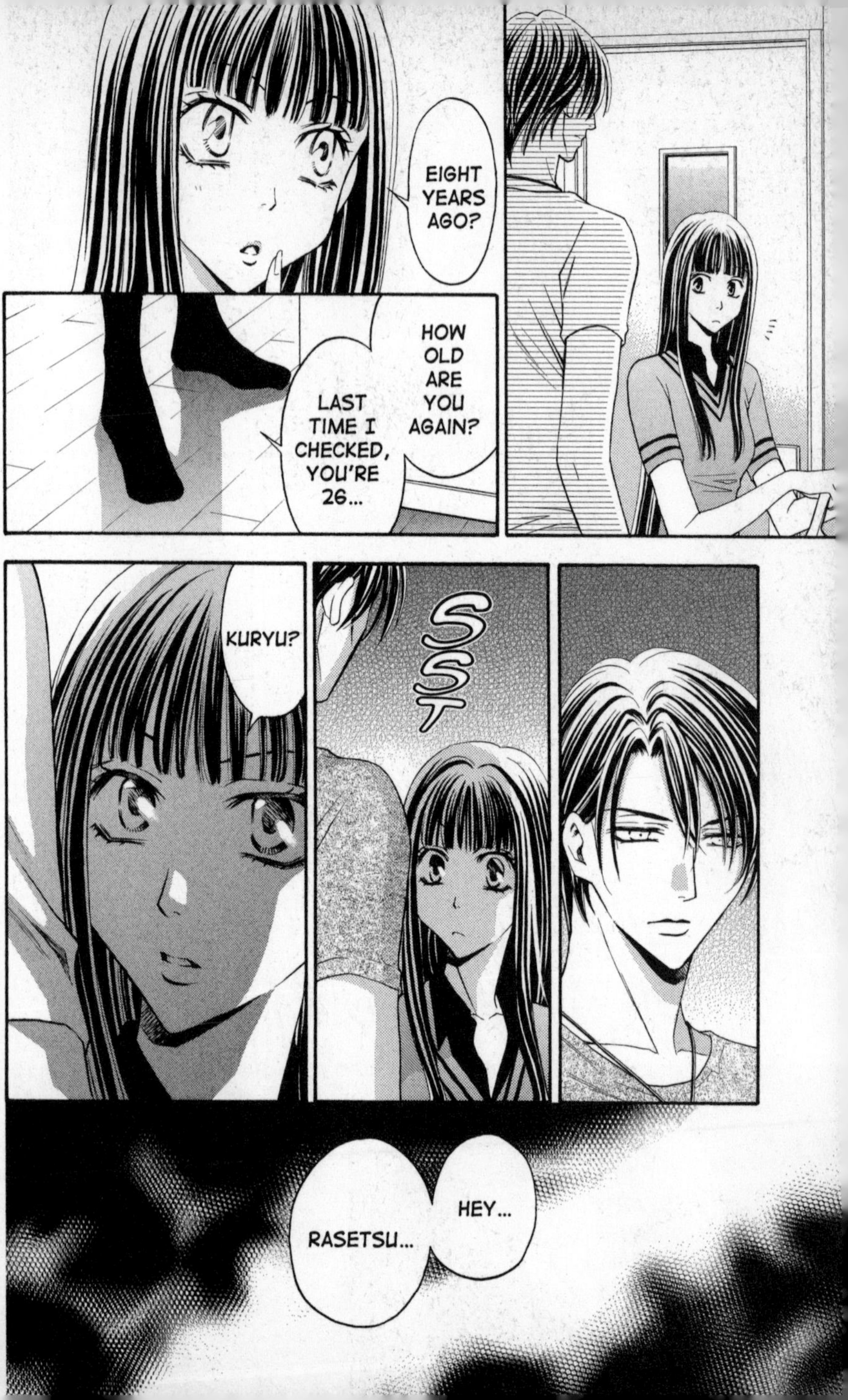
EIGHT YEARS AGO?
HOW OLD ARE YOU AGAIN?
LAST TIME I CHECKED, YOU'RE 26...
SST
KURYU?
HEY...
RASETSU...

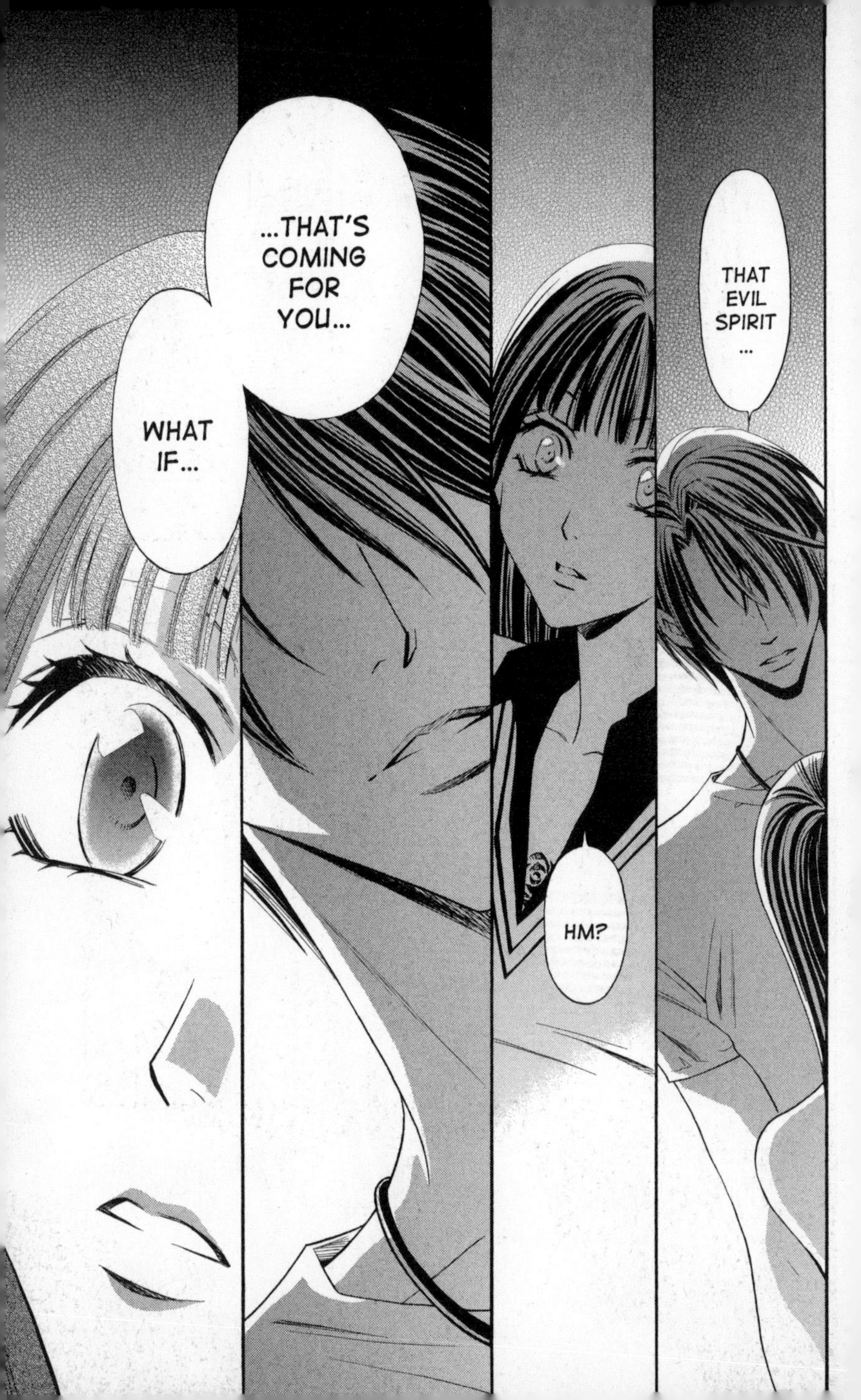

THAT EVIL SPIRIT ...
HM?
...THAT'S COMING FOR YOU...
WHAT IF...

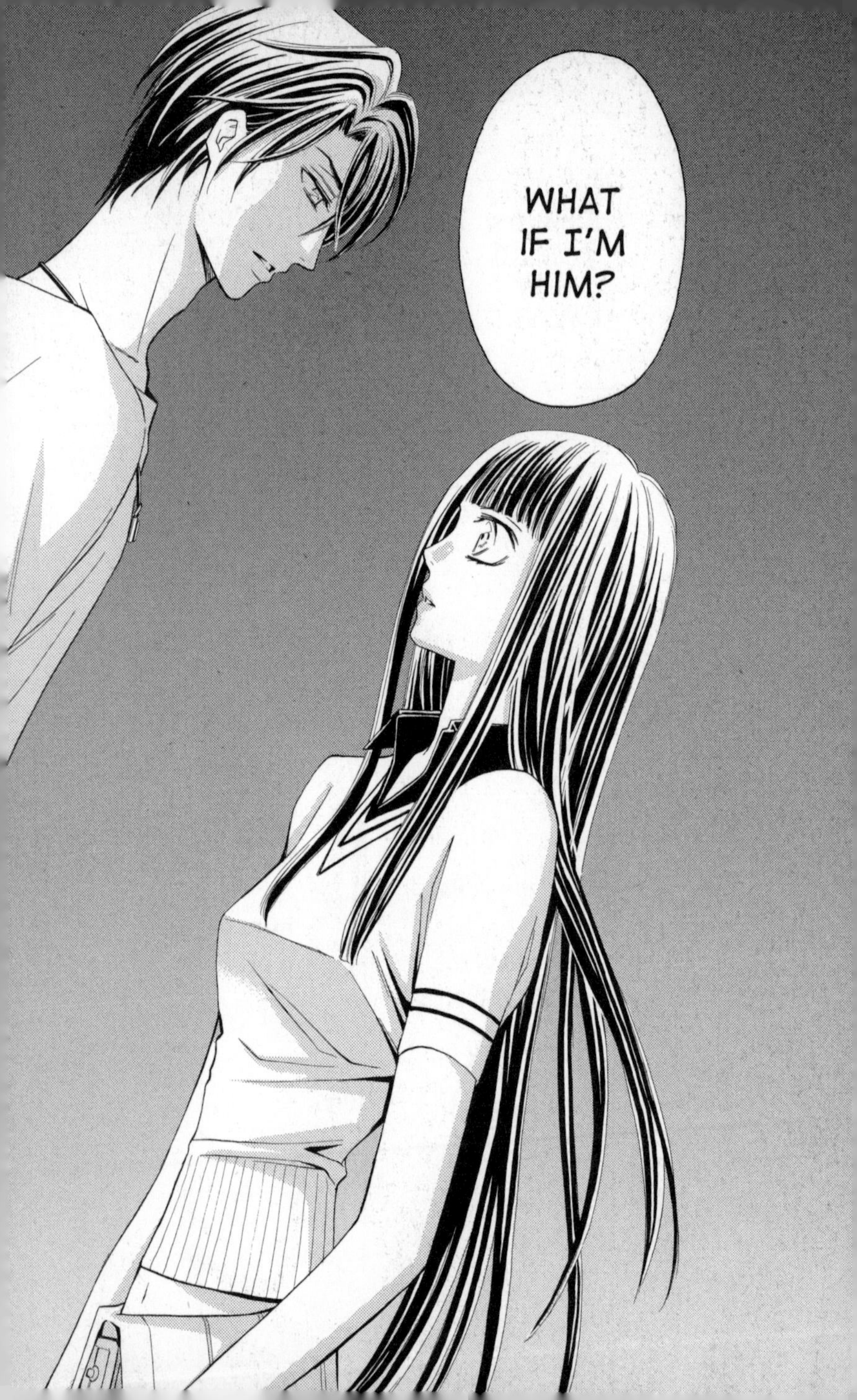
WHAT IF I'M HIM?

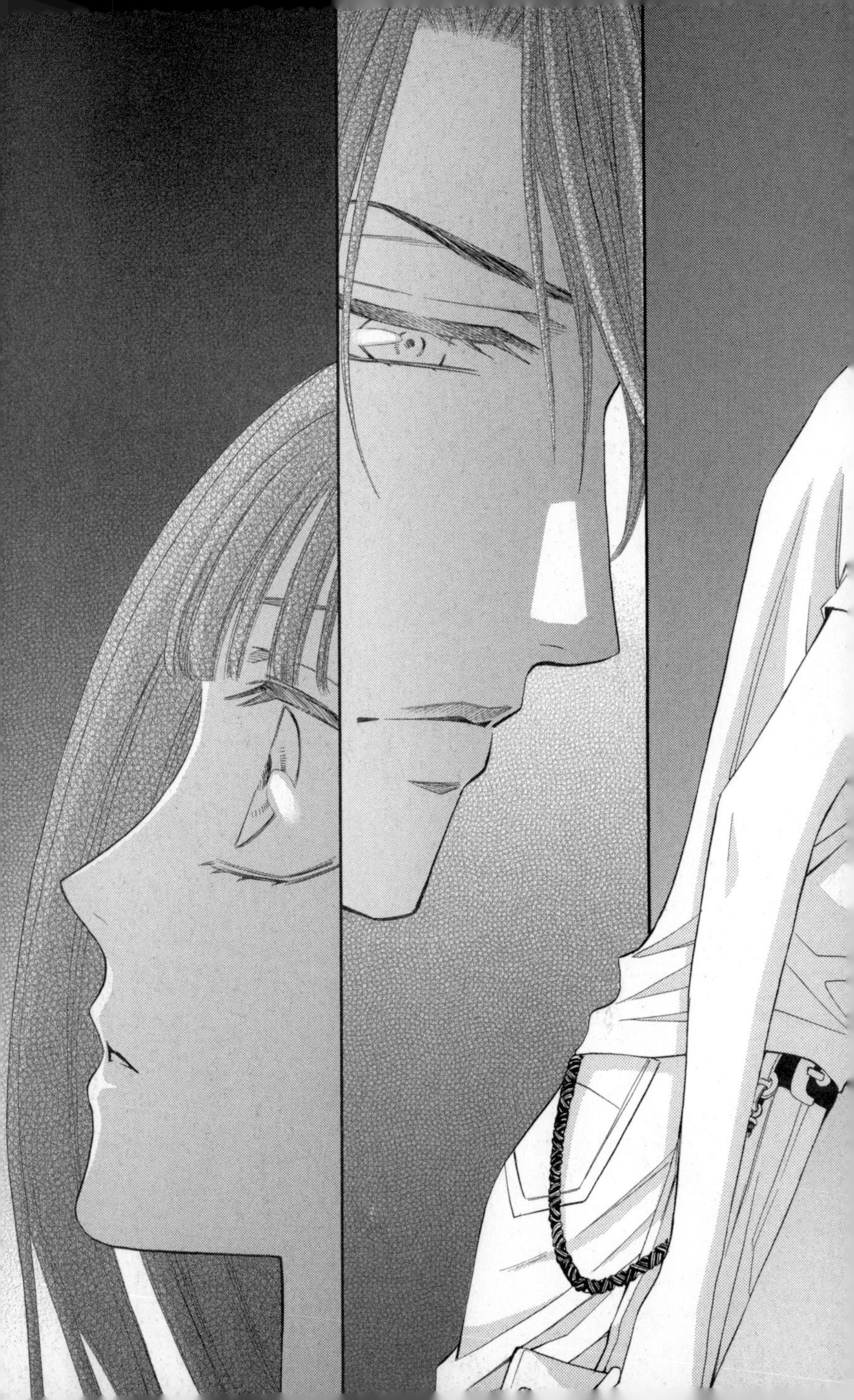

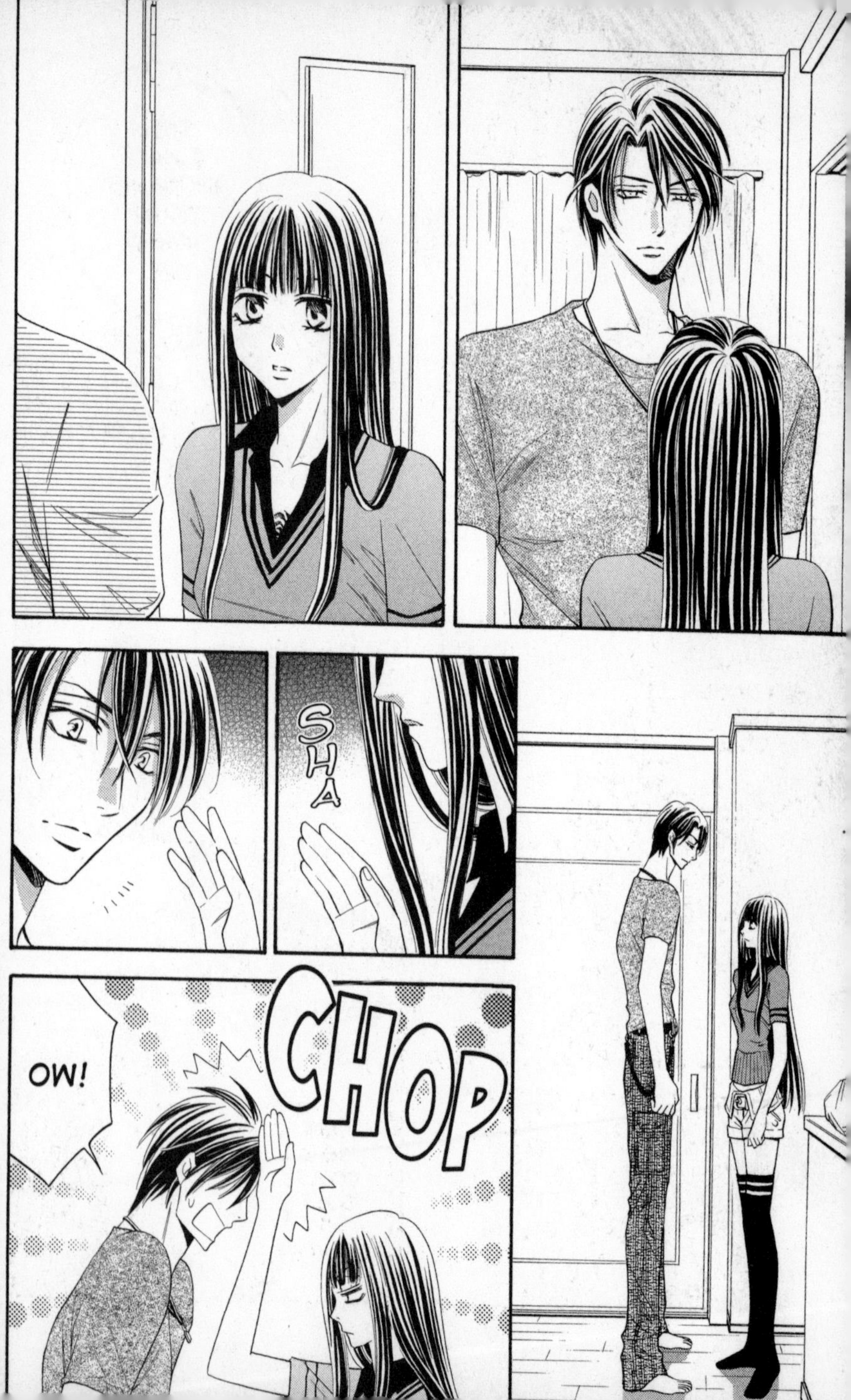
SHA
CHOP
OW!

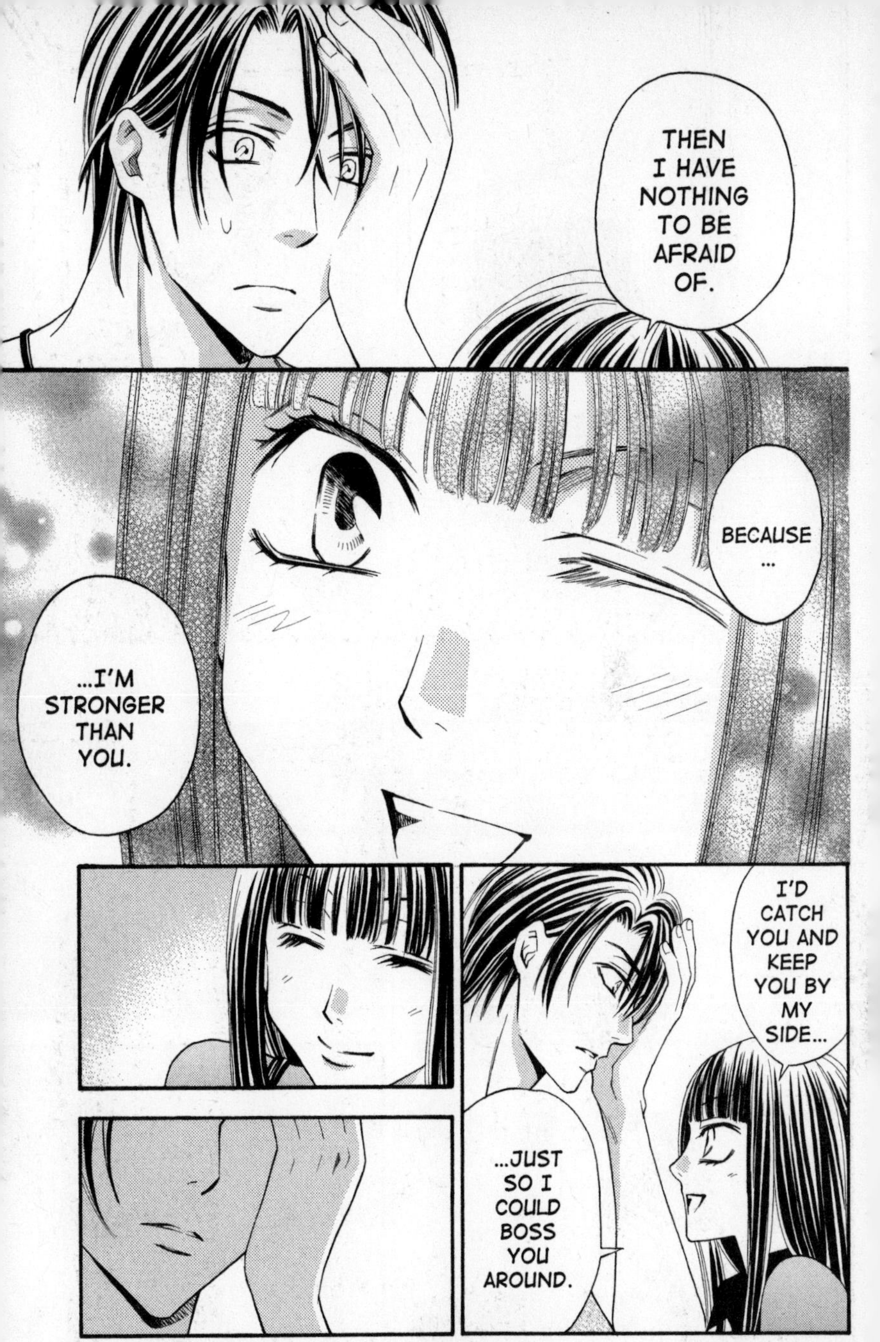
THEN I HAVE NOTHING TO BE AFRAID OF.
BECAUSE ...
...I'M STRONGER THAN YOU.
I'D CATCH YOU AND KEEP YOU BY MY SIDE...
...JUST SO I COULD BOSS YOU AROUND.

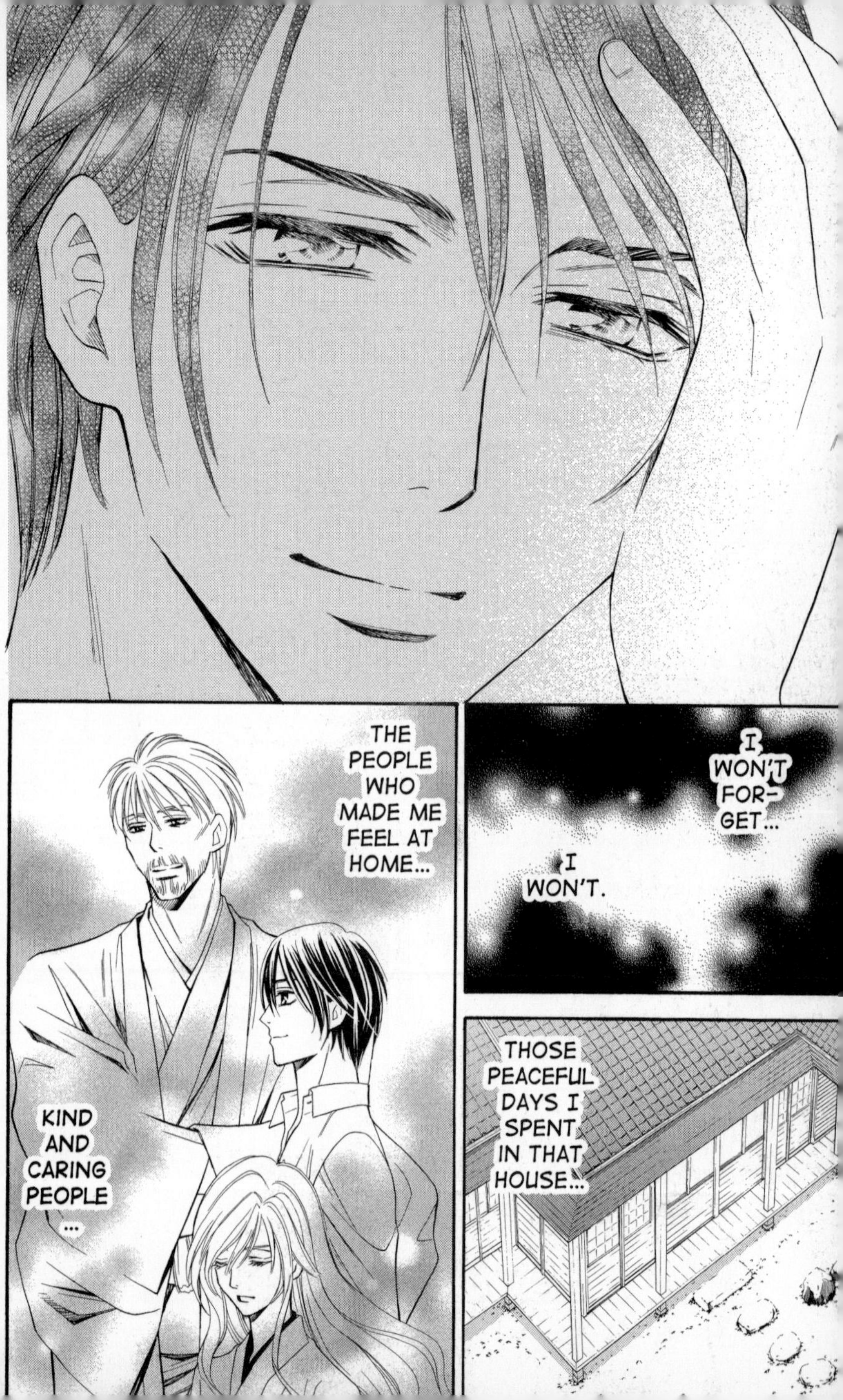
I WON'T FORGET...
I WON'T.
THOSE PEACEFUL DAYS I SPENT IN THAT HOUSE...
THE PEOPLE WHO MADE ME FEEL AT HOME...
KIND AND CARING PEOPLE ...

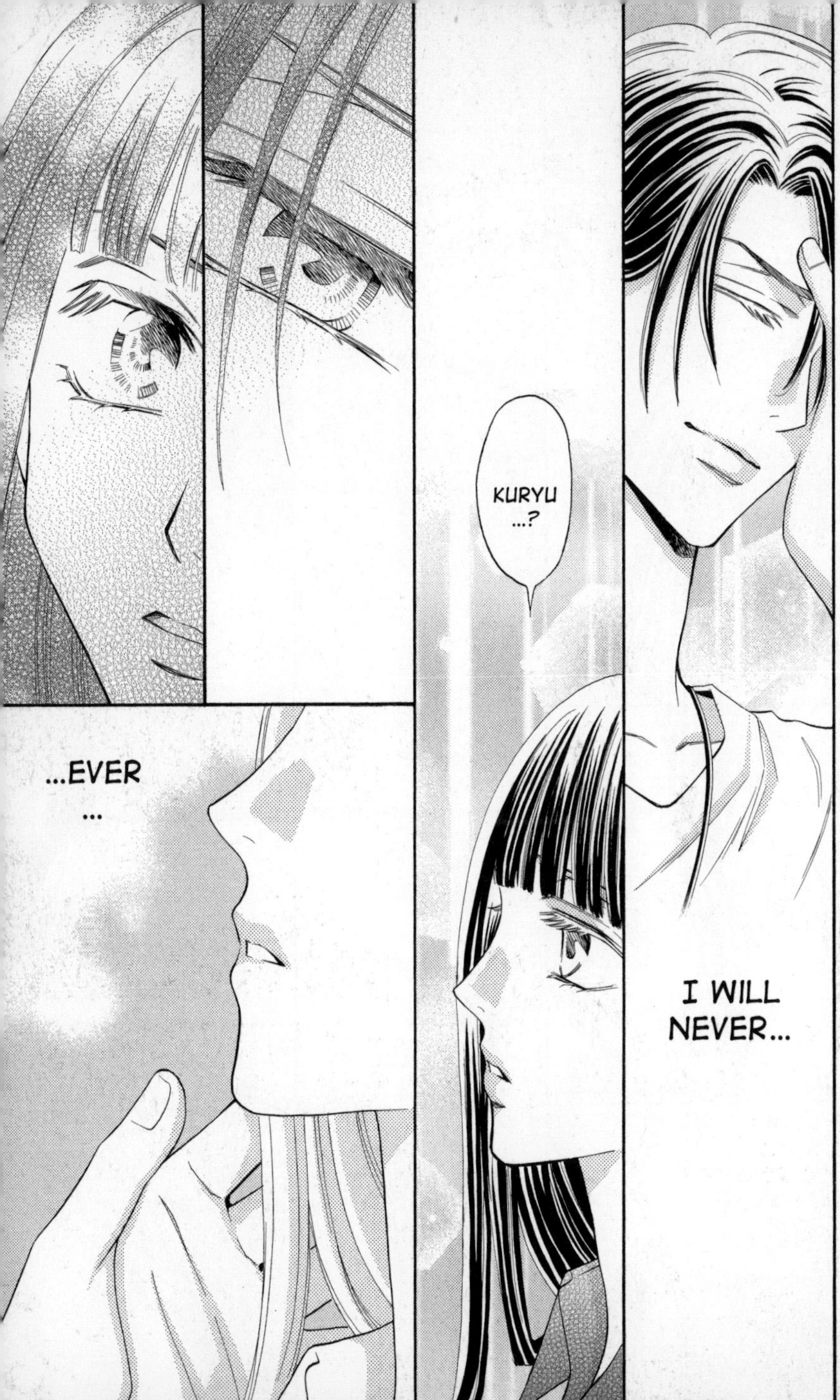
I WILL NEVER...
KURYU ...?
...EVER ...

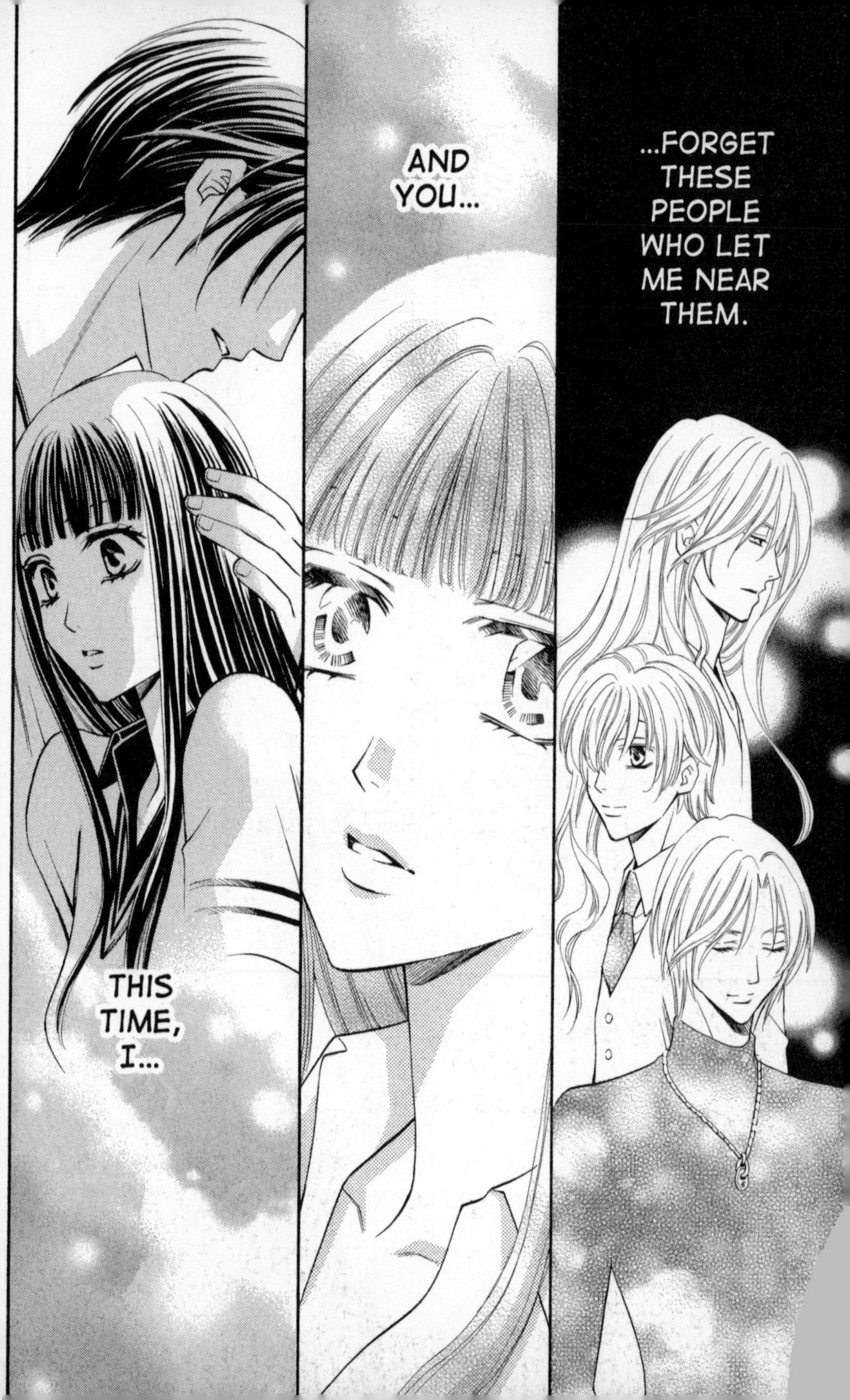
...FORGET THESE PEOPLE WHO LET ME NEAR THEM.
AND YOU...
THIS TIME, I...

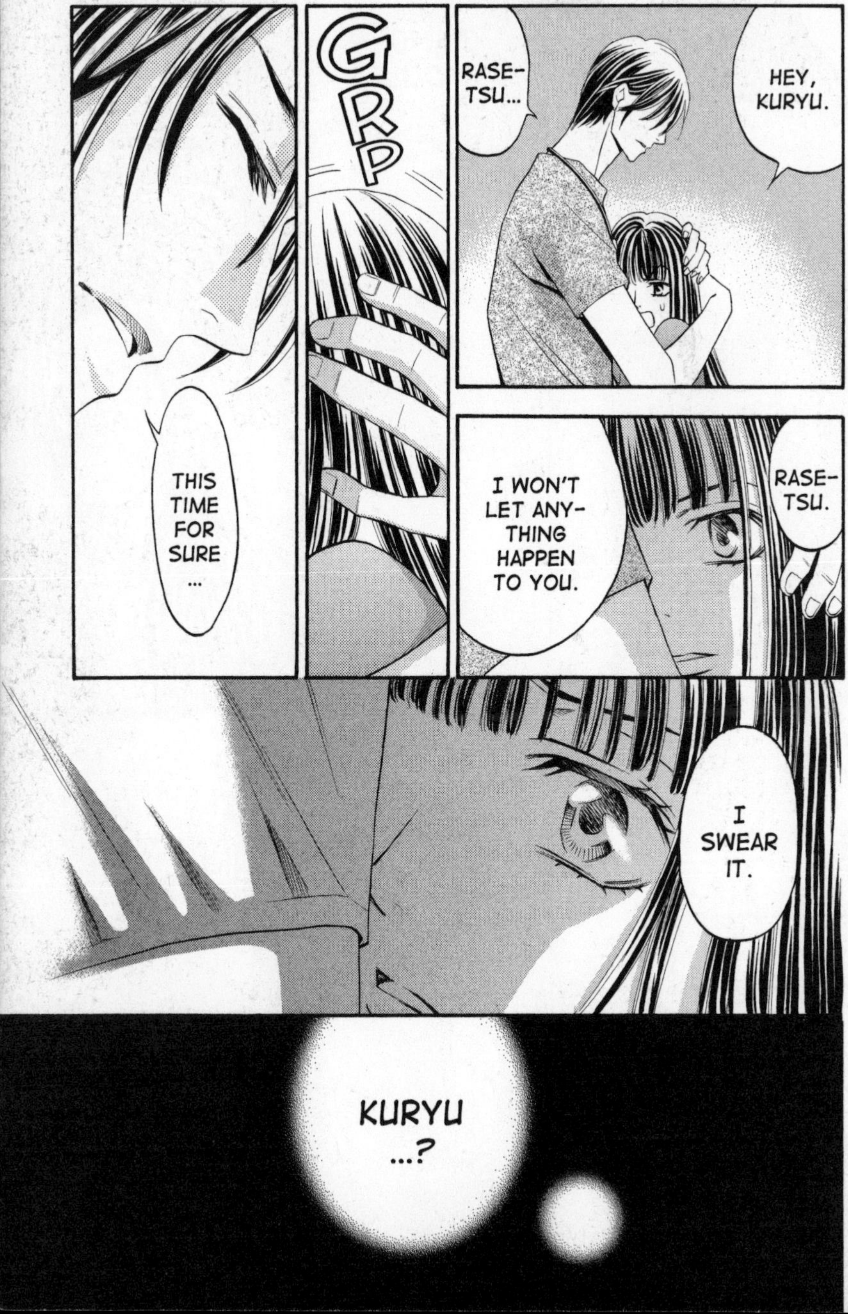
HEY, KURYU.
RASE-TSU...
RASE-TSU.
I WON'T LET ANY-THING HAPPEN TO YOU.
GRP
THIS TIME FOR SURE ...
I SWEAR IT.
KURYU ...?

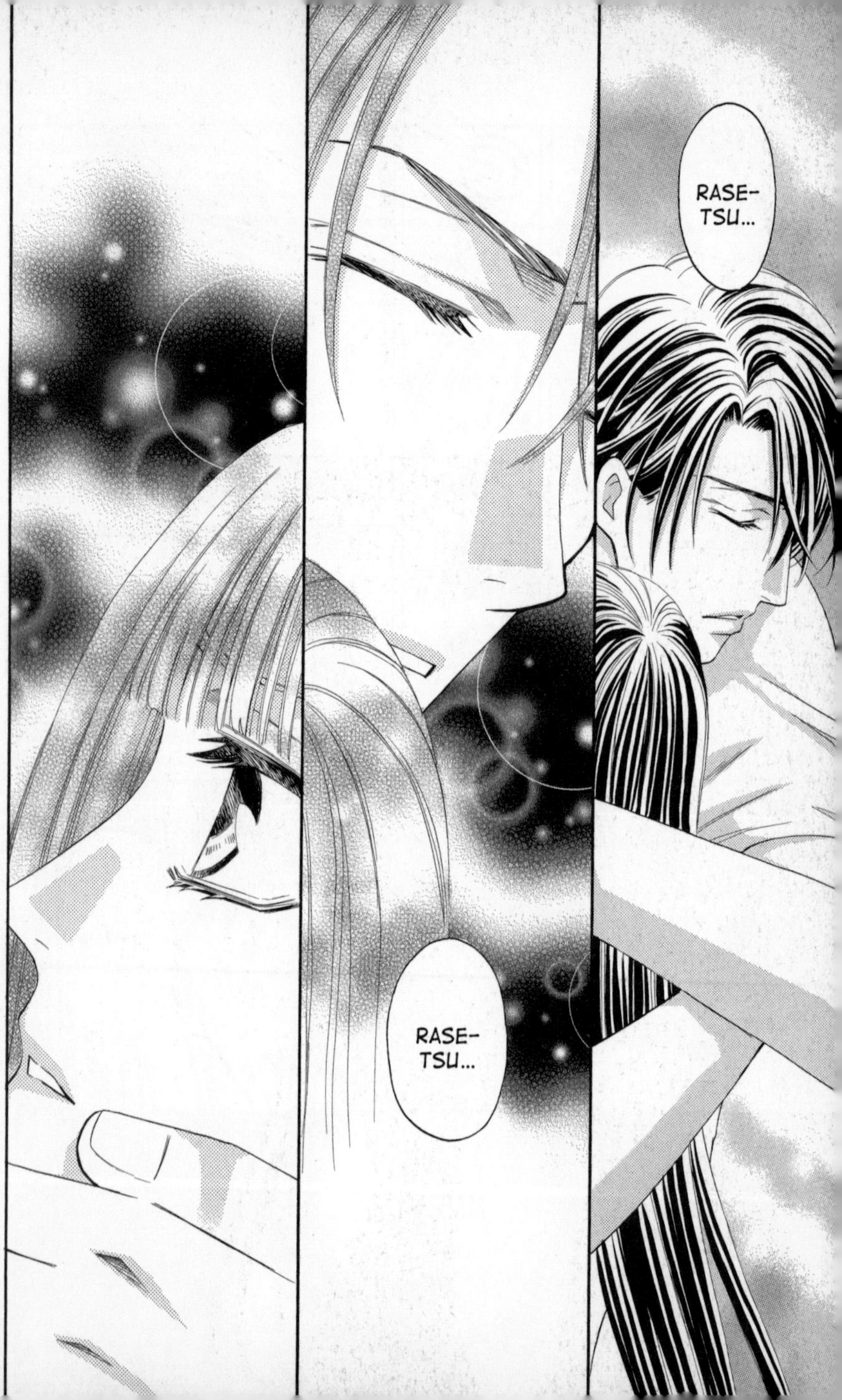
RASE-TSU...
RASE-TSU...

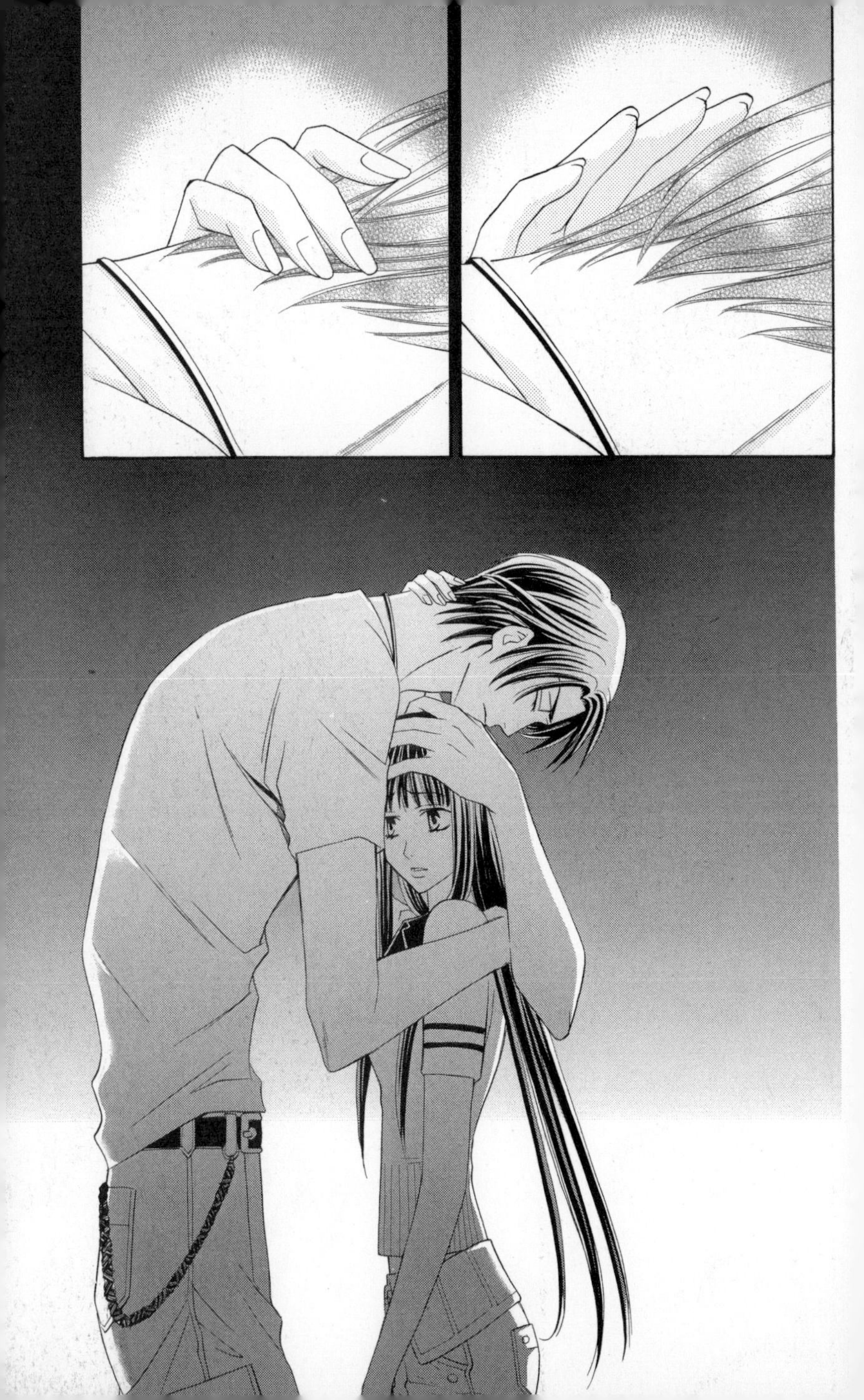

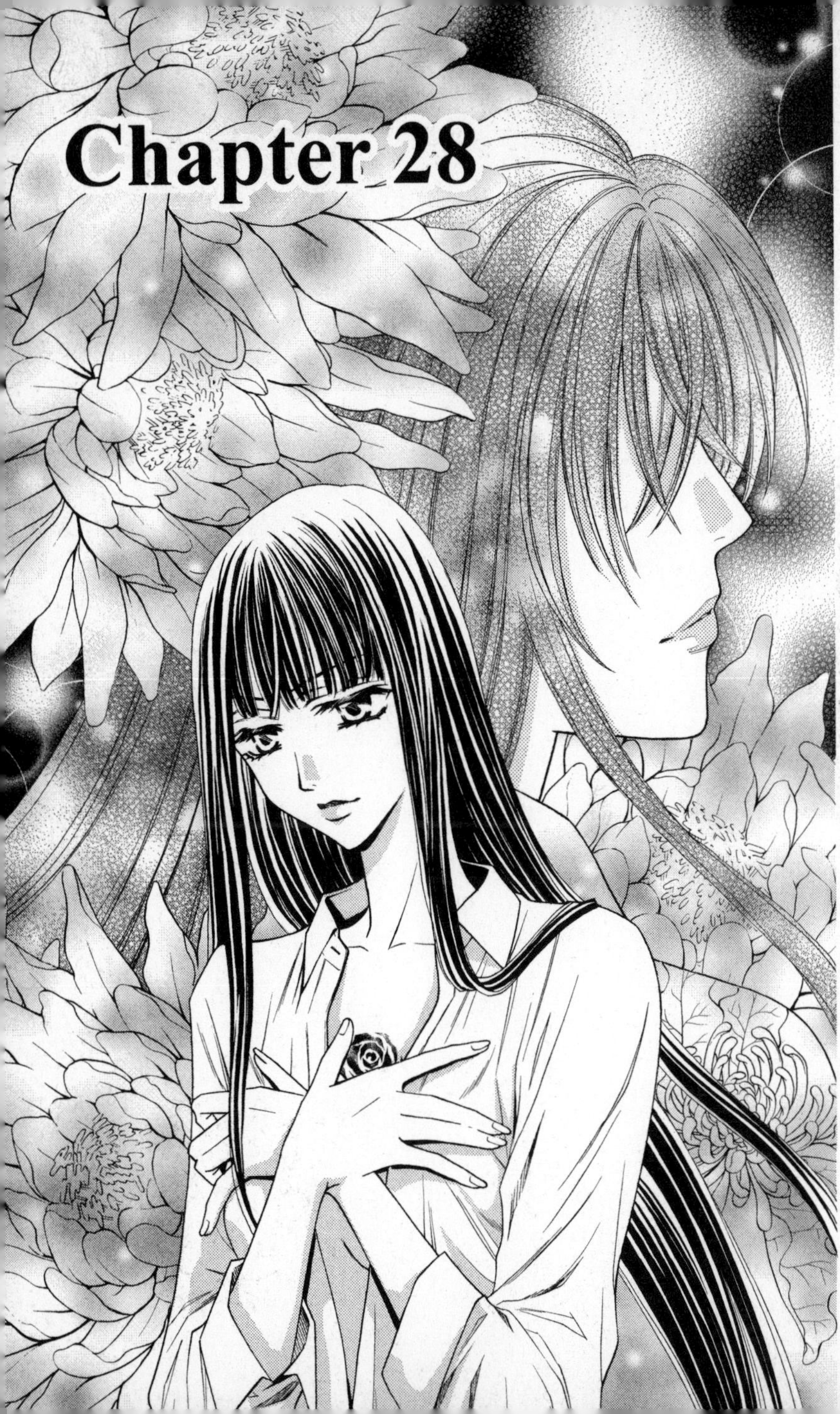
Chapter 28

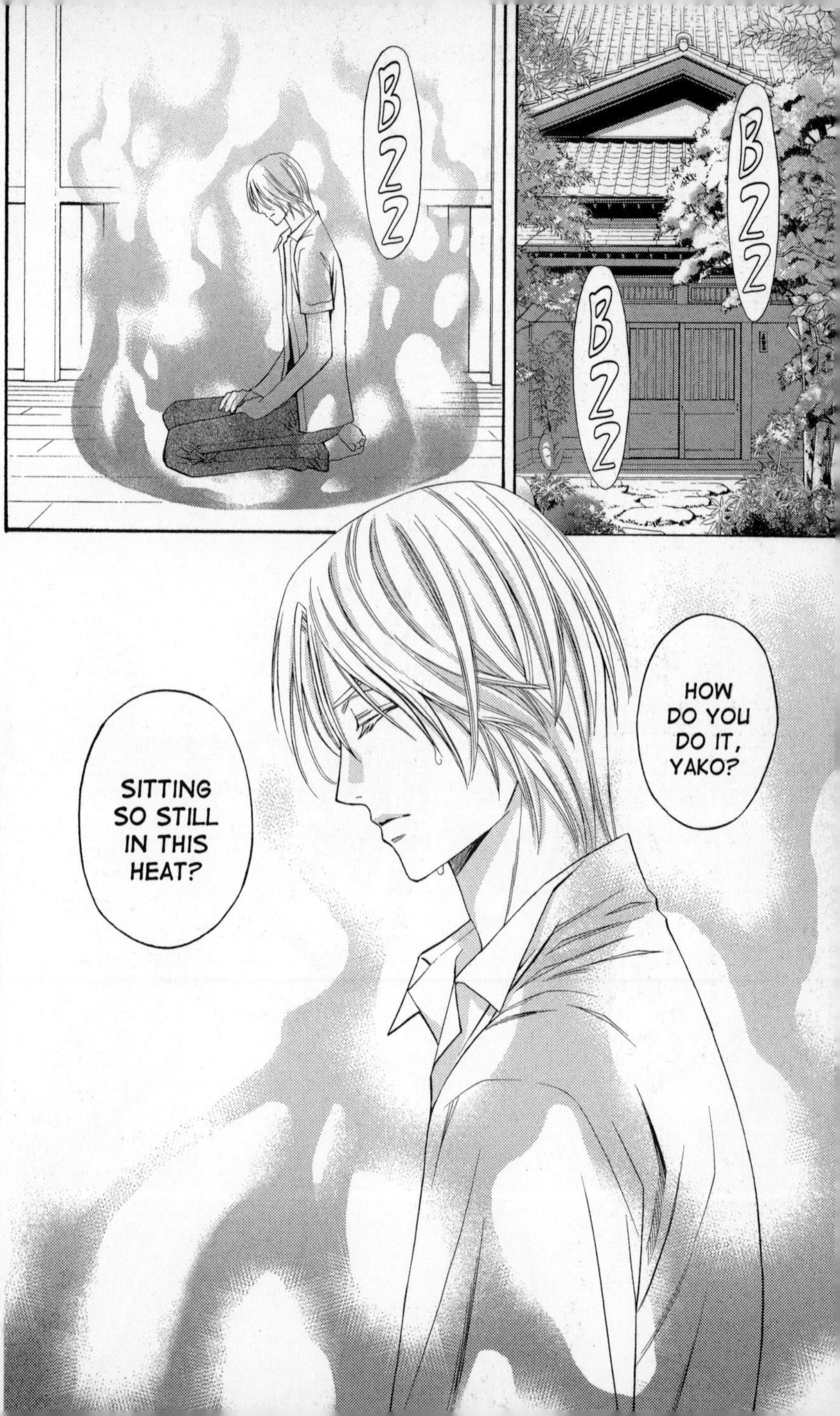
BZZ
BZZ
BZZ
HOW DO YOU DO IT, YAKO?
SITTING SO STILL IN THIS HEAT?

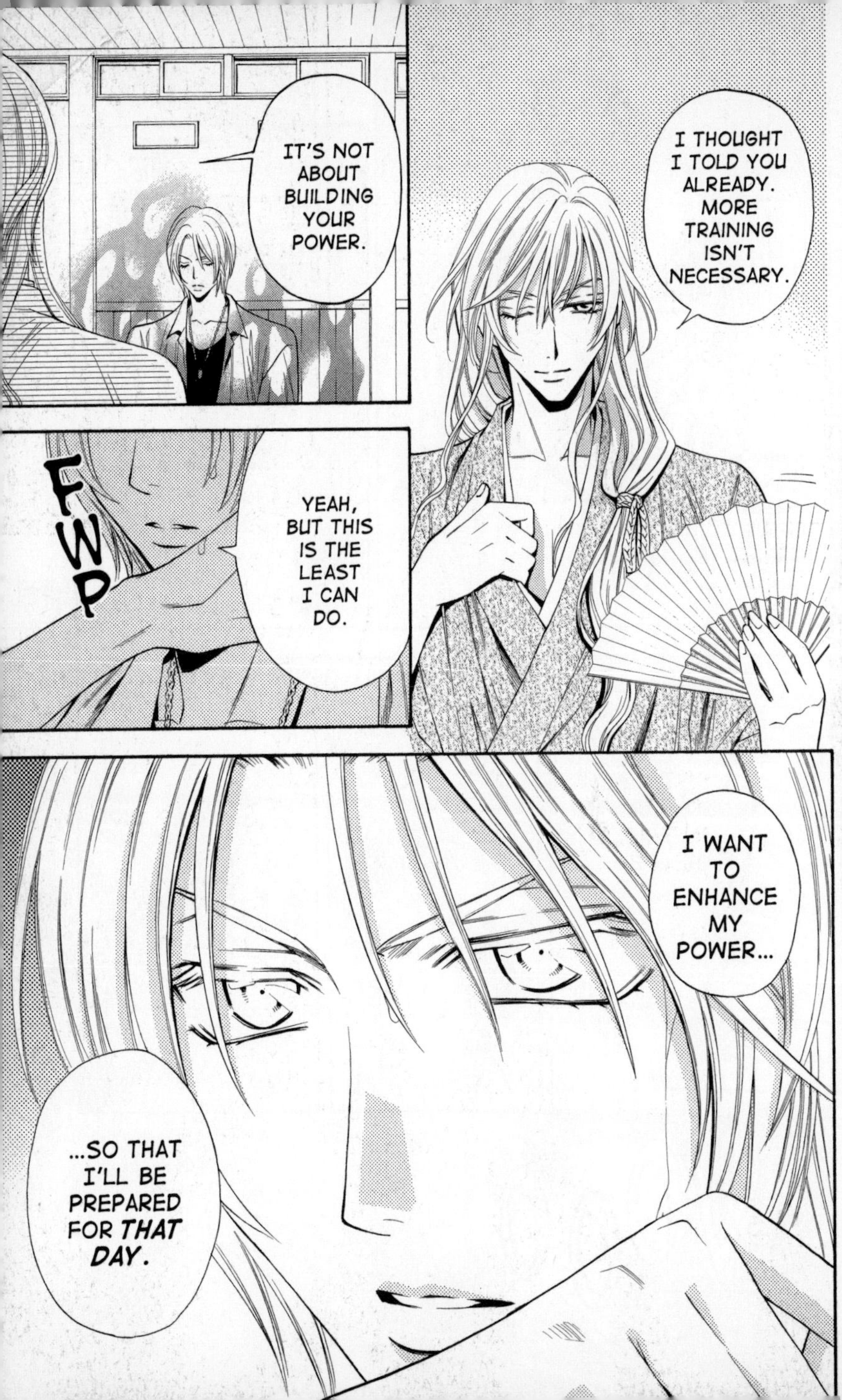
I THOUGHT I TOLD YOU ALREADY. MORE TRAINING ISN'T NECESSARY.
IT'S NOT ABOUT BUILDING YOUR POWER.
YEAH, BUT THIS IS THE LEAST I CAN DO.
FWP
I WANT TO ENHANCE MY POWER...
...SO THAT I'LL BE PREPARED FOR *THAT DAY*.

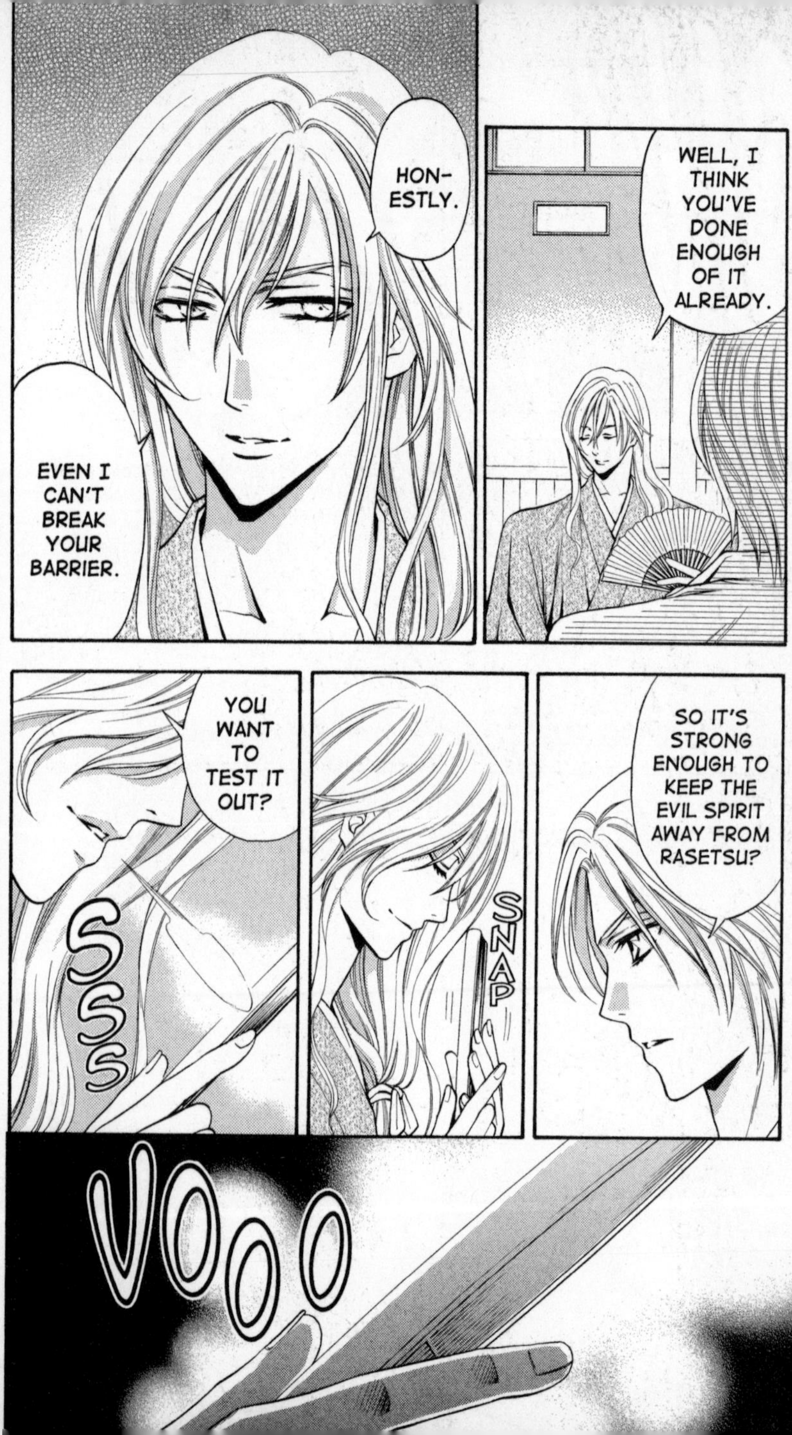
WELL, I THINK YOU'VE DONE ENOUGH OF IT ALREADY.
HON-ESTLY.
EVEN I CAN'T BREAK YOUR BARRIER.
SO IT'S STRONG ENOUGH TO KEEP THE EVIL SPIRIT AWAY FROM RASETSU?
SNAP
YOU WANT TO TEST IT OUT?
SSS
VOOO

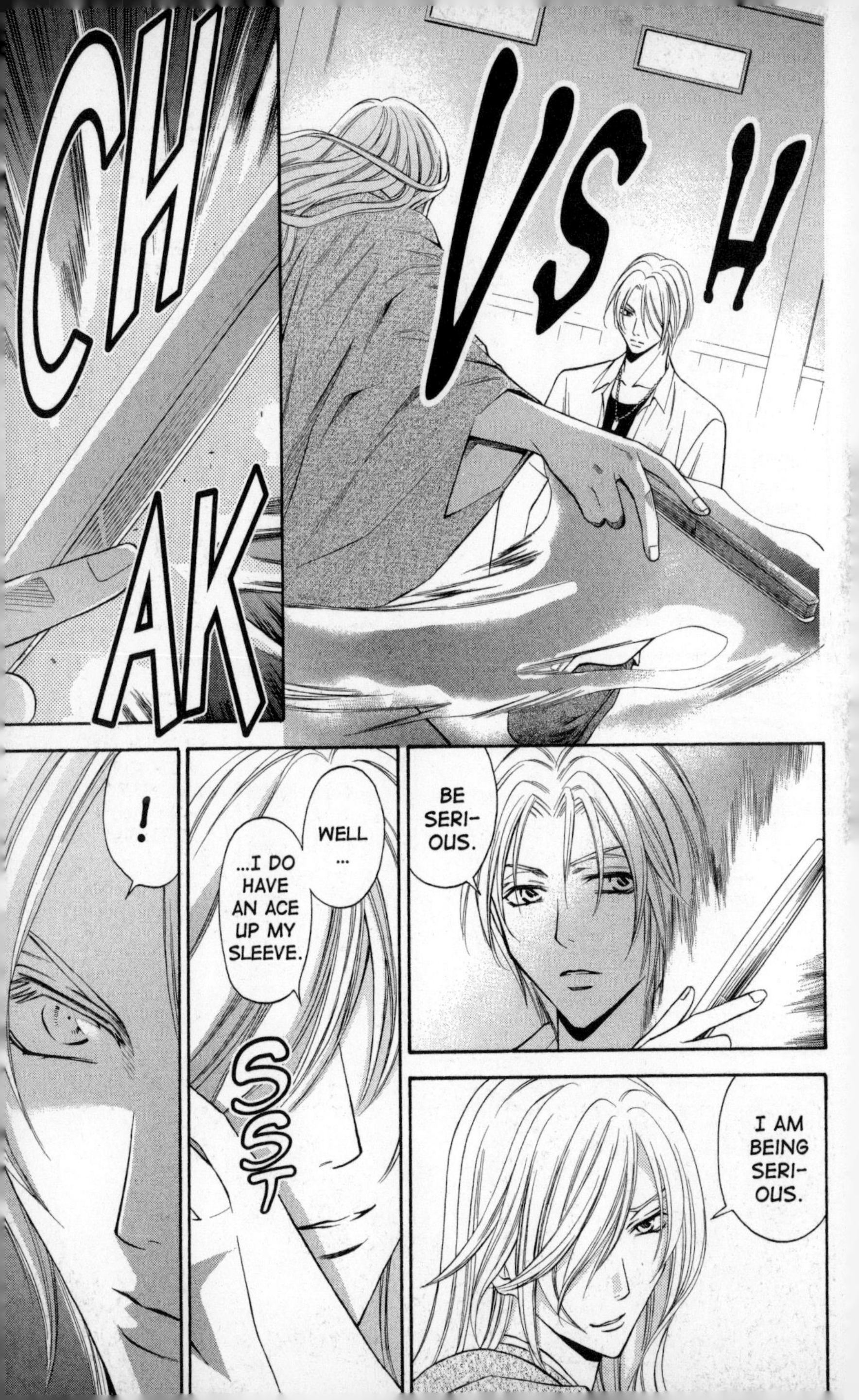
VSH
CH
AK
BE SERI- OUS.
I AM BEING SERI- OUS.
WELL ...
...I DO HAVE AN ACE UP MY SLEEVE.
SST
!

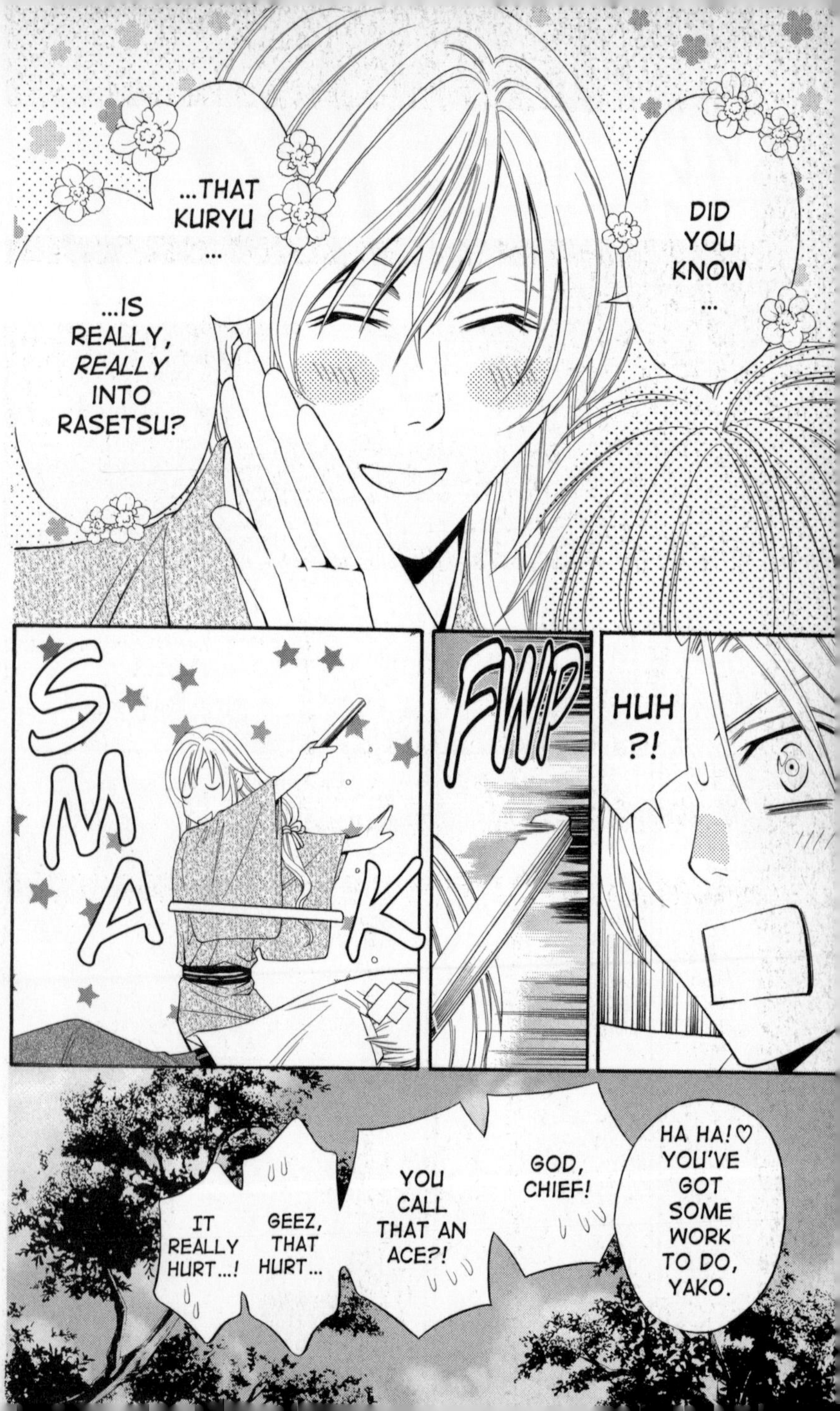
DID YOU KNOW ...
...THAT KURYU ...
...IS REALLY, *REALLY* INTO RASETSU?
HUH ?!
FWP
SMAK
HA HA! ♡ YOU'VE GOT SOME WORK TO DO, YAKO.
GOD, CHIEF!
YOU CALL THAT AN ACE?!
GEEZ, THAT HURT...
IT REALLY HURT...!

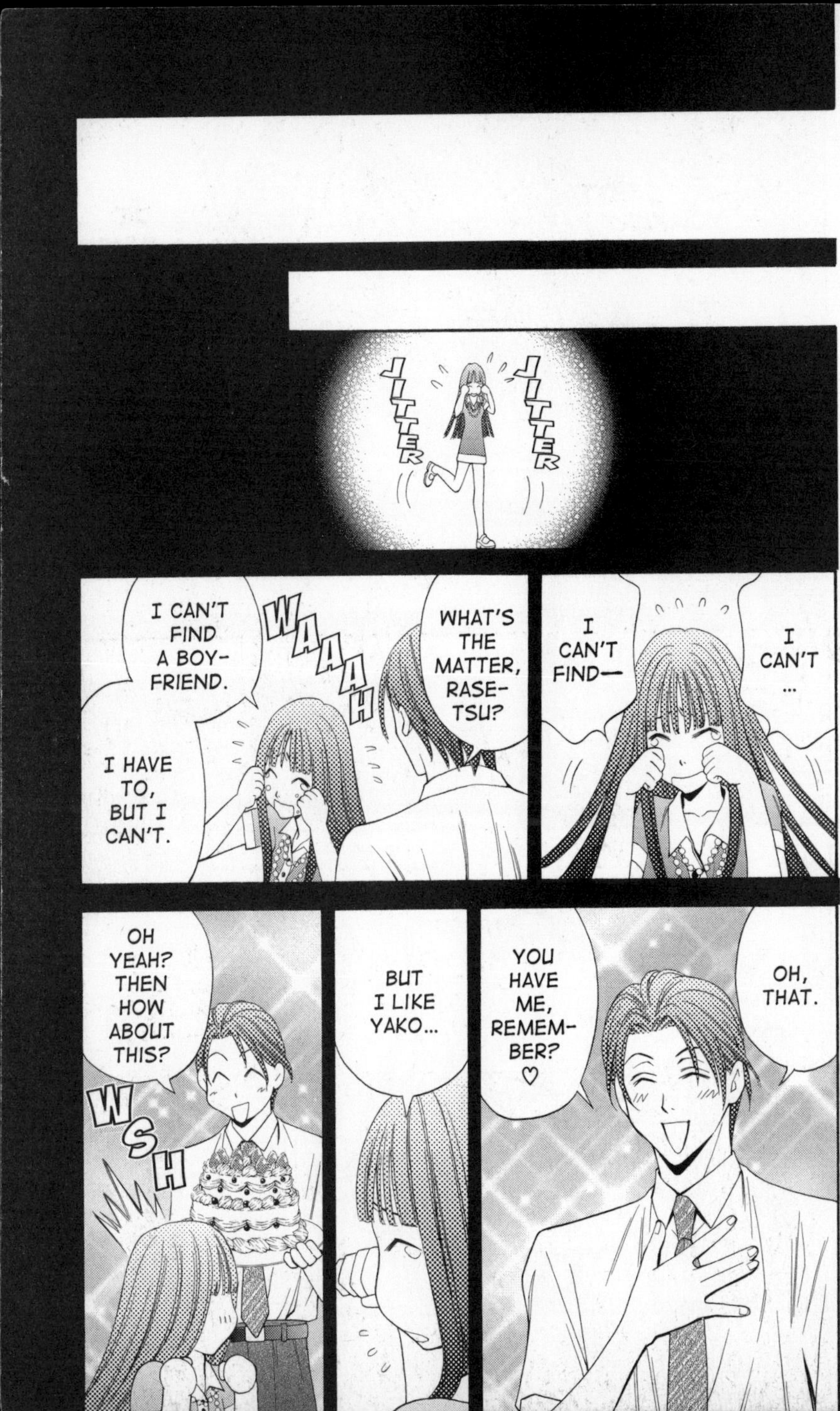
JITTER
JITTER
I CAN'T ...
I CAN'T FIND—
WHAT'S THE MATTER, RASE-TSU?
WAAAH
I CAN'T FIND A BOY-FRIEND.
I HAVE TO, BUT I CAN'T.
OH, THAT.
YOU HAVE ME, REMEM-BER? ♡
BUT I LIKE YAKO...
OH YEAH? THEN HOW ABOUT THIS?
WSH

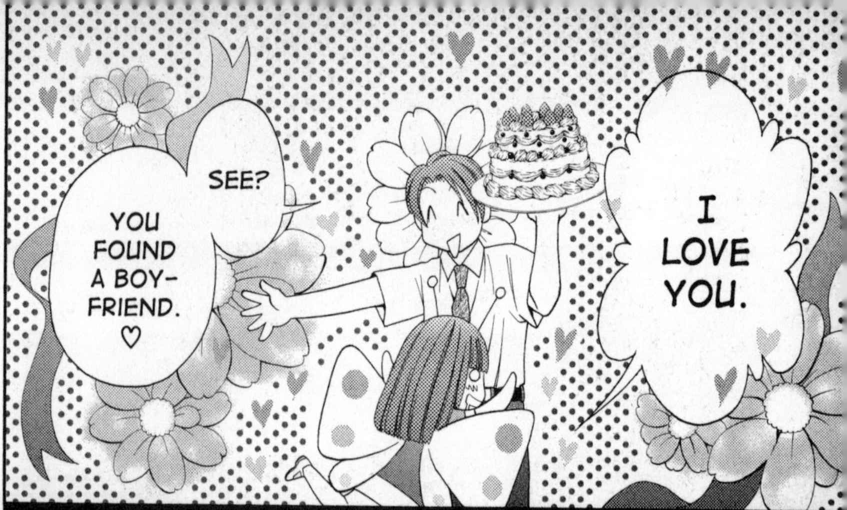
I LOVE YOU.
SEE?
YOU FOUND A BOY-FRIEND. ♡

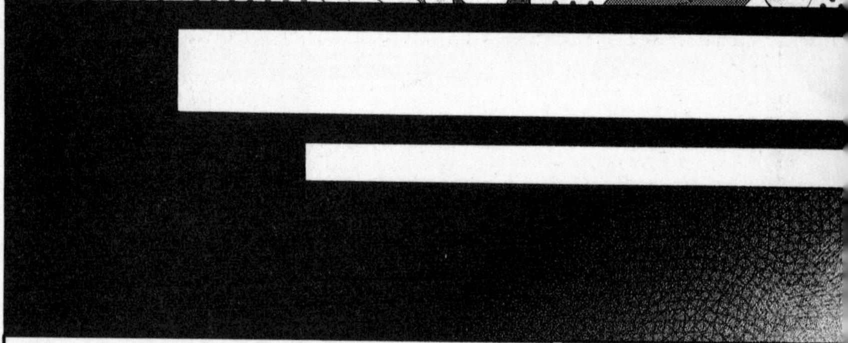

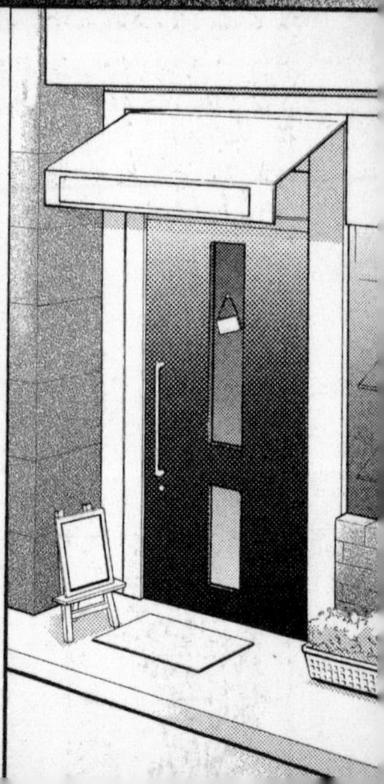

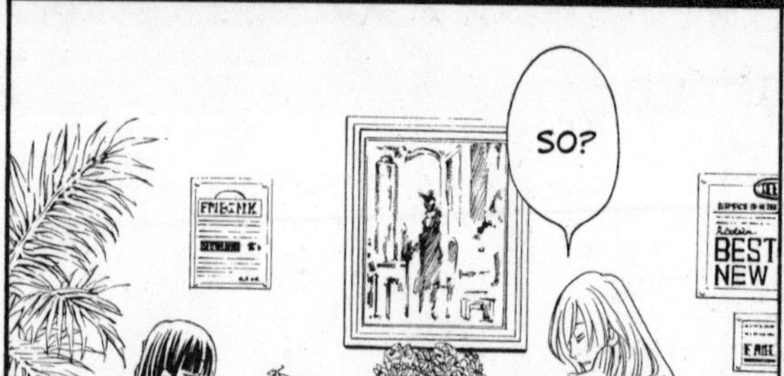
SO?

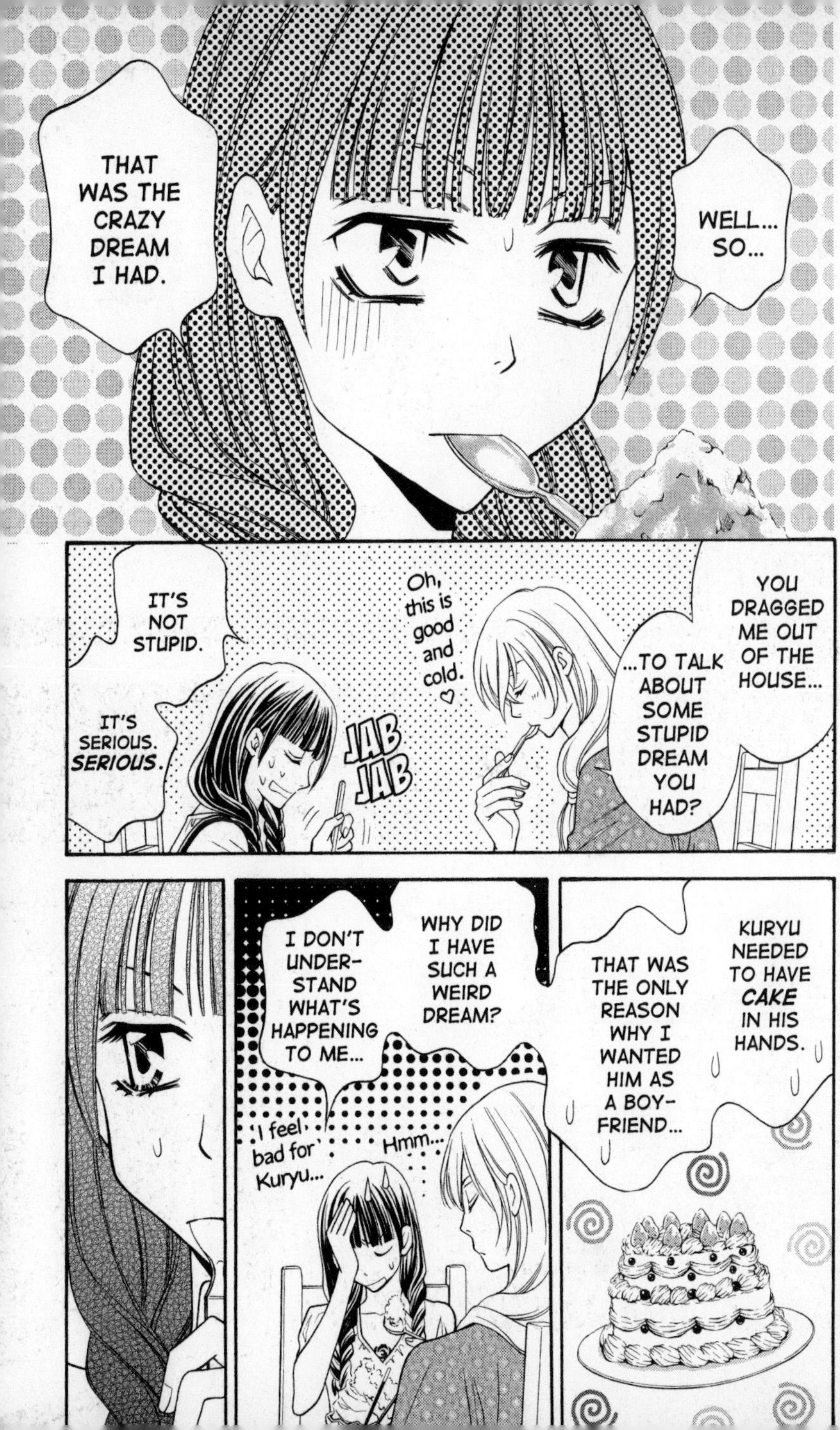
WELL... SO...
THAT WAS THE CRAZY DREAM I HAD.
YOU DRAGGED ME OUT OF THE HOUSE...
...TO TALK ABOUT SOME STUPID DREAM YOU HAD?
Oh, this is good and cold. ♡
JAB JAB
IT'S NOT STUPID.
IT'S SERIOUS. *SERIOUS*.
KURYU NEEDED TO HAVE *CAKE* IN HIS HANDS.
THAT WAS THE ONLY REASON WHY I WANTED HIM AS A BOY-FRIEND...
WHY DID I HAVE SUCH A WEIRD DREAM?
I DON'T UNDER-STAND WHAT'S HAPPENING TO ME...
Hmm...
I feel bad for Kuryu...

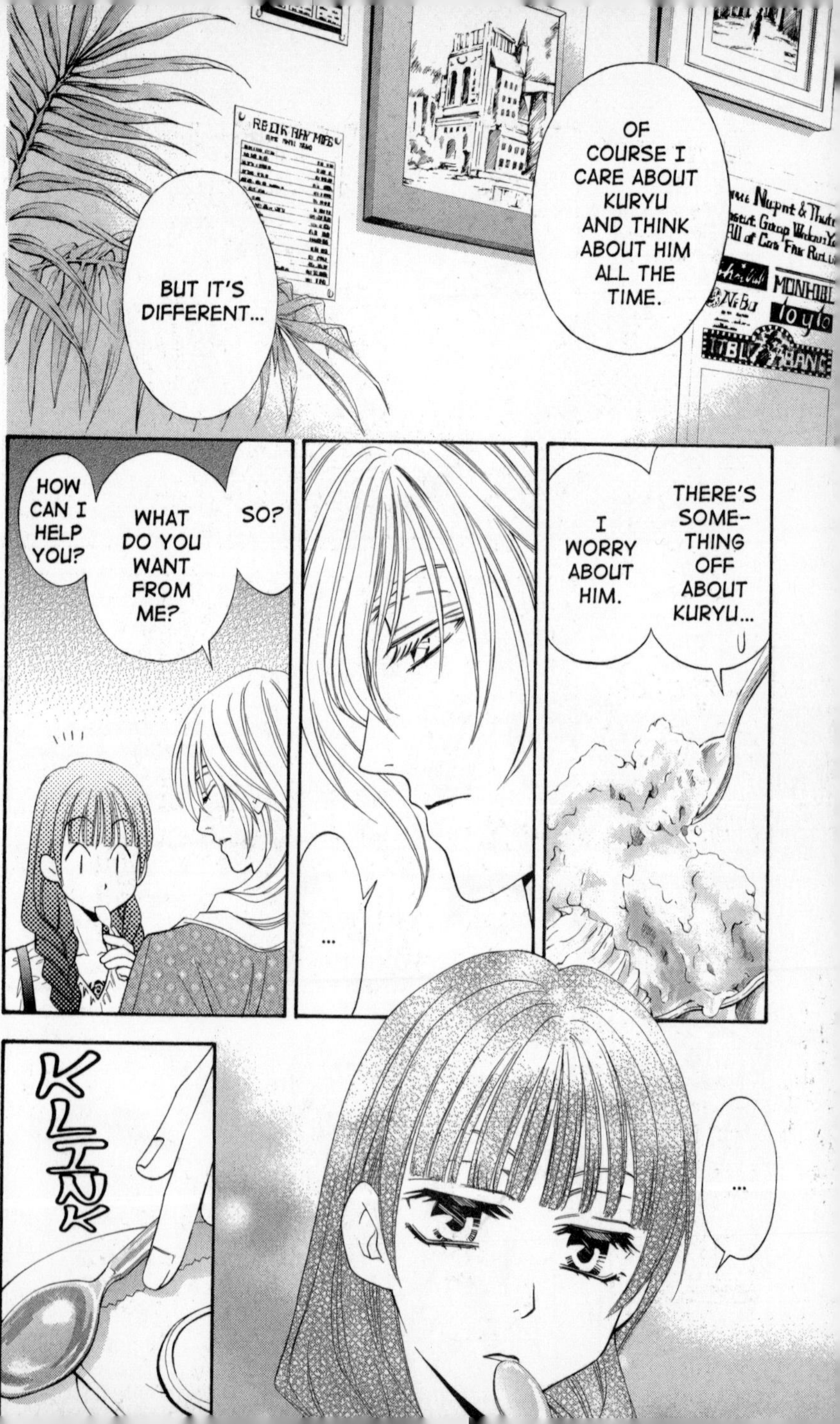
OF COURSE I CARE ABOUT KURYU AND THINK ABOUT HIM ALL THE TIME.
BUT IT'S DIFFERENT...
THERE'S SOME-THING OFF ABOUT KURYU...
I WORRY ABOUT HIM.
...
SO?
WHAT DO YOU WANT FROM ME?
HOW CAN I HELP YOU?
...
KLINK

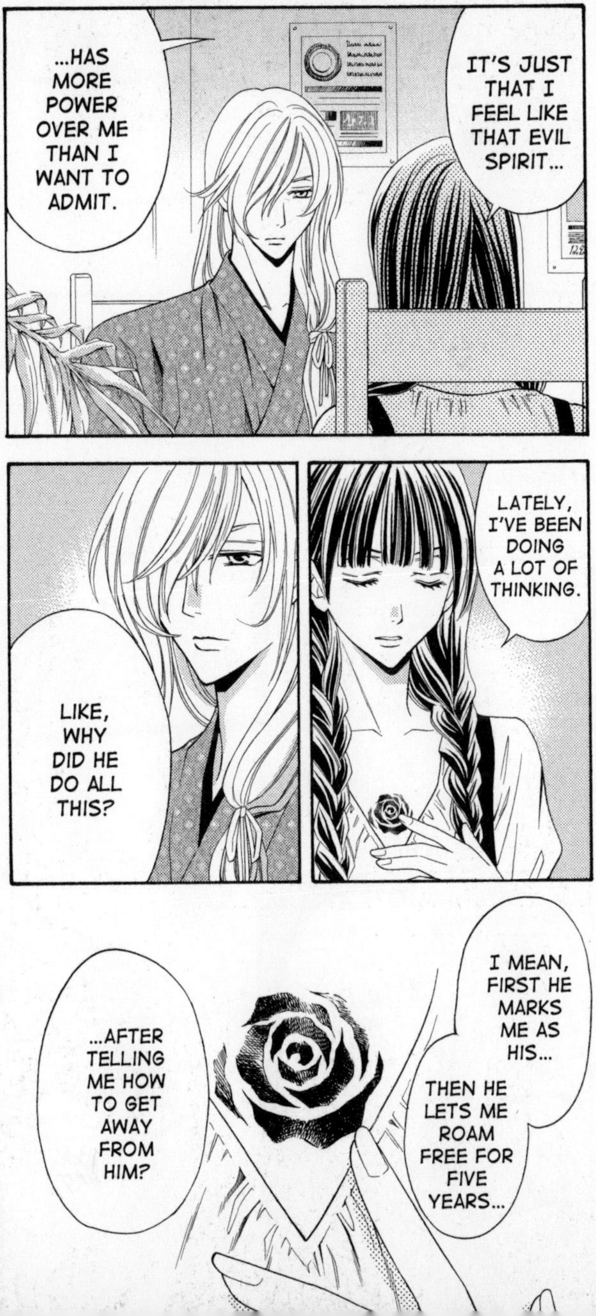
IT'S JUST THAT I FEEL LIKE THAT EVIL SPIRIT...
...HAS MORE POWER OVER ME THAN I WANT TO ADMIT.
LATELY, I'VE BEEN DOING A LOT OF THINKING.
LIKE, WHY DID HE DO ALL THIS?
I MEAN, FIRST HE MARKS ME AS HIS...
THEN HE LETS ME ROAM FREE FOR FIVE YEARS...
...AFTER TELLING ME HOW TO GET AWAY FROM HIM?

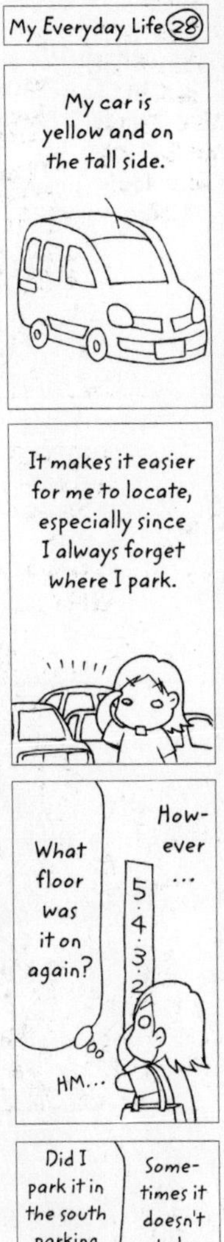
My Everyday Life 28
My car is yellow and on the tall side.
It makes it easier for me to locate, especially since I always forget where I park.
However...
What floor was it on again?
5 4 3 2
HM...
Sometimes it doesn't help a bit.
Did I park it in the south parking lot? Or was it in the north side?
HM...
DIRECTORY

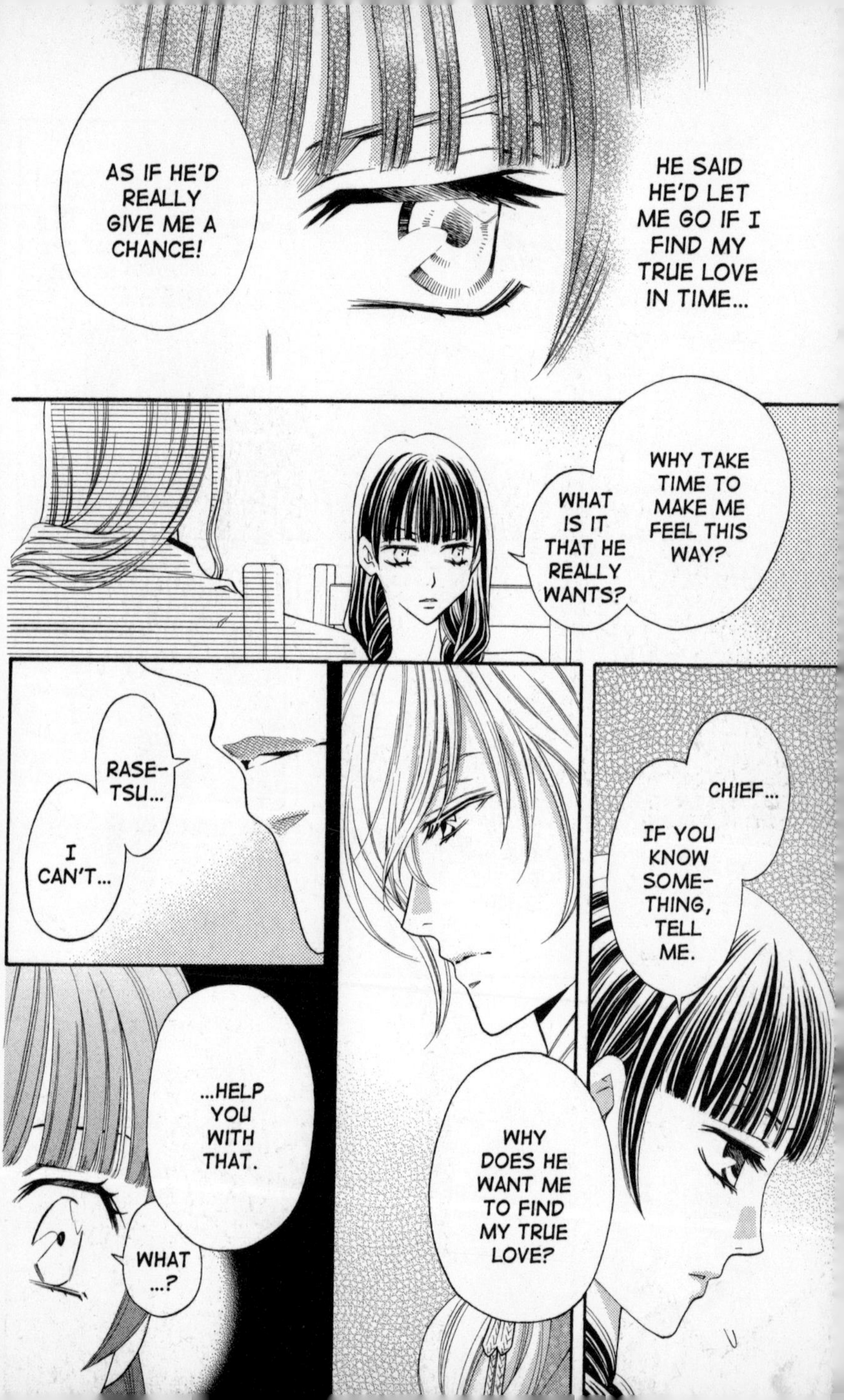
HE SAID HE'D LET ME GO IF I FIND MY TRUE LOVE IN TIME...
AS IF HE'D REALLY GIVE ME A CHANCE!
WHY TAKE TIME TO MAKE ME FEEL THIS WAY?
WHAT IS IT THAT HE REALLY WANTS?
CHIEF...
IF YOU KNOW SOMETHING, TELL ME.
WHY DOES HE WANT ME TO FIND MY TRUE LOVE?
RASE-TSU...
I CAN'T...
...HELP YOU WITH THAT.
WHAT ...?

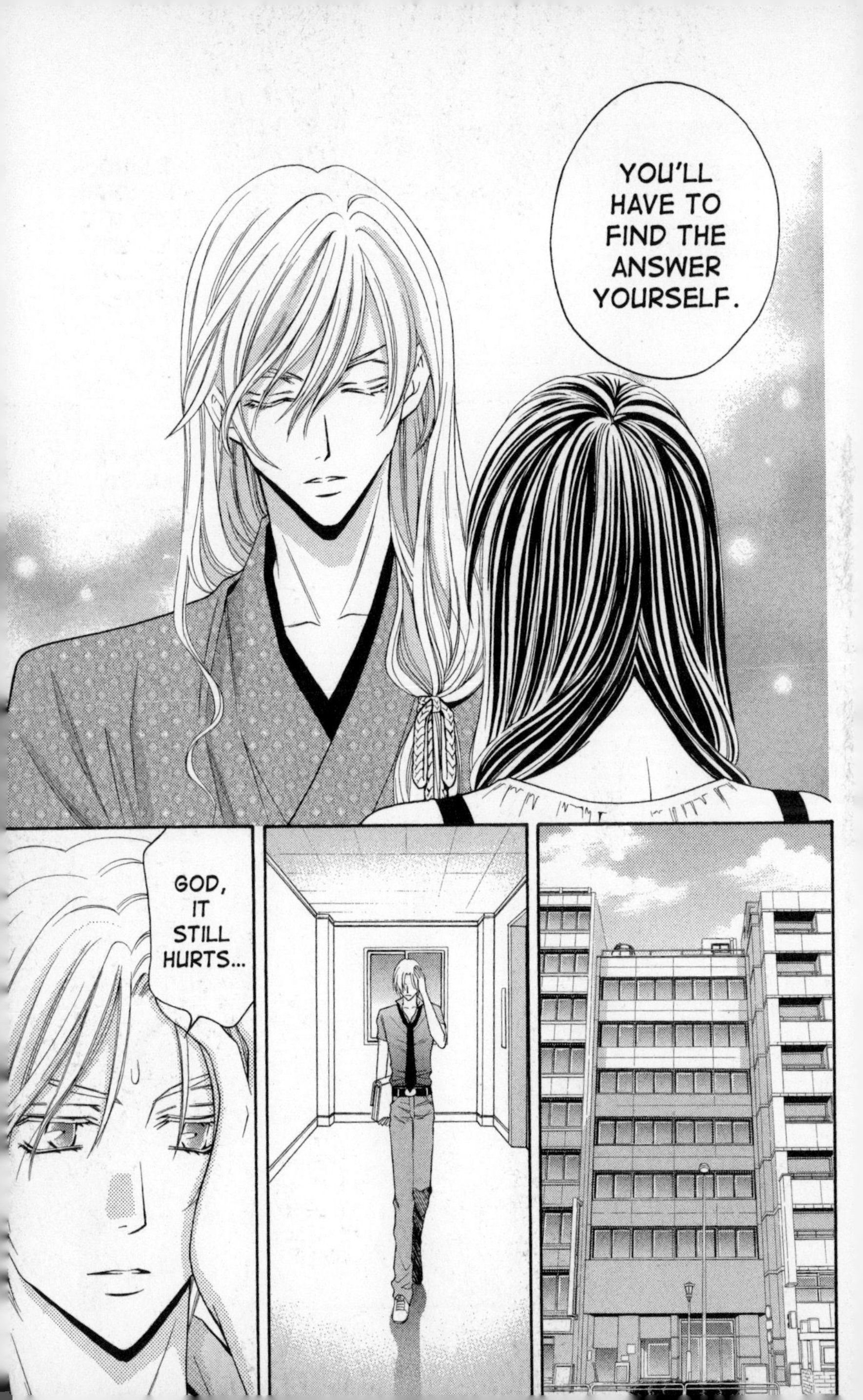
YOU'LL HAVE TO FIND THE ANSWER YOURSELF.
GOD, IT STILL HURTS...

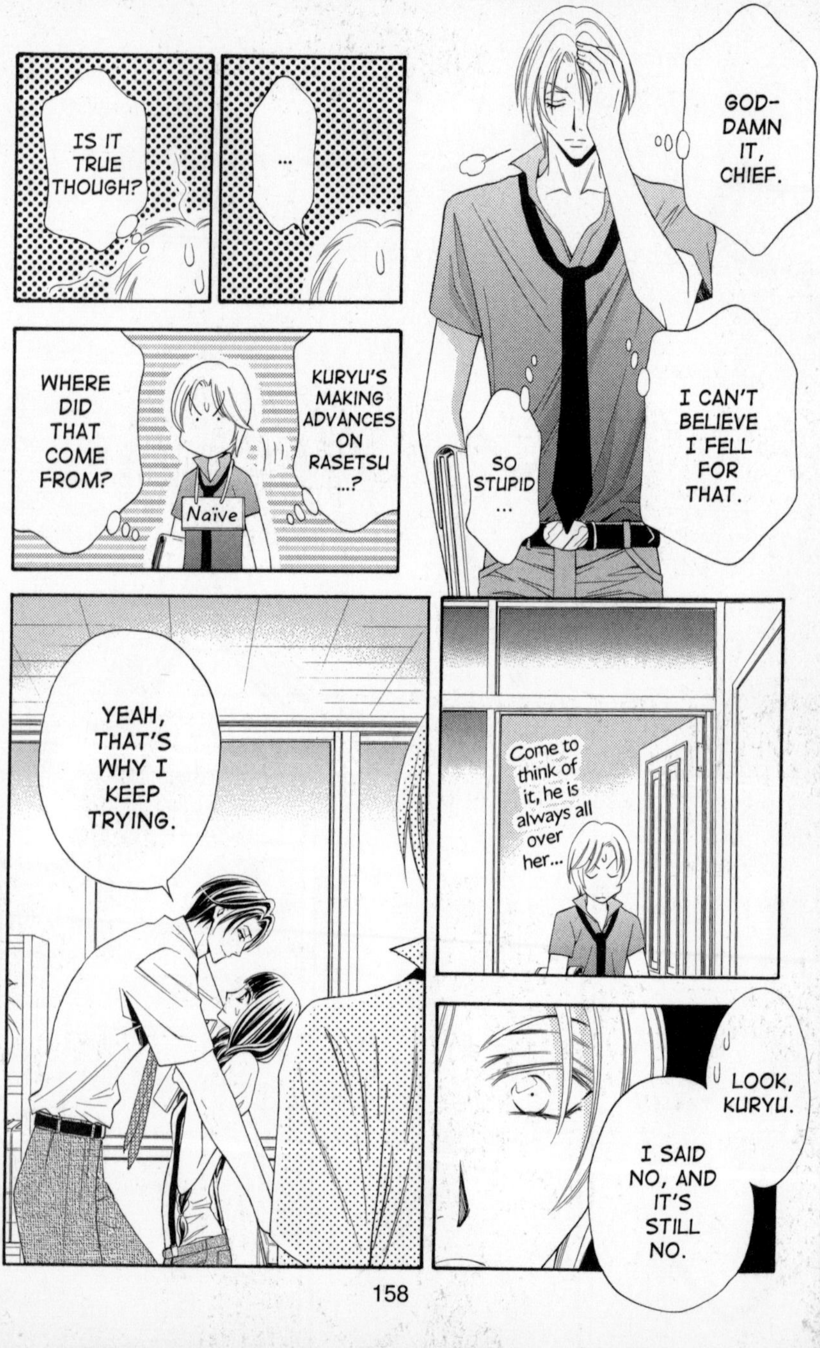
GOD-DAMN IT, CHIEF.
I CAN'T BELIEVE I FELL FOR THAT.
SO STUPID...
...
IS IT TRUE THOUGH?
KURYU'S MAKING ADVANCES ON RASETSU ...?
WHERE DID THAT COME FROM?
Naïve
Come to think of it, he is always all over her...
LOOK, KURYU.
I SAID NO, AND IT'S STILL NO.
YEAH, THAT'S WHY I KEEP TRYING.

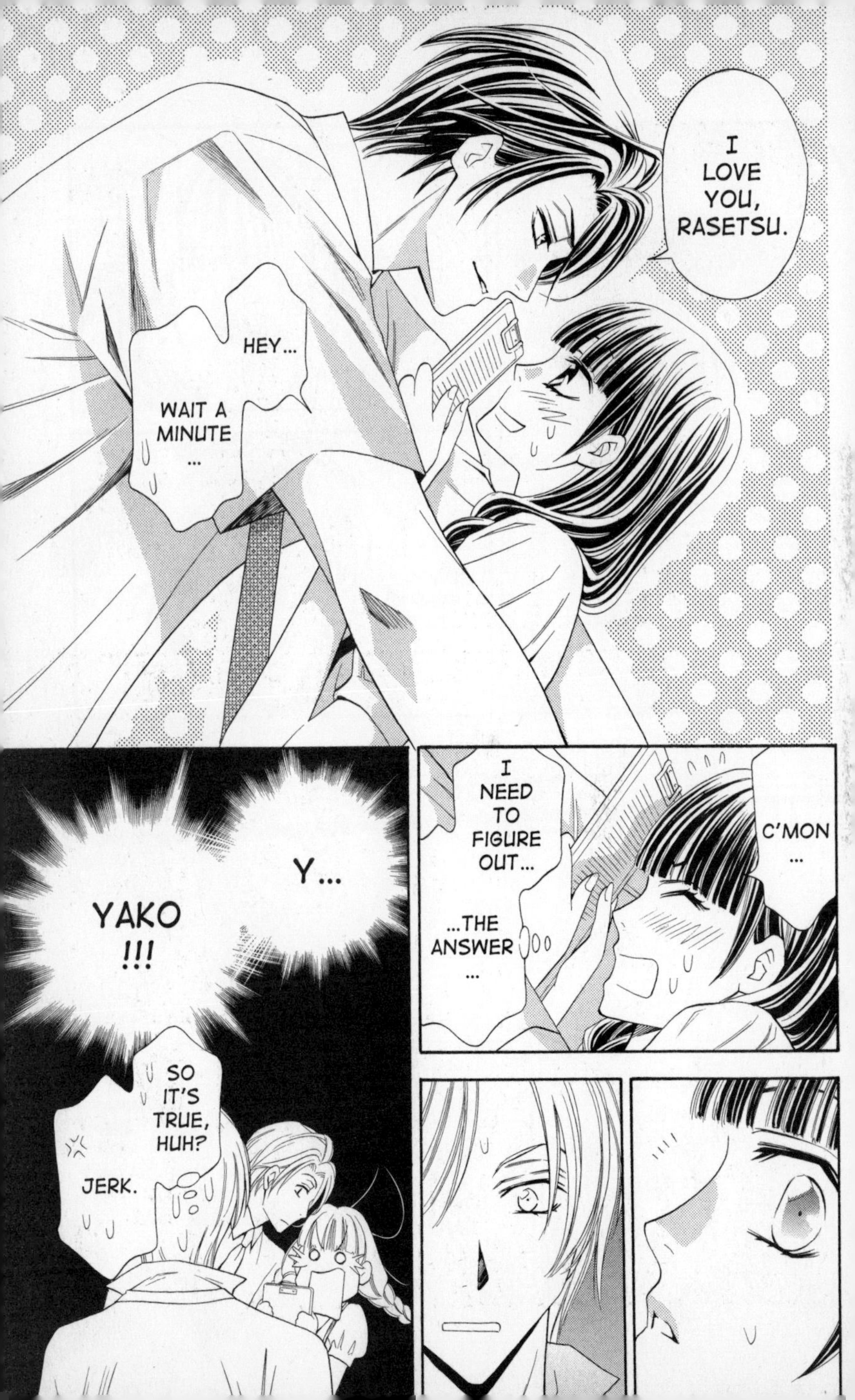
I LOVE YOU, RASETSU.
HEY...
WAIT A MINUTE ...
C'MON ...
I NEED TO FIGURE OUT...
...THE ANSWER ...
Y...
YAKO !!!
SO IT'S TRUE, HUH?
JERK.

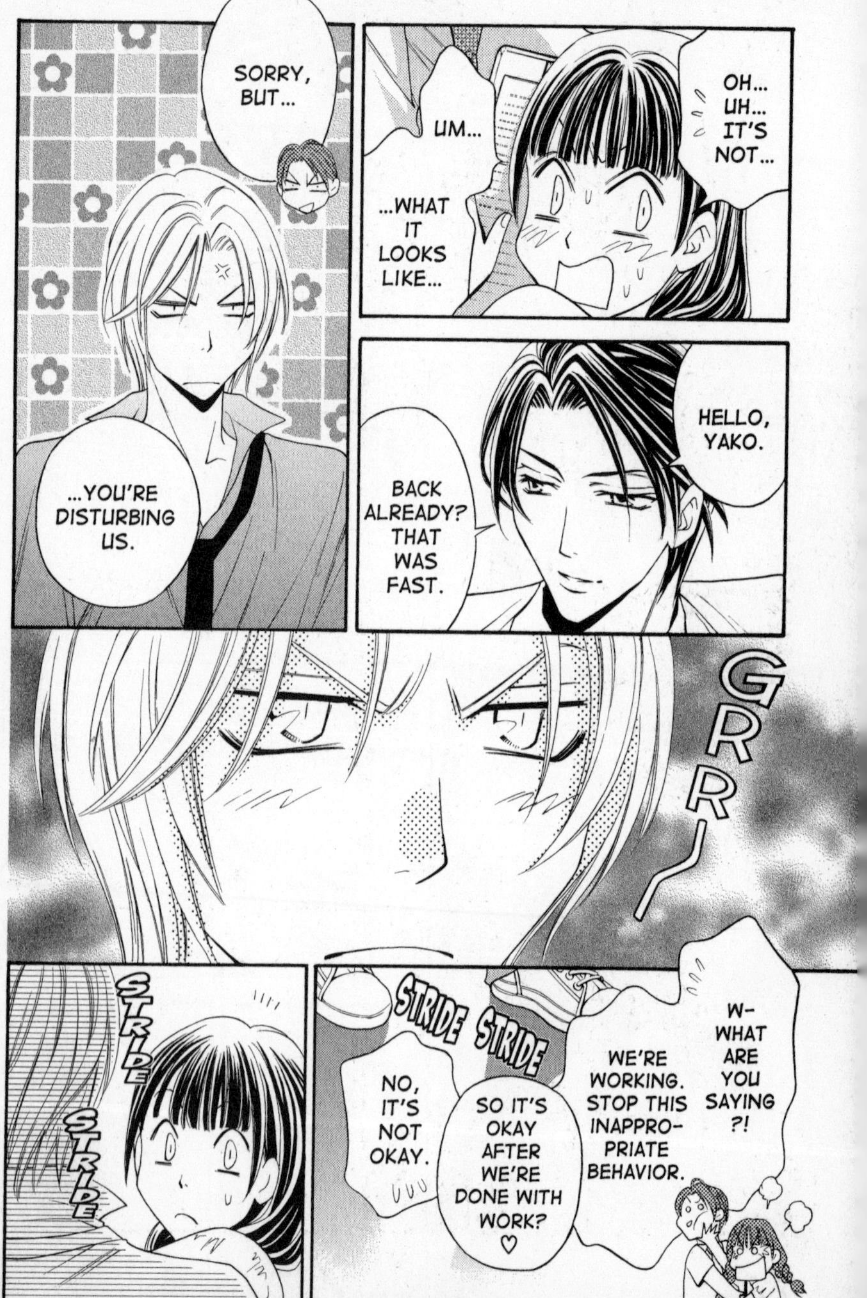
OH... UH... IT'S NOT...
UM...
...WHAT IT LOOKS LIKE...
HELLO, YAKO.
BACK ALREADY? THAT WAS FAST.
SORRY, BUT...
...YOU'RE DISTURBING US.
GRR
W-WHAT ARE YOU SAYING?!
WE'RE WORKING. STOP THIS INAPPRO-PRIATE BEHAVIOR.
SO IT'S OKAY AFTER WE'RE DONE WITH WORK? ♡
NO, IT'S NOT OKAY.
STRIDE STRIDE
STRIDE STRIDE

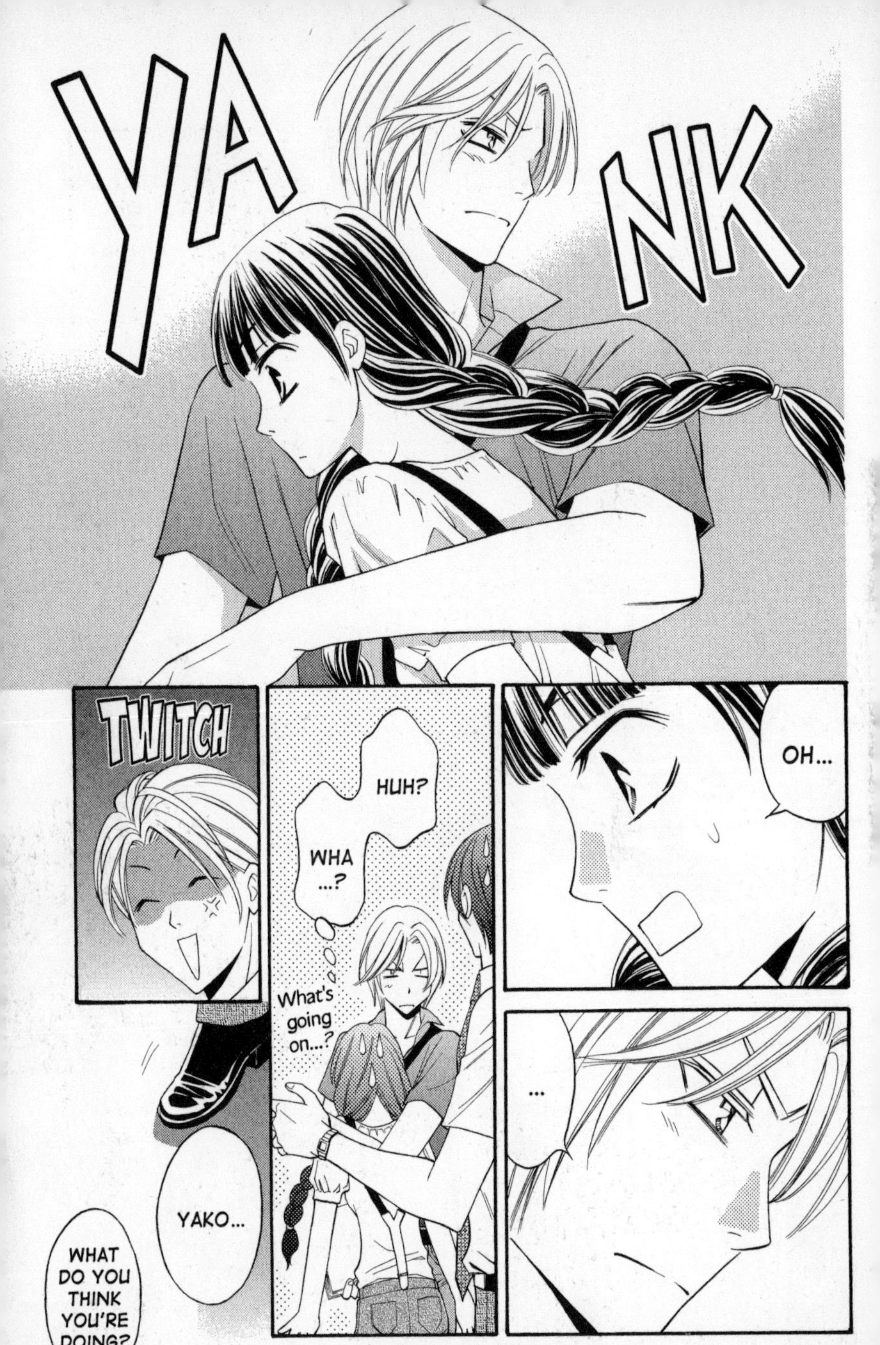
YANK
OH...
...
HUH?
WHA ...?
What's going on...?
TWITCH
YAKO...
WHAT DO YOU THINK YOU'RE DOING?

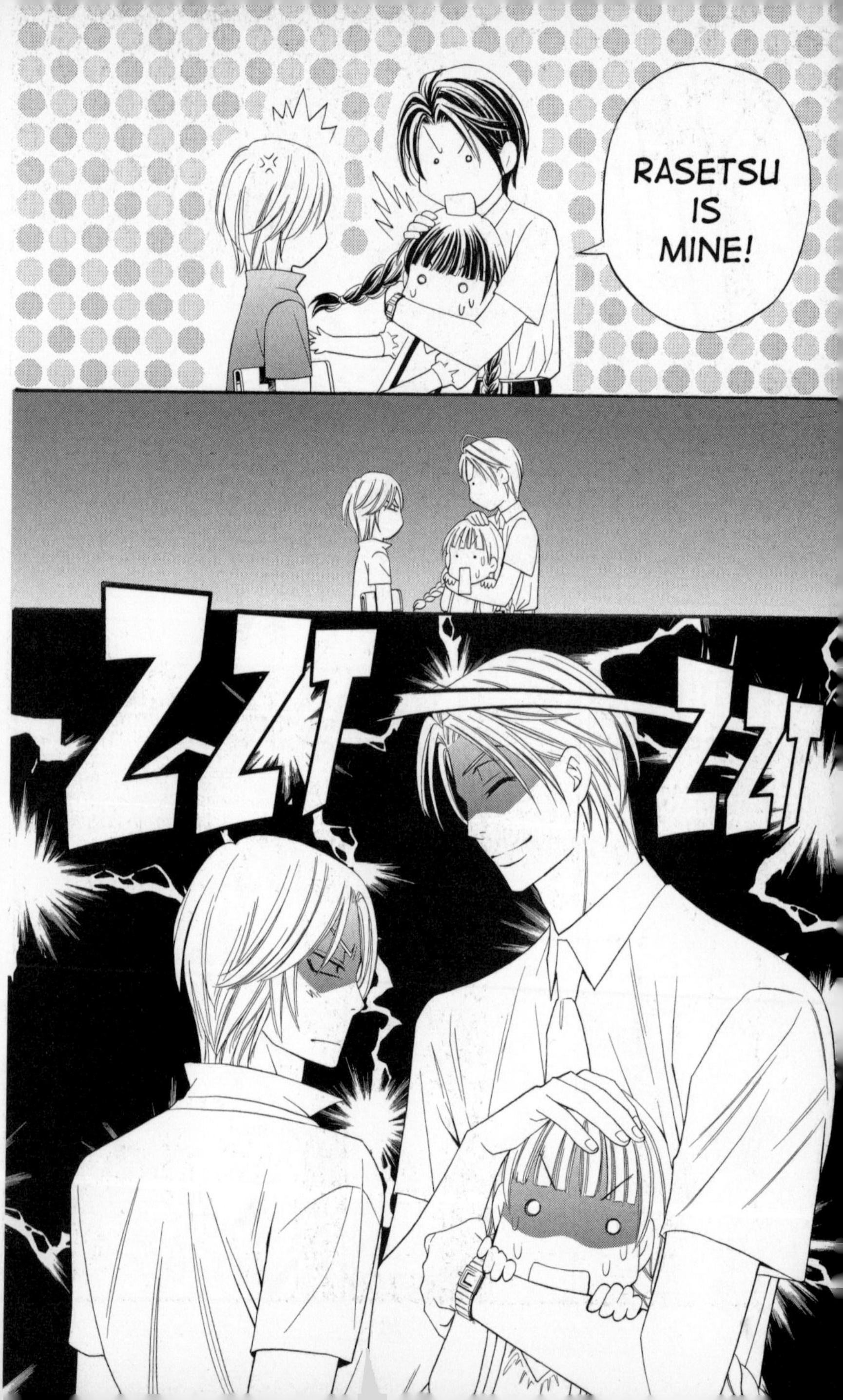
RASETSU IS MINE!
ZZT
ZZT

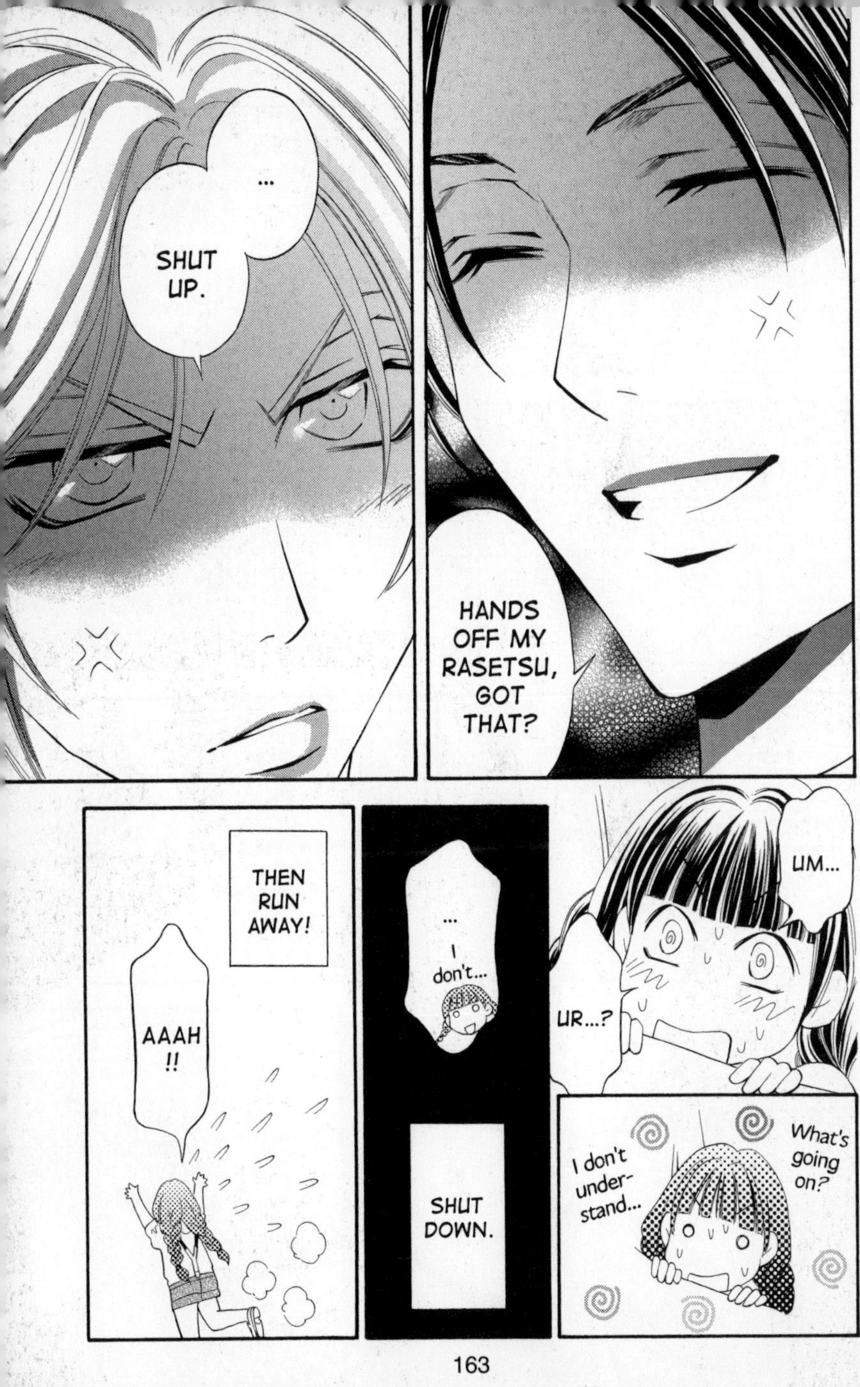
HANDS OFF MY RASETSU, GOT THAT?
...
SHUT UP.
UM...
UR...?
What's going on?
I don't under-stand...
...
I don't...
SHUT DOWN.
THEN RUN AWAY!
AAAH!!

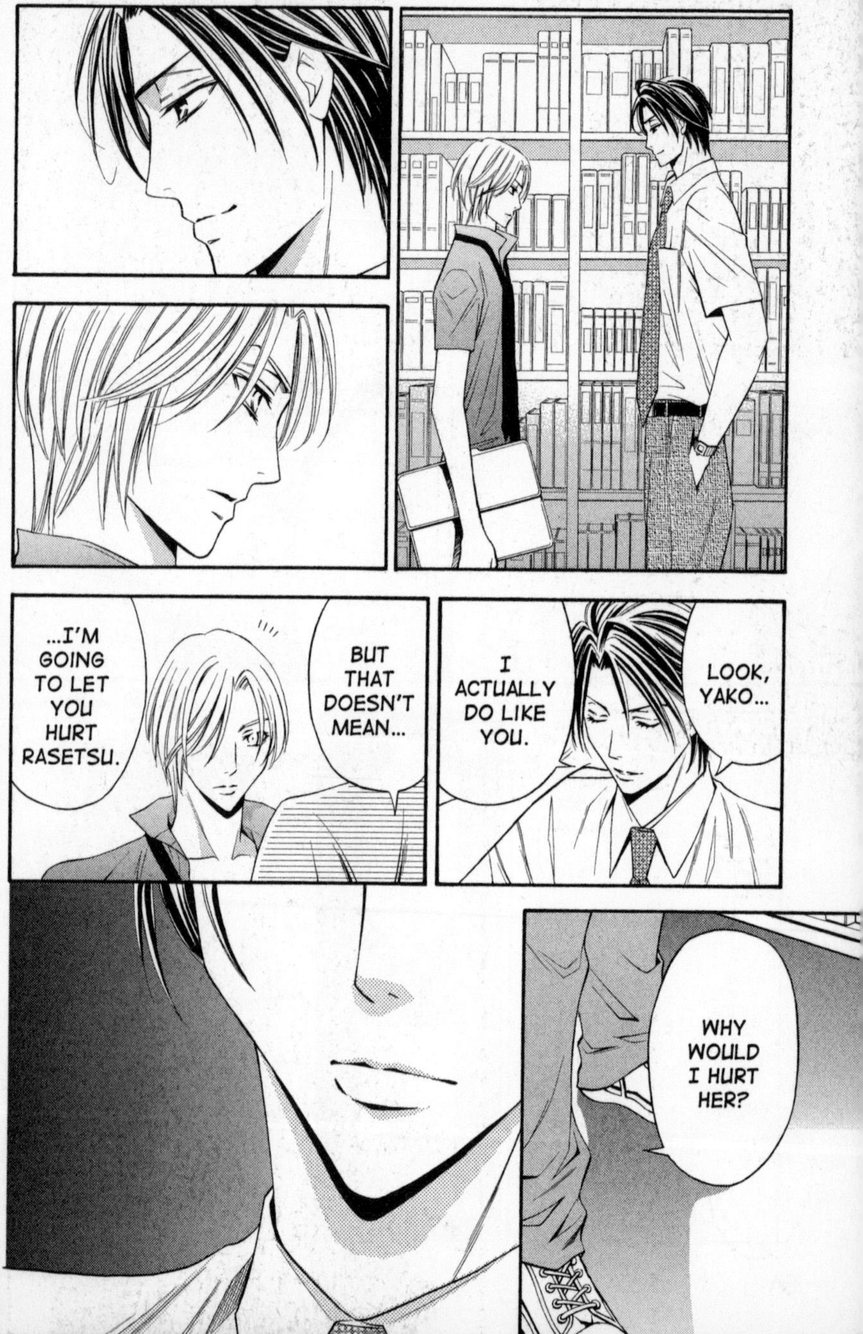
LOOK, YAKO...
I ACTUALLY DO LIKE YOU.
BUT THAT DOESN'T MEAN...
...I'M GOING TO LET YOU HURT RASETSU.
WHY WOULD I HURT HER?

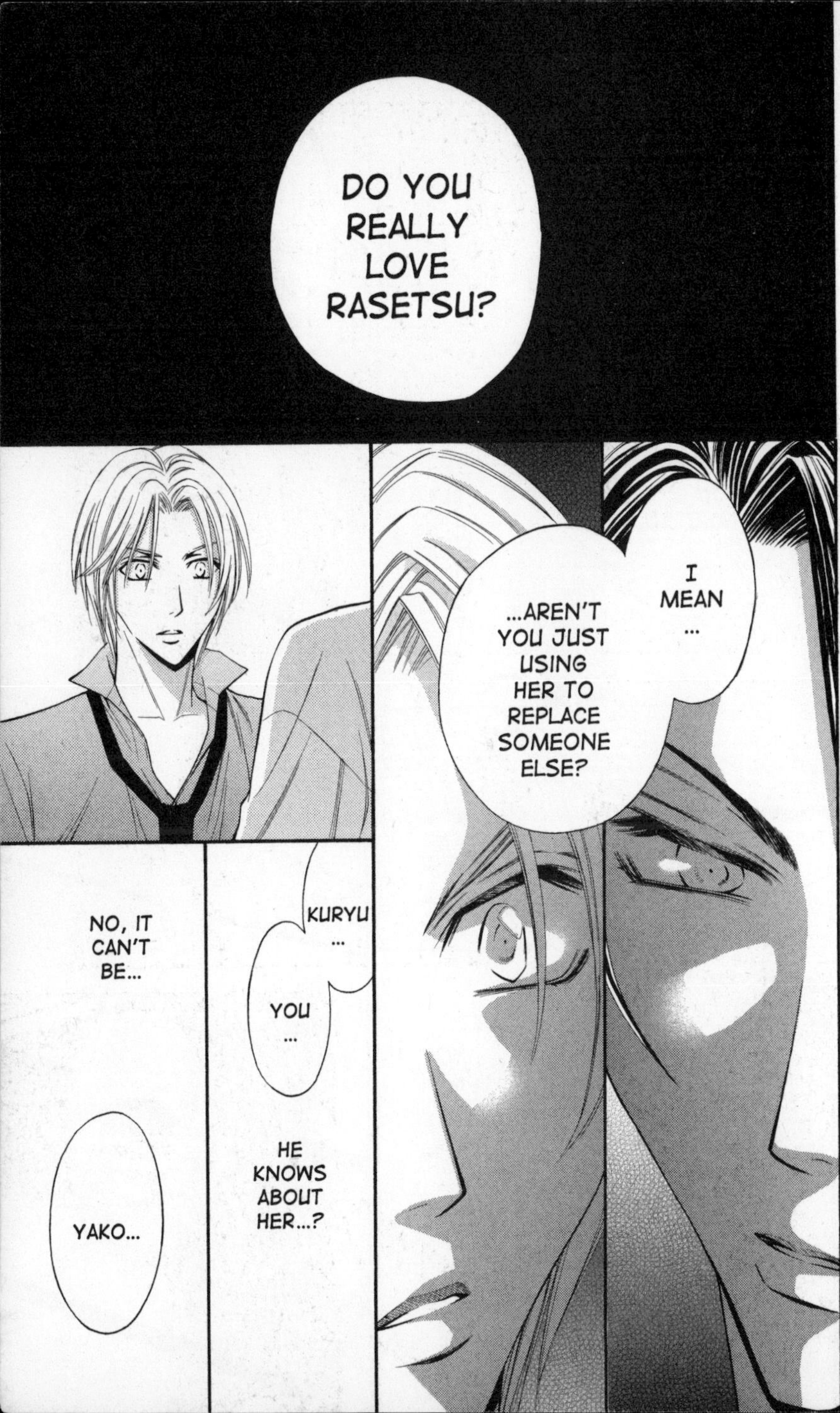
DO YOU REALLY LOVE RASETSU?
I MEAN ...
...AREN'T YOU JUST USING HER TO REPLACE SOMEONE ELSE?
KURYU ...
YOU ...
HE KNOWS ABOUT HER...?
NO, IT CAN'T BE...
YAKO...

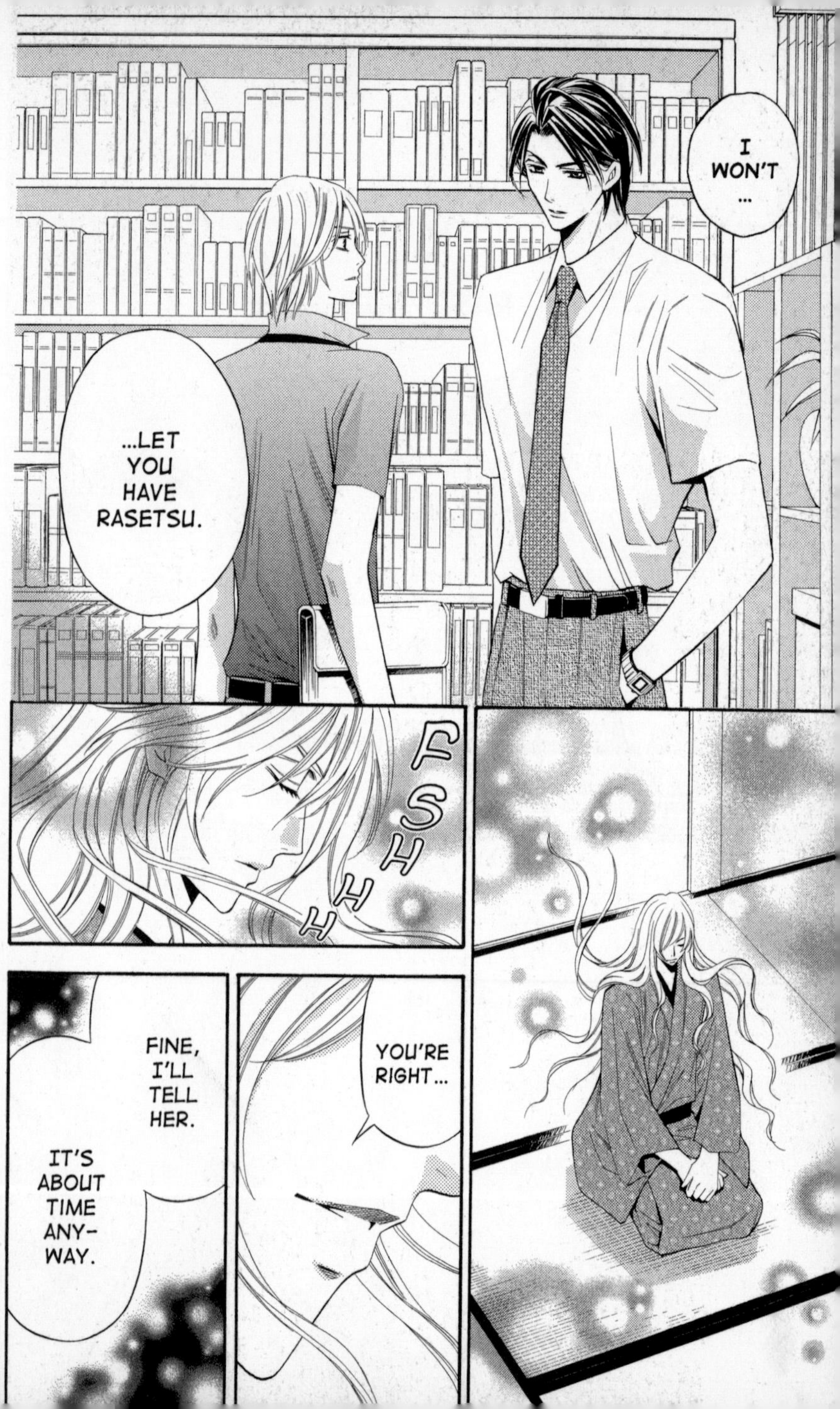
I WON'T ...
...LET YOU HAVE RASETSU.
FSHHHH
YOU'RE RIGHT...
FINE, I'LL TELL HER.
IT'S ABOUT TIME ANY-WAY.

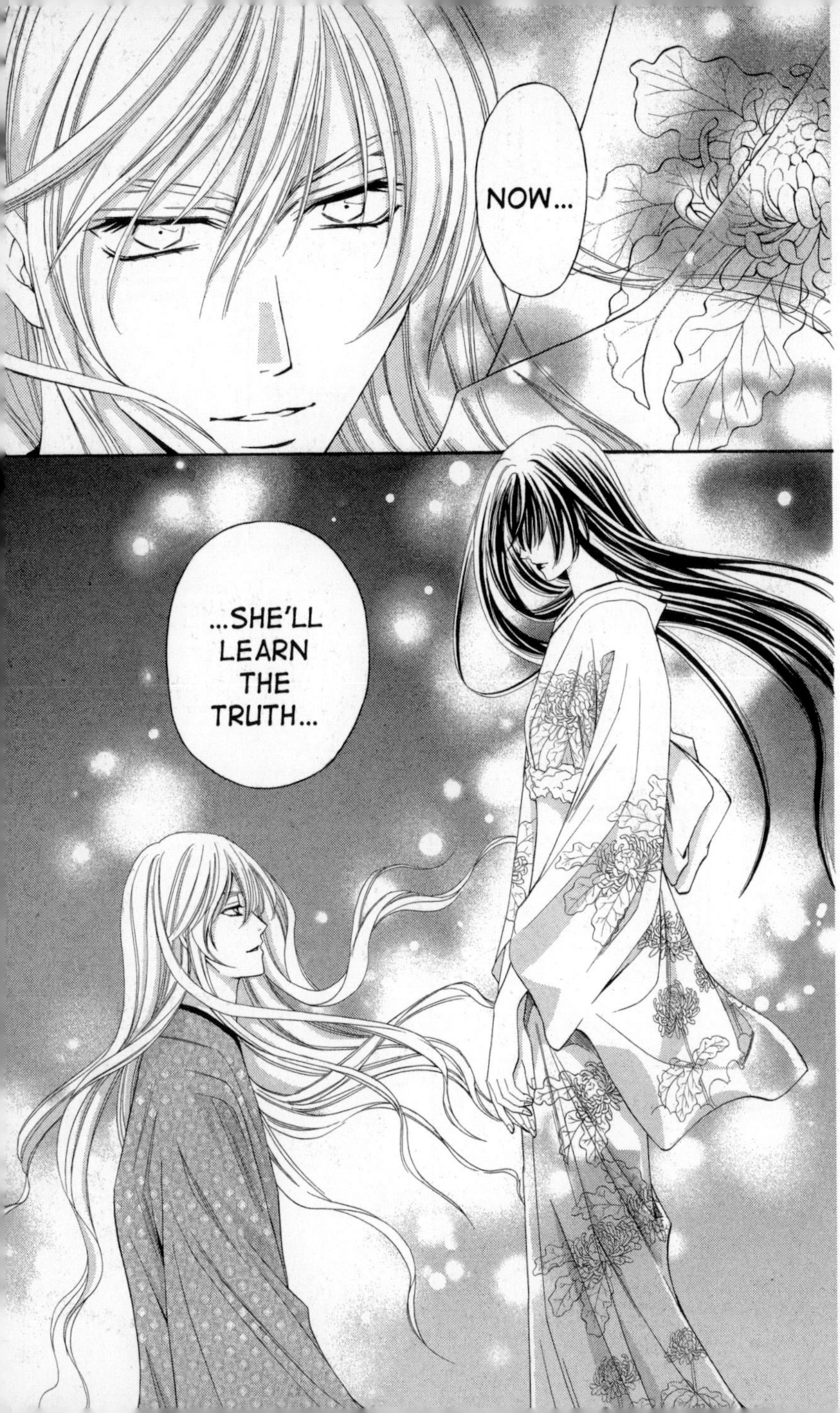
NOW...
...SHE'LL LEARN THE TRUTH...

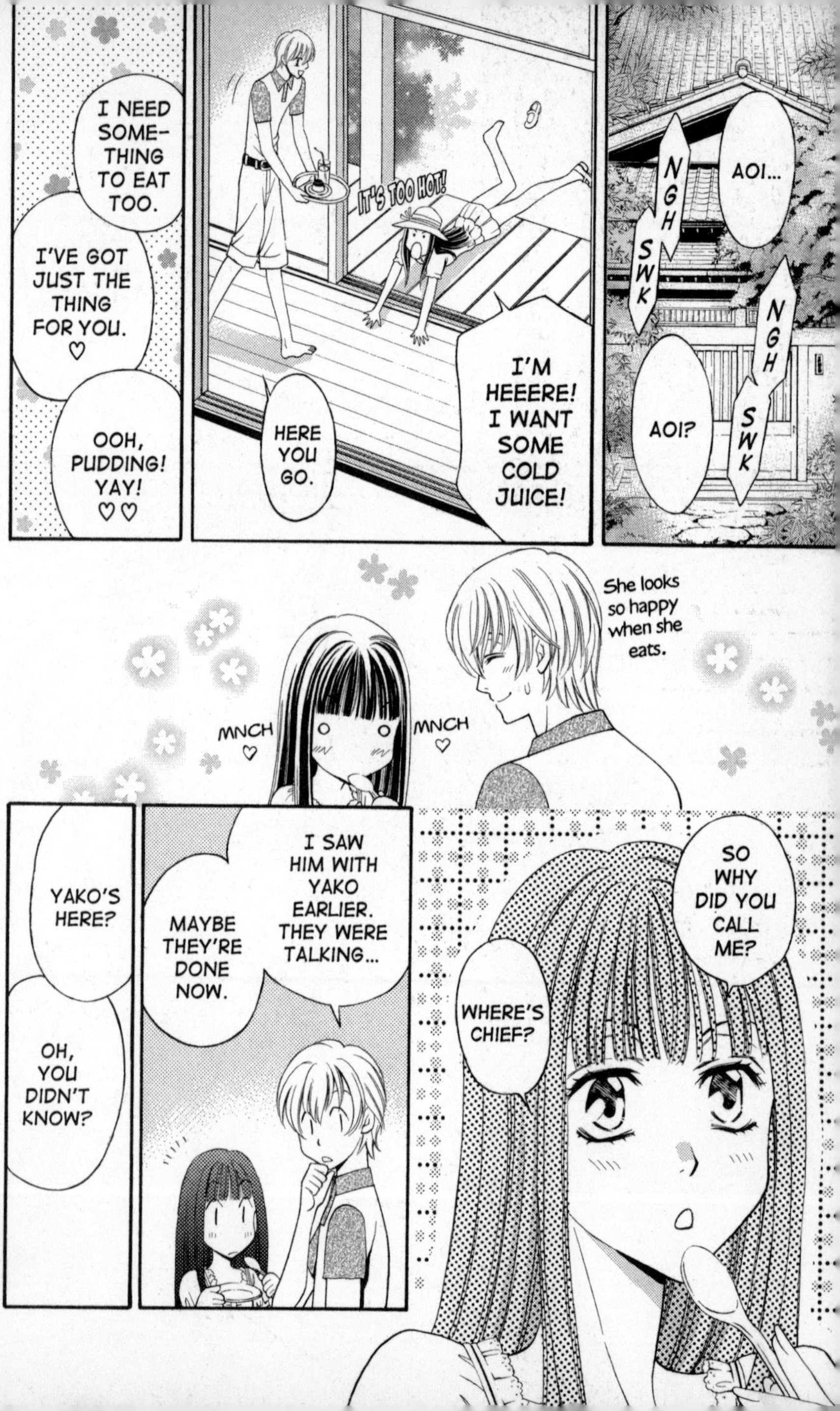
AOI...
NGH
SWK
AOI?
NGH
SWK
I'M HEEERE! I WANT SOME COLD JUICE!
IT'S TOO HOT!
HERE YOU GO.
I NEED SOMETHING TO EAT TOO.
I'VE GOT JUST THE THING FOR YOU. ♡
OOH, PUDDING! YAY! ♡♡
She looks so happy when she eats.
MNCH ♡
MNCH ♡
SO WHY DID YOU CALL ME?
WHERE'S CHIEF?
I SAW HIM WITH YAKO EARLIER. THEY WERE TALKING...
MAYBE THEY'RE DONE NOW.
YAKO'S HERE?
OH, YOU DIDN'T KNOW?

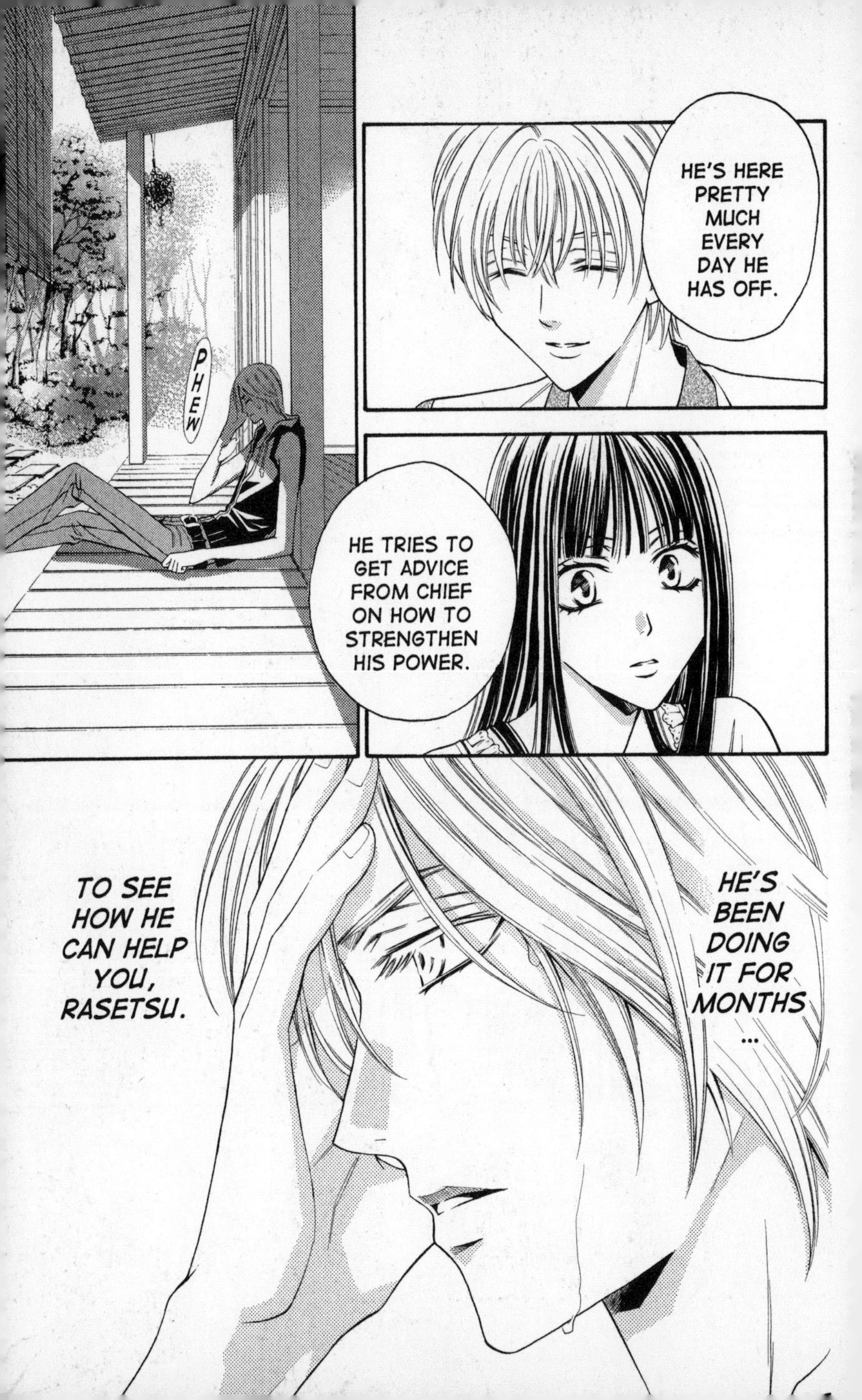
HE'S HERE PRETTY MUCH EVERY DAY HE HAS OFF.
HE TRIES TO GET ADVICE FROM CHIEF ON HOW TO STRENGTHEN HIS POWER.
PHEW
HE'S BEEN DOING IT FOR MONTHS...
TO SEE HOW HE CAN HELP YOU, RASETSU.

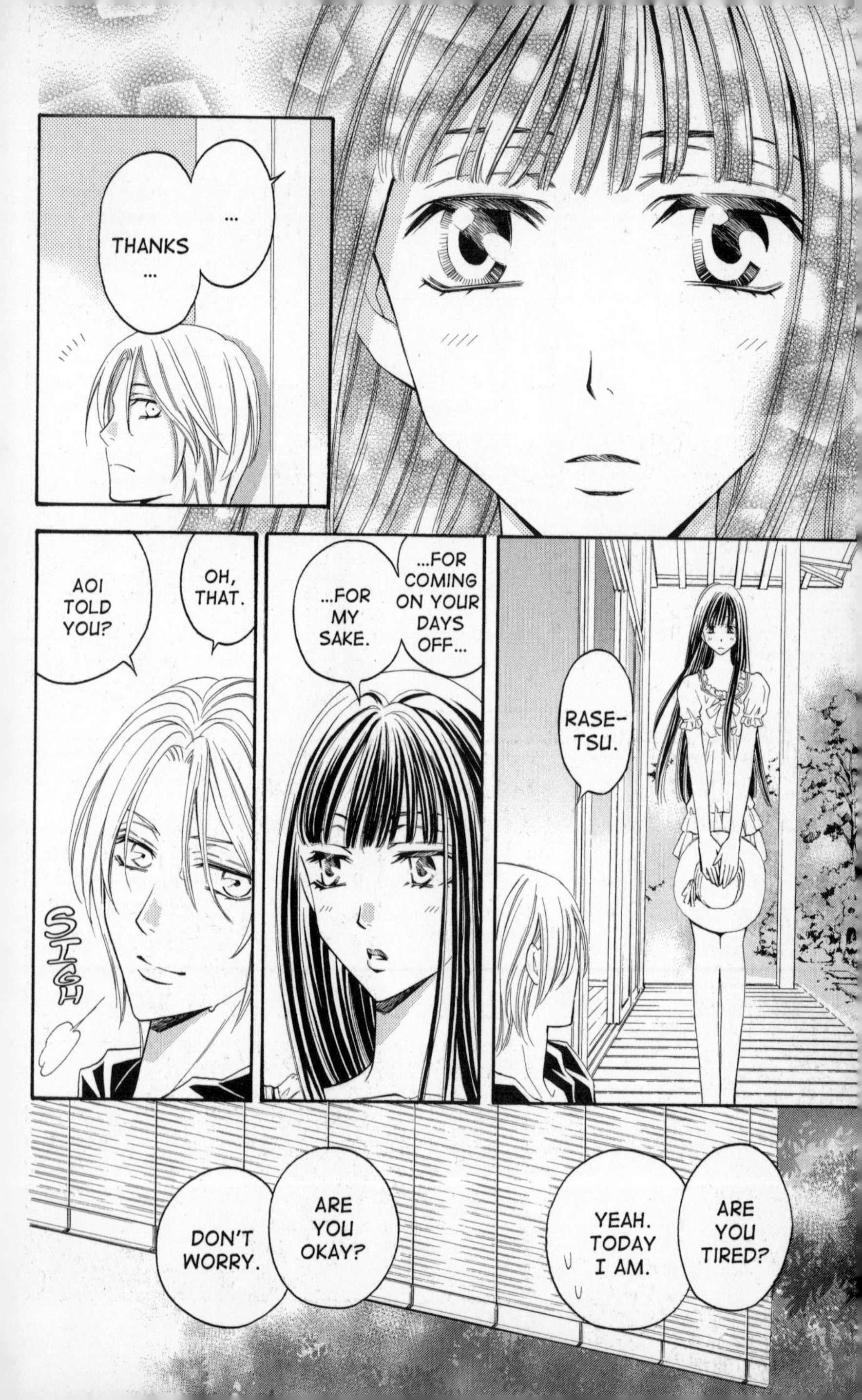
... THANKS ...
RASE-TSU.
...FOR COMING ON YOUR DAYS OFF...
...FOR MY SAKE.
OH, THAT.
AOI TOLD YOU?
SIGH
ARE YOU TIRED?
YEAH. TODAY I AM.
ARE YOU OKAY?
DON'T WORRY.

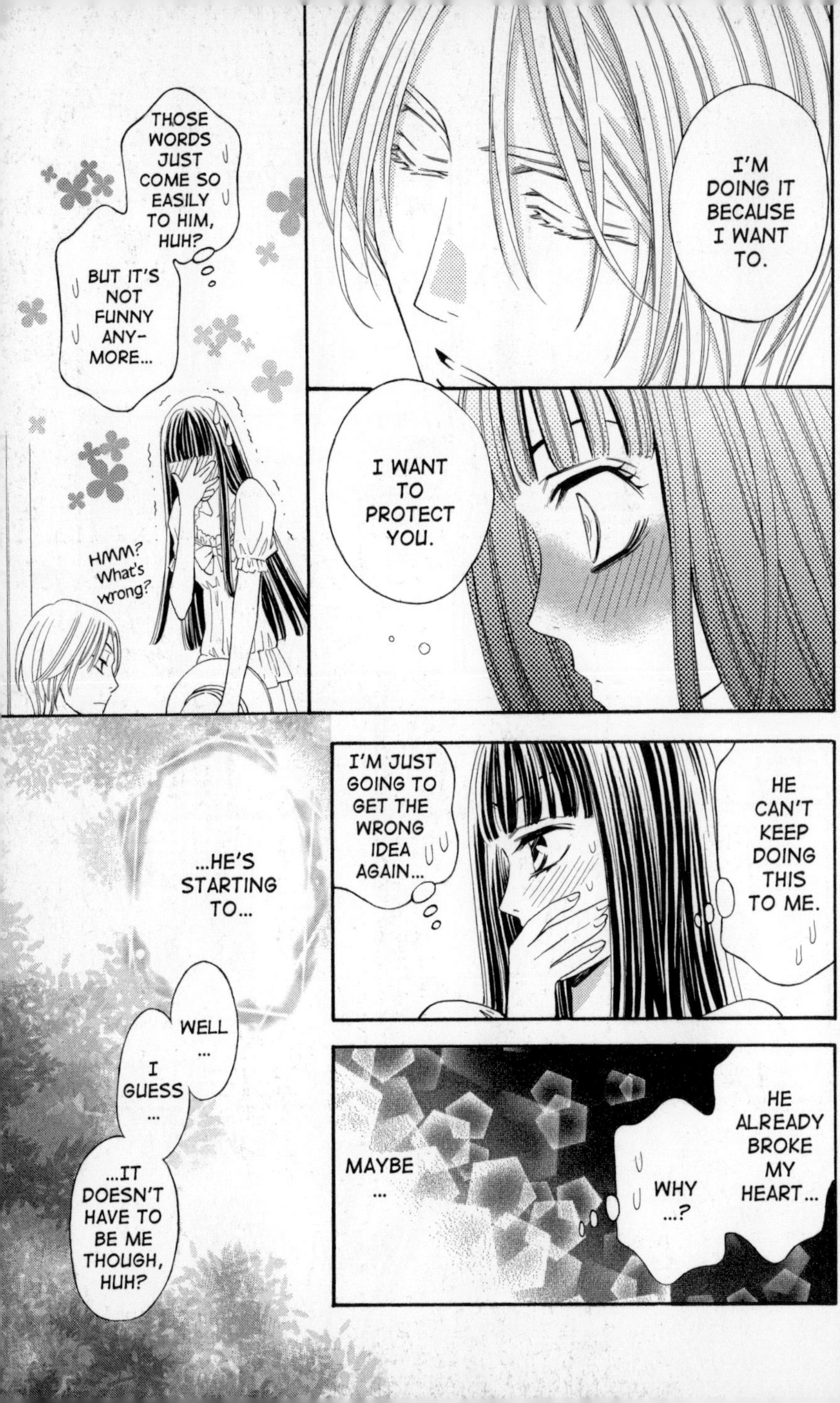
I'M DOING IT BECAUSE I WANT TO.
I WANT TO PROTECT YOU.
THOSE WORDS JUST COME SO EASILY TO HIM, HUH?
BUT IT'S NOT FUNNY ANYMORE...
HMM? What's wrong?
HE CAN'T KEEP DOING THIS TO ME.
I'M JUST GOING TO GET THE WRONG IDEA AGAIN...
HE ALREADY BROKE MY HEART...
WHY ...?
MAYBE ...
...HE'S STARTING TO...
WELL ...
I GUESS ...
...IT DOESN'T HAVE TO BE ME THOUGH, HUH?

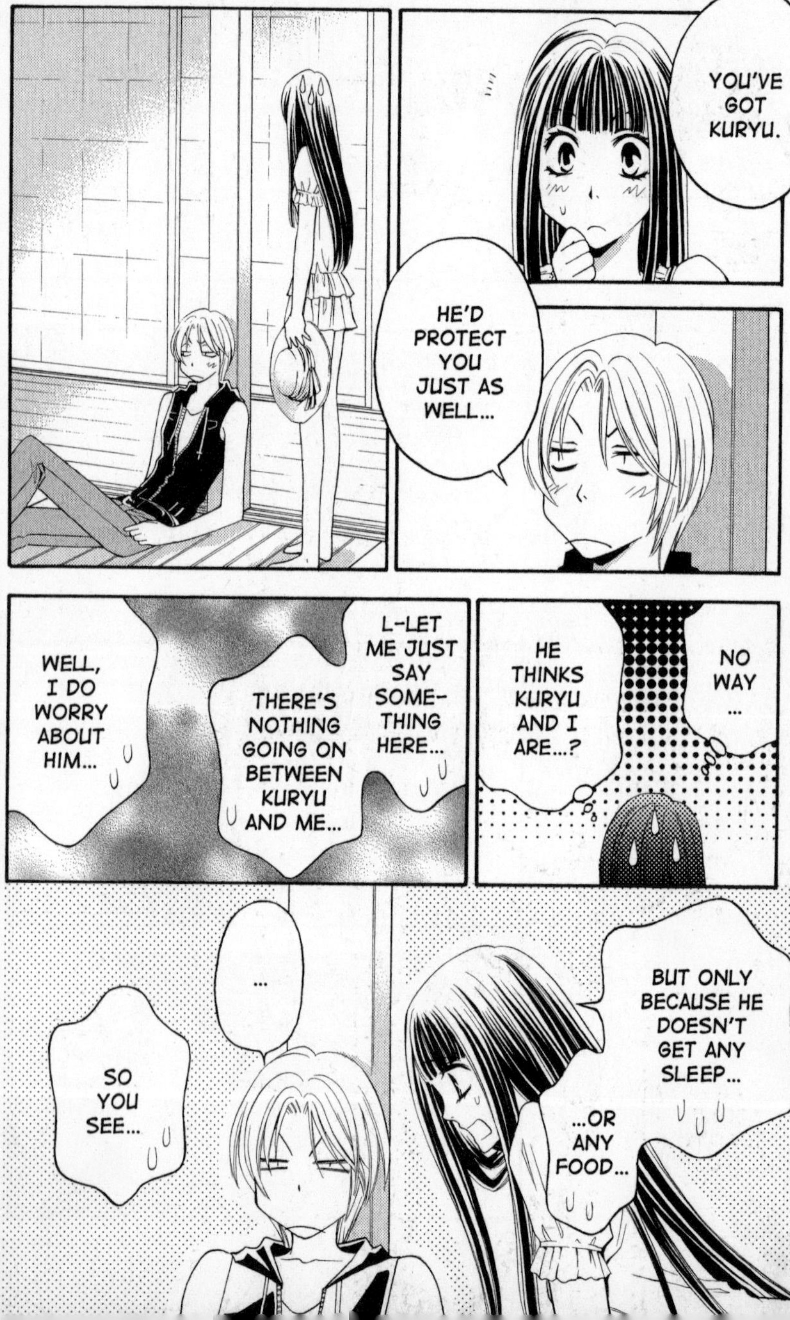
YOU'VE GOT KURYU.
HE'D PROTECT YOU JUST AS WELL...
NO WAY ...
HE THINKS KURYU AND I ARE...?
L-LET ME JUST SAY SOME-THING HERE...
THERE'S NOTHING GOING ON BETWEEN KURYU AND ME...
WELL, I DO WORRY ABOUT HIM...
BUT ONLY BECAUSE HE DOESN'T GET ANY SLEEP...
...OR ANY FOOD...
...
SO YOU SEE...

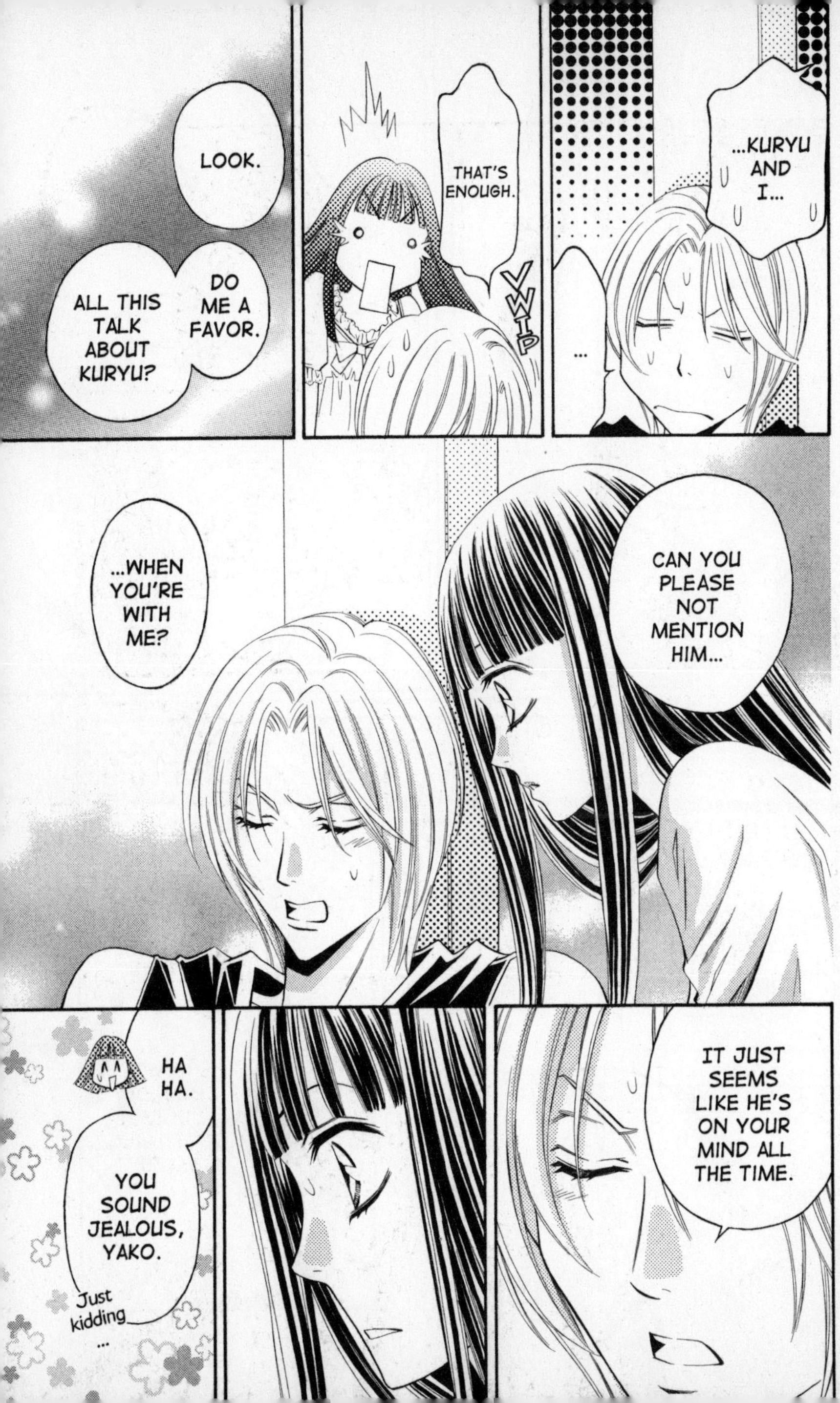
...KURYU AND I...
...
THAT'S ENOUGH.
VWIP
LOOK.
DO ME A FAVOR.
ALL THIS TALK ABOUT KURYU?
CAN YOU PLEASE NOT MENTION HIM...
...WHEN YOU'RE WITH ME?
IT JUST SEEMS LIKE HE'S ON YOUR MIND ALL THE TIME.
HA HA.
YOU SOUND JEALOUS, YAKO.
Just kidding...

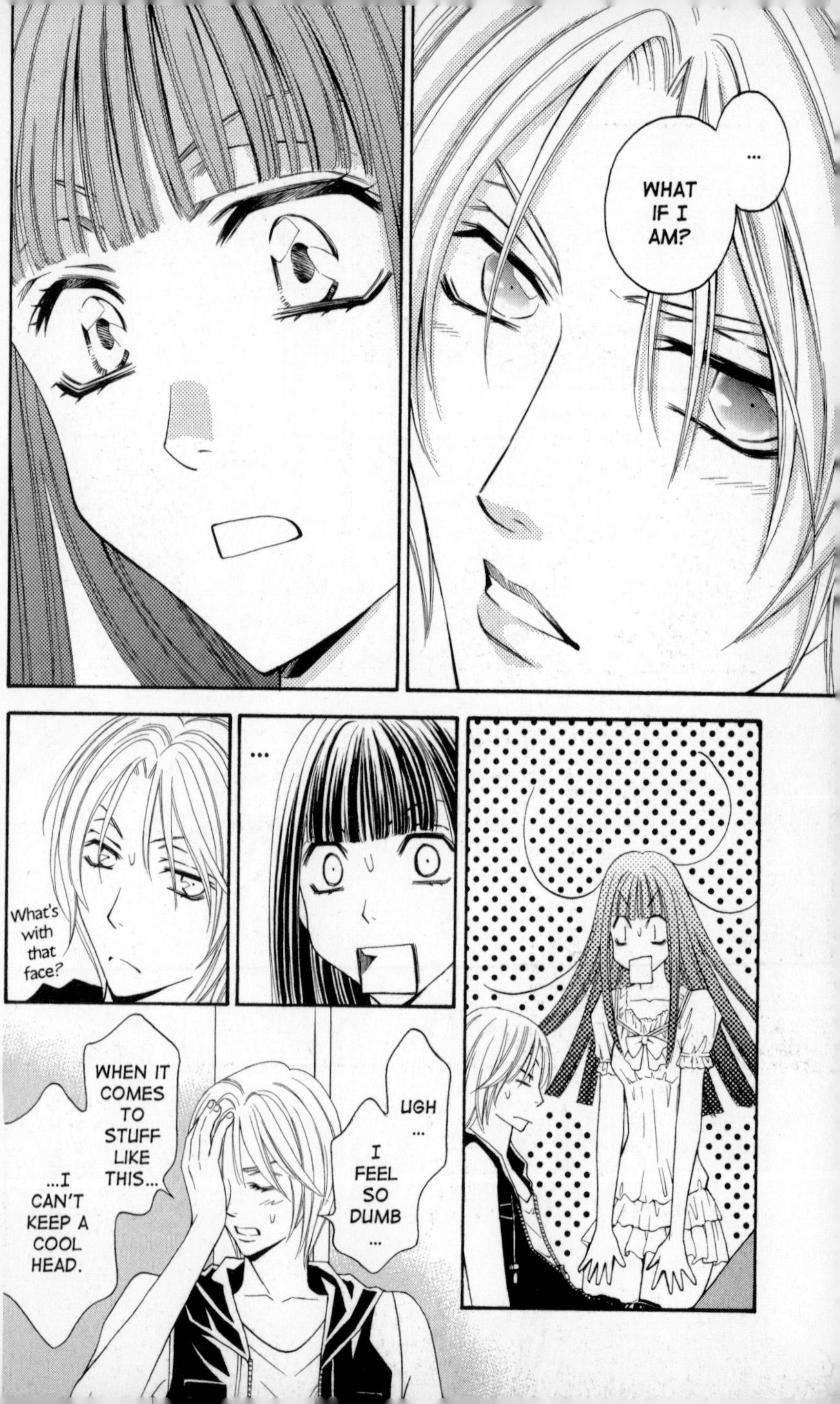

... WHAT IF I AM?
...
What's with that face?
UGH ... I FEEL SO DUMB ...
WHEN IT COMES TO STUFF LIKE THIS...
...I CAN'T KEEP A COOL HEAD.

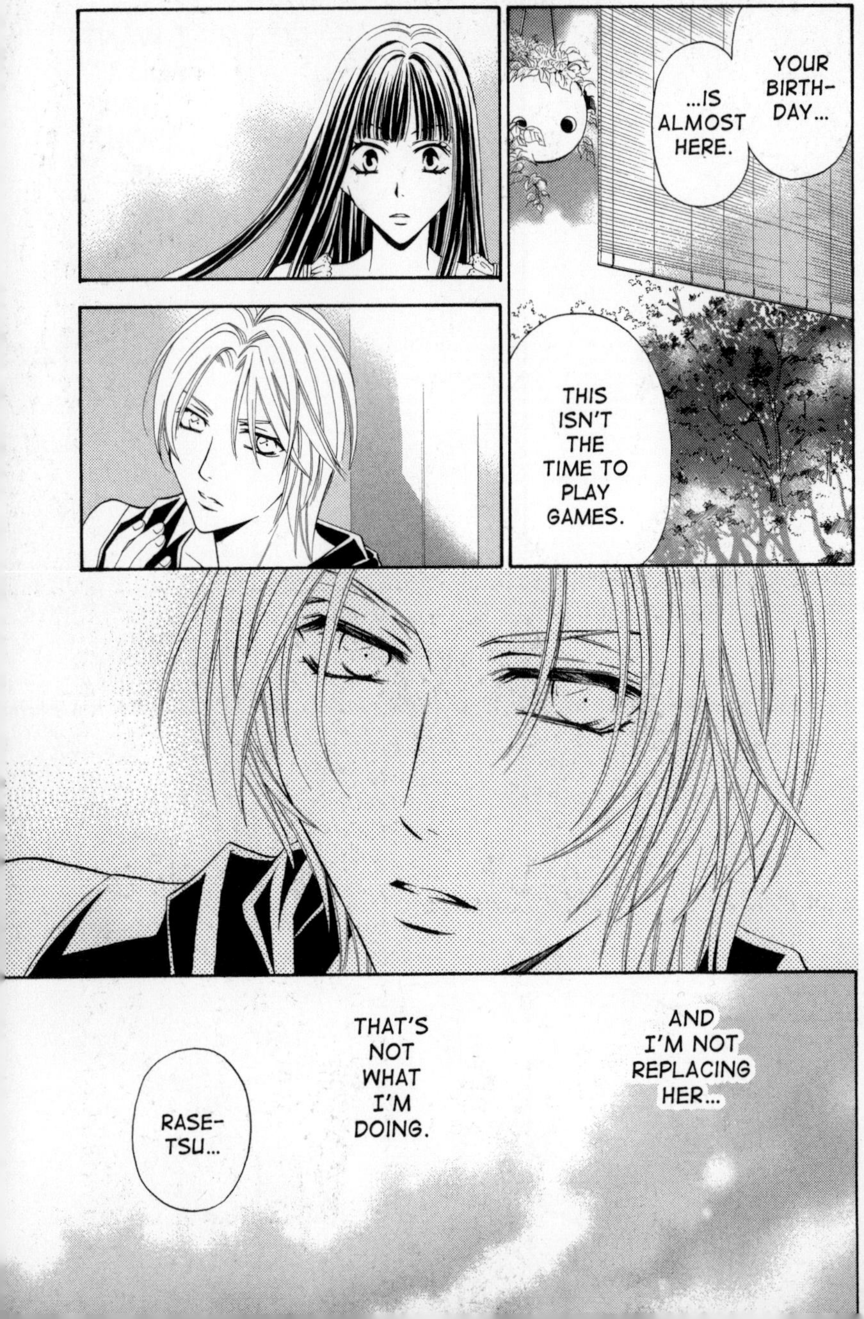
YOUR BIRTH-DAY...
...IS ALMOST HERE.
THIS ISN'T THE TIME TO PLAY GAMES.
AND I'M NOT REPLACING HER...
THAT'S NOT WHAT I'M DOING.
RASE-TSU...

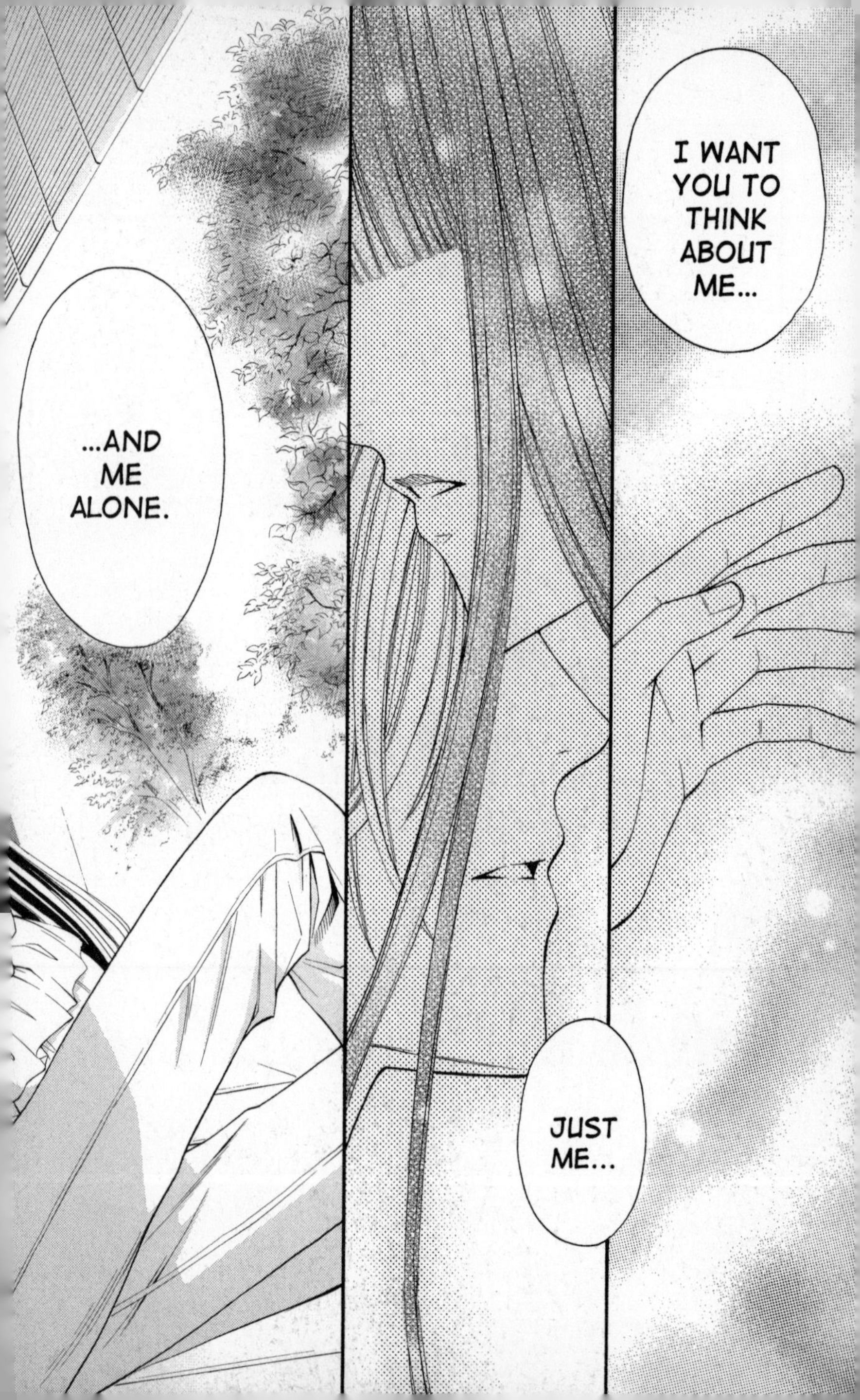
I WANT YOU TO THINK ABOUT ME...
JUST ME...
...AND ME ALONE.

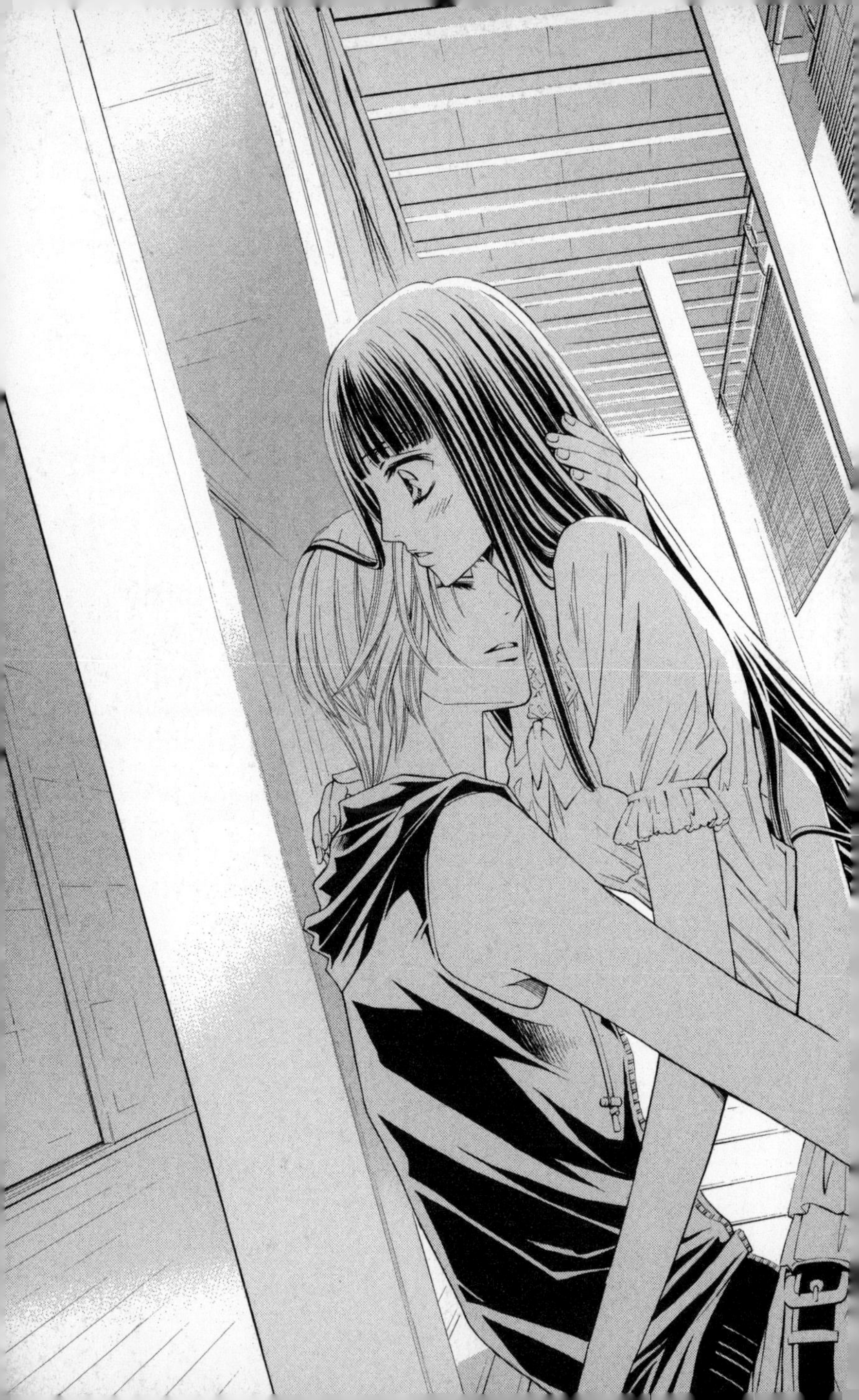

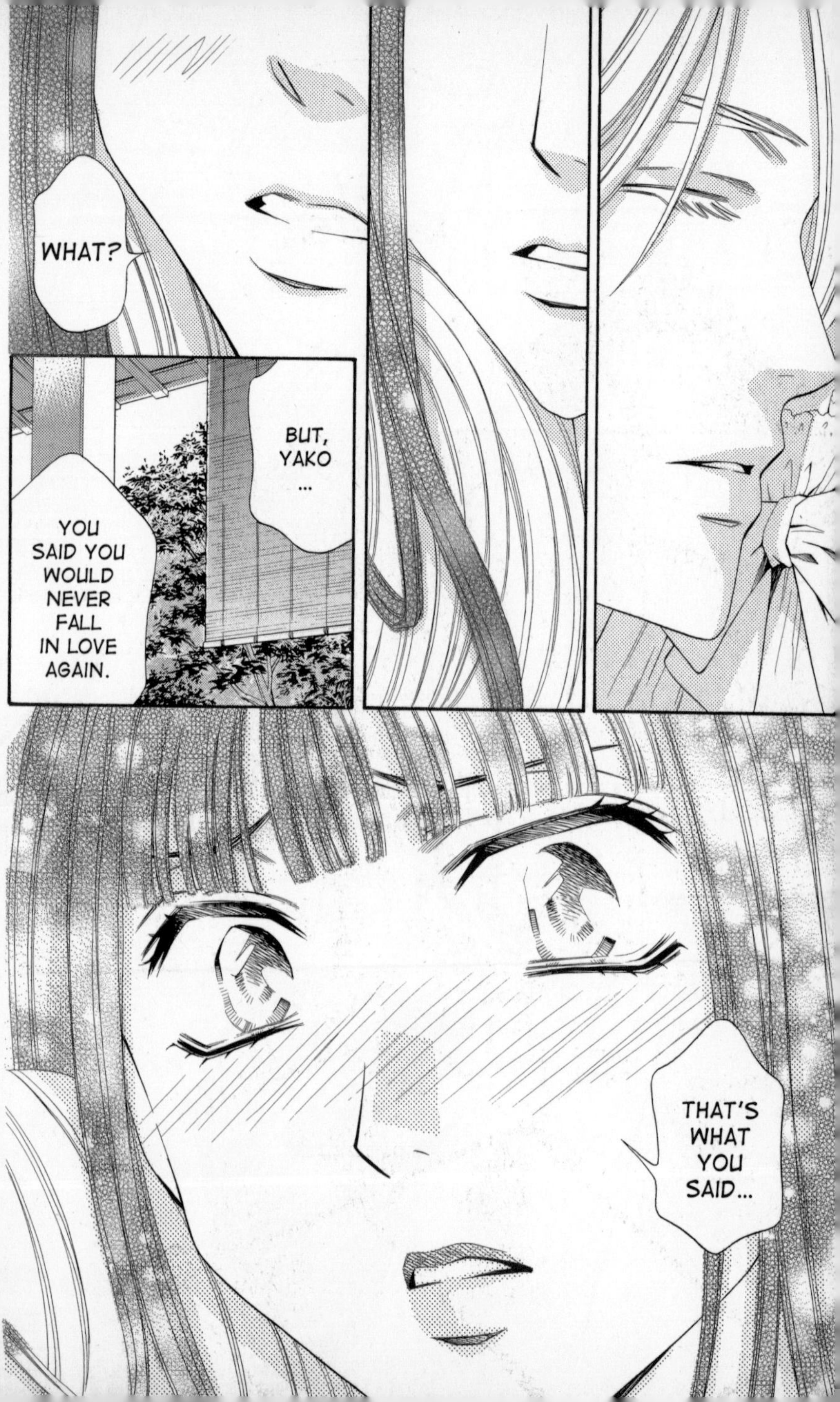
WHAT?
BUT, YAKO ...
YOU SAID YOU WOULD NEVER FALL IN LOVE AGAIN.
THAT'S WHAT YOU SAID...

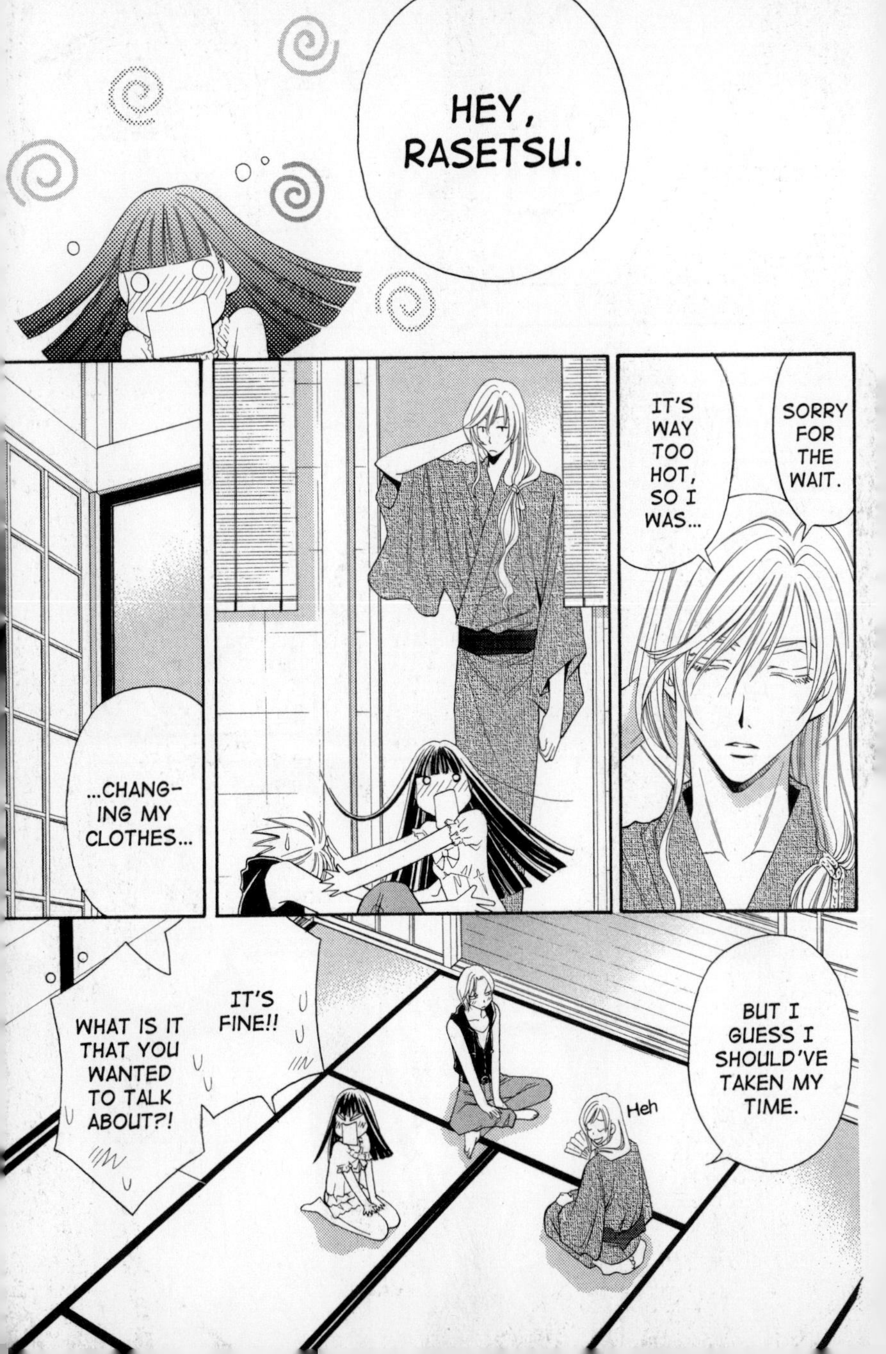
HEY, RASETSU.
SORRY FOR THE WAIT.
IT'S WAY TOO HOT, SO I WAS...
...CHANGING MY CLOTHES...
BUT I GUESS I SHOULD'VE TAKEN MY TIME.
Heh
IT'S FINE!!
WHAT IS IT THAT YOU WANTED TO TALK ABOUT?!

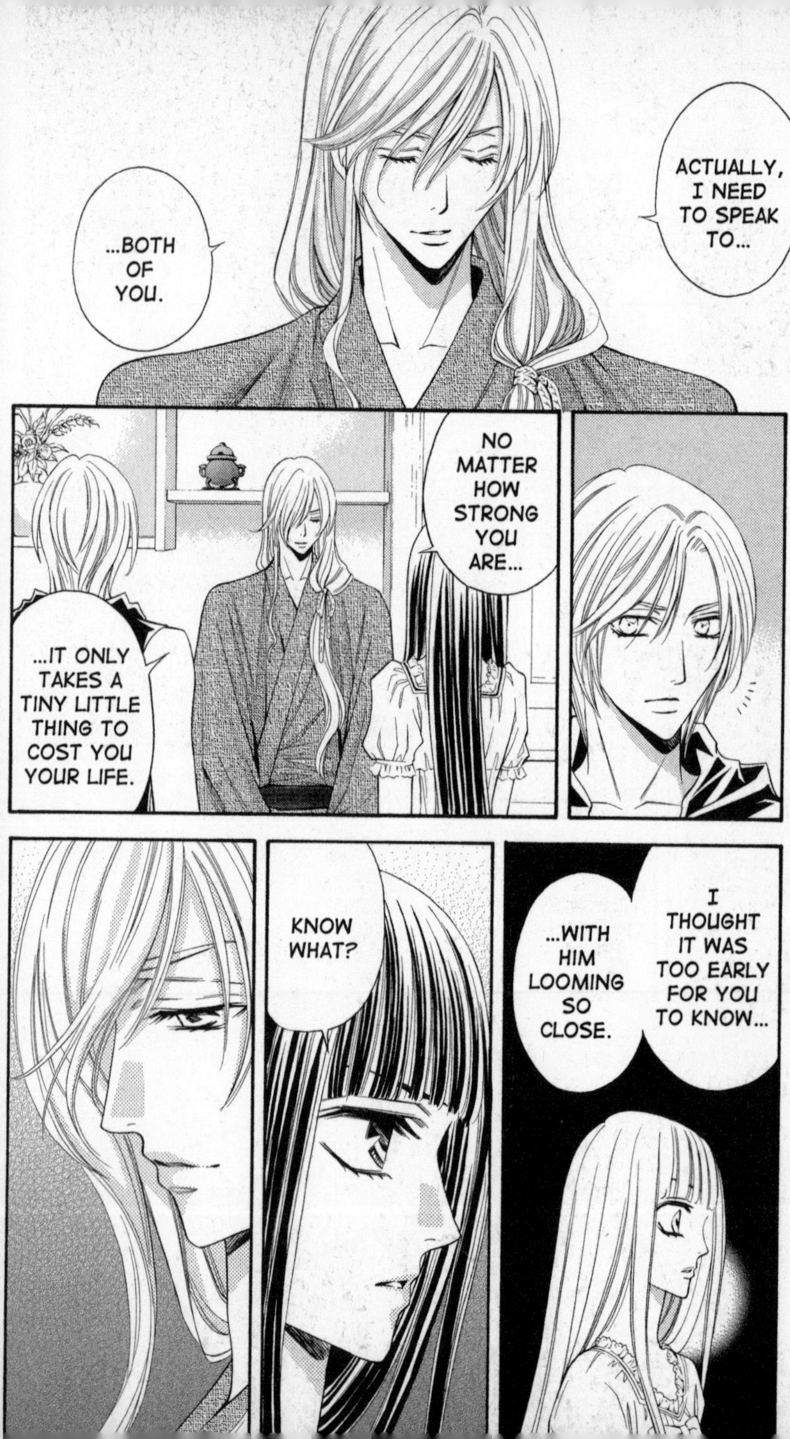
ACTUALLY, I NEED TO SPEAK TO...
...BOTH OF YOU.
NO MATTER HOW STRONG YOU ARE...
...IT ONLY TAKES A TINY LITTLE THING TO COST YOU YOUR LIFE.
I THOUGHT IT WAS TOO EARLY FOR YOU TO KNOW...
...WITH HIM LOOMING SO CLOSE.
KNOW WHAT?

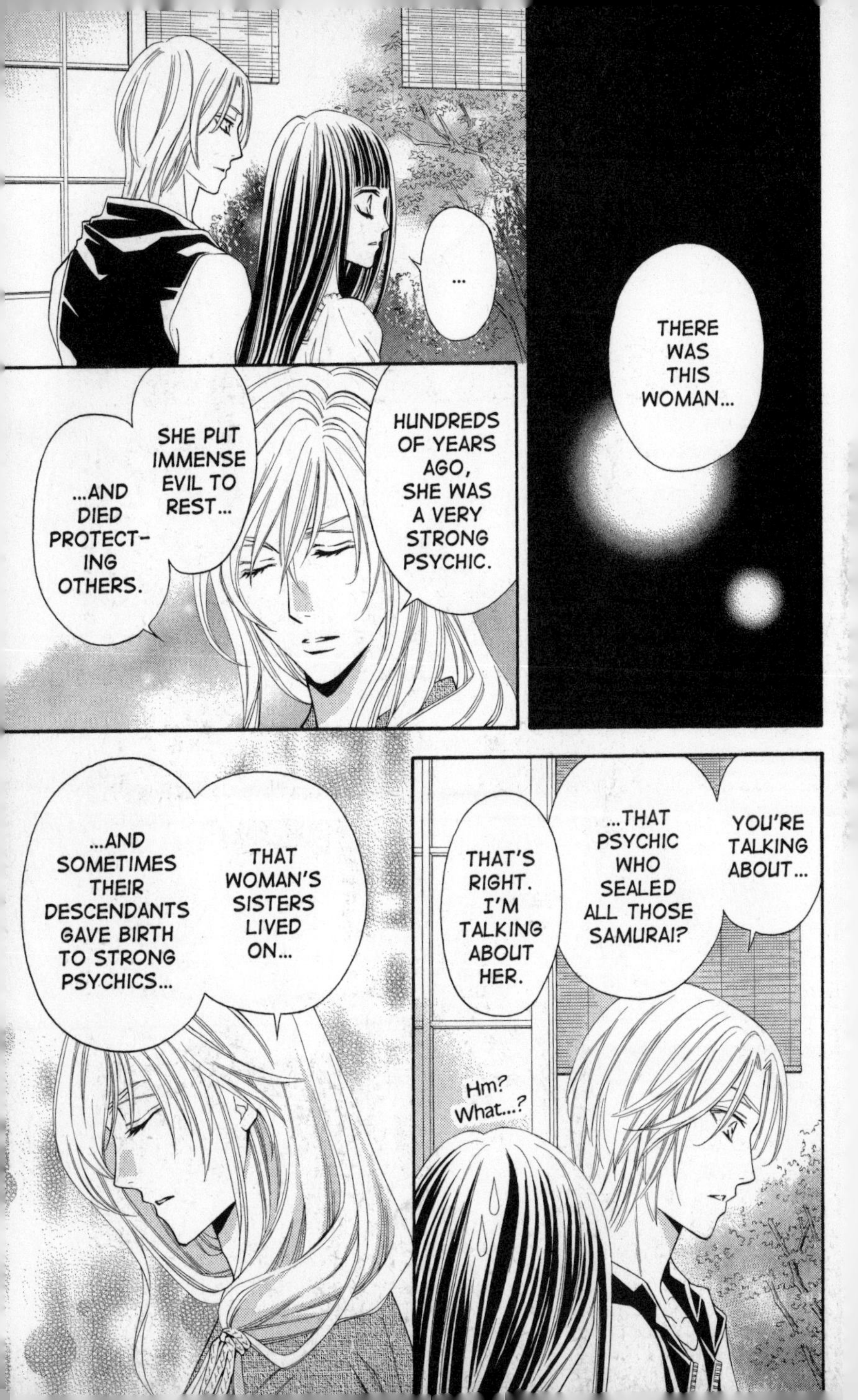
THERE WAS THIS WOMAN...
...
HUNDREDS OF YEARS AGO, SHE WAS A VERY STRONG PSYCHIC.
SHE PUT IMMENSE EVIL TO REST...
...AND DIED PROTECT-ING OTHERS.
YOU'RE TALKING ABOUT...
...THAT PSYCHIC WHO SEALED ALL THOSE SAMURAI?
THAT'S RIGHT. I'M TALKING ABOUT HER.
Hm? What...?
THAT WOMAN'S SISTERS LIVED ON...
...AND SOMETIMES THEIR DESCENDANTS GAVE BIRTH TO STRONG PSYCHICS...

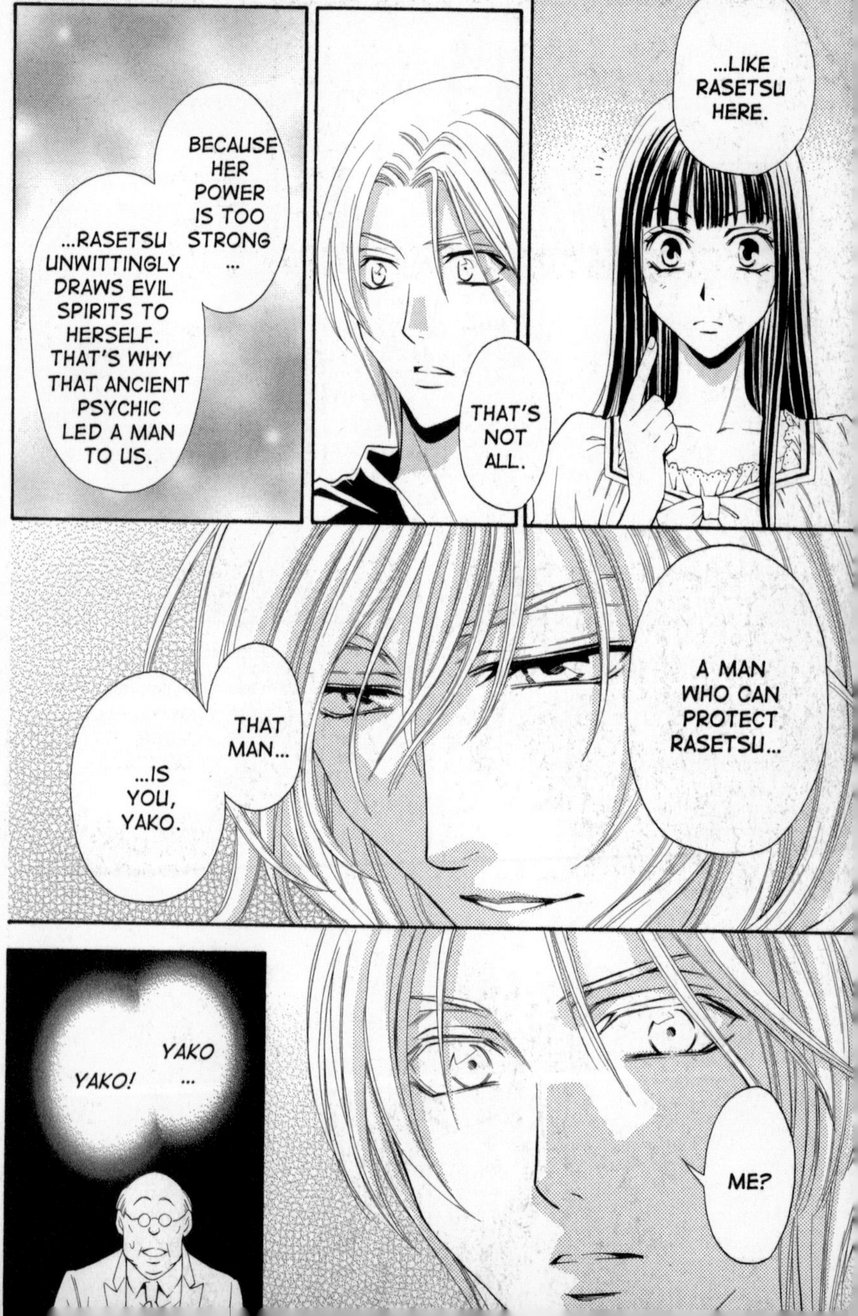
...LIKE RASETSU HERE.
THAT'S NOT ALL.
BECAUSE HER POWER IS TOO STRONG...
...RASETSU UNWITTINGLY DRAWS EVIL SPIRITS TO HERSELF. THAT'S WHY THAT ANCIENT PSYCHIC LED A MAN TO US.
A MAN WHO CAN PROTECT RASETSU...
THAT MAN...
...IS YOU, YAKO.
ME?
YAKO...
YAKO!

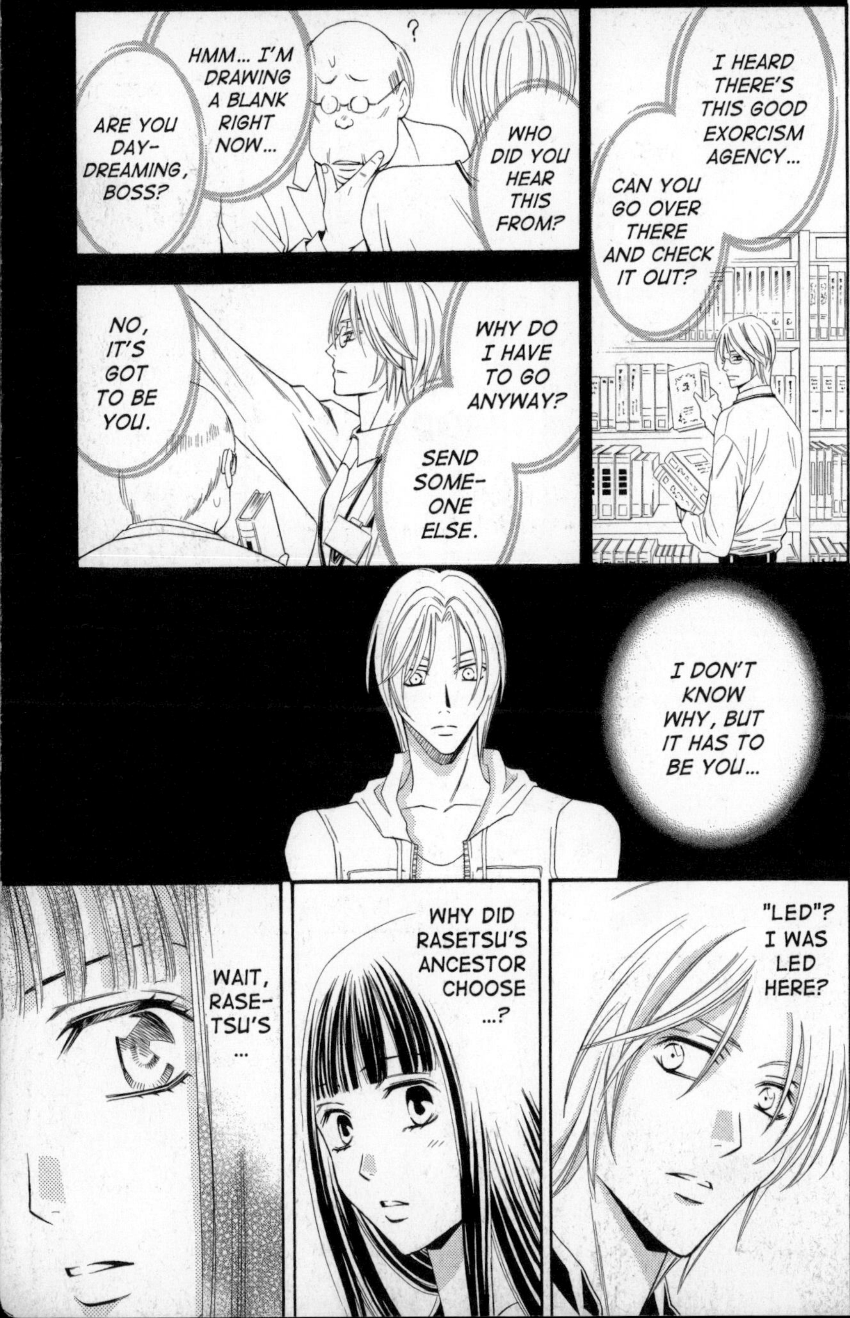
I HEARD THERE'S THIS GOOD EXORCISM AGENCY...
CAN YOU GO OVER THERE AND CHECK IT OUT?
WHO DID YOU HEAR THIS FROM?
?
HMM... I'M DRAWING A BLANK RIGHT NOW...
ARE YOU DAY-DREAMING, BOSS?
WHY DO I HAVE TO GO ANYWAY?
SEND SOME-ONE ELSE.
NO, IT'S GOT TO BE YOU.
I DON'T KNOW WHY, BUT IT HAS TO BE YOU...
"LED"? I WAS LED HERE?
WHY DID RASETSU'S ANCESTOR CHOOSE ...?
WAIT, RASE-TSU'S ...

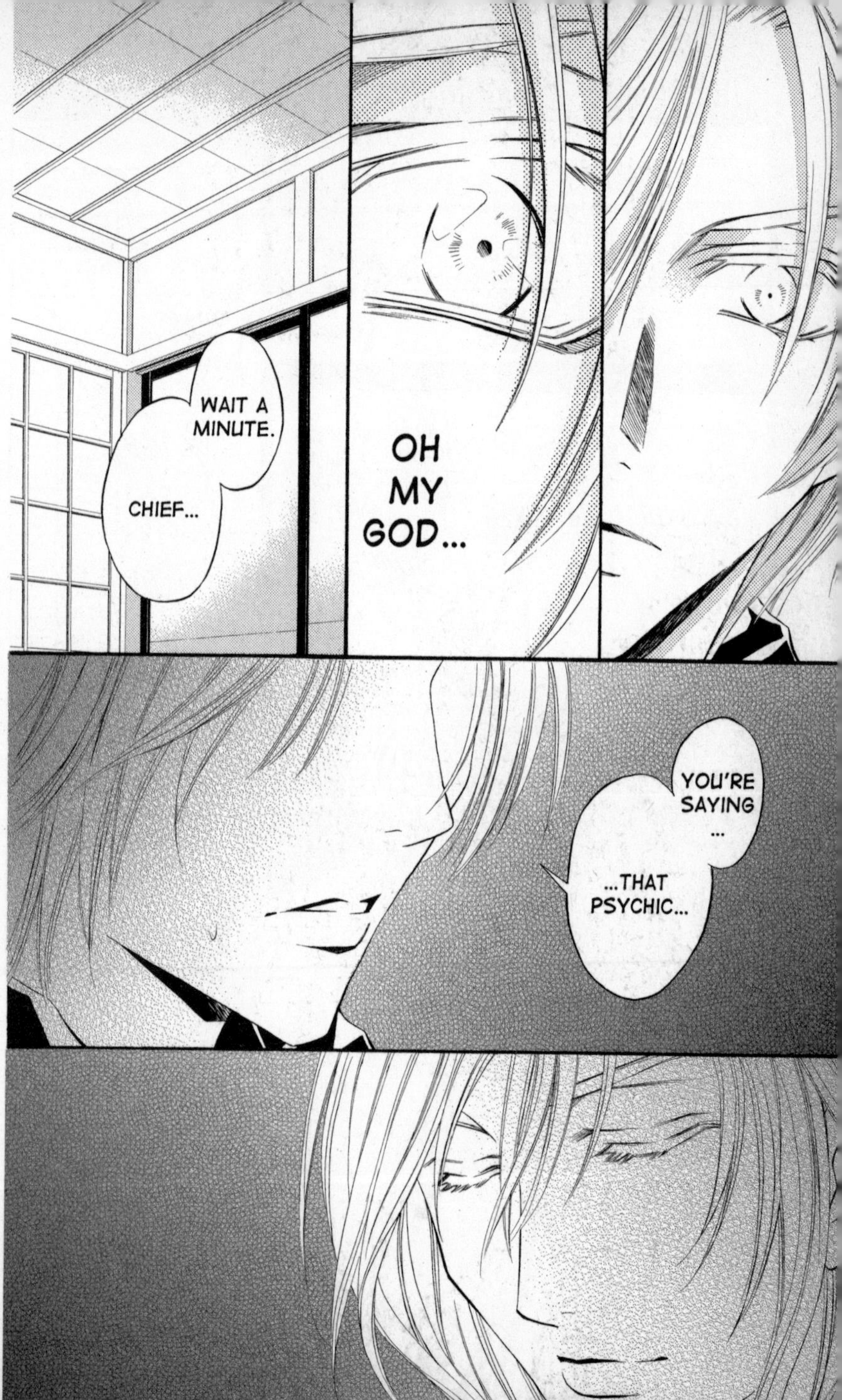
OH MY GOD...
WAIT A MINUTE.
CHIEF...
YOU'RE SAYING ...
...THAT PSYCHIC...

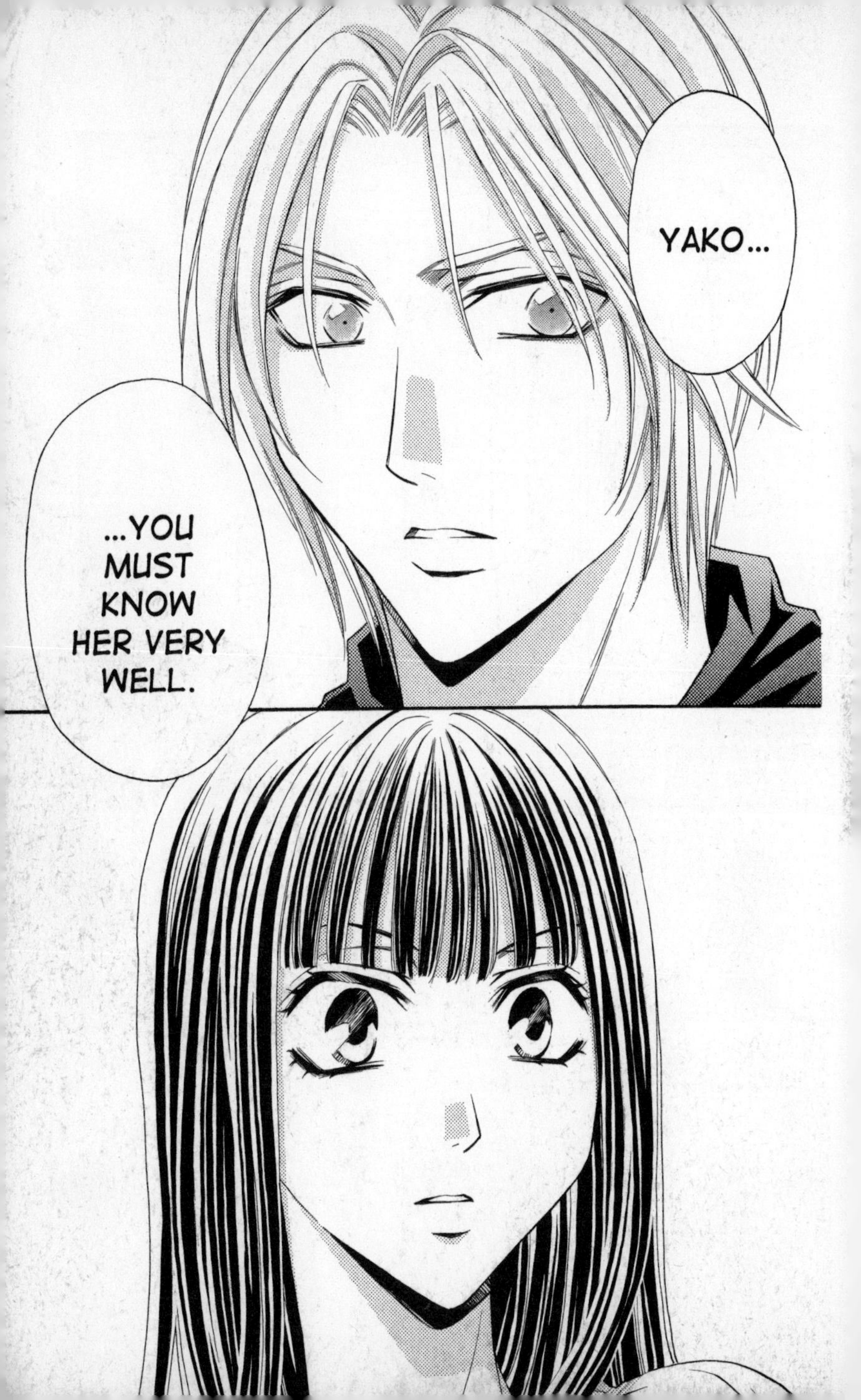
YAKO...
...YOU MUST KNOW HER VERY WELL.

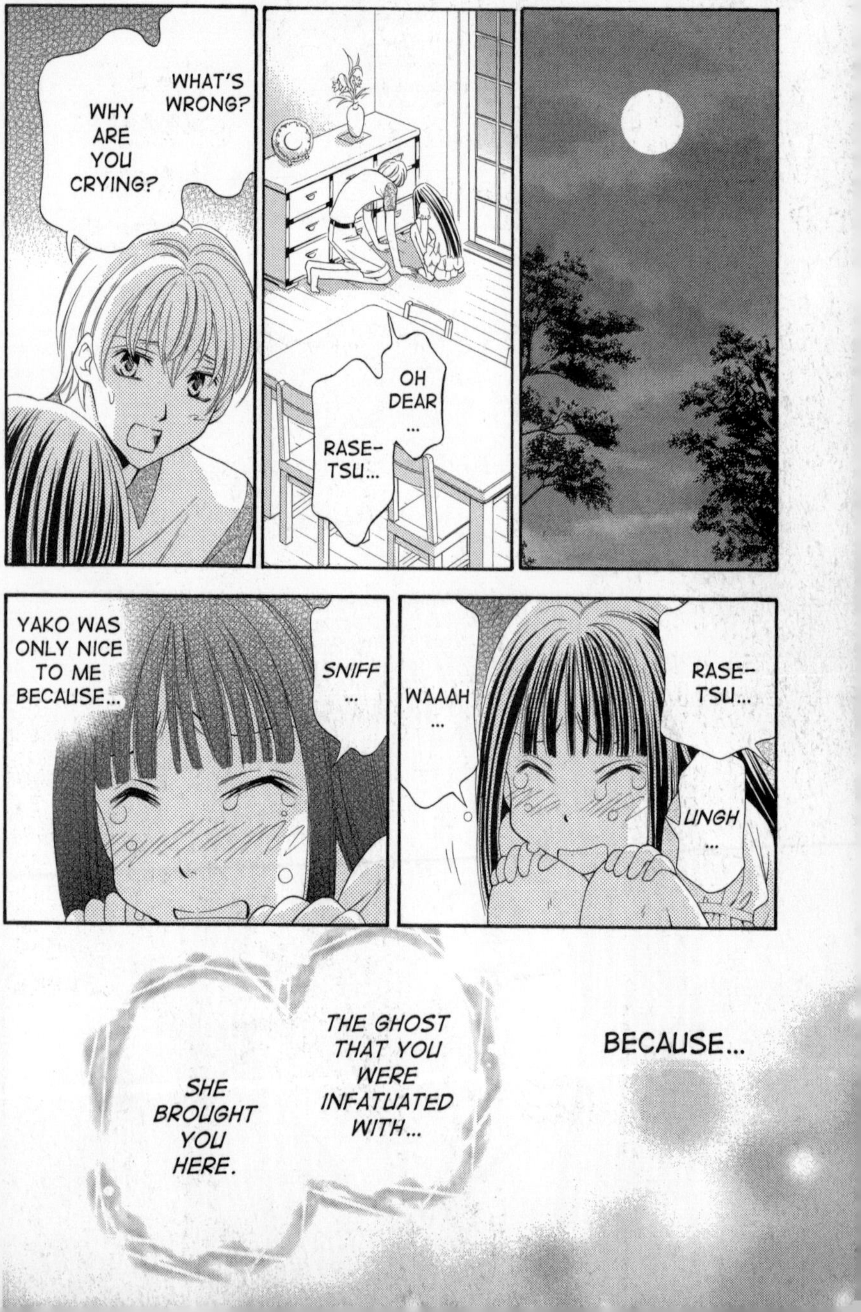
OH DEAR ...
RASE-TSU...
WHAT'S WRONG?
WHY ARE YOU CRYING?
RASE-TSU...
WAAAH ...
UNGH ...
SNIFF ...
YAKO WAS ONLY NICE TO ME BECAUSE...
BECAUSE...
THE GHOST THAT YOU WERE INFATUATED WITH...
SHE BROUGHT YOU HERE.

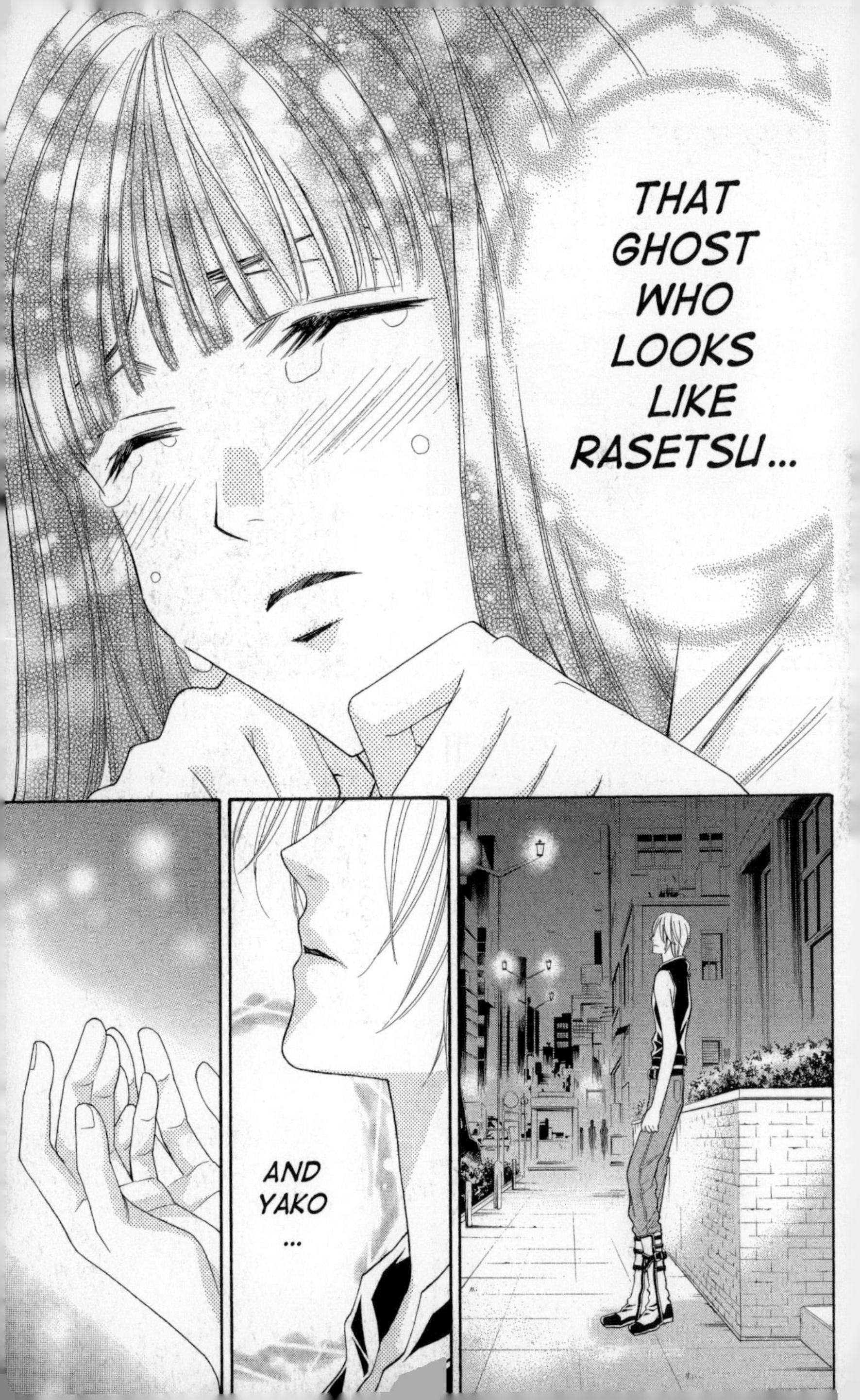
THAT GHOST WHO LOOKS LIKE RASETSU...
AND YAKO ...

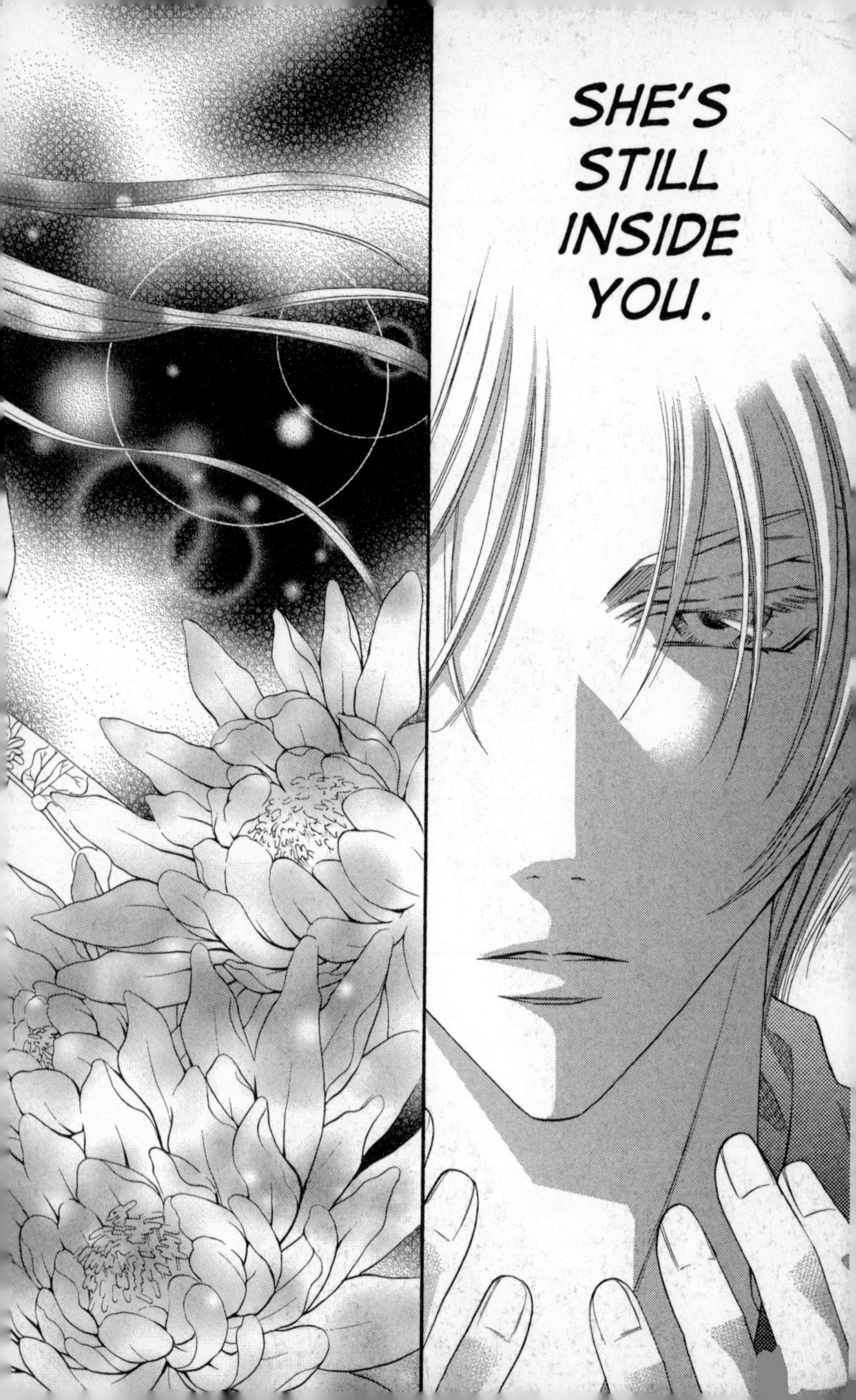
SHE'S STILL INSIDE YOU.

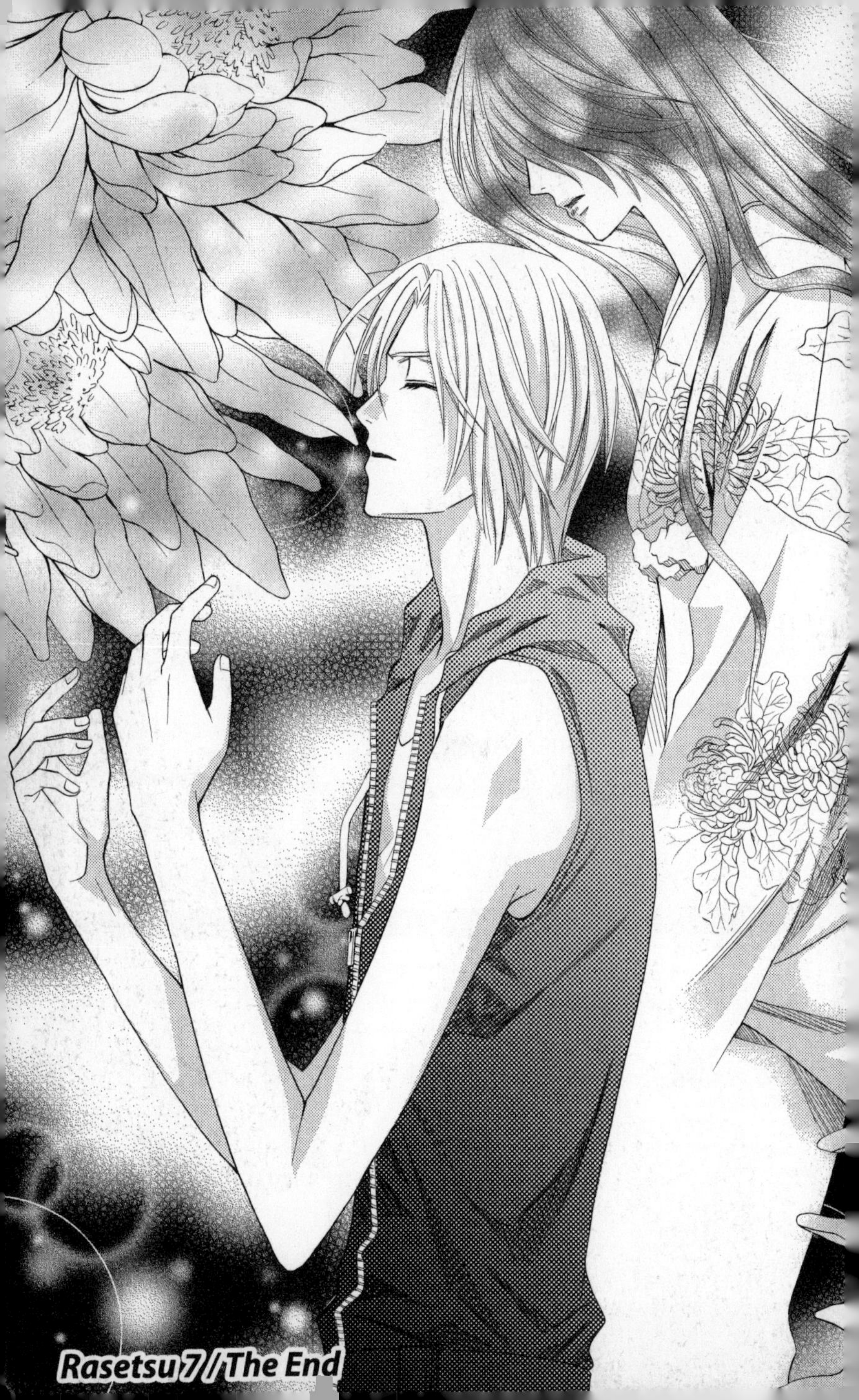

Rasetsu 7 / The End

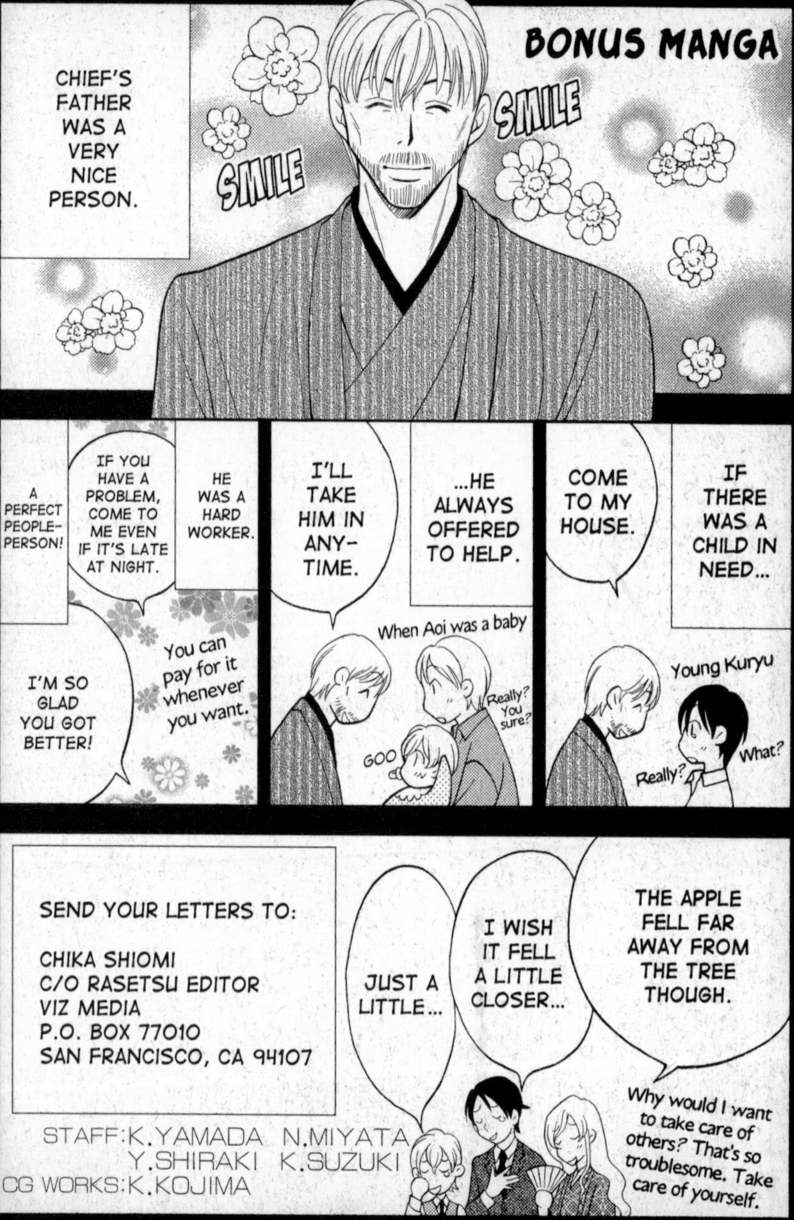
BONUS MANGA
SMILE
SMILE
CHIEF'S FATHER WAS A VERY NICE PERSON.
IF THERE WAS A CHILD IN NEED...
COME TO MY HOUSE.
Young Kuryu
What?
Really?
...HE ALWAYS OFFERED TO HELP.
I'LL TAKE HIM IN ANY-TIME.
When Aoi was a baby
Really? You sure?
GOO
HE WAS A HARD WORKER.
IF YOU HAVE A PROBLEM, COME TO ME EVEN IF IT'S LATE AT NIGHT.
A PERFECT PEOPLE-PERSON!
You can pay for it whenever you want.
I'M SO GLAD YOU GOT BETTER!
THE APPLE FELL FAR AWAY FROM THE TREE THOUGH.
I WISH IT FELL A LITTLE CLOSER...
JUST A LITTLE...
Why would I want to take care of others? That's so troublesome. Take care of yourself.
SEND YOUR LETTERS TO:
CHIKA SHIOMI
C/O RASETSU EDITOR
VIZ MEDIA
P.O. BOX 77010
SAN FRANCISCO, CA 94107
STAFF:K.YAMADA N.MIYATA
Y.SHIRAKI K.SUZUKI
CG WORKS:K.KOJIMA

Chika Shiomi lives in Aichi Prefecture, Japan. She debuted with the manga *Todokeru Toki o Sugitemo* (Even if the Time for Deliverance Passes), and her previous works include the supernatural series *Yurara*. She loves reading manga, traveling and listening to music. Her favorite artists include Michelangelo, Hokusai, Bernini and Gustav Klimt.

RASETSU
VOL. 7
Shojo Beat Edition

STORY AND ART BY
CHIKA SHIOMI

Translation & Adaptation/Kinami Watabe
Touch-up Art & Lettering/Freeman Wong
Cover Design/Hidemi Dunn
Interior Design/Ronnie Casson
Editor/Amy Yu

Rasetsu No Hana by Chika Shiomi
© Chika Shiomi 2009
All rights reserved.
First published in Japan in 2009 by HAKUSENSHA, Inc., Tokyo.
English language translation rights arranged with HAKUSENSHA, Inc., Tokyo.

The stories, characters and incidents mentioned in this publication are entirely fictional.

Printed in the U.S.A.

Published by VIZ Media, LLC
P.O. Box 77010
San Francisco, CA 94107

10 9 8 7 6 5 4 3 2 1
First printing, December 2010

www.viz.com

www.shojobeat.com